A GLORIOUS INSTITUTION

THE CHURCH IN HISTORY

20th Anniversary Edition

Dr. Stanford E. Murrell

Ichthus *Publications* · Apollo, Pennsylvania

A Glorious Institution: The Church in History
Copyright © 2018 by Stanford E. Murrell

This book was previously published by Chapel Library as four parts in two volumes. A study guide is also available from the original publisher. For a copy of the study guide or information about other Bible study materials and correspondence courses (often based on texts from prior centuries), please contact:

MOUNT ZION BIBLE INSTITUTE
2603 West Wright Street
Pensacola, Florida 32505 USA

Phone: (850) 438-6666 • Fax: (850) 438-0227
school@mountzion.org • www.chapellibrary.org

MZBI courses may be downloaded worldwide without charge from www.chapellibrary.org.

All rights reserved. No part of this publication may be reproduced, stored in a retrieval system, or transmitted, in any form or by any means, electronic, mechanical, photocopying, recording or otherwise, without prior permission of the publisher or the Copyright Licensing Agency.

Our goal is to provide high-quality, thought-provoking books that foster encouragement and spiritual growth. For more information regarding Ichthus Publications, other IP books, or bulk purchases, visit us online or write to support@ichthuspublications.com.

Stanford E. Murrell, Th.D., is an experienced pastor and Bible teacher in Viera, Florida. A complete overview of *Church History* is also available as a local seminar taught in your own church assembly. For more information, contact Dr. Murrell directly: *stanfordmurrell@yahoo.com* and *www.stanmurrell.org*.

Printed in the United States of America

ISBN: 978-1-946971-42-5

www.ichthuspublications.com

Contents

Introduction xv

// PART ONE: WHEN THE CHURCH WAS YOUNG //
A.D. 33–754

1 The Birth of the New Testament Church 23
    A Divine Interpretation | 23
    A Spiritual Kingdom | 24
    In the Fullness of Time | 25
    Courage and Corruption | 26
    Selected Early Church Leaders | 27
    Selected Early Writings of the "Fathers" | 28

2 The Suffering Saints, A.D. 33–313 29
    The Heroic Age | 29
    Enemies on Every Side | 29
    The Glory and the Power of the Roman Empire | 31
    A Beast Named Nero | 32
    Three Memorable Martyrs | 32
    Decline and Fall of the Roman Empire: A.D. 193–476 | 35
    Peace Before Persecution | 37
    Renewed Efforts of Destruction | 38
    The Promise of Jesus Realized | 39

3 The Foundations of Faith, A.D. 33–325 42
    Contending for the Faith | 42
    The Importance of Bible Doctrine | 42
    A Canon of Scripture for the Church | 43
    "Fathers" of the Church | 47
    Early Heresies | 49

Four Church Champions | 50
"I Believe": The Apostles' Creed | 51
New Forms of Church Government | 52

4 The Sign of the Saviour, A.D. 313 54
Constantine the Great | 54
The Donatists | 56
Julian the Apostate | 57

5 In the Councils of the Church, A.D. 325–451 58
A Multitude of Counselors | 58
Nicea: The First Ecumenical Council | 58
Important Question to Settle | 59
"Athanasius Against the World" | 61
Three More Champions of Orthodoxy | 66
The Council of Chalcedon | 66
The Latin Church Fathers | 68
The Manicheans | 70
The Donatists | 71
The Pelagians | 71
The Ecumenical Councils | 72

6 Sowing Seeds of Self-Destruction, A.D. 100–461 75
The Sins of the Saints | 75
The Rise of Monasicism | 77
Chrysostom, "Golden Mouth" | 78

7 New Trials and Great Triumphs, A.D. 376–754 79
German Tribes Invade the Empire | 79
The Fall of Rome: A.D. 410 | 81
A Divided People | 83
Evangelism and Education | 84
The Preservation of a People | 84
The Franks Find Christ | 85
The "Apostle of Ireland" | 85
The Missionary Work of Wynfrith and Willibrord | 86
Gregory the Great | 86

8 Diminishing Glory 89
The Arabs Attack the Eastern Part of the Empire | 89
A Man Named Mohammed | 89

The Influence of a False Prophet | 91
The Battle of Tours | 92
The Cross and the Sword: The Expansion of Islam | 92

9 New Political Alliances, A.D. 751–800 95
The "Longbeards" of Northern Italy | 95
Gregory I | 95
The Rise of Pepin III | 97
The Establishment of the Carolingian Dynasty | 97

10 The Growing Power of the Papacy, A.D. 461–1073 100
Growth Through Organization | 100
Growth Through Politics | 101
Growth Through Deception | 101
Growth Through Fantastical Claims | 102

11 The Church in the World; The World in the Church, A.D. 885–1049 104
Inner Division and Internecine Warfare | 104
Dependency on Emperors | 105
Simony: The Selling of the Papal Office | 106

12 A House Divided, A.D. 1054 109
The Eastern Church | 109
The Western Church | 111

// PART TWO: THE CHURCH IN THE MIDDLE AGES //

A.D. 754–1517

13 Monasticism and the Cluny Reforms 115
Asceticism | 115
Reform at the Monastery of Cluny | 116

14 The Church Cries out for Spiritual Reform, A.D. 1049–1073 118
The Cluny Reforms: A.D. 1049–1058 | 118
Pope Leo IX | 118
Pope Stephen X | 119
Hildebrand: The Power Behind the Throne | 120
Movement Toward Maturity: A.D. 1059–1073 | 120

15 The Struggle for Independence from the State, A.D. 1073–1122 124
    The Fight for Ultimate Authority | 124
    Contesting the Church | 124
    A Compromising Compact | 127
    The Doctrine of Repentance | 128

16 Killing in the Name of Christ: The Crusades, A.D. 1096–1291 137
    Raising an Army of God | 137
    "God Wills It!" | 139
    More Military Adventures | 139
    The Children's Crusade | 141
    The Results of the Crusades | 142

17 The Height of Eathly Power, A.D. 1198–1216 143
    The Zenith of Earthly Glory | 143
    Wealth and Wickedness | 145
    The Mendicant Orders | 146
    Teachers of the Church | 147
    Summary | 151

18 The Passing of Power, A.D. 1294–1417 152
    The Trouble with Taxes | 152
    Factors Contributing to Decline | 153
    The Papal Schism (1378–1417) | 154

19 The Search for Sanctification, A.D. 1200–1517 156
    The Return of Heresy | 156
    The Followers of Peter Waldo | 157
    Then Came the Inquistion | 157
    John Wycliffe, "Morning Star of the Reformation" | 158
    John Huss | 159
    Wounded Healers | 160
    The "Rebirth" of Learning | 161
    Savonarola | 162
    Educating Youth for Christ | 163
    Future Leaders | 163

// Part Three: The Reformation and Its Aftermath //
A.D. 1517–1648

20 The Reformation Begins, A.D. 1517 169
The Reformation Era | 169
The Day God Shook the World | 170
Ecclesiastical Power over People | 171
A System of Sacraments | 172
A Non-Salvation of Penance | 173
Indulgences | 174
Supererogation | 174
John Tetzel: A Master of Deceit | 175
A Man Named Martin | 175
A Religious Awakening | 176
Salvation in a Solitary Cell | 178
Ninety-Five Theses | 178
Initial Response to Luther | 179

21 Upheaval!, A.D. 1518 182
A Saint is Summoned to Rome | 182
Emissaries of the Pope | 183
Miltitz and Eck | 184
The Leipzig Debate | 185
The Gathering Assault | 186
The Emperor Joins the Fray | 187
Standing Resolute at the Diet of Worms | 189
Kidnapped! | 190
A Protestation | 191

22 A New Way of Life for Luther and Lutherans, A.D. 1525 193
A New Principle of Christian Liberty | 193
Transubstantiation | 194
Consubstantiation | 194
Spiritual Resources for the Righteous | 195
Master Melanchthon | 196
Luther at Home | 197
A Faithful Servant | 198

23 The Reformation Reaches beyond Germany, A.D. 1526 199
A Foundation for the Reformation | 199
A Mixed Heritage | 200

Ulrich Zwingli | 201
John Calvin | 202
The Beliefs of Farel | 204
A Great Work in Geneva | 205
Banished! | 206
Return to Geneva | 207
The Rule of the Righteous | 208
Pharisaic or Pure Religion? | 209
Calvin's Contributions | 210

24 Blood and Violence in the Body of Christ 212
A Spiritual Battle | 212
The Peasants Misunderstand | 213
Thomas Müntzer | 214
The Peasants' War Continues | 215
The Anabaptists | 215
Opposition to the Anabaptists | 216
The Movement Grows | 217
Transformed by the Power of God | 218

25 Reformation Faith Is Found in France 220
The Need for Reform | 220
The Waldenses | 221
Jacques d'E'taples Lefevre | 222
The Death of Jean Leclerc | 223
The Cruelty of a King | 223
The Gallic Confession of Faith | 224
The Reformation Reaches the Netherlands | 225

26 John Knox and the Scottish Reformation, A.D. 1513–1572 227
A Spark Ignites Scotland | 227
The Castilians and Their Capture | 228
Life as a Galley Slave | 229
Marriage and an Unusual Mother-in-law | 230
The "Black Rubric" | 230
Mary Tudor | 231
Compliments for Calvin | 232
A Political Mistake | 233
Spiritual Victory in Scotland | 234
Death of the "Thundering Scot" | 234

27 Reformation Comes to England, A.D. 1558–1603 236
    The "Morning Star" of the Reformation | 236
    The Powerful Prayer of a Dying Professor | 237
    A Potentially Splendid Sovereign | 237
    The Cardinal of the King | 238
    Weaving a Tangled Web | 238
    A Questionable Marriage | 239
    A Sovereign Wants a Son | 239
    The Pope Says, No | 240
    The Supremacy of the King | 241
    Flickering Hope | 242
    "Bloody Mary" | 242
    Hope Springs Eternal | 234

28 Counter Reformation and Conflict, A.D. 1545–1563 245
    The Religious Zeal of Ximenes | 245
    Realizing the Need for Reform | 246
    The Nightmare Years| 246
    The Council of Trent | 248
    The Cruelty of Charles V | 248
    The Power of Passionate People | 250
    A Fragmented Faith | 252

29 The Reformation in England Continues, A.D. 1647 255
    More Purity for the Church in England | 255
    The Authority of God's Word | 256
    Thomas Cartwright | 256
    The Independents | 257
    Persecution of the Puritans | 257
    King Charles I | 258
    The People and Parliament Challenge the Crown | 259
    A "Lord Protector" | 260
    An Assembly of Saints | 261
    The Restoration and Its Persecutions | 262
    John Bunyan and John Milton | 263
    Return England to Catholicism? | 264
    A Summary of the Thirty-Nine Articles | 265
    The Puritan Legacy | 266

30 The Rise of New Expressions of Religion 268
    A Fight without a Reasonable Finish | 268

A Tree of Life | 269
A Man of Conscience without Conviction | 270
A Burst of Anger and a New Bible | 271
A Short Chronology of Two Congregations | 273
Distinctive Baptist Beliefs | 273
The Savoy Synod | 275

31 The Changes in the Church Continue, A.D. 1618 276
Contending for the Faith | 276
Changing the Faith | 276
The Synod of Dort | 277
"Something" in the Soul | 279

// PART FOUR: THE CHURCH IN THE MODERN AGE //
A.D. 1648–PRESENT

32 The Continued Growth of Mysticism 285
Gnosticism Again! | 285
Reaction to Rationalization of Roman Theology | 286
Roman Catholic Rejection of Reform | 287
Lutheran Pietism | 288
The Unity of the Brethren | 289
A Concise Catechism on Conversion | 290

33 The Boundaries of Acceptable Beliefs 294
The Sin of Socinianism | 294
The Ugliness of Unitarianism | 295
The Spiritual Madness of Modernism | 295
The Message of Two Methodists | 295
The Very Interesting Edward Irving | 298
The Impeccability of Christ | 301

34 "This Is the Gospel!", A.D. 1714–1770 304
Wesley and Whitefield | 304
The Danger of Deism | 305
The Rise of the Age of Reason | 306
Three Parties of Anglicans (Mid-1700s–Mid-1800s) | 308
Attack on "Saving Faith" | 309
The Plymouth Brethren | 310

    Preaching the Gospel to Every Creature | 312
    The Work Continues | 313

35 Christianity Comes to the New World 315
    Christ in the Colonies | 315
    The Protestant Presence | 316
    The Dutch Reformed Church | 317
    Birth of the Baptists | 318
    Catholicism in the Colonies | 320
    The Courage of the Quakers | 321
    Religious Diversity | 321
    Reasons America Does Not Have a State Church | 323

36 Religious Revivals in the United States, A.D. 1741–1859 325
    A Great Awakening (1741–1744) | 325
    Jonathan Edwards | 326
    George Whitefield | 327
    Do It Again, Lord; Do It Again! | 328
    The Shame of Slavery | 329
    The Second Great Awakening (c. 1791–1835) | 330
    A Contrast of Two Christian Evangelists | 331
    A Third Great Awakening (1857–1859) | 332

37 Counterfeit Religions to Christian Revivals, A.D. 1844 335
    Ellen G. White and Seventh-day Adventism | 335
    A Modern Day Prophetess? | 336
    The Christian Sabbath is the First Day of the Week | 339
    Joseph Smith and Mormonism | 340
    The Doctrines of Mormonism | 343
    Charles Taze Russell and Jehovah's Witnesses | 344
    A New Leader of the Movement | 345
    A Time for Terminology | 346
    Jehovah's Witnesses vs. the Word of God | 347
    Christian Science | 348

38 A Return to Normalcy, A.D. 1858 352
    An Antidote for Anti-Christian Teachings | 352
    A Million Souls for the Savior | 353
    Gospel Progress in the United Kingdom | 355
    The General Next to God | 357
    "The Prince of Preachers" | 358

The Keswick Convention | 360

39 Challenges in the Twenty-First Century and Beyond 362
New Challenges | 362
The Church Faces the Future | 368
Legalism and Other Extremes | 370
Eastern Mysticism and the New Age | 371
Pragmatism and the Church Growth Movement | 372
Psychological Seduction | 373
The Battle for the Bible | 373
The Sovereignty of God | 374
The Next Chapter | 375

"Therefore let us repent and pass from ignorance to knowledge, from foolishness to wisdom, from licentiousness to self-control, from injustice to righteousness, from godlessness to God."

—*Clement of Alexandria,
Theologian of the second century*

Introduction

In 1998, when Bro. L. R. Shelton, Jr. (1923–2003) asked me to write something on Church history for his own interest and understanding, I had no idea that twenty years later the work he had Chapel Library in Pensacola, Florida publish would still be in circulation. I am very grateful to Bro. Shelton for promoting this project. Appreciation is also extended to Steven Frakes for his extensive editorial counsel and correction of the manuscript and to Mike Snyder who was the general manger of publications at the time. In the providence of God, this work on Church history has found wide circulation in many churches, prisons, schools, and centers of learning in America and abroad. Because there is an independent Study Guide, Sunday school classes, and home schoolers have learned a little more of the history of the Christian Church. Professor Leonardo Galanza Jr., a teacher at the Center for Biblical Studies Institute and Seminary in Calabarzon, Philippines, has been using this work on Church history for more than a decade. For all of these venues I am grateful for the study of Church history, which is essential for a vital Christian faith. The Psalmist said, "We have heard with our ears, O God, our fathers have told us, what work thou didst in their days, in the times of old" (Psa 44:1).

Consider several important reasons why Christians should devote time to studying the past in general, and Church history in particular.

First, the past is a great stimulus to faith. When David faced Goliath, he did so because he had already seen God's faithfulness and power. David carried in his soul the memories of some dramatic moments when the Lord delivered his life from the mouth of a ferocious hungry lion and the jaws of a ravenous bear. When the lion carried away a lamb that was entrusted to David, the "Sweet Singer of Israel" went after that lion. And when the lion dropped the lamb and turned to devour David, the Shepherd fought back and slew him (1 Sam 17:32–36). In like manner, Christ protects His own by dealing with the Great Lion who spiritually seeks to destroy the sheep.

Time passed and another enemy came forth. The enemy was an uncircumcised Philistine named Goliath (1 Sam 17:38–51). Standing over nine feet tall, Goliath had been trained in fleshly warfare since childhood. But he was no match for David because this soldier of God had been trained in spiritual warfare since childhood. Goliath might trust the strength of the carnal weapons he possessed, but David would rely on the mighty arm of the living Lord. God had always been faithful. And so David remembered the past in order to face a present ordeal.

Not only is the study of the past a stimuli to faith, *but the study of history pleases God.* Many times in Scripture God reminds His people of His great exploits on their behalf and bids them to remember. "Remember the former things of old: For I am God, and there is none else; I am God, and there is none like me" (Isa 46:9). And, "Seek the Lord and His strength, seek His face continually. Remember His marvelous works that He hath done, His wonders, and the judgments of His mouth" (1 Chron 16:11–12).

There are particular truths God wants His people to remember.

Christians are to remember the works of creation for "The heavens declare the glory of God; and the firmament sheweth his handiwork" (Psa 19:1).

Christians are to remember the Sabbath day. "Remember the sabbath day, to keep it holy" (Exod 20:8).

Christians are to remember the commandments of God. The Law was given "That ye may remember, and do all my commandments, and be holy unto your God" (Num 15:40).

The church is to remember the general mercies of Divine favor in being delivered from the land of bondage. "And thou shalt remember that thou wast a bondman in Egypt: and thou shalt observe and do these statutes" (Deut 16:12).

Christians are to remember the Lord's death until He comes (1 Cor 11:26).

It is in the study of history that the greatest story ever told is reviewed. The heart remembers the death, burial, and resurrection of Jesus Christ. And the world is invited to authenticate or discredit Christianity on a simple historical question: "Who moved the stone?"

If the Disciples of Christ moved the stone to steal the body of Jesus, then Christianity is a lie and the most monstrous of all religions because it sets itself up to be the most moral. However, if an angel rolled the stone away from the tomb, not to let Christ out, but to let the world in, then Christianity is vindicated and we serve a risen Savior. There is a Man in the heavens, and His name is Jesus.

As the study of history stimulates faith, pleases God, and validates the Christian message *it also encourages the Church to contend for the faith once and for all delivered to the saints.*

There is such a faith as per Jude 3. "Beloved, when I gave all diligence to write unto you of the common salvation, it was needful for me to write unto you, and exhort you that ye should earnestly contend for the faith which was once delivered unto the saints."

In every generation the body of truth has been divinely preserved and protected in order to be passed on and preached afresh. Unfortunately, one of the great challenge to the truth are men and women, filled with good intentions, who think they have to add to, or improve upon the gospel, rather than receive and proclaim it. And a lesson is learned: good intentions can kill!

I tell you a true story. A number of years ago a young female college student went to Mexico City with a friend on vacation. Just as they were ready to come home, one of the girls spotted what she thought was a wounded little Chihuahua. Moved with compassion she took the little animal and was determined to nurse it back to health. After returning home she took the creature to a veterinarian for advice. As soon as the doctor saw the creature, he took it from the girl and put it in a cage.

"Do you know what you were holding so close to you," asked the doctor.

"A Chihuahua," replied the young lady.

"That was no Chihuahua," responded the doctor. "That was a Mexican gutter rat dying of rabies."

Doctrinally, millions of religious people are holding a gutter rat to their heart. Not having a sense of the historical faith of the church, new ideas and concepts are constantly being presented, in sincerity, but with the voice of authority of the ancient prophets. And that is wrong.

It is more than wrong—it kills souls. The truth of the matter is that much popular thinking finds no support in the creeds of Christendom or in the writings of the Church: Self-esteem theology; Health and Wealth Gospel; Liberation Theology; certain forms of Dispensationalist; Rationalism; the gospel of Sophia; the Cults etc. Our generation needs to heed the biblical exhortation of Jude 1:3. "Beloved, when I gave all diligence to write unto you of the common salvation, it was needful for me to write unto you, and exhort you that ye should earnestly contend for the faith which was once delivered unto the saints."

What will happen when God's people seriously begin to study church history?

First, there will be a greater appreciation for the saints that have gone before. I think of the young people in particular now. Christian young people need heroes to believe in. Role models are important. Therefore study the lives of the saints.

Let me suggest to the young people one person in particular. His name was William Borden, and he was the heir to a large American fortune. Having graduated from Yale and attended Princeton Seminary, Borden was committed to being a missionary for Jesus Christ. Despite an upper-class upbringing, his travels around the world had challenged him to the needs of the lost to hear about Jesus Christ. He wanted to make his own life count for Christ. As William Borden trained for a life of service to the Kansu people of China, his heart and labor went out in practical ways to the widows, orphans, and cripples, in the backstreets of Chicago. A quiet yet powerful young man, William Borden sought to win other young college men for Christ and His service. In 1913, Borden finally fulfilled his dream to move towards the mission field. He arrived in Egypt and was soon battling cerebral meningitis. William Borden understood there were risks to serving the Savior—and he accepted those risks. Nearly every newspaper in the United States covered his untimely death at the age of twenty-five. William Borden made a great decision. Like Moses he forsook the pleasures of this world to lead others to a better world to come. Though his life was waste, in the eyes of the world, his life and death have been a testimony and a challenge beyond his own generation to "keep eternity's values in view." *Those who study history will be challenged* by other such stories.

Second, in the study of history there will be a greater confidence in witnessing for there will be no apology for the Church. One of the dangers of modern thinking is that the Church is a corrupt institution living in the last days—and this is taught by those within the body of Christ. We are not of that persuasion. We believe the Church is the most glorious institution. To know her story is to invite others to come to the only kingdom that will never end.

Third, there will be the enjoyment of great stories. There is, for example, the dramatic narrative of men such as John Wycliffe (1320–1384) and John Huss (1369–1415). John Huss, as a servant of the Savior, remained uncorrupted during the dark ages of human history when the glory of the gospel was darkened by the superstitions of the Church. John Wycliffe who preceded Huss had tried to turn the minds of the common people away from the vain superstitions of the Church by placing the Scriptures into their hands. Official opposition to Wycliffe by the Church was so severe that he had to flee to Bohemia.

While the "Morning Star of the Reformation" continued to criticize the sale of indulgences, the doctrine of transubstantiation (the magical turning of the communion elements into the literal body and blood of Christ), and papal hierarchies, darkness continued to descend the Church.

Another voice was needed to carry on the work of Wycliffe in Bohemia. That voice was found in the ministry of John Huss. John Huss was bold enough to criticize churchmen who rode on horses with brilliant tassels trailing behind in order to beat their fellow citizens with silver clubs. For his cries against injustice Huss was hated. He was arrested and brought to trial at a council of the Church of Constance (in present-day Germany) where, over a seven-month period, Huss was accused of teachings contrary to the official Church dogma.

In defense, Huss declared that he had never taught what he was accused of teaching. How could he recant or take back what he never said or wrote? Nor could he renounce the truth that the Church had become corrupt in some areas. The practice of penance was wrong for salvation is by grace through faith alone. Because of his stand for an alien righteousness, on July 6, 1415, Huss was condemned to be burned at the stake. He was taken outside the city limits and tied to a stake where a fire was lit. He died with these words upon his lips: "Jesus, Son of David, have mercy."

There are great men and movements to be read about in the study of history. Therefore, cultivate a greater appreciation for the saints of old, learn to witness with confidence, and learn the interesting stories of the Church.

The study of history need not be overwhelming. Let me share some practical ways to study this subject.

First, read the excellent biographies that are available. Barbour publishing House has an excellent series of biographies called *Heroes of the Faith*. The books can be read by old and young. The names of faithful men and women will live again: John Bunyan, William Carey, Amy Carmichael, Fanny Crosby, Corrie ten Boom, Jim Elliot, David Livingstone, Martin Luther, D. L. Moody, and George Muller, to name but a few.

Second, subscribe to *Christian History*, a very informative magazine. Several times a year this excellent work will be received. Several times a year some great person or event can be read about.

Third, find out what happened on some of the most important dates in Church history. We are familiar with secular dates.

July 4, 1776	The Declaration of Independence was signed
December 7, 1941	Pearl Harbor was attacked
September 11, 2001	The iconic Twin Towers of the World Trade Center in New York City were felled by terrorists

As we are familiar with dates in secular history let us become familiar with specific dates and events in sacred history.

A.D. 70	The city of Jerusalem is destroyed according to prophecy
A.D. 312	The conversion of Constantine took place
A.D. 1095	Pope Urban II launches the First Crusade
A.D. 1380	John Wycliffe oversees the English Bible Translation
A.D. 1478	The Spanish Inquisition was established
A.D. 1517	Martin Luther posts his Ninety-Five thesis
A.D. 1735	The Great Awakening under Jonathan Edwards begins
A.D. 1949	Billy Graham's Los Angeles Crusade is held

There are dates with destiny.

History need not be boring and will not be when it is remembered that the past is really His-Story. It is the story of God working in the lives of His people to conform them into the image of Christ and bring them back to glory. May it be said of the next generation as it was said of another, " We have heard with our ears, O God, our fathers have told us, what work thou didst in their days, in the times of old" (Ps 44:1).

I commend to you the study of Church history.

Stanford E. Murrell
Viera, Florida
May 2018

PART ONE
WHEN THE CHURCH WAS YOUNG
A.D. 33—754

CHAPTER 1

The Birth of the New Testament Church[1]

A Divine Interpretation

The story of human history may rightly be called "His-Story," or the story of God's work in the affairs of man. There is a grand central theme to be found in history and that is *God's redeeming love*. Viewing history from this perspective, where God is actively working out His plan of redemption in the affairs of men, could be called a "divine interpretation" of history. The Bible teaches us that, "God so loved the world he gave his only begotten Son, that whosoever believeth in him should not perish but have everlasting life" (John 3:16). The Son was given about 2,000 years ago.

Born in humility, raised in obscurity, Jesus Christ came in the fullness of time (Gal 4:4-5) to accomplish the great act of redeeming His people from their sins (Matt 1:21). The Lord of Glory came to earth through the lineage of the house of David in the nation of Israel. The Hebrew people were privileged to be the recipients of divine truth. Their prophets had predicted the Messiah was to come, and He came. Matthew was careful to record many incidents in the life of the Lord and then wrote, "That it might be fulfilled which was spoken through the prophets" (Matt 2:15; 4:14; 8:17; 12:17; 21:4).

During the days of the Lord's earthly ministry, most people in Palestine did not believe that the ancient prophecies were being fulfilled in the person of Jesus Christ. Because of this, the religious leaders arrested Jesus; He was tried, sentenced, and executed on a wooden cross at Calvary (Matt 27:27–35). But on the third day Jesus

---

[1] I am particularly indebted to B. K. Kuiper who greatly influenced my thoughts in writing A Glorious Institution: The Church in History When the Church was Young A.D. 33–754, and the companion volume, A Glorious Institution: The Church in History The Reformation and its Aftermath 1517 to the 1900s. Gratitude is also extended to Wm. B. Eerdmans Publishing Co. for permission to use The Church in History by B. K. Kuper under Eerdman's Fair Use policy.

arose from the dead (Matt 28:1–6). His resurrection became the foundation on which the New Testament Church would be built (1 Cor 15:3–8).

A Spiritual Kingdom

It was the Lord's desire to establish a *spiritual kingdom* (John 18:36) that would touch all the nations of earth (Matt 28:19–20). It was the Lord's design to call unto Himself a peculiar people (1 Pet 2:9) from every tongue and tribe (Rev 5:9), who would be indwelt and empowered by the Holy Spirit (John 14:16, 26). This called-out assembly would be *a most glorious institution, the Church* (Eph 5:25–27)!

Here we must draw a careful distinction between the *visible* and the *invisible* church. In the New Testament, the word "church" is the translation of the Greek word *ecclesia*, which means simply "an assembly." We find the word *ecclesia* used in the following senses in the New Testament (taken from *Easton's Bible Dictionary*):

(1) It is sometimes translated "assembly" in the ordinary sense (Acts 19:32, 39, 41).

(2) A few Christians associated together in observing the ordinances of the gospel are an *ecclesia* (Rom 16:5; Col 4:15).

(3) All the Christians in a particular city, whether they assembled together in one place or in several places for religious worship, were an *ecclesia*, as at Antioch (Acts 13:1), Jerusalem (Acts 8:1), and Ephesus (Rev 2:1).

(4) The whole *visible* body of professing Christians throughout the world are called the church (1 Cor 15:9; Gal 1:13; Matt 16:18). It is called "visible" because its members are known and its assemblies are public. God has ordained His people to organize themselves into distinct visible church communities, for the great purpose of giving visibility to His kingdom, of making known the Gospel of that kingdom, and of gathering-in all its chosen subjects.

In our day, as throughout history, the visible professing church is a mixture of "wheat and chaff," of the saved saints and the unsaved (Matt 13:24–30). It simultaneously has become polluted with the values of the world. In the visible church, great discernment is required in order not to judge but yet correctly to follow God's ways of holiness.

Ecclesia also denotes the *invisible* church, the whole body of the redeemed, all those whom the Father has given to Christ (Eph 5:23–29; Heb 12:23). The church invisible is a pure society, the church in which Christ dwells, the body of Christ. It is called "invisible" because the greater part of those who constitute it are already in heaven or are yet unborn, and also because its members still on earth cannot be distinguished with certainty. The qualifications of membership in it are internal and hidden. It is unseen except by Him who "searches the heart." "The Lord knoweth them that are his" (2 Tim 2:19). The church to which the promises appertaining to Christ's kingdom belong, is a spiritual body consisting of all true believers. It can be characterized by:

- *Its unity.* God has ever had only one church on earth. The Apostles did not set up a new organization. Under their ministry, disciples were "added" to the church already existing (Acts 2:47).
- *Its universality.* It is the "catholic" church: not confined to any particular country or outward organization, but comprehending all believers throughout the whole world. This use of the word "catholic" does not refer to any specific religious institution.
- *Its perpetuity.* It will continue through all ages to the end of the world. It can never be destroyed. It is an "everlasting kingdom."

For our purposes in this history of the Church, we treat the recognized visible Church up until the time of Constantine (chapter four), as approximately representing Christ's true invisible Church on earth. This was true in times of persecution because it was mainly only true believers who were willing to pay the costs (in suffering) associated with outward profession. However, as the State entered into Christian decisions beginning with Constantine, the resulting "institutions" of the visible Church became increasingly corrupt through sensuality, greed, pride, and political intrigue (1 John 2:16), creating a great departure from the principles given by God in Scripture.

Therefore, especially from the time of Constantine, we should understand our use of the word "church" herein to mean only the visible Church. Christ's true invisible Church would continue in the hearts of men, not in the institutions of mankind!

In the Fullness of Time

Physical preparation

To enhance the physical spread of the Gospel in "the fullness of time" (Gal 4:4), God used the Roman Empire. Peace and safety replaced tribal warfare. Widespread and easy travel became possible through a network of roads and bridges, like the famous Via Apia on the Italian peninsula. The pirates were driven from the sea to protect travelers and trade. Roman justice was swift and severe, which reduced robbery and rioting.

Spiritual preparation

While physical conditions of Roman life helped the cause of Christ, there was a spiritual and intellectual hunger in the hearts of people. The Greek altars and philosophy that had "conquered" Rome caused many people to doubt the multitude of gods with their fatal flaws. Myths and legends abounded. Superstitious travelers considered it wise to sail under the figurehead of two Greek gods, the Dioscuri or "Twin Brothers," Castor and Pollux, sons of Zeus and patrons of seafarers. The state religion of Rome offered no real change of heart or life. There was a moral vacuum as individuals became saturated with sins of the flesh. Then came the Gospel with its promises of peace from troubled consciences, pardon from all sin, and rest for heavy hearts. In Christ, people could find assurance of salvation, divine forgiveness, and eternal life—for Jesus was the Son of God.

Rapid expansion

Armed with a powerful message of hope, the early Church was poised for rapid expansion. The primary cause for the expansion was the sovereign movement of God visiting people and converting hearts. The book of Acts is careful to record that "the Lord added to the Church daily such as should be saved" (Acts 2:47). As God worked directly, so He also worked through secondary causes, such as the stoning of Stephen (Acts 7:54–60) and the persecution by Saul and other religious leaders (Acts 8:1–3). The Church was forced to flee for protection. In the flight to safety the Gospel was shared continuously, many were saved, and the Church grew.

Courage and Corruption

People looked at the suffering saints and were impressed by their faith, commitment, and perseverance. The Gentiles wanted to come to Christ and were welcomed (Acts 10:44–48). People looked at the spiritual body of the earthly Church and found it attractive. An enthusiastic belief that Jesus was alive, the good news of eternal life, high moral standards, followed by miraculous power (Acts 4:33), all these caused sinners to seek out the Savior. In addition, individuals were impressed with the unity of the saints (Acts 2:44), their firm doctrinal conviction (Acts 2:42), their acts of generosity (Acts 2:45), their joy (Acts 2:46), and the success that was present (Acts 2:41, 47).

Unfortunately, the early New Testament Church soon knew the pain of corruption and dissension as the world, the flesh, and the devil found a way into the local assemblies. Division, taking others to court, drunkenness during communion, open immorality, greed, pride, posturing for position, and many other sins were manifested. Still, in spite of transgressions, in spite of human failures, in spite of outward fears and inward corruption, the gates of hell would not prevent the Church's expansion (Matt 16:17–18). In the power of the Holy Spirit, the Stone which the builders rejected was about to fill the earth (Luke 20:17; Acts 4:11; 1 Pet 2:7; cp. Dan 2:35).

Selected Early Church Leaders

Apostolic Fathers

Clement of Rome	died *c.* A.D. 100
Ignatius	died *c.* A.D. 107
Hermas of Rome	died *c.* A.D. 150
Polycarp of Smyrna	A.D. 70–156
Barnabas of Alexandria	died *c.* A.D. 130
Papias	A.D. 60–130
Justin Martyr	A.D. 100–165

Church Fathers

Melito of Sardis	A.D. 100–170
Hegesippus	*c.* A.D. 120–190
Tatian	died *c.* A.D. 180
Irenaeus	*c.* A.D. 175–195
Tertullian	*c.* A.D. 160–225
Clement of Alexandria	*c.* A.D. 155–220
Origen	*c.* A.D. 185–254
Hippolytus	*c.* A.D. 160–236
Cyprian	*c.* A.D. 200–258
Lactanius	*c.* A.D. 240–320

Selected Early Writings of the "Fathers"
The Didache
Apology of Aristides
Apologies (Justin Martyr)
Shepherd of Hermes
Dialogue with Trypho
Epistle of Diognetus
Epistle of Ignatius
Epistle of Barnabas
Epistle to the Corinthians (Clement)
Epistle to the Philippians, Sayings of the Lord (Polycarp)
First and *Second Epistles* (Clement of Rome)
Address to the Greeks, Harmony of the Gospels (Tatian)
Apologetics (Tertullian)
Against Heresies (Irenaeus)
Miscellanies, Outlines of Scriptures (Clement of Alexandria)
Against Celsus, Hexapla, Tetrapla (Origen)
Ecclesiastical History (Eusebius)
Confessions, Retractions (Augustine)
Concerning the Trinity, Concerning Doctrine (Augustine)
The City of God (Augustine)

CHAPTER 2

The Suffering Saints
A.D. 33–313

The Heroic Age

The Greek word *thilipsis* is a very important word in the Christian vocabulary, for it speaks of tribulation. Christ had forewarned His disciples that they shall know something about suffering for righteousness by saying, "If they have persecuted me, they will also persecute you" (John 15:20). During the first three hundred years of its existence, sometimes called "The Heroic Age of the Church," the people of God knew persecution.

Enemies on Every Side

Peter was put in prison for preaching the gospel, *"but prayer was made without ceasing of the church unto God for him"* (Acts 12:5). Stephen and James died violently as faithful witnesses to Christ. Stephen was stoned, while James was put to death by the sword (Acts 7:59–60; 12:1–2). During his first visit to Corinth, Paul was taken by force into the presence of the Roman proconsul of Achaia, Gallio (Acts 18:12). The Lord inter-vened for when the governor discerned that the Jewish enemies of Paul were opposed to him based on a religious dispute, and not civil disorder, he had them ejected from the court (Acts 18:12–17).

    At first the sufferings of the Church came primarily from the Jewish community because the message of Christ threatened the social and economic fabric of their society in many ways. The early Christians were turning the world upside down (Acts 17:6). The attitude of the Jewish community towards Christians influenced the attitude of the Roman government officials when specific charges were heard. Of Paul and Silas it was said, *"These all do contrary to the decrees of Caesar"* (Acts 17:7).

Christians were also accused of atheism, cannibalism, immorality, and antisocial behavior. The charge of atheism arose because Christians refused to worship the emperor or the gods of Rome. The charge of cannibalism was based upon a misunderstanding of the celebration of the Lord's Supper. Spiritual language of "eating the body of Christ and drinking His blood" was taken literally by those who were not spiritually minded (1 Cor 11:23–26). Because religious services were often condu-cted in secret or after dark out of necessity, and because Christians displayed great love for each other, they were accused of immorality. Finally, Christians were charged with being antisocial, since many found it necessary to remove themselves from public life, rather than honor false gods in the same social gathering, or engage in unholy relationships (2 Cor 6:14).

The blood of the early Church flowed freely. Leading the path to martyrdom were the Apostles (1 Cor 4:9). According to tradition, each of the Apostles met a violent death with the exception of John (but even he suffered for righteousness sake).

- **Simon Peter** the first notable leader of the Church (Acts 1–15; Gal 2:9) was executed at Rome. It is said that he was crucified upside down (cf. John 21:18–19).
- **James**, the son of Zebedee, preached in Judea. He was beheaded by Herod Antipas about A.D. 44 (Acts 12:1–2).
- **John**, the son of Zebedee, labored in Jerusalem, and then from Ephesus among the Churches of Asia Minor. He was banished to the isle of Patmos, liberated, and died a natural death at Ephesus (cf. John 21:20–23).
- **Andrew**, once a disciple of John the Baptist, preached in Scythia, Greece, and Asia Minor. He died by crucifixion.
- **Philip** preached in Phrygia, and died a martyr's death at Hierapolis.
- **Bartholomew** became a missionary in Armenia. He was flayed to death.
- **Thomas** labored in Parthia, Persia, and India. He suffered martyrdom near Madras, at Mount St. Thomas.
- **Matthew** ministered in Ethiopia and was martyred.
- **James** the Less preached in Palestine and Egypt, where he was finally crucified.
- **Jude** preached in Assyria and Persia, where he was martyred.

- **Simon** the Zealot was crucified.
- **Judas** Iscariot hanged himself following his betrayal of Christ (Matt 26:14–16; 27:3–5; Acts 1:16–20).

Of the original Twelve Disciples, one committed suicide, one died a natural death, and ten suffered martyrdom—four of them by crucifixion.

The Glory and the Power of the Roman Empire
(The Roman Emperors from Augustus to Commodus)

The Julio-Claudian Dynasty
30 BC–AD 14	Augustus
AD 14–37	Tiberius
AD 37–41	Gaius (Caligula)
AD 41–54	Claudius
AD 54–68	Nero

The Year of the Four Emperors and the Flavian Dynasty
AD 68	Galba
AD 69	Otho
AD 69	Vitellius
AD 69–79	Vespasian
AD 79–81	Titus
AD 81–96	Domitian

The Antonine Emperors
AD 96–98	Nerva
AD 98–117	Trajan
AD 117–138	Hadrian
AD 138–161	Antoninus Pius
AD 161–180	Marcus Aurelius
AD 161–169	Lucius Verus
AD 180–192	Commodus

A Beast Named Nero

There was another reason why the attitude of the Roman government changed toward the Christians. There was a need to blame someone for a tragic fire in Rome itself that occurred in A.D. 64, during the reign of the emperor Nero. Beginning on June 18, the fire burned brightly for six days and seven nights, destroying the greater part of the city. Ten of the fourteen sections of the city were destroyed. Initially, Nero himself was suspected of starting the fire. His dreams of rebuilding the ancient city were well known. In all probability, Nero was several miles away in his palace at Antium. As soon as he heard the news he went to Rome and tried to fight the fire. Still, the people clamored for justice.

In order to dispel the rumors and growing hostility away from himself, Nero accused the Christians of starting the fire. The accusation seemed plausible—the Church taught that Jesus was coming again and that the earth was to be destroyed by fire (2 Pet 3:10). And so terrible persecution came to the Church. Some Christians were sewn up in the skins of wild beasts. Fierce dogs were let loose upon them and their bodies were ripped to pieces. On at least one occasion, Nero held a dinner party in which he burned Christians at the stake. His purpose was to use them to illuminate the nighttime skies when daylight ended. And so the slaughter of Christians went. The tides of hostility ebbed and flowed in strength from A.D. 68 onward. Only one thing was constant: Christians were made to hurt and die because of their faith. The martyrs became witnesses to a watching world.

Three Memorable Martyrs

Standing out among the martyrs of the early Church were Ignatius, a Syrian bishop of Antioch; Polycarp, bishop of Smyrna; and Justin the Apologist, who wrote extensively and spoke verbally in defense of Christianity. These leaders and others are sometimes called *Church Fathers* because of the esteem in which they were held by other Christians in the local assemblies. The men who led God's people from A.D. 90 to 460 are frequently divided into four groups:

- Apostolic Fathers   A.D. 90–150
  edified the Church
- Apologists   A.D. 130–180
  defended the Church against Roman persecution

- Polemicists   A.D. 180–225
  led the Church against internal heresy
- Theologians   A.D. 225–460
  attempted to harmonize Christianity with popular philosophy

Ignatius (A.D. 67–107)

About A.D. 110, Ignatius was ordered by the Roman authorities to be arrested because of his Christian profession and was sent to Rome to be executed by being thrown to the wild animals. The emperor at this time was Trajan (A.D. 98–117) who was usually a moderate ruler. Though he did fear secret societies, it was not Trajan's official policy to engage in random persecutions of Christians. He allowed no arrests to be made solely on the basis of anonymous tips. However, an open profession of faith could be dangerous as Ignatius discovered. Because of his confession of Christ, he was arrested and sent to Rome. Along the way Ignatius wrote letters to different congregations stressing the importance of Church unity. Unity, he taught, was to be enhanced by rooting out all heresies denying the deity of Christ. Finally, the time of death came. Ignatius wanted to die for Jesus. He did not want other Christians to interfere in his commitment. "I fear your kindness, which may harm me," he wrote to the saints in Rome who desired to set him free; "you may be able to achieve what you plan. But if you pay no heed to my request, it will be very difficult for me to attain unto God."

Justin Martyr (c. A.D. 100–165)

As Ignatius faced death bravely, so did the philosopher Justin Martyr, who was scourged and beheaded in Rome with six other Christians. Born about A.D. 100 in a small town in Samaria, Justin was a natural scholar. After studying the various philosophical systems of his day, he embraced Christianity and became a capable defender of the faith. He wrote two apologies[1] to the emperor Antionius Pius (A.D. 138–161) and to his adopted son Marcus Aurelius, who would one day reign from A.D. 161 to 180. He also wrote a dialogue with Trypho the Jew, in which Justin contended that Jesus was the Messiah.

---

[1] The word *apologies* is here used to mean verbal or written defenses of a particular doctrine; the word is so used by the Apologists.

On his second stay in the city of Rome, Justin engaged in a public debate with a Stoic philosopher by the name of Crescens who attacked Christians with great acrimony saying they are atheists and impious. Shortly thereafter, about A.D. 166, Justin was beheaded during the reign of Marcus Aurelius. He faced death bravely. When threatened with execution Justin said, "If we are punished for the sake of our Lord Jesus Christ, we hope to be saved."

Polycarp (A.D. 70–156)

Perhaps the best known of the early martyrs is Polycarp, who ministered in Asia Minor (modern Turkey) as bishop of Smyrna. He was a disciple of the Apostle John. In his messages to the Church, Polycarp emphasized faith in Christ and the necessity of working out faith in daily life. When the hour of his execution came, the proconsul offered Polycarp a way to escape. But Polycarp stood firm in his faith. On the day of his execution, after being bound with his hand behind him like a sacrificial ram, Polycarp lifted his eyes to heaven and prayed. "I bless Thee for that Thou hast granted me this day and hour, that I might receive a portion amongst the number of martyrs in the cup of [Thy] Christ unto resurrection of eternal life, both of soul and of body, in the incorruptibility of the Holy Spirit."

Though he is now famous for his thoughtful *Meditations,* the emperor Marcus Aurelius (A.D. 161–180) proved to be a terrible opponent of Christianity. According to the Christian historian, Eusebius, Christians were shut out from many forms of public life. Some were arrested without cause, brought before magistrates, convicted, and condemned. Their property was confiscated and given away.

In Lyons and Vienne in southern Gaul (France) the assault on Christians was intense. Those who could not be compelled to renounce their faith were beheaded even if they possessed Roman citizenship. Some were taken to the arena of the amphitheater to be splattered in blood. They were part of a cruel spectacle known as damnatio ad bestias—literally "condemnation by beasts." The men who orchestrated the show were known as bestiarii. Vicious and starving animals were trained to pounce upon human flesh. One such martyr was Blandina, a slave girl of Lyons (A.D. 177). She had personally endured numerous tortures, and witnessed the killing of others. Through her many ordeals, Blandina was a source of inspiration as she encouraged fellow prisoners under terrible torture to be faithful to Christ. Among those who died was Ponticus, a boy who was about fifteen years old. Finally, Blandina's moment came. She faced her death bravely rejoicing that she could suffer for the Lord. After much abuse a net was thrown over her. She was tossed about and gored by a bull until death overcame her. The body of Blandina along with others were exposed for six days and then burned. Their ashes were thrown into the Rhone River. The pagans did not want to acknowledge the hope of resurrections which Christians believed.

Decline and Fall of the Roman Empire: A.D. 193–476

(The Roman Emperors from Pertinax to Romulus Augustulus)

The House of Severus

Pertinax	A.D. 193
Didius Julianus	A.D. 193
Septimius Severus	A.D. 193–211
Pescennius Niger	A.D. 193–195
Clodius Albinus	A.D. 195–197
Caracalla	A.D. 211–217
Geta	A.D. 211
Macrinus	A.D. 217–218
Elagabalus	A.D. 218–222
Severus Alexander	A.D. 222–235

The Struggle for Survival

Maximinus I	A.D. 235–238
Gordian I	A.D. 238
Gordian II	A.D. 238
Balbinus	A.D. 238
Pupienus	A.D. 238
Gordian III	A.D. 238–244
Phillips I	A.D. 244–249
Trajanus Decius	A.D. 249–251
Trebonianus Gallus	A.D. 251–253
Aemilian	A.D. 253
Valerian	A.D. 253–260
Gallienus	A.D. 253–268
Postumus	A.D. 260–268

The Period of Military Rule
    Claudius II Gothicus   A.D. 268–270
    Quintillus   A.D. 270
    Aurelian   A.D. 270–275
    Tacitus   A.D. 275–276
    Florian   A.D. 276
    Probus   A.D. 276–282
    Carus   A.D. 282–283
    Carinus   A.D. 283–285
    Numerian   A.D. 283–284

The Tetrarchy and the Dynasty of Constantine
    Diocletian   A.D. 284–305
    Maximian   A.D. 286–305/307–308
    Carausius   A.D. 286/287–293
    Constantius I Chlorus   A.D. 305–306
    Galerius   A.D. 305–311
    Severus II   A.D. 306–307
    Maxentius   A.D. 306–312
    Constantine the Great   A.D. 306–337
    Licinius   A.D. 308–324
    Maximinus II Daia   A.D. 310–313
    Constantine II   A.D. 337–340
    Constantius II   A.D. 337–361
    Constans I   A.D. 337–361
    Magnentius   A.D. 350–353
    Julian the Apostate   A.D. 361–363
    Jovian   A.D. 363–364

The House of Valentinian Rulers of the West
    Valentinian I   A.D. 364–375
    Valens [East]   A.D. 364–378
    Gratian   A.D. 375–383
    Valentinian II   A.D. 375–392
    Theodosius I the Great   A.D. 379–395

[East only, then the whole empire]

Magnus Maximus	A.D. 383–388
Arcadius [East]	A.D. 395–408
Honorius	A.D. 395–423
Constantine III	A.D. 407–411
Theodosius II [East]	A.D. 408–450
Constantius III	A.D. 421
Johannes	A.D. 423–425
Valentinian III	A.D. 425–455

The Survival of the Eastern Part of the Roman Empire and the Fall of the West

Marcian [East]	A.D. 450–457
Petronius Maximus	A.D. 455
Avitus	A.D. 455–456
Leo I the Great [East]	A.D. 457–474
Majorian	A.D. 457–461
Libius Severus	A.D. 461–465
Anthemius	A.D. 467–472
Olybrius	A.D. 472
Glycerius	A.D. 473–474
Julius Nepos	A.D. 474–475/477–480
Zeno [West]	A.D. 474–475
[East]	A.D. 476–491
Basiliscus [East]	A.D. 475–476
Romulus Augustulus	A.D. 475–476

Peace Before Persecution

Following the death of Marcus Aurelius on A.D. March 17, 180, the church enjoyed a time of relative peace. It was not to last due to the reign of Septimius Severus (A.D. 200–211). In the early years of his reign, Christians were not treated badly. But then, in A.D. 202, the emperor issued a decree which forbid anyone to convert to Christianity or Judaism. The reason for this official change in policy is uncertain. What is certain is that believers in Alexandria, Egypt experienced a fiery trial of their faith. Along with many others who suffered for Christ was Origen (c. A.D. 185–254), the most famous of the Alexandrian writers. His father Leonides had been beheaded for the Lord. His son was to suffer for the Savior as well. In A.D. 250, the emperor Decius imprisoned Origen and had him tortured. In the providence of God, Origen initially survived his ordeals. Then, Decius died and Origen was released. However, his health was destroyed. He died shortly after his release. He was faithful to Christ to the end.

Origen encouraged the *allegorical interpretation* of the Scriptures. Simply stated, this method of understanding the Scriptures holds that the literal meaning of the Bible conceals a deeper meaning that can only be perceived by the mature believer. He taught that this concealing of the truth by God under the guise of common words was designed to prevent "pearls" from being cast before the uninterested and unbelieving (Matt 7:6).

Renewed Efforts of Destruction

In A.D. 249 another general persecution of the Church broke out under the emperor Decius. In the providence of the Lord, his reign only lasted two years (A.D. 249–251). Then came Valerian (A.D. 253–260) and the Church suffered again. There was hardly any reprieve. Hostility was endured through the reigns of Galienus (A.D. 260–268), Aurelian (A.D. 270–275) and on into the reign of the emperor Diocletian (A.D. 284–305).

Perhaps the most severe of all the persecutions came under Diocletian. Beginning in February 303, three edicts of persecution were issued in quick succession. The Churches were to be burned, all sacred books were to be confiscated, and the religious leaders were to be imprisoned or compelled to offer a sacrifice. Many lives were lost. Mental cruelty was added to physical hardships, as Satan's servants assaulted the Church in order to destroy it completely.

During these dark days many Christians in the city of Rome found a small place of security. Under the city were the catacombs. The catacombs existed because, as early as the fifth century before Christ, burials were forbidden inside the city of Rome. Burial vaults could be carved into the underground tunnels of Rome which winded and crisscrossed in every direction making up over 500 miles of subterranean passages thirty or more feet below the surface. In the sides of the galleries or passages, excavations were made in rows upon rows so that the dead could be properly buried. Here, among the dead, the living found a hiding place.

The Promise of Jesus Realized

Despite her great hardships, the Church never lost hope, and the Lord began to honor such faith. When the emperor of the East, Galerius, became ill, he suffered excruciating torment. A Christian writer named Lactantius recorded that the body of Galerius rotted and was eaten by maggots as he twisted on his bed in agony. In his final days Galerius had opportunity to reconsider the pain of the Christians which he had caused. In A.D. 304, Galerius had issued an edict requiring everyone in the empire to sacrifice to the gods on pain of death or forced labor. When Christians refused they were imprisoned or executed. Precious Bibles were destroyed. However, in the will of the Lord, Galerius manifested a belated measure of repentance. Believing he was being judged by the Christian God for the sufferings he had caused the followers of Christ, from his deathbed, Galerius issued in the year A.D. 311, a proclamation which allowed Christians permission to worship freely. He even invited prayers for his own welfare. By receiving more freedom to worship, and by manifesting a willingness to pray for one's enemies, little by little, the Church began to gain the spiritual triumph that Jesus had promised (Matt 16:18).

* * *

THE DOCTRINE OF TRIBULATION

(1) The word *tribulation* is found twenty two times in the Authorized Version. The word *tribulations* is found four times.

(2) To suffer tribulation (Gk. *thilipsis*) is to suffer affliction, to be troubled, to suffer due to the pressure of circumstances or the antagonism of persons.

(3) In examining the passages that speak of tribulation, it becomes evident that all God's people in all ages have known emotional, spiritual, and physical affliction (Deut 4:30; Jdgs 10:14; 1 Sam 26:24; 1 Sam 10:19; Matt 13:21).

(4) Tribulation also comes to those who are not God's people, in the form of divine discipline (Matt 24:21, 29; Mark 13:24; 2 Thess 1:6; Rom 2:9).

(5) Of particular concern is the Christian and tribulation. The Bible clearly makes the following statements.

- For as long as they are in the world, the disciples of Christ shall have tribulation (John 16:33).
- Only through much tribulation will the saints enter into the kingdom (Acts 14:22).
- The value of tribulation is that it works patience (Rom 5:3; 12:12).
- To endure tribulation is not to be loved less by Christ, for nothing shall separate Christians from His faithful love (Rom 8:35).
- God finds a special way to comfort the saints who suffer (2Co 1:4).
- Paul could find reasons to rejoice in the very midst of tribulation (2 Cor 7:4; Rom 5:3; 2 Thess 1:4), and therefore did not want anyone else to worry on his behalf (Eph 3:13).
- When believers at Thessalonica were surprised at the suffering they had to endure, Paul reminded them he had taught that Christians must suffer (1 Thess 3:4).
- John on the isle of Patmos does not divorce himself from tribulation, nor does he ever say of himself that he represents those who shall not suffer tribulation. On the contrary, John considers himself at the moment of his writing to be a companion in suffering (Rev 1:9).
- The tribulation of the saints is well known to the Lord (Rev 2:9–10), and is for a stated purpose.
- Always, God's people emerge victorious out of tribulation, no matter how great (Rev 7:14).

(6) In all the biblical passages, there is not a single word that God will spare His people from the purifying effects of tribulation. Just the opposite is stated and demonstrated time and again.

(7) The story of the Old Testament, the writing of the New Testament, and the documentation of 2,000 years of history testify to the blood of the saints in the Church.

(8) Any teaching that seeks to exempt God's people from tribulation during any period of human history, will not find support from the twenty-six passages in the Scriptures that use this word.

CHAPTER 3

The Foundations of Faith
A.D. 33–325

Contending for the Faith

Bible doctrine is essential to proper spiritual maturity (Prov 4:2; 1 Tim 4:13). Sound doctrine is the foundation of faith (Titus 1:9). What people believe about sin, salvation, the Scriptures, and the Savior will determine their eternal destiny, as well as their relationship with God the Father (John 7:17). Doctrine does not divide the Church as much as it unites the saints around the truth that has been entrusted for preservation and proclamation (Jude 1:3). Any attempt to minimize the importance of doctrine should be challenged (2 John 1:9–10). The Church of Jesus Christ would not be the powerful force it is in the world today apart from the faithful defense of basic Bible doctrine. While it is unfortunate that controversies about doctrine occur, such discussions are necessary (1 Cor 11:18–19) as they form an essential part of the history of the Church. Christians are exhorted by Jude to "earnestly contend for the faith which was once delivered unto the saints" (Jude 3).

The Importance of Doctrine

The importance of Bible doctrine is demonstrated in the life of Christ. People were astonished at His words (Matt 7:28; 22:33; Mark 11:18; Luke 4:32). Through doctrinal teaching Jesus set forth the reality of His kingdom and how the citizens of His domain should live. The disciples the Lord chose to be with Him learned His thoughts well; His doctrine become their doctrine. Following the Lord's ascension into heaven, new converts were taught, so that they continued steadfast in the apostle's doctrine (Acts 2:42). As a result, the Church grew stronger (Acts 5:28).

A Canon of Scripture for the Church

The Old Testament Canon

The early Church trusted the Apostles' doctrine because they knew it was grounded in the teachings of the Old Testament, which they believed to be inspired by God (2 Tim 3:16). While the Christian community did not embrace the idea that God inspired all men and all writings, there was selected material considered unique. By the end of the first century A.D., thirty-nine books were listed as being canonical (inspired and given by God) according to Bishop Melito of Sardis in modern Turkey.

Bishop Melito had been asked by a friend to provide an accurate listing of the ancient books as to their number and order. He honored the request. Leaving out the book of Esther, the list Melito provided is recognized by Jews and Protestants today. It had taken many centuries to determine which books would be held in high esteem, and which writings would not be received. But finally, the canon on the Old Testament was closed after centuries of consideration. God had been faithful to preserve His Word.

The process of preserving the sacred Scriptures started immediately after the first recording of the same. The divine revelations of the Old Testament began when specific speeches and sayings were written down. God Himself was the first author of Holy Scripture, according to Deuteronomy 5:22: it was the Lord who wrote the Ten Commandments in stone. Later, Moses put into writing the Book of the Covenant, including the Ten Commandments (Exod 20:1—23:33). The people of Palestine promised to obey all that had been written and rehearsed in their hearing (Exod 24:3–8), because they received it as the Word of God through Moses (Deut 31:24–26).

Subsequent generations would also submit to these Scriptures. In 625 B.C., for example, when repairs were being made on the temple in Jerusalem, a scroll containing the Law of God was discovered. King Josiah had it read before all the people; this led to a time of spiritual renewal (2 Kgs 22—23).

As the centuries passed, other speeches and wise sayings were written down and recognized by the Hebrew people as being the authoritative voice of God. The message of Micah (Mic 3:9–12), for example, caused King Hezekiah to repent (Jer 26:17–19). Ezra is credited with gathering the many Old Testament writings into the approximate collection we have today.

When the collection of inspired material became larger, Judas Maccabeus and his associates (c. 164 B.C.) divided the canonical books into three divisions: the Law, the Prophets, and the Writings. It was this division and this canon that Jesus accepted (Luke 24:44) and that the early Church embraced.

The Old Testament Canon as History

The Pentateuch

Genesis, Exodus, Leviticus, Numbers, Deuteronomy

12 Historical Books

(Pre-Kingdom) Ezra, Joshua, Judges, Ruth
(Kingdom) 1 and 2 Samuel, 1 and 2 Kings, 1 and 2 Chronicles
(Exile and after) Ezra, Nehemiah, Esther

5 Books of Poetry

Job, Psalms, Proverbs, Ecclesiastes, Song of Solomon

5 Major Prophets

Isaiah, Jeremiah, Lamentations, Ezekiel, Daniel

12 Minor Prophets

(Pre- and Assyrian) Hosea, Joel, Amos, Obadiah, Jonah, Micah, Nahum
(Chaldean/Babylonian) Habakkuk, Zephaniah
(Post-Exile) Haggai, Zechariah, Malachi

The New Testament Canon

While the Old Testament had taken many years to formulate, the New Testament Scriptures were written within one hundred years of each other. However, like the Old Testament canon, it would take time until the multitude of various writings (Luke 1:1) could be duly considered by Church leaders and a canon carefully formulated.

There were good reasons why the Church wanted to settle upon an official body of Scripture. First, there was the matter of persecution. Soon after the ascension of

Christ into heaven (Acts 1:9–11), physical acts of hostility were inflicted upon the saints. Initially, the Jewish community was responsible for the ill treatment of believers in Christ as the true Messiah (Acts 8). Later, the Roman government officially attacked the people of God (Jas 1:1; Rev 13:1–7). If Christians were called upon to suffer for their faith, they would do so (1 Pet 2:21), but there was no need to suffer needlessly for non-canonical books, which were found only to be offensive to religious and civil authorities. Those spurious writings gladly could be given up or destroyed.

Second, there was the matter of heresy. Some of the enemies of Christ and the Gospel were brazen enough to tell those in the Christian community which books in their possession were inspired of God and which were not. These heretics tried to set the scriptural boundaries for the Church!

One such bold enemy of Christ was a man named Marcion. Around the year A.D. 140 Marcion arrived in Rome to spread his heretical ideas about God and Christ. Marcion denied the physical resurrection of Christ and the Judeo heritage of the Church. Therefore, he excluded the early apostolic writings, which placed great emphasis upon the doctrine of the resurrection and the deity of Christ. The *Canon Muratori* forced the Church to consider more closely and more formally which books should make up the New Testament.

It was not always easy. Writing in the early part of the fourth century, Eusebius of Caesarea confessed that some texts were still being debated, such as the letters of James and Jude, the second letter of Peter, the second and third letters of John, and the letter to the seven churches of the Revelation. And yet progress was being made. By the middle of the fourth century, the *Codex Vaticanus*, a Greek volume of both Old and New Testaments, listed the complete New Testament as it is known today. The discussion continued, however. There were other writings that were under consideration for canonicity, such as the *Letter of Barnabas* and *The Shepherd of Hermas*.

It was not until A.D. 367, in his annual Easter Festal Letter, that Athanasius, Bishop of Alexandria, explained to all the churches and monasteries within his sphere of authority what the Old Testament and the New Testament canon of Scripture should be. Though his list did not conclude the discussion for everyone, it hastened the day when the debate over the canon would end.

By the first part of the fifth century, the consensus of tradition concerning the canon of Scripture was established and honored. Jerome, in a letter written in 414, accepted the New Testament books listed by Athanasius, though he was also willing to include the *Letter of Barnabas* because, in his opinion, the author was the traveling companion of Paul and was therefore an apostle.

A key in understanding the formation of the New Testament canon, is that it was never an arbitrary choice based on the decisions of men. Four criteria were used powerfully by the Holy Spirit among widely dispersed groups to bring unity in the formation of the canon. Inspired books should have:

(1) authors who had been in direct contact with Christ or the Apostles;
(2) consistency in doctrine;
(3) wide acceptance and use by churches in all regions, through the guidance of the Spirit; and,
(4) produced dynamic changes in lives, as used by the Spirit.

The New Testament canon meets these criteria in a unique and special way; it truly has been formulated by the hand of God!

Finally, all the discussions were over. In the providence of God since the days of Jerome, the twenty-seven books that make up the New Testament have been confirmed by the Church. Spiritual healing has come to those who read the sacred words. Worthy men have debated and defended these particular books of the Bible against unworthy opponents (Jude 1:4). God has been faithful to give to His people a particular body of truth (Jude 1:3). Fundamental to Christian faith is the fact that we have a God-breathed book without error, the Bible. There is a canon of Scripture for the Church!

Development of the New Testament Canon

Marcion	*The Canon Muratori*	*Eusebius*	*Athanasius*
c. 140	c. 200	c. 325	367
	Matthew	Matthew	Matthew
	Mark	Mark	Mark
Luke	Luke	Luke	Luke
	John	John	John
	Acts	Acts	Acts

Marcion	*The Canon Muratori*	*Eusebius*	*Athanasius*
c. 140	c. 200	c. 325	367
Romans	Romans	Romans	Romans
1 Corinthians	1 Corinthians	1 Corinthians	1 Corinthians
2 Corinthians	2 Corinthians	2 Corinthians	2 Corinthians
Galatians	Galatians	Galatians	Galatians
Ephesians	Ephesians	Ephesians	Ephesians
Philippians	Philippians	Philippians	Philippians
Colossians	Colossians	Colossians	Colossians
1 Thess.	1 Thess.	1 Thess.	1 Thess.
2 Thess.	2 Thess.	2 Thess.	2 Thess.
	1 Timothy	1 Timothy	1 Timothy
	2 Timothy	2 Timothy	2 Timothy
	Titus	Titus	Titus
Philemon			Philemon
			Hebrews
			James
		1 Peter	1 Peter
			2 Peter
	1 John	1 John	1 John
			2 John
			3 John
	Jude		Jude
	Revelation	Revelation	Revelation
	The Wisdom of Solomon		
	The Revelation of Peter		

"Fathers of the Church"

The leaders of the churches during the first century after the Apostles are called the "Apostolic Fathers" because they effectively continued the work of the Apostles. They too believed that, "All Scripture is given by inspiration of God, and is profitable for doctrine, for reproof, for correction, for instruction in righteousness, that the man of God may be complete, thoroughly equipped for every good work" (2 Tim 3:16–

17). By teaching the Scriptures, men like Clement, Hermas of Rome, Ignatius of Antioch, Polycarp of Smyrna, and Barnabas of Alexandria were able to establish others in the doctrines of grace.[1]

Clement of Rome (died A.D. 100) was a presbyter and bishop in Rome. In A.D. 96 he wrote a letter to the Church at Corinth, admonishing the Christians to restore some older presbyters who had been ousted by younger members. Quoting extensively from the Old Testament and from the words of Jesus, Clement tried to teach the way of humility that yields to God's divine order and peace (Titus 2:10).

Hermas of Rome (died c. 150) also taught the doctrines of Christ in his writings such as *The Shepherd*. After providing some biographical information as to how he came to faith, Hermas' book set forth a series of visions about Christian life and morality. *The Shepherd* contains three main parts: five visions, twelve mandates, and ten similitudes concerning an ethical life.

Ignatius (died c. 107) was bishop of Antioch in Syria. Prior to suffering martyrdom for his faith, Ignatius was able to teach the Church to stand against false doctrines. He opposed the Ebionite heresy, which demanded that the regulations of the Jewish faith be kept as a means of salvation. He also challenged Docetism, which held that Christ only *appeared* to have a real birth, death, and resurrection.

Polycarp (c. 70–156), bishop of Smyrna, joined Ignatius in a martyr's death. By life and by lip he defended sound doctrine, through opposing some of the Valentinian heretics who had embraced Gnosticism. When Polycarp encountered Marcion, a leader of Gnosticism, he fearlessly characterized him as "the first born of Satan." Only one of Polycarp's letters has been preserved, and that is the letter addressed to the Philippians.

Barnabas of Alexandria in North Africa (died c. 130) may have gone a little too far in his zeal to combat false doctrine. He became so anti-Judaic as to almost deny a historical connection between Judaism and Christianity. Still, his life throbbed with missionary zeal as he taught individual responsibility.

Justin the Apologist (born c. 100) was probably the most dramatic defender of the faith. He was a prolific writer. Around the year A.D. 153, while in Rome, Justin wrote his famous *Apology*, whereby he defended Christianity against the charges of atheism

---

[1] While the Apostolic Fathers were not without their own theological biases, they did want to exhort and edify the Church. In some instances, the Apostolic Fathers seem to assign a rather significant place to baptism as a medium of forgiveness of sin. Martyrdom and celibacy are also thought to have special power to atone for sin. Therefore, in reading the Apostolic Fathers, much spiritual discernment is needed.

and immorality. He tried to prove that Christians were loyal citizens by teaching that the Lord's kingdom was not of this world. Therefore, the Roman Empire had no reason to fear a social insurrection from the Christian community. In the midst of his many literary efforts and his faithfulness to sound doctrine, Justin was beheaded for his faith in A.D. 165.

Early Heresies

Heresy may be defined as a radical departure from the truth. It differs from "incorrect" teaching by matter of degrees. In the last half of the second century, several heresies emerged that shook the foundation of the Church. They were Gnosticism, Montanism, and Arianism.

Gnosticism

The name "Gnosticism" derives from the Greek word *gnosis*, which means "knowledge." According to the Gnostics, they possessed a special mystical knowledge that was the secret key to salvation. Salvation was their main concern. Unfortunately, the Gnostics came to believe that all matter is evil, or at best unreal. A human being, they said, is an eternal spirit trapped or imprisoned in a body that is evil, being made of matter.

How did this happen? Gnosticism taught that the supreme being had no intention of creating a material world, but only a spiritual one. Therefore, only a number of spiritual beings, called eons, were made. One of these eons, far removed from the supreme being, fell into error, and created the material world.

Since this world was made by a spiritual being, there are still "sparks" or "bits" of spirit in it. These are imprisoned in human bodies and must be liberated through "gnosis" (knowledge). This liberation is accomplished by listening to special heavenly messengers who have been sent to give individuals that knowledge, without which there is no salvation. One messenger, some believed, was Christ.

Since Christ was a heavenly messenger, and since body and matter are evil, Gnostics rejected the idea that Christ had a body like ours. Some said that His body was just an *appearance* of a real body. Later, the Church would call this heresy Docetism, meaning "to seem," and would refute it totally (1 John 1:1–4).

Montanism

Montanism is named after its founder, Montanus, who had been a pagan priest until his conversion to Christ in A.D. 155. After a time, Montanus began to teach that he was possessed by the Holy Spirit. Soon two women, Priscilla and Maximilla, followed him and also began to prophesy. Together, they claimed that their movement was the beginning of a new age demanding a rigorous moral life. To claim, as the Montanists did, that the end of time was beginning with the giving of the Spirit to Montanus and his followers, was to deny the significance of the Person and work of Christ. His teachings made the Gospel into just one more stage in the history of salvation. Because of these issues, the rest of the Church opposed Montanism.

Arianism

The Arian Controversy began in Alexandria, Egypt, when Licinius ruled in the East and Constantine ruled Rome in the West. The bishop of Alexandria, Alexander, clashed with Arius, one of the most prestigious and popular presbyters of the city. The main issue at stake was whether the Son of God (Christ) was co-eternal with God. One important phrase of the Arian motto said, "There was when the Son was not." With these words the Arians denied both the deity of Christ and His eternal pre-existence.

From its foundation, the Church had worshipped Jesus Christ. Arius' proposal forced the Church to decide whether it would cease such worship, or to declare that it was worshipping a creature. At the Council of Nicea the Church solved the Arian Controversy, by declaring that Jesus Christ was "very God of very God," and Arianism was rejected as heresy (discussed further in chapter 5).

Four Church Champions

The Church found spiritual champions to combat these heresies. These are called "Church Fathers" (as distinguished from "Apostolic Fathers") because (1) they too were used of the Lord to teach and strengthen the churches, and (2) they lived in the second and third centuries and therefore were not close to the Apostles. Among the most capable of these defenders of the faith were Irenaeus, Tertullian, Clement, and Origen.

Irenaeus was born into a Christian family during the first half of the second century, though the exact date is uncertain. The years A.D. 115 through 142 have been suggested. He is believed to have been a Greek from Polycarp's home town of Smyrna, now Izmir, Turkey. While in Smyrna, Irenaeus saw Polycarp and heard him preach. Moving to Lyons in Gaul, now France, Irenaeus became a bishop in the Church. In the year A.D. 200 he suffered the death of a faithful witness to the cause of Christ having defended Christianity in such works as *Against Heresies*. Irenaeus had felt compelled to speak against those who falsified the Word of God in order to overthrow the faith of many, by drawing them away.

Tertullian was born sometime between the years A.D. 150 and 155 in the North African city of Carthage. He has been called "The Father of Latin Christianity." A prolific writer, he spoke out against heresy, including Gnosticism which stresses salvation through special knowledge, which is contrary to the message of salvation through Christ alone, by faith alone (Acts 4:12; Rom 1:17). Converted to Christ, when he was about forty, while practicing law in Rome, Tertullian eventually returned to Carthage and became a presbyter in the Church. Some of his writings were controversial because he encouraged Christians to embrace persecution rather than to flee from it. "The blood of the martyrs is the seed of the Church," he famous noted. Ironically, Tertullian died peacefully sometime after the year A.D. 229.

Clement of Alexandria was a very able instructor in the theological school in Egypt. During his years as a teacher (A.D. 190–202), Clement wrote the majority of his works, in which he covered almost every aspect of Christian conduct. Later, when religious persecution broke out under the Roman emperor Septimius Severus, about A.D. 202, Clement fled Alexandria. He died in Asia Minor.

Origen (c. 185–254), a student of Clement of Alexandria, was a great scholar in the Church. As a prolific writer he wrote many books in defense of Christianity, including *Against Celsus*. One of his monumental works was the *Hexapla*, a comprehensive edition of the Bible arranged in six columns. It contained the text from the Hebrew Scriptures, a Greek translation of the Hebrew, the Septuagint, and the Greek versions by Symmachus, Aquila, and Theodotion. But he was not without controversy. Origen notoriously espoused an allegorical interpretation of Scripture, which ultimately led to a number of erroneous and peculiar interpretations of the Bible, including universalism redemption. His life ended as a teacher in Caesarea.

"I Believe": The Apostles' Creed

The difficulties of the Church with the early heresies necessitated, and produced, a creed for Christendom. The word "creed" comes from the Latin word *credo* and means, "I believe." Chief among ancient articulations of the Christian faith was a creed known as *The Apostles' Creed*, the most universally accepted Christian creed in the early Church period. Being Roman in origin, the Apostles' Creed is known and used only in churches of Western origin, such as the Roman Catholic Church and those stemming from the Protestant Reformation.

> I believe in God the Father Almighty, Maker of heaven and earth,
>
> And in Jesus His only Son our Lord, Who was conceived by the Holy Ghost, born of the Virgin Mary, suffered under Pontius Pilate, was crucified, dead, and buried. The third day He rose again from the dead. He ascended into heaven and sitteth on the right hand of God the Father Almighty; from thence He shall come to judge the quick and the dead.
>
> I believe in the Holy Ghost, the holy universal Church, the communion of saints, the forgiveness of sins, the resurrection of the body, and the life everlasting. Amen.

New Forms of Church Government

As the Church struggled to formulate a core set of beliefs based upon an accepted canon of Scripture, so the Church was determined to preserve what it professed. Many felt a strong form of Church government had to be found, and it was. The controversy with the Gnostics and Montanists produced the episcopal form of government, whereby Church authority was invested in spiritual rulers who came to be called "bishops" (Greek: *episcopos*; overseer). Organizational complexity had found Christianity. But it had taken a long time, for at first the organizational structure had been very simple. The Church officers were presbyters or elders, and deacons (1 Tim 3:1–13; Acts 14:23; 1 Tim 5:17; 1 Pet 5:1).

As the Church grew in number and the affairs of the Church grew more complex, local assemblies would chose a priest or layman in each city to be an *episcopos*, overseer or bishop, to help manage its affairs. As the number of bishops grew, they in turn required superintendence and co-ordination. By the fourth century we hear of archbishops, metropolitans, or primates, governing the bishops and the churches of a province. Over all these levels of clergy were the patriarchs who ruled at the apostolic sees in Constantinople, Antioch, Jerusalem, Alexandria, and Rome. During this time, the foundations were laid for the Bishop of Rome to begin to feel that additional power was within his grasp, especially since Rome was the only city in the Latin-speaking West that traced its origins to an Apostle (whereas the other four sees resided in the Greek-speaking East). The Bishop of Rome could claim authority over other bishops by virtue of being in the capitol city of the Empire, as well as could interpret "the keys of the kingdom" to mean Jesus entrusted Peter exclusively, and his subsequent successors, with the authority of His Church (Matt 16:19).

A patriarch or an emperor could also call the bishops and archbishops to convene in synods, or councils, to discuss important matters and to make rules and regulations that were binding. If a council represented only a county or region, it was called a *provincial* council; if it represented the whole number of bishops of some given territory, it was called a *plenary* council. Sometimes an *ecumenical* council, also called a *general* council, was convened to discuss Church dotrince and practice that was binding on the entire Church. In this way, the Church grew in organizational intricacy.

CHAPTER 4

The Sign of the Savior
A.D. 313

Constantine the Great

Constantine the Great (c. 285–337) is known as the first "Christian emperor" of the Roman Empire. He ruled from A.D. 306 to 337. Constantine's parents were Constantius Chlorus, the western co-emperor of the Roman Empire, and Helena, a concubine. When his father died in 306, the Roman army in Britain proclaimed Constantine emperor. This meant that he ruled over Britain, Gaul [France], and Spain. Maxentius ruled over Italy and North Africa. A military conflict for power was inevitable.

In a surprise move made in order to get the military advantage, Constantine marched into Italy leading an army of forty thousand men. At Saxa Rubra, ten miles from Rome and a little to the north of the city, the two great armies of Maxentius and Constantine met. The date was October 27, 312. On the morning of October 28, the battle would begin. During the night, the only thing separating the army of Constantine from the army of Rome was the Tiber River, and the Milvian Bridge, which crossed the river.

Constantine had reason to be concerned as his soldiers made their final preparations for battle. He was outnumbered three to one and the army of Maxentius contained the Praetorian Guard, the elite of all the Roman armies. As the twilight faded away, the outcome of the engagement on the next day was in grave doubt. Constantine felt he needed spiritual help.

Like his father, Constantine's heart was drawn toward the worship of Mithra, the Persian sun god, who was believed to be a great warrior and the champion of truth and justice. Mithra was a soldier's god. Perhaps Constantine was thinking of Mithra when he fell into a fitful sleep that night and dreamed an unusual dream. According to one account, Constantine dreamed of a monogram composed of the first two Greek letters—chi and rho—of the name of Christ (*Christos*) ☧. The next day he had his soldiers inscribe the monogram on their shields. According to another version, on the evening before the battle, as he watched the setting sun, Constantine suddenly saw a cross above the sun. In letters of light the cross bore the words: *Hoc Signo Vinces*, "In this sign, conquer." On October 28, Constantine and his soldiers won the victory. The army of Maxentius was completely defeated. Although the Praetorian Guard fought like lions, they were cut down where they stood.

Finding Freedom to Worship

Constantine believed he had won the battle because he had received help from the God of the Christians. He too would become a Christian and worship the true Light of the world. Whether or not Constantine was indeed converted has been a subject of great debate; certainly he was very tolerant toward Christians. During the winter of A.D. 312–313, he instructed an officer in North Africa to provide money to the bishop of Carthage so that the ministers could be paid. At Milan in 313, he issued an edict granting all persons the freedom to worship as they wished. Persecution of Christians stopped! They were placed upon a level of equality, before the law, with the other religions of the Empire. New laws allowed bishops to decide civil lawsuits. The branding of the face was banned because it marred the image of God. Law courts and workshops were closed on Sundays, and the gladiatorial games were stopped.

Building for the Glory of God

While the Edict of Milan did not establish Christianity as the only and official religion of the Empire, it did mark the victory of the Church over heathenism. Despite three hundred years of fierce persecutions, the Church had not only survived, it had triumphed. The blood of the martyrs had not been spilt in vain. Upon the throne of Rome finally sat a man who confessed Christ. Buildings where Christians met were once burned; majestic buildings were to be erected to the glory of God. The Church of the Holy Sepulchre would be constructed in Jerusalem. In Constantinople the Hagai Sophia would be erected to the glory of God. In Bethlehem, the Church of the Nativity would stand.

A.D. 313: A Date to Remember

All Christians should remember the date 313, for in that year the Church was granted the same rights and privileges that the followers of other religions had. But as the date is remembered, let it also be remembered that the Church won her rights not by fighting, but by suffering. The Church survived not by might or power, but by the Spirit of the Living God (Zech 4:6).

The Eagle and the Cross

After A.D. 313 the emblem of the Roman armies was replaced. The eagle gave way to a cross. However this was not all good, for as the Church transformed the world, the world invaded the Church. Suddenly, the Christian name became an avenue to political, military, and social promotion. Individuals became Christians in name only.

The Relation between Church and State

Because Constantine granted the Church freedom of religion and many special favors, he felt freedom to take an arbitrary and active role in the internal affairs of the Church. For example, when the appointment of Caecilian as bishop of Carthage was challenged in A.D. 313, Constantine intervened to settle the dispute in Caecilian's favor.

The Donatists

The Donatists were named after their leader, Donatus. While orthodox in faith, the Donatists caused division in the Church by teaching that those who had denied the faith during periods of severe persecution should not be re-admitted to the Church. Constantine instructed the bishops of Rome to hold a formal hearing to review the matter. When the Donatists were not satisfied with the opinion of the commission, Constantine heard the case himself, and in 316 declared Caecilian to be the rightful bishop. Constantine also summoned the Council of Nicea in 325, which ruled against Arianism, a heresy that denied that Christ as the Son of God was co-eternal with the Father. It was the Edict of the emperor that provided legal force to the Nicene council.

This merging of Church and state became a mixed blessing to the nations of the earth. While some good did come out of the arrangement, the blending of the two became the occasion for misunderstanding, hostility, and bloodshed. It can be argued that more harm than good was done by the merging of Church and state. Certainly the spiritual vitality of the Church was weakened because of the many concessions that had to be made to sinful men and worldly practices, in order to survive politically in a sinful society. Instead of transforming the kingdoms of this world by truth, righteousness, holiness, and separation, the Church was transformed and then corrupted by the world. In many ways, the Church first embraced and then practiced all that makes up the satanic world system (2 Cor 4:4).

Julian the Apostate

Born in A.D. 332, Julian, a nephew of Constantine the Great, became emperor in A.D. 361. His reign was to be brief, ending in A.D. 363 when he was killed in battle fighting the Persians. Though blessed with a Christian home, Julian was never converted. He became enamored with the classical philosophers and forsook his spiritual heritage. Once he was in political power, Julian made it clear that his heart preferred the old gods. Because he abandoned Christianity, and promoted Hellenistic philosophy, he is known as Julian the Apostate.

In his hostility to the Church, Julian did persecute the Christians. He reversed the land and financial privileges that Christians had been given. His primary weapon against the Church was the pen. As a gifted writer, Julian attacked Christianity with scorn and mockery. All the while Julian tried to restore polytheistic worship by rebuilding pagan temples. There is a wonderful legend that Julian acknowledged his failures in A.D. 363 when he was mortally wounded in battle against the Persians. A spear pierced his thigh. As the blood spurted out, Julian took some in his hand, threw it toward heaven and cried, "Thou hast conquered, O Galilean." He was 32 years old.

CHAPTER 5

In the Councils of the Church
A.D. 325–451

A Multitude of Counselors

The Bible teaches that there is safety in a multitude of counselors (Prov 11:14). When the early Church became concerned over problems that arose as a result of the conversion of the Gentiles, a council was held by the apostles and elders in Jerusalem (Acts 15). This established an important precedent followed in the centuries to come.

Different types of councils were established. A provincial council acted for and spoke on behalf of only one province. A national council took into consideration the religious concerns of an entire nation. A general or ecumenical council assembled ecclesiastic representatives of the Christian Church of all countries. In a small town in Asia Minor called Nicea in A.D. 325 the first general or ecumenical council was held.

Nicea: The First Ecumenical Council

It was at Nicea that the important issue was fully discussed which had engaged the constant attention of the Church for over three hundred years as it debated whether Jesus Christ, the Son, was really God. Because the Church was unable to successfully answer the Arian Controversy concerning the deity of Christ, there was lingering and deep division in the Church.

Finally, Emperor Constantine (c. 285–337) called a general council to resolve the controversy in a definitive manner. According to early Church historian and eyewitness, Eusebius, more than three hundred bishops made their way to a lovely city called Nicea, located on the eastern shore of Lake Ascania (now Lake Iznik, Turkey) along the Bosporus strait, forty-five miles from Constantinople. The men met in a magnificent hall in the palace of the emperor who presided over the opening session and took an active part in the discussions. Some of the bishops in the council had endured for Christ physical suffering, which left permanent scars in their bodies.

The atmosphere was euphoric as the ministers of God began to discuss many legislative matters. They approved a standard procedure for bringing back into the Church those who had not been faithful in the days of persecution. They also established the procedure for the election and ordination of presbyters and bishops. But the most difficult issue that the Council faced was the Arian Controversy.

An Important Question to Settle

Arius (d. 336), a presbyter in the Church in Alexandria, Egypt, taught that Jesus was not truly God while Athanasius (born c. 295), another presbyter in the same Church, taught he was. The question was important to settle. The value of the saving work of Christ depends upon what kind of Person He is. If Christ is not God, He cannot be the Savior of man for only God can save man from the desperate state of sin into which he has fallen. Only God can forgive sins (Mark 2:7) Jesus claimed the authority to forgive sins (Matt 9:1–8). Did Jesus have this authority? The Church needed to know. Athanasius understood the importance of the controversy and affirmed that Christ was "One in being with the Father" (*homoousios*), and "begotten not made." Like the apostle John, Athanasius declared his Redeemer was his Lord and his God (John 20:28).

The debate grew fierce between the young Athanasius and the more mature Arius, a man of integrity and a capable orator. Still, the young "David" was ready to challenge his "Goliath," who was popular with a large number of people.

Arius truly thought that to believe that the Son is God as well as the Father is God, would mean to believe that there are two Gods. If this were true, then the Church was in danger of falling back into heathenism and polytheism, the belief in many gods. To stop this from happening, Arius thought that Jesus, although He is somewhat like God, is not after all fully God, with all of God's attributes and virtues. According to Arius, Jesus Christ is the first and highest of all created beings and is worthy of honor and veneration, but Jesus does not exist from eternity past, and is not of the same substance or essence as the Father.

Athanasius argued that if Jesus were not God, then He would be a great blasphemer—for He certainly claimed to be God (John 8:28, 58). Furthermore, if Jesus is not God, then millions upon millions of people have been foolishly misled into idolatry, for Christ has been worshipped. Only God is worthy of worship. Athanasius defended the worshipping of Christ in a famous book entitled *On the Incarnation of the Word of God*.

The debate concerning the deity of Christ was monumental in importance. Man's salvation was at stake, for Christ's Person and work are inseparably united. At His birth an angel had announced, "Thou shalt call his name Jesus; for he shall save his people from their sin" (Matt 1:21).

At this historic Council of Nicea in the year A.D. 325, and after much debate, the views of Arius were condemned as heresy. A statement of the true doctrine of the Person and work of Christ was finally adopted and articulated in the Nicene Creed. This creed is accepted by both the Western churches and those of the East, including the Greek Orthodox and Russian Orthodox churches. The following is an early version reviewed at the council.

The Nicene Creed

We believe in one God, the Father Almighty, maker of all things visible and invisible.

And in one Lord Jesus Christ, the Son of God, the only-begotten of the Father, that is, from the substance of the Father, God of God, light of light, true God of true God, begotten, not made, of one substance [Greek: *homoousios*] with the Father, through whom all things were made, both in heaven and on earth, who for us humans and for our salvation descended and became incarnate, becoming human, suffered and rose again on the third day, ascended to the heavens, and will come to judge the living and the dead.

And in the Holy Spirit.

But those who say that "there was when He was not," and that before being begotten He was not, or that He came from that which is not, or that the Son of God is of a different substance [*hypostasis*] or essence [*ousia*], or that He is created, or mutable, these the universal Church anathematizes.

The Greek words are very significant, speaking as forcibly as possible for the deity of Christ, and unity in the Godhead:

homoousios   one and the same substance
hypostasis   person, distinction, mode of subsistence
ousia   essence, substance, nature, being

The final version included an expansion of the third paragraph, and in Christian charity omitted the judgments of the last paragraph, so that it ended in this way:

> And we believe in the Holy Spirit, the Lord and Giver of life, who proceedeth from [Latin: *filioque*, "from" and not "through"] the Father and the Son; who with the Father and the Son together is worshipped and glorified; who spoke by the prophets.
>
> And we believe in one catholic [universal] and apostolic Church; we acknowledge one baptism for the remission of sins; and we look for the resurrection of the dead, and the life of the world to come. Amen.

"Athanasius Against the World"

As the Nicene Creed exalts Christ by declaring Him to be God, it also serves to remind the Church to be grateful for faithful men such as Athanasius (c. 295–373), Bishop of Alexandria, Egypt. Who would want to forget his famous saying, *Athanasius contra mundum*, which means "Athanasius against the world"? The point was made that even if he were the only person in the whole world defending the truth of the deity of Christ, he still would defend it against all opponents. Athanasius was responsible more than anyone else for the defeat of Arianism in 325. One of the three Ecumenical Creeds is associated with his name (the other two being the Apostles' and the Nicene).

The Athanasian Creed

> Whosoever will be saved: before all things it is necessary that he hold the universal Faith: Which Faith except every one do keep whole and undefiled: without doubt he shall perish ever-lastingly.

And the universal Faith is this: That we worship one God in Trinity, and Trinity in Unity; Neither confounding the Persons: nor dividing the Substance [Essence]. For there is one Person of the Father: another of the Son: and another of the Holy Ghost.

But the Godhead of the Father, of the Son, and of the Holy Ghost, is all one: the Glory equal, the Majesty co-eternal. Such as the Father is: such is the Son: and such is the Holy Ghost. The Father uncreated: the Son uncreated: and the Holy Ghost uncreated.

The Father incomprehensible [unlimited, infinite]: the Son incomprehensible: and the Holy Ghost incomprehensible.

The Father eternal: the Son eternal: and the Holy Ghost eternal. And yet they are not three eternals: but one eternal. As also there are not three uncreated: nor three incomprehensibles [infinites], but one uncreated, and one incomprehensible [infinite]. So likewise the Father is Almighty: the Son Almighty: and the Holy Ghost Almighty. So the Father is God: the Son is God: and the Holy Ghost is God. And yet they are not three Gods: but one God.

So likewise the Father is Lord: the Son Lord: and the Holy Ghost Lord. And yet not three Lords: but one Lord. For like as we are compelled by the Christian verity, to acknowledge every Person by himself to be God and Lord; So are we forbidden by the universal religion to say, There be [are] three Gods, or three Lords.

The Father is made of none: neither created, nor begotten. The Son is of the Father alone: not made, nor created: but begotten. The Holy Ghost is of the Father and of the Son: neither made, nor created, nor begotten: but proceeding.

So there is one Father, not three Fathers: one Son, not three Sons: one Holy Ghost, not three Holy Ghosts. And in this Trinity none is afore, or after another; none is greater, or less than another. But the whole three Persons are co-eternal, and coequal.

So that in all things, as aforesaid: the Unity in Trinity, and the Trinity in Unity, is to be worshipped. He therefore that will be saved, must [let him] thus think of the Trinity. Furthermore it is necessary to everlasting salvation: that he also believe rightly [faithfully] the Incarnation of our Lord Jesus Christ.

For the right Faith is, that we believe and confess: that our Lord Jesus Christ, the Son of God, is God and Man; God, of the Substance [Essence] of the Father; begotten before the worlds: and Man, of the Substance [Essence] of his mother, born in the world. Perfect God; and perfect Man, of a reasonable soul and human flesh subsisting.

Equal to the Father, as touching his Godhead: and inferior to the Father as touching his Manhood. Who although He be [is] God and Man: yet He is not two but one Christ. One; not by conversion of the Godhead into flesh: but by taking [assumption] of the Manhood into God.

One altogether: not by confusion of Substance [Essence]: but by unity of Person. For as the reasonable soul and flesh is one man: so God and man is one Christ; who suffered for our salvation: descended into hell [Hades, the sphere of the dead]: rose again the third day from the dead.

He ascended into heaven, he sitteth on the right hand of the Father God [God the Father] Almighty. From whence [thence] He shall come to judge the quick and the dead.

At whose coming all men shall rise again with their bodies; And shall give account for their own works.

And they that have done good shall go into life everlasting: and they that have done evil, into everlasting fire. This is the universal Faith: which except a man believe faithfully [truly and firmly], he can not be saved.

* * *

THE DOCTRINE OF THE DEITY OF CHRIST

(1) The Gospel of John declares that Jesus is the eternal divine Word (*logos*), and the source of life and light (John 1:1, cp. 1:14; 1:1–5, 9).

(2) Through becoming flesh, the Word was revealed as the Son of God and the source of "grace and truth," as "the only begotten of the Father" (John 1:14, 18).

(3) The Lord used the divine name (cp. Exod. 3:14) for Himself seven times. The claims to deity are explicit:

- The bread of life   John 6:35, 48, 51
- The light of the world   John 8:12; 9:5
- The door for the sheep   John 10:7, 9
- The good shepherd   John 10:11, 14
- The resurrection and the life   John 11:25
- The way, truth, and life   John 14:6
- The true vine   John 15:1, 5

(4) Thomas worshipped Jesus declaring Him to be, "My Lord and my God" (John 20:28). The Lord pronounced a blessing on all who share the faith of Thomas (John 20:29–31).

(5) Paul declares that in Christ "dwells all the fullness of the Godhead bodily" (Col 2:9; cf. 1:19).

(6) Jesus is the Father's image and His agent in creating and upholding all things (Col 1:15–17).

(7) All who would be saved must call upon Christ for salvation, just as one calls upon Jehovah (Joel 2:32; Rom 10:9–13).

(8) Jesus is "God over all" (Rom 9:5), our "God and Saviour" (Titus 2:13), and the source of divine grace (2 Cor 12:8–9; cp. 2 Cor 13:14).

(9) In Hebrews, the perfection of Christ's high priesthood is presented, declaring Him to have full deity and unique dignity as the eternal Son of God (Heb 1:3, 6, 8–12).

(10) There are many other passages that teach the deity of Christ.

- In the Old Testament, study: Psa 2:6–12; cp. Heb 1:5; Ps 45:6–7; cp. Heb 1:8–9; Psa 110:1; cp. Heb 1:13; Isa 9:6; Jer 23:6; Dan 7:13; Mic 5:2; Zec 13:7; Mal 3:1.

- In the New Testament, study: John 1:1–3, 14, 18; 2:24–25; 3:16–18, 35, 36; 4:4, 15; 5:18, 20–22, 25–27; 11:41–44; 20:28; 1 John 1:3; 2:23; 4:14–15; 5:5, 10–13, 20; Rom 1:7; 9:5; 1 Cor 1:1–3; 2:8; 2 Cor 5:10; Gal 2:20, 4:4; Phil 2:6; Col 2:9; 1 Tim 3:16; Heb 1:1–3, 5, 8; 4:14; 5:8.

Three More Champions of Orthodoxy

Unfortunately, the Nicene Council did not put an end to the Arian Controversy. Falsehood does not die easily. There were still many in the Church who agreed with Arius. Until the day of his death, Athanasius had to contend for the doctrine of the deity of Christ as expressed in the Nicene Creed. Following the death of Athanasius (c. 373), other champions of orthodoxy (historic Christian truth) emerged. Among the most capable were three men from the province of Cappadocia in Asia Minor: Basil of Caesarea, Gregory of Nazianzus, and Gregory of Nyssa.

Basil of Caesarea (c. 330–379) came from a very famous Church family and studied at Athens. In 356 he started a monastic community in Pontus. In 370 Basil became Bishop of Caesarea in Cappadocia, which put him in the middle of the Trinitarian controversy. He was influential in the eventual triumph of orthodoxy, and worked to heal the schism at Antioch.

Gregory of Nazianzus (c. 330–389) was a friend of Basil of Caesarea. He was a notable Eastern theologian and leader in the monastic movement. In 379 Gregory was called to become the orthodox bishop in Constantinople. He faithfully preached the doctrines of grace[1] and presided at the start of the Council of Constantinople in 381. After being persecuted for his faith, Gregory resigned as bishop in 381 and devoted the rest of his life to study and meditation.

Gregory of Nyssa (c. 330–395) was the younger brother of Basil of Caesarea. He was a champion of orthodox doctrine during the years of the Trinitarian controversy. He was a great preacher and a faithful theologian.

---

[1] The historic doctrines recovered in the Reformation that exalt God's sovereignty and holiness, especially in the realm of salvation.

When the Council of Constantinople was called in 381 to reaffirm the Nicene Creed and to articulate the beliefs of the Church in the deity of the Holy Spirit, the influence of these three great Cappadocians was felt. Because of their strong defense of the teachings of Scripture, Arianism was completely and finally rejected by the Church.

The Council of Chalcedon

As there had been a variety of views in the Church concerning the deity of Christ, so there was diversity regarding His humanity and His two natures in their relation to each other. How could Jesus be both God and man? Was He two persons or one? Did Jesus cease to be God during the days of His humiliation? Was there ever a moment when He was not God?

Nestorius (late fourth century, c. A.D. 451), Bishop of Constantinople, was one of those who saw the two natures of Christ in a loose mechanical co-existence, so that neither nature partook in the properties of the other. According to Nestorius, the divine did not have a part in the sufferings of the human nature of Christ. This teaching needed to be contested, for if Nestorius was right, a sinner would be redeemed by the suffering sacrifices of a mere man. But a mere man could accomplish no eternal redemption. In 431 a Third Ecumenical Council was called at Ephesus, which condemned Nestorius and his followers. When the Nestorians arrived to defend their position, they were not welcomed, so they established a rival council. When the controversy continued to rage, the Emperor finally decided the matter against the Nestorians. Nestorius himself entered into a monastery afterwards.

Following the Council of Ephesus, there was a great deal of dissatisfaction on the part of many. Eutyches, abbot of a monastery near Constantinople, in an effort to demonstrate the unity of the person of Christ, began to teach that after the incarnation of Christ the two natures fused into one so that the one nature partook of the properties of the other. Distinctions between the two natures were obliterated. This teaching only served to heighten the controversy considerably.

Complete confusion would have reigned if Eutyches were right! *Omniscience* is an attribute of Deity only; according to the flesh, Christ grew in wisdom and knowledge and favor with God and men (Luke 2:52). *Omnipresence* is an attribute of Deity only; one of the characteristics of the human body is that it is confined to a specific locality. If Christ is already physically omnipresent, how can He come a second time from heaven?

Because of these considerations the stage was set for another Church council. In the year 451 a Fourth Ecumenical Council was held in Chalcedon near Nicea. Over six hundred bishops were present. Finally, after much debate a creed was formulated which stands equal in importance as the Creed of Nicea. The Church affirmed that Jesus has two complete natures. One nature of Jesus, fully human, and one nature, fully divine. This is called the "Hypostatic union." The term hypostatic means personal. The hypostatic union is the personal union of the two natures of Jesus. Christ was complete and true humanity without loss or diminishing of His divine attributes. The human and the divine natures of Christ existing together is a great mystery, which the Church acknowledged. However, the Church stated that they exist in Christ without confusion, change, division, or separation. While Christ has two natures, He is uniquely one person, not two persons.

The Creed of Chalcedon

> We, then, following the holy Fathers, all with one consent, teach men to confess one and the same Son, our Lord Jesus Christ, the same perfect in Godhead and also perfect in manhood; truly God and truly man, of a reasonable [rational] soul and body; con-substantial [co-essential] with the Father according to the Godhead, and con-substantial with us according to the Manhood; in all things like unto us, without sin; begotten before all ages of the Father according to the Godhead, and in these latter days, for us and for our salvation, born of the virgin Mary, the mother of God, according to the Manhood; one and the same Christ, Son, Lord, Only begotten, to be acknowledged in two natures, inconfusedly, unchangeably, indivisibly, inseparably the distinction of natures being by no means taken away by the union, but rather the property of each nature being preserved, and concurring in one Person and one Subsistence, not parted or divided into two persons, but one and the same Son and only begotten—God the Word, the Lord Jesus Christ, as the prophets from the beginning [have declared] concerning Him, and the Lord Jesus Christ Himself has taught us, and the Creed of the holy Fathers has handed down to us.

The Latin Church Fathers

The passing of the Apostolic Fathers (who were taught the Christian faith by the Apostles directly) brought forth the Eastern and Latin [Western] Church Fathers. These men were ordained by God to keep on defending the truth of the Scriptures against heretical teachers. In their writings we find the history, doctrines, and traditions of the Church. Three of the Latin Fathers were Ambrose, Jerome, and Augustine.

Ambrose (A.D. 339–397), the son of a Roman governor in Gaul (France), became the Bishop of Milan. Educated in the law in Rome, he became a faithful defender of the faith for the Western Church against Arianism. Ambrose wrote extensively. More than half of his many writings were commentaries on Scriptures. In his interpretation of the Bible, Ambrose used the allegorical-mystical method. He admits to a literal sense of the text, but sought a deeper mystical meaning. A lover of music, Ambrose wrote many songs. A lover of souls, he sought to bring people to Christ. It was to him that Augustine owed his conversion. When he died many mourned his passing, for they greatly loved him. People remembered that he remained firm in the face of intense opposition.

For one event in particular Ambrose should always be remem-bered. It concerned the atrocious behavior of the Emperor Theodosius. Despite a confession of faith, Theodosius had murdered 7,000 people in the city of Thessalonica as punishment for a rebellion in which Roman officers had been killed. Ambrose wrote a letter to the Emperor but received no reply. When the Emperor presented himself at the Lord's table, the Bishop met him at the door to the Church and turned him away by saying, "How will you lift up in prayer the hands still dripping with the blood of the murdered? How will you, with such hands, receive and bring to your mouth the body and blood of the Lord? Get out of here, and do not dare to add another crime to the one you have already committed!" This bold move caused the Emperor, eight months later, to make a public confession of his sins and seek forgiveness.

Jerome (A.D. 341–420) was born in Eastern Europe but was converted in Rome. He labored for thirty-four years in a monastery at Bethlehem (A.D. 386–420), and gave to the Church the Vulgate, the Latin translation of the Bible from the Hebrew of the Old Testament and from the Greek of the New Testament. For over 1,000 years, the Vulgate became the only form in which the Bible was known to Western Europe. It remains to this day the authorized version of the Roman Catholic Church. He was careful about his sources of information and extensively used early manuscripts of the Bible that no longer exist. Jerome did much to promote asceticism and celibacy.

Augustine (A.D. 354–430) was born in the province of Numidia, North Africa, near ancient Carthage. Little did anyone realize that he would one day become the Bishop of Hippo, North Africa. His father Patricius was a pagan, but his saintly mother Monica prayed earnestly for many years that her son might be converted. A good bishop living near her home assured her that, "A son of so many prayers and tears would not be finally lost." By the grace of God, Augustine did come to faith and helped to change the world. His conversion happened in a very dramatic way.

At the age of thirty-one Augustine was in a garden in Milan, weeping and pleading with God to deliver him from sin. In despair he suddenly heard the voice of a child from a house nearby repeating in a kind of chant, "Take and read; take and read." Augustine immediately took up a New Testament and read Romans 13:13–14. The first words on which his eyes fell: "Let us walk honestly, as in the day; not in rioting and drunkenness, not in chambering and wantonness, not in strife and envying. But put ye on the Lord Jesus Christ and make not provision for the flesh to fulfill the lusts thereof." At once, all shadows of doubt were removed from Augustine. In a moment of time, he passed from death into life!

His journey, from moral darkness and philosophical speculation to a spiritual crisis of the soul and conversion, is told in two volumes. His *Confessions* tells of his moral change, while his *Retractions* describes the changes in his intellectual thought over the years.

Following his salvation, Augustine gave his life to the Church and to defending the faith. As a student of the Bible, Augustine stands pre-eminent among the theologians of all time. His influence upon all faiths has been notable. His teaching that the millennium (Rev 20:1–6) referred to the period between the Lord's first and second comings, during which time the Church would conquer the world, has influenced amillennial[2] and post-millennial[3] writers of past and present.

---

[2] *Amillennial.* That doctrine which holds the millennium to be a picture of the present reign of Christ ("the kingdom of God is within you," Luke 17:21) and of the saints in heaven (analogous to Rev 6:9–10). The "first resurrection" (Rev 20:5) is either the life of Christians who have died and are with Christ in heaven, or life in Christ that starts with spiritual new birth (Rom 6:8–11; Eph 2:6; Col 3:1–4). Satan has been bound through the triumph of Christ in His crucifixion and resurrection (John 12:31; Col 2:15).

[3] *Post-millennial.* That doctrine in which the kingdom of Christ and the Church will experience much more expansion on earth before the Second Coming. The thousand years are understood by

A prolific writer of about 250 volumes, Augustine's greatest book might be *The City of God*, which took fourteen years to write. In this work, Augustine traces the development of the city of earth and the city of God through two cities: the former to eternal judgment and the latter to eternal happiness. It sets forth the sovereignty of God in the affairs of men and the ultimate triumph of good over evil, despite the fact that the reverse seems more often true. Much of Augustine's pastoral time and energy were spent contending with the Manicheans, the Donatists, and the Pelagians.

The Manicheans

This religion had its origin in southern Babylonia, having been founded by Mani in the third century A.D. (c. 240). It spread rapidly through Persia, India, China, Egypt, North Africa, and Italy. It became the official religion of Turkey. Like Gnosticism, Manicheism was a dualistic system. According to Mani, the internal conflict of good and evil found in each person is because of the presence of two principles. One principle, called "light," is spiritual; the other principle, of "darkness," is matter. Throughout the universe are these two principles, both eternal: light and darkness. Somehow the two have mingled and the present human condition of good and evil is a result of that mixture. Salvation consists in separating the two elements, and in preparing the spirit for its return to the realm of pure light, in which it will be absorbed. Since any new mingling of the principles is evil, true believers must avoid such things as the sexual act of procreation. According to Mani, what he taught had been revealed in various fashions to a long series of prophets, including Buddha, Zoroaster, Jesus, and Mani himself.

For a short period, as a young man, Augustine embraced Manicheism, because the system seemed to offer an answer to some of his perplexing concerns about the Scriptures and the origin of evil. As Augustine considered the problem of evil in particular, he wondered where it came from. He had been taught by his Christian mother, Monica, that all things were created by the Divine, who was supreme and good. However, if God did not create evil, who did? How did it come into existence? Perhaps God was not altogether good or wise. Augustine wanted to know and Manicheism offered an answer.

---

some as a final period of earthly Christian triumph following the spread of the gospel. Others agree with amillennialists in identifying Revelation 20:1–6 with the entire period that begins with the resurrection of Christ.

The Bible, taught Mani, was not in truth the word of the eternal principle of light. Nor was evil a creation of that principle, but of its opposite, the principle of darkness. What do all of these metaphysical phrases mean? Who really knows!

Because Augustine was not satisfied with such speculative teaching, he continued to search until he found the Savior, the true Light of the World. His heart returned to trusting the Bible, which reveals the true origin of sin in the rebellion of Satan (Isa 14) and in the fall of man (Gen 3).

The results of the teaching of Mani had far reaching repercussions for the Church because it was so divisive. In the system of Manicheism there were two classes: the elect and the auditors. The elect were ascetic and concerned themselves with religious activity. The auditors participated in the holiness of the elect, in return for supplying the elect with the necessities of life. Manicheism encouraged an ascetic spirit in the churches, while dividing Church members into clergy and laity. It also promoted the concept that the primary function of the priest was to be an intermediary between God and man. The priest was believed to have extraordinary power with God.

The Donatists

The Donatists received their name from their leader, Donatus. It was his position that professing Christians who had denied the faith during the days of persecution in the reign of Diocletian (284–305), should not be re-admitted to the Church. Because some bishops had given their copies of the Scriptures to the government officials to be burned, Donatus did not believe that they were worthy to minister the sacraments or to ordain others as bishops. The Donatists withdrew and started their own churches.

The Pelagians

Far more serious were the teachings of the Pelagians. Pelagius was a British monk who denied the doctrine of original sin (that the human race had fallen into moral corruption in Adam). Pelagius argued that man was *not* born corrupt; he was not totally depraved; and he was not predestined to heaven or hell. Denying original sin, Pelagius said that babies are born innocent. The influence of others causes a person to do what is wrong. Each person has a free will that determines his eternal destiny.

Augustine believed that every person is born physically alive but spiritually dead, having been conceived in sin (Psa 51:5). Only the grace of God can save a soul (Eph 2:8-9). The grace of God is based on His divine pleasure (Eph 1:9). The Church agreed with Augustine over Pelagius. The General Council of Ephesus in 431 officially condemned the teachings of Pelagius. Later, in 529 the Synod of Orange condemned the teachings of Semi-Pelagianism which hold that individuals have the final determination in salvation. It is up to the individual to accept or refuse the gift of God's grace, which he can discern because although he is depraved, there is still a spark of goodness in him. The Bible teaches that salvation is of the Lord (John 2:9). The Church contended for God's sovereign act of free grace, not man's free will to choose (Rom 9:16).

The Ecumenical Councils

(1) In A.D. 325 the First Council of Nicea was held. It condemned Arianism by saying that the Son is of one substance with the Father and that Christ is divine. The Nicene Creed was adopted.

(2) In A.D. 381 the First Council of Constantinople took place. It restated the decisions embraced at Nicea, established the divinity of the Holy Spirit, and condemned Apollinaris.

(3) In A.D. 431 at Ephesus, the Church council condemned Nestoranism and upheld the doctrine of the natural depravity of man.

(4) In A.D. 451 at the Council of Chalcedon, Eutyches was condemned, while the divine and human natures of Christ were contended for.

(5) In A.D. 553 the Second Council at Constantinople was held. Theodore of Mopsuestia was condemned, as were Theodoret and Ibas of Edessa. The Council also settled the Monophysites controversy.

(6) From A.D. 680 to 681, the Third Council of Constantinople took place. This Council condemned polytheism and Pope Honorius.

(7) In A.D. 787 the Second Council of Nicea was held. It officially condemned iconoclasts,[4] but allowed that some images were worthy of veneration, though they were not to be worshipped.

(8) From A.D. 869 to 870, the Fourth Council at Constantinople was in session. This Council ended the schism of Photius.

---

[4] *Iconoclast*–a person who destroys religious images or opposes their veneration.

(9) In A.D. 1123, the First Lateran Council met to confirm the *Concordat of Worms* between the Papacy and the Empire. It was decided that Bishops would be appointed by the Pope.

(10) In A.D. 1139 the Second Lateran Council met. Celibacy was made compulsory. It also tried to heal the schism between East and West.

(11) In A.D. 1179 the Third Lateran Council took place. It determined the method of papal election.

(12) In A.D. 1215 the Fourth Lateran Council convened to embrace the terrible doctrine of transubstantiation,[5] while condemning Joachim of Fiore, the Waldensians, and the Albigensians. It was determined that the Inquisition would be regulated.

(13) In A.D. 1245 the First Council of Lyons met. It declared Emperor Frederick II to be deposed, thus settling the quarrel of Pope and Emperor.

(14) In A.D. 1274 the Second Council of Lyons came together. New regulations for papal elections were adopted.

(15) From A.D. 1311 to 1312, a council met in Vienne (France). Here the Templars were suppressed.

(16) From A.D. 1414 to 1418 at Constance, another Church Council met to put an end to The Great Schism. This Council condemned John Huss. It also decided that the Pope was to be subject to Church Councils. Plans were made for reformation and future councils.

(17) From A.D. 1431 to 1435, another Church Council met at Basel/Ferrara, Florence. There was a token effort to be re-united with Constantinople, Armenia, and with the Jacobites.

(18) From A.D. 1512 to 1517, the Fifth Lateran Council met. It condemned the schismatic Council of Pisa.

(19) From A.D. 1545 to 1563, the important Council of Trent was in session. This Council condemned the Protestants. It officially established the authority of tradition alongside that of Scripture.

(20) From A.D. 1869 to 1870, the First Vatican Council met to establish papal infallibility.

---

[5] *Transubstantiation*–the doctrine that Christ's physical body and blood are present in the bread and wine of the Lord Supper, upheld to this day by the Roman Catholic Church.

(21) From A.D. 1962 to 1965, the Second Vatican Council met to renew Catholic liturgy, and to respond to modern concerns such as nuclear war, religious freedom, and openness to other Christians.

CHAPTER 6

Sowing Seeds of Self-Destruction
A.D. 100–461

The Sins of the Saints

The study of Church history is the study of men and women of great faith and courage. Those who have known so little of physical suffering for the cause of Christ have to be humbled by the testimony of the blood of the martyrs. The Church has a rich spiritual heritage to look back upon with thanksgiving.

However, there is a tendency to idealize the past and to think that somehow it was better than the present. We are inclined to believe that the early Christians were more godly, more spiritual, and less sinful than the Church today. That is not the case. From the very start, the Church struggled against a hostile society from without the sanctuary, and personal sins of the saints from within. In Acts 6, the story is told of inner conflict among the brethren:

"And in those days, when the number of the disciples was multiplied, there arose a murmuring of the Grecians against the Hebrews, because their widows were neglected in the daily ministration."

As the New Testament narrative continues, a host of problems are set forth— including the most heinous sins against nature (1 Cor 5:1–6). In the letters to the seven churches in Asia (which Christ Himself dictated to John on the isle of Patmos), direct references are made to spiritual deterioration (Rev 1–3).

Following the close of the Apostolic Age (c. A.D. 100), the spiritual climate of the Church did not improve. By the end of the fifth century, a number of unscriptural doctrines and practices had become deeply rooted in the Church.

Demonism. As demonic activity was part of the evil which the Lord had to face while on earth during His incarnation, so the demons of darkness plagued the

Church, as people opened themselves up to the Wicked One. Exorcism, the expelling of an evil spirit, was practiced by the Church leaders.

Prayers for the Dead. While it is normal to remember loved ones, it is not right to pray for the dead, or to the dead as if their state of existence could be changed, or as if they have influence in human affairs.

Purgatory. In the name of humility, the teaching was introduced to the Church that no person was good enough to go directly into the presence of the Lord. It seemed "logical" to some to believe that an intermediate state existed between heaven and earth where purification takes place. In essence, what this doctrine really teaches is that all men go to a form of hell. Apparently, the hell of purgatory does not last forever, because individuals will move from there into heaven, but only after having helped to redeem themselves through suffering. The whole concept of purgatory goes against the teaching of the Bible, for it diminishes the glorious and finished work of redemption which Christ accomplished at Calvary on behalf of His own (Matt 1:21). Worst of all, purgatory makes man his own partial savior (cp. Eph 2:8–9).

The Forty Day Lenten Season. The emphasis is again placed upon man doing something for salvation and for sanctification. Set aside is the biblical doctrine that "the just shall *live by faith*" (Rom 1:17).

Mass. The Lord's Supper was transformed from a memorial service, "*Do this in remembrance of me,*" (1 Cor 11:24) into a daily sacrifice of the body and blood of Christ.[1]

Veneration. It was encouraged to give adoration to the martyrs, saints, Apostles, and above all others, Mary. The Seventh Ecumenical Council (A.D. 787) declared that "we adore and respect God our Lord; and those who have been genuine servants of our common Lord we honor and venerate because they have the power to make us friends with God the King of all." The bones of the martyrs were treated as precious stones. The Church began to celebrate the martyr's day of death as their birthday in heaven. The old heathen gods of Rome were being replaced by the new "gods" of the Church.

Relics. Miraculous powers were attributed to pieces of wood, said to be part of the Cross of Christ. There were so many pieces in Europe, that the Church taught that the wood was reproducing itself! Healing powers were ascribed to the relics of

---

[1] The word mass, is from the Latin *missa*, so called from the words of dismissal at the end of the service: *Ite, missa est*, "Go, [the congregation] is dismissed.)

the saints and martyrs, such as bones, hair, and fragments of clothing. The Church became the object of ridicule. Emperor Julian the Apostate called Christians "bone worshipers."

Iconoclasts. Pictures, images, and altars in the churches were endorsed, not as aids of worship but as objects of spiritual power.

Vestments. Gorgeous and expensive garments began to be worn by the clergy as the trappings of regal power found expression in the kingdom of God. Justification was found by giving symbolism to the garments. The alb, the long gown worn by the clergy, the white garment, became the symbol of purity, both of soul and body. The cincture, made of braided linen, or sometimes of wool, is a sash indicating a perpetual priesthood (Exod 29:9). The stole, a long narrow vestment, has been adopted from the court uniform of Roman judges to denote authority. The chasuble, the large vestment worn on the shoulders and hanging down in front and behind, ornamented with a large cross, speaks of a "casual," meaning, "a little house," designed to be a shelter for the clergy.

Ritual. Rather than pray and preach spontaneously in natural acts of worship, formal ritual services were encouraged. Individuals forget that a religious ritual without any corresponding spiritual reality is meaningless to the Lord. People can draw near to God with their lips, but their hearts are far from Him (Isa 29:13).

Monasticism. In an effort to be truly spiritual, some Christians began to withdraw from society to become monks and nuns. The word "monk" is derived from the Greek *monachos*, which means "solitary."

The Rise of Monasticism

Christian monasticism began in Egypt when men like Anthony of Thebes took up the life of a monk. The year was A.D. 270. According to Athanasius, Anthony was born in a small village on the left shore of the Nile River, the son of well-to-do parents. When they died, Anthony was able to live off of his inheritance. One day in church, the text was read of the story of the rich young ruler. Anthony took the words of Matthew 19:21 literally. He disposed of his property and gave the proceeds to the poor. He left for the desert, after placing his sister under the care of the virgins of the Church (who served as nuns dedicated to the work of the Lord, later gathering in convents, similar to the monasteries for monks). After about fifteen years, Anthony went to live alone in a tomb in an abandoned cemetery.

Others followed the example of Anthony, such as Pachomius. Pachomius was born around A.D. 286, in a small village in the southern portion of Egypt. As a young man he was drafted into the army. Finding himself far from home and lonely, Pachomius was impressed by a group of Christians who came to console him. He decided to devote himself to the service of others. The opportunity came when he was allowed to leave the army. He sought someone to instruct him in the Christian faith, and to baptize him. Years later he decided to go to the desert, where he was able to establish a monastery. There was one basic rule and that was the rule of service. By the time he died, Pachomius had founded nine communities. Meanwhile Mary, his sister, founded similar communities for women.

Chrysostom, "Golden Mouth"

Chrysostom (c. 347–407), patriarch of Constantinople, was a preacher of great ability. His name means "golden mouth." This name was given to him because of his oratorical skills. Born in Antioch into a wealthy Christian family, Chrysostom was a natural and brilliant student. He studied philosophy, logic, and rhetoric with a view to becoming a lawyer. However, being a religious man, Chrysostom desired to join a monastic order, but was unable to do so because of responsibilities to his family. But even at home, he lived an austere life. Finally, in A.D. 373 he retired to the mountains where he stayed for about ten years. His health broke under the physical stress. Returning to Antioch, Chrysostom studied under the bishop Melitius, who ordained him a deacon in 381. Five years later he became a priest.

As a gifted preacher, Chrysostom attracted a wide following. When the patriarch of Constantinople died in 397, Chrysostom was appointed to replace him. Reluctantly he was made a bishop. In the years to follow, Chrysostom preached boldly against the vices of the congregation and corruption in high places of government. He even criticized the empress Eudoxia and the immorality of the imperial court. Outraged, Eudoxia enlisted the support of the bishop of Alexandria to remove Chrysostom from office based upon frivolous charges. Exiled in 403, he was recalled, but soon offended the empress again and was banished once more to Pontus. Forced to march through the hot sand without any covering on his head, he died on the way. Such unnecessary sufferings bore bitter fruit in the years to come.

CHAPTER 7

New Trials and Great Triumphs
A.D. 376–754

By the fifth century A.D. the Church had grown in power, prestige, wealth, and numerical strength. The army of Christ had marched victoriously through many lands: Palestine, Greece, Italy, Gaul, Spain, Egypt, and North Africa. In cities, large and small, the gospel had taken hearts captive for Christ. Because of the missionary labors of Paul and others, Christians preached the gospel to the nations in obedience to the known will of Jesus (Matt 28:19).

Disciples of Christ could also be found in remote and dangerous places. They lived in caves and dwelt in the desert. Many confined themselves to small cells as monks and served in dark dungeons. Christian men, women, and young people went bravely to a martyr's death as wild beasts devoured them in public arenas. The saints prayed and worshipped among the dead in damp catacombs. However, overall, the Church militant had become the Church triumphant—despite all that the world, the flesh, and the devil could do to destroy and discredit her. While the empires of this world crumbled, the kingdom of Christ grew stronger and stronger, moving from one spiritual victory to another.

German Tribes Invade the Empire

The success of the Church can only be explained according to God's sovereign grace. God the Father had promised many souls for the labors of His Son at Calvary (Heb 2:10). Without the divine undergirding, the kingdoms of this world will always collapse illustrated in the Roman Empire. That mighty empire did not trust in the true God. Her spiritual strength was placed in myths and pagan gods. Her moral strength existed only in the form of a social contract, which her subjects grew weary of trying to implement. No man can be more moral than his nature. The nature of man apart from Christ is depraved (Jer 17:9).

It was inevitable that the social contract which bound Roman society together would not be honored. The culture of Rome collapsed as men "did that which was right in their own sight" (Jdg 21:25). The Roman Empire, for all of its military might, was but a shadow that passed on the dial of time. In the dusty pages of the history books, people can still read at their leisure about the rise, decline, and fall of the Roman Empire. The fall of Rome was all the sadder because of the glory that she once held in the eyes of this world.

In its advance to glory and greatness, through assimilation and acculturation, the city of Rome extended power over Italy, Sicily, Carthage, Spain, and North Africa. Its legions continued to spread around the Mediterranean. Rome conquered many of the territories of Greece, the Balkans, Turkey, France, the Middle East, Egypt, Morocco, Germany, and Britain in A.D. 43. When it had reached its highest point, the boundaries of the Roman Empire was generally defined in the north by following the course of major rivers as the Rhine and the Danube. The Euphrates River marked the eastern border. The southern border lay along the deserts of Arabia in the Middle East and the Sahara in North Africa. The Atlantic Ocean formed a natural boundary on the West.

It was on the northern frontier of the Empire that Rome would find new and terrible enemies to fight. East of the Rhine and north of the Danube were two great German tribes. The Ostrogoths [bright Goths] were in the Ukraine. The Visigoths [wise Goths] settled in the area that is now called Romania.

Warring against the German tribes were the Mongolian Huns. These fierce horsemen instilled fear into the hearts of German tribes. As a result, in 376, two hundred thousand Visigoths crossed the lower Danube fleeing before the Huns. It was the first tribe of barbarians to enter into the Roman Empire.

At first they were allowed to settle in a peaceful manner. But then the Visigothic settlers protested that they were being exploited and oppressed by the east Roman administration. Open revolt resulted. Under the leadership of their chieftain Fritigern, the Visigoths ravaged the Balkan Peninsula. At the same time, new waves of German invaders moved across the Danube.

Valens (ruler, A.D. 364–378), the Roman Emperor of the East, hastened from Asia to engage in battle with the Visigoths near the city of Hadrianopolis. The year was 378. In the battle that followed, the Roman army was severely defeated. Valens was killed but his body was never found. Ambrose (c. 339–397), the Bishop of Milan in northern Italy, viewed the catastrophic battle as "the massacre of all humanity, the end of the world." Ambrose was not far from being right. The world was changing but it was the western, not the eastern part of the Empire that was destined for destruction.

The conflict with the barbarians was not to be halted until the days of Theodosius I, who ruled A.D. 379–395. Unable to continually battle against the Visigoths or expel them, Theodosius instead, in 382, concluded a treaty with their leaders, accepting them all as one block of federates within the imperial borders. By virtue of this new arrangement they were given lands in Thrace and permitted to live under their own laws and rules on the condition that they provide soldiers and farm workers to the Roman government.

While relative peace came to the eastern part of the Roman Empire, the Goths, together with other German tribes, attacked the western part. Years of constant conflict depleted Rome of her strength to the point that she was ready to collapse. During these last and dark days of the Roman Empire lived Ambrose, Jerome, and Augustine.

As the barbarians overran the Roman Empire, they left behind violence, destruction, tears of despair, and death. Virgins were molested and raped. Children were terrorized. Babies were hacked to pieces. No respect was shown to bishops and priests who were ridiculed, and murdered with relish. Churches were looted or desecrated by being used to stable horses and livestock. Valuable and venerated religious objects were confiscated as trophies of conquest. Majestic monasteries, constructed with hard earned resources provided by the people of God, were pillaged, torn down, and burned. The monasteries had been designed to be sanctuaries of safety and peace. The water of local creeks and streams mixed with blood pouring out of wounded people fleeing in terror. So many people were wounded and slaughtered without mercy. Men and women and young people were compelled to serve as slaves as captives of conflict. Rome, "eternal city" was about to fall. It was to be the end of the civilized world as many knew it.

The Fall of Rome: A.D. 410

On August 24, 410 Rome was finally attacked by the Visigoths under Alaric. His invading army reached the edge of the city, which had been left without any defense. For several days and nights the barbarians ravaged the city. The streets were wet with puddles of blood. People shrieked and cried in pain and terror. The palace of the emperors and the residences of the wealthy citizens were looted of their costly furniture, expensive vessels and valuable jewelry. Silken and velvet hangings and beautiful objects of art were plundered.

The defilement of Rome shocked many Christians, including Jerome (c. 345–c. 419), who was living in Bethlehem. When he heard the news of the fall of Rome, he was distraught. "If Rome can perish, what can be safe?" Like Jerome, Augustine (354–430) lamented the fall of Rome. However, he did not despair. He wrote many letters to refugees attempting to comfort them.

Then, in the midst of the mass destruction and loss of all that was beautiful and holy, Augustine began his work on *The City of God*. Augustine wanted to prove in part that the Church was not to be blamed for the fall of Rome. Rome had fallen because of her own pride and sins.

When the Visigoths were through plundering Rome, the Vandals came. After occupying Spain and North Africa, they crossed the Mediterranean Sea and took Rome in the year 455.

Meanwhile, the Huns had been waging war against and subduing various tribes under the leadership of Attila, king of the Huns. Known as the "Scourge of God," Attila had annihilated his enemies or absorbed them into his vast domain. At the height of his power, he commanded an army of seven hundred thousand men, held together by a large number of vassal kings. For nine years Attila made war in the Eastern Empire. At one point, his forces were ready to destroy the walls of Constantinople, but this did not happen. Attila was promised an annual tribute, and given the immediate payment of six thousand pounds of gold!

At the request of a Frankish king, who had been drawn to the east side of the Rhine River, Attila turned his army away from Constantinople, and invaded Gaul. In one of the most important and greatest conflicts in the history of the world, the Huns were defeated at the Battle of Chalons in 451, by an alliance of Romans, Franks, and Visigoths, led by Western Emperor Aetius, the "Last of the Romans." One hundred sixty-two thousand of the barbarians were killed! Attila retreated back across the Rhine into Germany—but only temporarily.

He was defeated, but not destroyed as a military might. In the spring of 452, Attila moved his army into Italy to attack Rome itself. This time, only the political negotiating intervention of Pope Leo I spared the city from certain destruction. (Leo died 461; Bishop of Rome, 440–461). Peace was made with the Emperor

Valentinian III, and Attila retired from the area. In the providence of God, Attila died the next year in 453 from a burst blood-vessel! Thereafter, the Huns ceased to be a threat to the Empire.

But the damage had been done; the empire in general, and Rome in particular, could not recover from the repeated invasions of immense hordes of barbarians. The Goths, Vandals, Huns, and various other tribes had desolated the area, constantly attracted by the rich fertile plains which were its earlier source of strength. The city of Rome had been taken repeatedly, and pillaged twice. Finally, every province of the western part of the Roman Empire had been conquered, including Italy, North Africa, Spain, Gaul (France), the Netherlands, and Britain. Yet, despite all of the political chaos and a world in upheaval, the Church would remain steadfast.

A Divided People

While Rome was given over to the barbarians, the eastern part of the Empire survived. It was not conquered nor occupied. The eastern part of the Empire embraced the Balkan Peninsula, Asia Minor, Syria, Palestine, and Egypt. It is known as the Eastern or Byzantine Empire. Its capital was Constantinople.

The invasion of the western part of the former Roman Empire brought new people to settle the land. After the invasion by the barbarians, the Ostrogoths settled in Italy among the native population. They embraced the established Church, having been converted to Christianity before they invaded the Empire. One human instrument of their salvation was Ulfilas (c. 311–383).

Born in Cappadocia (east Asia Minor), Ulfilas may have been taken captive by Gothic raiders as a youth. As an adult he found his way to Constantinople, the eastern capital of the Roman Empire. It was here that Ulfilas was educated and began his service to the Church. In 341 Eusebius of Nicomedia, bishop of Constantinople, consecrated Ulfilas as bishop. Soon afterward the young bishop went to Dacia (north of the Danube River), where he served as a missionary to the western Goths in this region. He was very successful in winning converts to Christ, in part because of his translation of the Old and New Testaments into the Goths' vernacular language. Just as the Ostrogoths had settled in Italy, the southern part of Gaul and the northern half of Spain were occupied by the Visigoths. Like their near relatives, the Ostrogoths in Italy, the Visigoths had accepted Christianity.

In addition to the Goths, there were many other German tribes that settled in the newly conquered territory, such as the Burgundians, who settled in eastern Gaul.

They too were Christians. Finally, the Vandals conquered southern Spain and North Africa, and they too claimed to be Christian. Unfortunately, the Goths, the Burgundians, and the Vandals were Arian Christians.

In Northern Gaul and in Britain the situation was far different. Heathenism still claimed the lives of the Franks who took northern Gaul, Belgium, and the southern Netherlands; the Frisians, who lived in the northwestern part of the Netherlands; the Saxons, who settled in the eastern part of the Netherlands; and the Anglo-Saxons, who conquered Britain.

Then there were the people who lived in countries which had never been part of the Roman Empire, such as the Celts in Ireland; the Scandinavians in what is now called Denmark, Norway, and Sweden; the many German tribes east of the Rhine; and in the east beyond them, the tribes in what is now called Russia. These vast territories were populated with millions of people who still needed to hear the name of Christ.

Evangelism and Education

With the fall of Rome and the division of the Empire into so many diverse groups, two challenges faced the Church. The people of God had the opportunity (1) to evangelize the barbarians and (2) to educate the newly formed nations. Would the Church be obedient to cultivate these open doors, and would it be successful?

The Preservation of a People

In the midst of economic chaos, social unrest, and cultural readjustment caused by the collapse of the Roman Empire, the Church found itself trying to preserve as much of her own culture and heritage as possible. Difficult days descended upon a large portion of the earth. The sword seemed to be more powerful than anything else. Still, while strong military arms fought for supremacy, godly men sat in small cells and began to copy the Scriptures. Slowly, laboriously, they copied the Bible and other important books in an effort to keep education and the knowledge of the true God alive. The day would come when men would grow weary of bathing themselves in blood and would want a better way to live. The Church would then be ready to make new disciples of all nations and to fulfill the mandates of the Great Commission (Matt 28:19–20).

The Franks Find Christ

Among the first of the unconverted Germanic warriors to embrace Christianity were the Franks. Their king was a man named Clovis. The story of his conversion is recorded by church historian Gregory of Tours (c. 539–594) in his History of the Franks. The Frankish king is believed to have been converted to Christ because he saw the sign of the cross in the sky. He believed that Christ had given him a military victory over the Alemanni, a rival German tribe. Following his great victory, on Christmas day, A.D. 496, in the city of Rheims, Clovis was baptized, along with three thousand of his soldiers.

As a new convert, Clovis made a decision to reject Arianism and embrace orthodox Christianity set forth in the Nicene Creed. This set the stage for religious civil warfare between the Franks against other German tribes who had embraced Arianism and thus were officially heretics.

Something else of significance happened with the conversion of Clovis. Up to this time in history individuals had accepted Christianity. Now, whole tribes technically became Christians when their kings were converted to Christ. As a result, many mere "professors," *i.e.*, Christians in name only, were coming into the church, bringing their worldly ways with them.

The "Apostle of Ireland"

Known as the "Father of English History", the Venerable Bede (born c. 672–735) states in his History of the English Church and People that in 156, a British king named Lucius wrote to the bishop of Rome requesting instruction in the Christian faith. "This pious request was quickly granted, and the Britons received the Faith and held it peacefully in all its purity and fullness until the time of the Emperor Diocletian." The gospel came to England and then to Ireland through the efforts of a British monk named Patrick (c. 390–c. 461). When he was sixteen years old Patrick was captured in a raid by Irish pirates and sold to a chieftain. He was forced to serve as a slave attending to sheep and pigs on Mount Slemish in Antrim. Six years later Patrick escaped to Gaul where he became a monk. Following a desire to minister the gospel as a missionary in Ireland, Patrick returned about 431 meeting with great success until his death.

The Missionary Work of Wynfrith and Willibrord

Fully embracing the message of God's redeeming love many Englishmen became committed to disseminating the gospel. One of the most effective missionaries was Boniface (680–754), "The Apostle of Germany." His real name was Wynfrith. He was an Anglo-Saxon, born in Devonshire. Boniface became a monk. He was a gifted preacher and excellent scholar.

After ministering successfully in Frisia, Hesse, and Thuringia in the Netherlands (719–722), Boniface went to Rome where he was consecrated a bishop. With that title he crossed the Rhine into Germany to win many converts to Christianity. His initial success came when Boniface cut down a large oak tree which was believed to be sacred to the god of thunder named Thor. When he was not struck down by lightening people were willing to listen to the gospel message and believe. Boniface used the wood of the oak tree in the building of a chapel. When he was 73 years old Boniface returned to minister among the Frisians. In 754 while ministering in Frisia, he and fifty three of his helpers were martyred.

Willibrord (c. 658–739) was another English monk who labored in the Netherlands from 690–739. A native of Northumbria, Willibrord was educated at the monastery of Ripon near York. As a young man he went to Ireland to the monastery at Rathmelsigi where he remained from 678–690. He was ordained a priest and began to minister in the cause of Christ. Leaving Ireland in 690 with eleven companions he went to preach the gospel in the Frisian Islands (which extend in an arc from the Netherlands through northern Germany to the west of Denmark), where the Lord blessed him with great success. Multitudes of conversions were witnessed in all northwestern Europe. Buildings erected for the glory and service of God could be found everywhere. The monastery and cathedral Willibrord constructed at Utrecht became the center for the Frisian work, from which he emphasized the training of native Church leaders. Like a grain of mustard seed, the kingdom of God continued to grow as the gospel went into the nations of the earth (Matt 13:31–32).

Gregory the Great

Gregory was born in A.D. 540 to a rich and influential family in Rome which provided him with educational and social advantages. Though a gifted politician, in his maturity, Gregory desired to take his Christianity more seriously. He gave away a large portion of the family fortune, converted the family home in Sicily into a monastery, and began his spiritual quest to be closer to God. He wanted to be more holy. To that end he prayed to the Lord saying, "Make me understand what great peace there is in a heart that desires nothing of this world." With a humble spirit Gregory labored faithfully to advance the kingdom of God. He moved through the organizational structure of the Church until he was elected Bishop of Rome in 590. He would serve until his death on March 12, 604.

Gregory called himself *Servus Servorum Dei*, "the servant of the servants of God." However, his stated humility did not stop him from becoming a strong leader. With ecclesiastical power securely in his hand Gregory turned his attention to acquiring for the Church broad political power. He appointed heads of cities, formed armies, and then arbitrated and enforced treaties among contending factions. He neutralized the effects of the Lombards who had conquered northern Italy. The power and prestige of the Church was further enhanced when the Church took on the responsibilities of education of the less fortunate population, improving the welfare of the people, and the preserving social justice. John Calvin admired the personal piety of Gregory and wrote in his *Institutes of the Christian Religion* that Gregory was the last good Bishop of Rome.

Apart from the good he did by giving much alms to the poor, promoting piety and prayer, establishing several cloisters, creating a new musical form, the Gregorian Chant, and sending out missionaries, Gregory also brought much harm to the cause of Christ. He readily embraced stories of miracles performed by the relics of saints, taught on the existence of purgatory, endorsed the medieval penitential system, believed in the efficacy of saying masses for the dead, accepted the intercession of departed saints, and believed in the merit of good works as a basis for justification. Despite this mixture of truth and error, goodness and corruption, the Lord had mercy on His people. The Church went forth to conquer and grow. However, as the Church increased in power and wealth, she faced many challenges to her spiritual effectiveness in the centuries to come.

Map of the Roman Empire

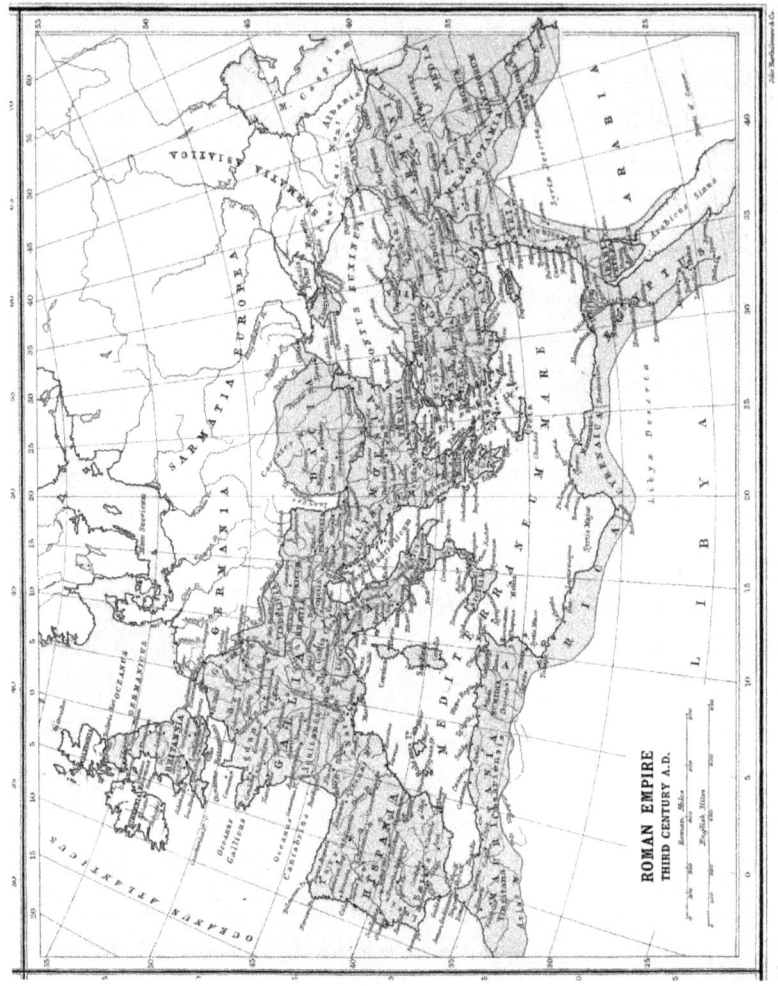

CHAPTER 8

Diminishing Glory

The Arabs Attack the Eastern Part of the Empire

Between A.D. 325–681, six great ecumenical councils were held. These were turbulent times in the political and religious history of the world. The Church was torn apart by theological controversies; but these controversies produced great statements of faith. Meanwhile, the barbarians continued to challenge the borders of the Roman Empire, until they finally conquered the whole western portion of it.

In the East, the Empire struggled for survival against the German tribes from the north, and then against the Persians. A desperate war was fought against the Persians by the Emperor Heraclius (c. 574–641; ruler of the East 610–641), ending at the Battle of Nineveh in the year A.D. 628. The Persian army was destroyed, while the Empire in the East survived despite the advances of the Arab army. The Arab warriors were Semitic by race, and Muslim (followers of Mohammed) in their religion.

A Man Named Mohammed

As the inhabitants of Arabia, the Arabs were the descendants of Ishmael, the son of Abraham and his wife's handmaiden, Hagar (Gen 16). Therefore, Ishmael was also the half brother of Isaac whose mother was Sarah. With the passing of time, many of the Arabs had forsaken the God of Abraham, Isaac, and Jacob to embrace many gods. In this idolatrous country of Arabia, there was born in the city of Mecca a boy named Mahomet, who came to be known as Mohammed. The year was A.D. 570. Mohammed claimed descent from the family of Hashem and the tribe of Koreish.

During his childhood Mohammed was in poor health because he suffered from epilepsy. Being orphaned when he was very young, he was reared by his uncle, Abu Talib. At the age of 25, Mohammed was employed by Kajijah, a rich widow. He carried on her husband's business and prospered. He also married Kajijah, who was fourteen years older than himself.

Being a merchant, Mohammed moved often with his caravan of camels, traveling the traditional trade routes of the Middle East. His journeys brought Mohammed into contact with both Jews and Christians. After considering their claims and customs, he rejected both as the basis for religious truth. In his fortieth year, Mohammed temporally retired from society to meditate in a mountain cave near Mecca called the Cave of Hira. He returned to his friends and family to announce that he had received a revelation from an angel which said to him, "O Mohammed! You are the prophet of Allah and I am Gabriel."

This was the first of many revelations allegedly given by Gabriel, who came to teach Mohammed the way of truth. Later, the teachings of the prophet were collected and written in a sacred book called the Koran, meaning literally "Rehearsal" or "Readings." Many of Mohammed's sayings had first been recorded on bones or palm leaves. While the prophet could neither read nor write, Mohammed claimed that the various sections of the Koran came down to him from heaven during a period of twenty-three years.

The Koran teaches that God used prophets to bring reformation to men. Such prophets included Jesus and Moses, but Mohammed himself was the greatest of them all and is to be followed above all others (cp. John 16:23; Acts 10:43). Because of this, Mohammedans deny that Jesus is the Son of God (cp. John 5:19–23). They also deny His deity (cp. John 5:17–18) and His resurrection from the dead (cp. 1 Cor 15:1–3). They hold the atoning death of Christ in contempt, while embracing a system of salvation by good works (cp. Eph 2:8–9). The main tenets of the Islamic faith are five in number.

(1) Confession is made that there is no other God but Allah and that Mohammed is his prophet.
(2) Five times each day, prayer is offered with the supplicant facing Mecca.
(3) Alms are to be given.
(4) Fasting is to take place during the period of Ramadan. The fast is to last from sunrise to sunset each day.
(5) A pilgrimage to Mecca must be made at least once in a person's lifetime.

Going to the city of Mecca, Mohammed began to share his new beliefs, which challenged many of the merchants of that city who sold idols. While the Prophet gained a few converts, the opposition to his teachings was so strong, he and his followers had to flee to the city of Medina in the year A.D. 622, where his thoughts were better received. This flight, which began on July 16, is called the Hegira.

In Medina, Mohammed formed his faithful followers into a killing war machine, and then went forth to conquer by the sword. In 630 Mohammed returned to Mecca in military triumph and destroyed the 360 idols of the city. Overwhelmed by his success, the inhabitants of Mecca shouted, "There is one God, Allah, and Mohammed is his prophet." This encouraged many others to embrace Islam, which means "Obedience" or "Surrender."

The Influence of a False Prophet

In A.D. 632 Mohammed died at the age of 63, leaving no son and only one daughter, Fatima. His body was buried in a grave dug under the same bed on which he departed this life. Though Mohammed died, his tremendous influence lived on. He taught his followers not to argue or discuss the different religions, but to kill with the sword all who refused obedience to the law of the Koran. Those who died in this spiritual battle were promised to receive a glorious reward in paradise. While prayer leads half-way to God, and fasting leads to the gates of heaven, and alms-giving opens the door, it is only Jihad (waging holy war) that gives actual entrance into heaven.

During the next 100 years, the leaders who succeeded him were known as Caliphs. Four of them founded the Mohammedan or Moslem Empire. The Muslims took their bloody swords and butchered their way over the hot deserts of Arabia to conquer Persia, penetrate India, and defeat the imperial province of Asia Minor. Twice Constantinople was attacked. While the city was able to protect itself, other places such as Syria, Palestine, Egypt, and North Africa fell to Islamic conquest.

In the year 637, Caliph Omar took Jerusalem, and built on the site of the old Jewish temple the mosque that bears his name to this day. It was Omar who also destroyed the famous library located at Alexandria in Egypt. He believed that no book other than the Koran was needed, and so he destroyed some of the greatest pieces of literature of the ancient world.

North Africa, where once Augustine and Cyprian had labored for the cause of Christ, fell to the Arabs. In 711, the Muslims crossed the Straits of Gibraltar to conquer Spain. After Spain, the Islamic forces crossed the Pyrenees Mountains to penetrate into the Roman province of Gaul (France). During these many years of bloody violence, thousands of Christian churches were destroyed or converted into mosques.

The Battle of Tours

Just when it seemed as if all of Europe might become Mohammedan, Charles Martel ("The Hammer") led a great army against the Islamic forces. In the year 732, on a Saturday in October, the battle lines were drawn on the Plain of Tours. The Arab army consisted mainly of cavalry, while the Frankish army consisted of foot soldiers.

The Franks drew up their army in close order. There was no gap to be found in the ranks. The Arabs charged swooping down headlong and furiously. Bodies began to fall as swords flashed in the sun. It was to be a fight to the finish. The banners of the cross waved defiantly and in the end; the Arabs retreated from the field of conflict.

Accepting defeat on the Plain of Tours, the Arabs retreated behind the Pyrenees into Spain, where they would remain influential for over 700 years. It was not until 1492 that Ferdinand of Aragon was able to drive the Moors (as the Mohammedans were then called) out of their last stronghold in Granada to force them back into Africa.

The Cross and the Sword: The Expansion of Islam

Though the Islamic conquest had been halted, there were permanent wounds that had been inflicted upon the Church, for the Christian Church lost many potential mission fields. India fell under the influence of the Islamic faith. Persia was dominated by the Mohammedans. Lands in the Orient were closed to Christian evangelism. Historic places that once housed believers of the Lord were conquered—such as Jerusalem, the cradle of the Church. Other places that fell under the Islamic sphere of influence included Bethlehem, where Jerome once lived and had given the Church his Latin translation of the Bible. Antioch in Syria was no longer Christian, the place that Paul used as the gateway to bring Christianity into the Roman Empire. Alexandria in Egypt fell to the Arabs, which had been the home of Clement, and of Origen the great scholar of the East, and of Athanasius, the champion of the deity of Christ against Arianism. Carthage and Hippo in North Africa now belonged to the Muslims, where men like Tertullian, Cyprian, and

Augustine had taught. Seville in Spain fell as well, where Isidore, the leader of the Church of Spain, had labored to impart the knowledge of the cultured Greeks and Romans of the ancient world to the German barbarian tribes of the Middle Ages. All these places and more were officially lost to Christianity.

Looking back upon this time period, the question arises as to why the Church suffered such a strategic setback. Several reasons may be discerned from a human point of view.

First, the mindset for world conquest was radically different for the Mohammedans than for the Christians. The Lord said that He did not come bearing a sword to advance His kingdom by physical violence (John 18:10; John 18:36), but Mohammed did. He was ready from the first to kill anyone who did not accept his teachings. People that were not killed were compelled to pay a poll tax to Muslim called the *jizya*, a reminder of their inferior status (Quran 9:29). Slavery was another form of Muslim conquest. Mohammed was a slave owner and trader. The Quran authorizes Muslim men to keep women as slaves for intimate sensual pleasure (Quran 33:50).

Second, the harsh enviromnet of desert life strengthened the Mohammedans, which suited them for the vigors of violent warfare. The Church was more civilized and therefore physically softer.

Third, Mohammedanism promised paradise to those who died while fighting for the faith. Arabs fought on foot, on camels, and on horseback with incredible courage without regard for life or limb. They fought unto death believing in the special privileges and pleasures in the world to come (Quran 56:15–21).

Finally, to a certain extent, the Church, as the salt of the earth, had lost much of its savor (Matt 5:13). The simple purity of the gospel message had been replaced by sacramentalism. Heartfelt worship had been replaced by formal ceremonialism. Endless religious debates discouraged evangelism. An uncertain message cannot be persuasively presented. In the Western church, the dark side of the soul of clergymen emerged to persecute other Christians for a variety of reasons, not the least of which was to maintain purity of faith!

Map of the Mohammedan Crescent

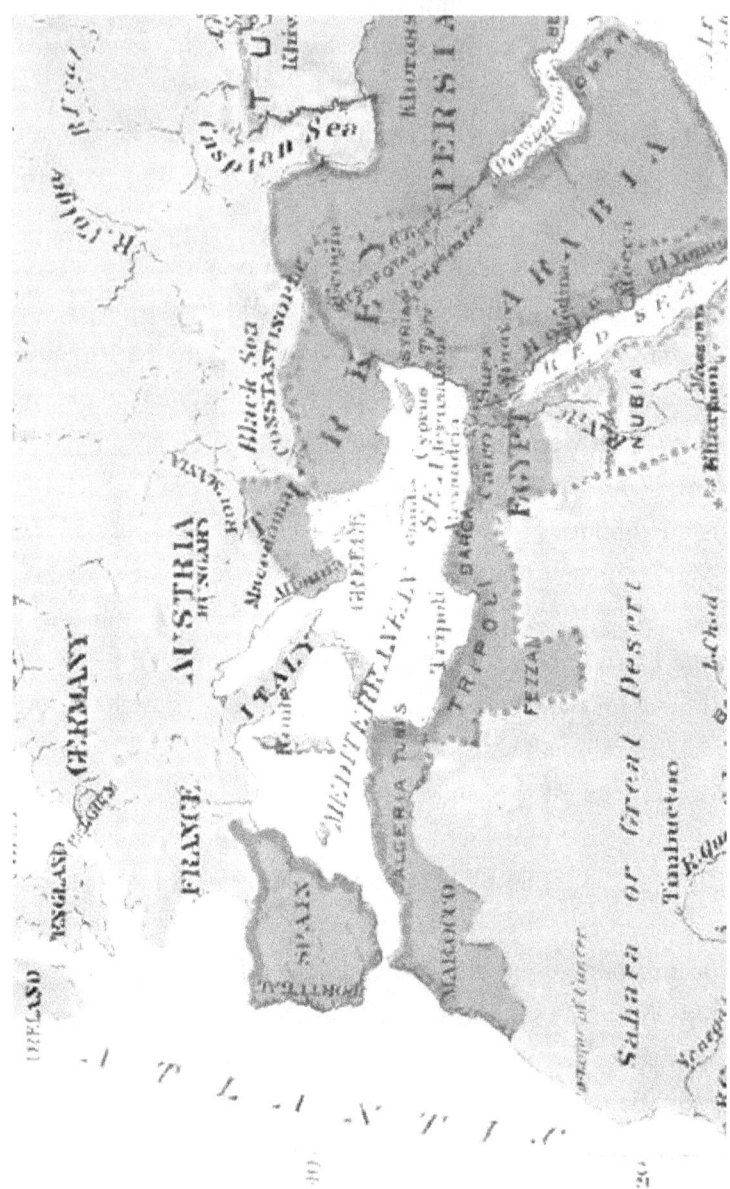

CHAPTER 9

New Political Alliances
A.D. 751–800

The "Longbeards" of Northern Italy

In the sixth century the fertile valley of the Po River was overrun by the barbarian Lombard hordes. These people were the last Germanic invaders of Italy. Coming from the north in 568, the "Longbeards" were unsuccessful at conquering any city with walls and so they settled for what they could occupy in the countryside.

During their military adventures, the Lombards came into contact with the gospel. Many were converted to Christ. Embracing the teachings of Arius for a while, the Lombards eventually accepted Christian orthodoxy (Greek: *orthodoxia*, "right opinion") reflected in the Nicene Creed.

Anxious to establish friendly relations with the Lombards, Pope Gregory I (c. 540–604; Pope, 590–604), placed a lovely crown upon their first king, Alboin (569–c. 527). It was called The Iron Crown because it contained a circlet of gold and jewels fitted around a central silver band, which tradition holds to be made of iron beaten out of a nail of the True Cross. The last Lombard to rule as king was Desiderius who reigned from 756 to 774 when Charlemagne not only conquered the Lombard kingdom, but took for himself the title "King of the Lombards." From the Lombard land the Papal States were created. The Papal States refer to those territories over which the Bishop of Rome is the civil ruler.

Gregory I

Despite this unhealthy honoring of religious relics, Gregory I was a believer in the *verbal* (word for word), *inerrant* (without error), *plenary* (in all parts) inspiration of Scripture. He thought it was fruitless to investigate the authorship of the books of the

Bible. He said, "When we are persuaded that the Holy Spirit was its author, in stirring a question about the human author, what else do we do than in reading a letter inquire about the pen?"

Unfortunately, Gregory went beyond the logical boundaries of his own confession concerning the Bible, by teaching things that are not found in the Scriptures. He taught that sin might be forgiven on condition of repentance, which he defined to involve contrition, confession, and satisfaction. Satisfaction could be found in penance, with the penance being in proportion to the sin. In this system, man can earn and deserve not only salvation but also sanctification. On this understanding of holiness, a vast and complex penitential system was constructed in the Middle Ages. The fruit of this system produced a meaningless theory of penance which culminated in the selling of indulgences, against which Martin Luther and others would one day vigorously protest. The grace of God was cheapened.

Other doctrines that Gregory developed would also be challenged later by the Reformers, such as purgatory and transubstantiation, which is the belief that in the mass or communion the bread and wine are transformed in a miraculous way to become the verible body and blood of Christ.

Whatever his failures as a scholar and a theologian, Gregory did manage to enhance the prestige of the Church. He successfully withstood the claim of the Patriarch of Constantinople to the title of "Universal Bishop." By the time he died in 604, the pope was viewed as the chief bishop of the Church in the West, the natural arbiter and court of appeal in ecclesiastical (Church) cases, and the one person who could intervene with authority in cases involving serious scandal. One of his best decisions was made in 596, when he sent Augustine of Canterbury (died c. 604) on a mission to convert the English to Christ.

In his personal life Gregory was known for his humility as "the servant of the servants of God." As a lover of music Gregory reorganized the Schola Cantorum in Rome, a center for singing. The Gregorian Chant is named for him. The Church mourned his death in A.D. 604.

While Gregory was able to establish a good relation with the Lombards, succeeding popes were never certain of their status for a long time. Civil war with the Lombards was a matter of constant concern. This caused the popes to look to the Franks of Gaul (in modern day France) for military and political support.

The Rise of Pepin III

One notable Frankish monarch was Clovis, who converted to Christianity in 496. Clovis was a strong and influential ruler. However, his descendants were not. This fact allowed Pepin III (Pepin the Short, c. 714–768), to rise to power. Pepin was the son of Charles Martel. By convincing the military that he was a better commander and could provide soldiers with the booty of war, Pepin was able to depose Childeric III, the last of the Merovingian dynasty, to establish his own, the Carolingian dynasty. Pepin put Childeric in a monastery where he died c. 751. Pepin then assumed the throne from which he ruled from 751–768. Additional military conquests enhanced his power.

Looking for ecclesiastical approval for all his actions, Pepin received it when he was anointed by Archbishop Boniface in 752 and again by Pope Stephen II in 754. The pope was willing to crown Pepin because he was in need of aid. The Lombards had marched south, surrounded Rome, and were prepared to lay siege to its walls. Making his way over the stormy mountain passes to Paris, Stephen anointed Pepin king. His sons, Charles and Carloman would be heirs of the crown. By reviving an Old Testament practice recorded of the Davidic monarchy (1 Sam 16:13), Pepin symbolically placed the State, as well as the military, beneath the authority of the pope. The precedent was set to believe that the pope had the right to give kingdoms and to take them away. The pope had the right to raise and command an army. The State had become subservient to the Church.

Within this new religious and political context, Pope Zacharias (d. 752, Last of the Greek Popes, 741–752) did not hesitate to ask Pepin to help bring stability to the Lombards, who were still perceived to be a threat to papal power and safety. Pepin agreed to help. He marched against the Lombards and forced them to relinquish much of their territory to the pope, thereby beginning the Papal States. The pope now held not only ecclesiastical power, but secular power and would do so until 1870 when the new Kingdom of Italy was established.

The Establishment of the Carolingian Dynasty

Following the death of Pepin the Short in 768, his two sons succeeded him, Carloman and Charles. When Carloman died in 771, Charles was free to rule alone. On December 25 of A.D. 800, while kneeling in St. Peter's Church in Rome, Charles was crowned King of the Franks by Pope Leo III, and became known as Emperor Charlemagne, which means Charles the Great.

Pope Leo III was born in Rome of humble origins (d. 816; Pope, 795–816). Little is known of him until his election to the papacy in 795. During his time in this office, Leo was beset by many aristocratic conspirators and dissidents who had been deprived of their power following the death of his predecessor, Pius IX. To secure his position in Rome, Leo became indebted to Charlemagne. In gratitude, at St. Peter's in Rome, on Christmas day in A.D. 800, Leo crowned Charlemagne emperor. The significance of this act produced scholarly and legal controversy. While this act allowed the prestige of Leo to be enhanced in Rome, it led Charlemagne to view the pope, and all other bishops, as his subjects.

As emperor, Charlemagne (742–814) was able to enforce law and order, promote civilization, and advance Christianity. None of these things came easily for the empire was filled with lawlessness, barbarians, and the encroachment of the Islamic faith.

Charlemagne ruled from 768 to 814 over France, the Netherlands, Belgium, and western Germany. He increased the borders of his empire by military force, but maintained power by a wise administrative system. Dividing the realm into districts called counties, supervised by appointed officials called counts, Charlemagne was able to keep effective control on what was happening. Border areas were administered by military leaders of operation. New regions were called marks or marches and a "count of the march" (or marquis) was basically unrestrained to govern as he pleased. The counts were overseen by two nomadic officials called "missi," who were continuously visiting the regions. One was a layman and one was a minister.

Though he considered himself a Christian, Charlemagne was not always faithful to the morals of the Church as he engaged in violence, bloodshed, and infidelity. Against the Saxons, a Germanic tribe of pagan worshippers, Charlemagne waged a bloody campaign that lasted for three decades. In 792 he slaughtered some 4,500 Saxons, leaving to history the Massacre of Verden. Anyone who did not receive baptism was subject to death. In his personal life, Charlemagne had multiple wives and mistresses which produced many children. This behavior necessitated social and ecclesiastical reforms following his death in January 814.

Also, during his reign, feudalism reached many of its distinctive medieval characteristics with the main feature being a rigid class system: kings and queens, vassals, lords, and serfs who were the common labors. Charlemagne has been regarded as the founder of Europe. When Charlemagne died in 814, there were three great empires in the world. The oldest was that of the Eastern Roman Empire consisting of the Balkans, Asia Minor, and southern Italy. The largest empire was that of the Mohammedan Arabs. It stretched from the border of India through Persia, Syria, Palestine in Asia, and all of north Africa up to the Ebro River in Europe. The newest and strongest of the empires was that of Charlemagne, which consisted of the northern half of Italy; the northeast corner of Spain; all of France, Belgium, and the Netherlands; and a large portion of Germany and Austria (Kuiper, B. K. *The Church in History*, p. 73).

CHAPTER 10

The Growing Power of the Papacy
A.D. 461–1073

Growth through Organization

As the Church grew larger and more complex, it was necessary for efficient administration to take place for both practical and doctrinal reasons. One *practical* need for a strong centralized voice to help solve concerns was manifested in the actions of Novatian, Bishop of Rome (251–253). Novatian was a very zealous Christian. When individuals who had renounced their faith during days of persecution wanted to be readmitted to the Church, Novatian denied the right of the Church to restore such people. He advocated a position of absolute fidelity to the cause of Christ at all times. The result was a schism that extended over the entire Empire, lasting until the sixth century! Many of the clergy thought that only a strong authoritative voice could keep the Church from continuing to fragment into splinter groups over non-essential issues; for this reason they supported a strong papacy.

Doctrinally the Church felt a strong voice was needed to combat heresy. One of the earliest errors, found in the second century, was *Ebonism* [Hebrew: "poor"], which insisted on law-keeping as a way of life. Many who embraced Ebonism denied the deity of Christ, His virgin birth, and the efficacy of His sufferings.

Another early heresy was *Manicheanism*, which struggled with the unity of the Godhead in the face of Trinitarianism. It stressed the unity [Greek: *monarchia*] of the divine nature as opposed to personal distinctions within the Godhead. It was believed by some that the Father alone possessed true personality; the Word [*logos*] and the Holy Spirit were merely impersonal attributes of the Godhead. Thus, the power of God came upon the man Jesus Christ and gradually saturated His soul until

His humanity became deity. The Manicheans said that Jesus must not be considered God in a pure and absolute sense.

Other Manicheans believed the three persons of the Godhead were merely modes of expression or ways of describing God. They were not distinct divine persons at all. Later, this modalistic type of Manicheanism became known as *Sabellianism* and *Nestorianism*, after two of its leading exponents.

Sabellius, who lived in the third century, affirmed that there is but one divine essence, which became operative in three temporally successive manifestations: as Creator and Law-Giver in the Father, as Redeemer in the Son, and as Life-Giver in the Holy Spirit.

Growth through Politics

In addition to practical problems and doctrinal disturbances, the power of the papacy grew because of political intrigue in the secular world and social unrest. The rivalries and uncertainties of political rulers were in plain contrast to the steadiness and uniformity of the government of the Church. Rulers came and went. After the Roman Empire fell in the fifth century, Europe was in constant chaos until the Empire of Charlemagne was established in the ninth century, a period known as the Dark Ages. People cried out for an extensive and enduring authority, and they found it in the papacy.

Growth through Deception

It is unfortunate that the men who held the office of the papacy did not realize just how powerful the Church was becoming. Foolishly, a number of "pious frauds" were committed to ensure popular and widespread support for the authority of Rome. One of these "pious frauds" was the forged documents called the *Donation of Constantine*. These bogus papers were circulated purporting to show that Constantine, the first Christian emperor, had legally given to the bishop of Rome, Sylvester I (A.D. 314–335), ultimate authority over all the European provinces of the empire. The documents proclaimed the bishop of Rome to be the true ruler of the western empire, even above the emperors.

While secular rulers probably smiled at such fraudulent documents, they took seriously the *Decretals of Isidore*, published about A.D. 830. These false documents pretended to be decisions handed down by the early bishops of Rome, beginning with the Apostles, declaring the absolute supremacy of the pope of Rome over the Church universal, and the independence of the Church from the State. In practical terms this meant that in matters pertaining to the clergy or the Church, no secular court could act as judge.

Growth through Fantastical Claims

In addition to using these false documents, other fantastic claims were made by such men as Pope Gelasius (Pope, 492–496), who instituted the concept of moral supervision over political rulers on the part of the pope. The thinking was that while there are two spheres of rule, the spiritual and the temporal, it is the Church that must one day give an account to God for the deeds of kings. Therefore, the kings should submit to the Church in spiritual matters. Symmachus (Pope, 498–514) added the axiom that no civil tribunal could compel the appearance of a pope or sentence him in his absence.

Pope Nicholas I (d. 867, Pope, 858–867) embraced these thoughts and embellished upon them to gain even more power for the papacy. He was the son of an aristocratic Roman family. Receiving an excellent education, Nicholas was well suited for service in the papal court, which he entered in 844. During the fourteen years that followed, Nicholas held various important offices that further prepared him for his election to the papacy.

His tenure as pope was controversial and stormy, as he strove to consolidate the power of the papacy in Rome—even over the Eastern Church! The great issue was control of the office of the bishop at Constantinople, which was the second most important place in the Church. The eastern Emperor Michael III replaced Ignatius (the duly elected bishop and head of the Church of Constantinople), with his own choice, named Photius. Pope Nicholas (in Rome) vigorously opposed the appointment, and he excommunicated Photius at the Synod of Rome in A.D. 863!

In retaliation, Photius excommunicated Nicholas in A.D. 867. Then Photius took the situation a step further by accusing the Western church of "heresy" for accepting the Filioque Doctrine, a true dogma that contends the Holy Spirit proceeds from both the Father and the Son (see the third paragraph of the Nicene Creed in chapter 5). In this bid for papal power, Nicholas set the stage for a full break between Eastern Orthodoxy and Roman Catholicism in the eleventh century.

Nicholas would have better success in the other major controversy of his tenure in office: control of the bishop's office at Soissons (northwest Gaul). In 861, Rothad, bishop of Soissons, was deposed by Hincmar, the leading Church figure of Gaul. Rothad appealed this decision to Nicholas, who ruled in his favor. Hincmar accepted the papal decision, so that in this and other matters Nicholas enhanced the power of the papacy.

CHAPTER 11

The Church in the World; The World in the Church
A.D. 885–1049

Inner Division and Internecine Warfare

Following the death of Charlemagne in 843, the Empire fell to his son Louis "The Pious." Though he tried to be a conscientious ruler, he was not the strong ruler his father had been. Louis did the best he could by endorsing the reformation of monasteries under the leadership of Benedict of Aniane, and ordering that two thirds of the money received as tithes be given to the poor. He encouraged the bishops to be elected by the people and the clergy. Unfortunately, the last years of his reign saw the outbreak of civil wars in which Louis' own sons fought him. When Louis died, the empire was divided among his three sons.

One of them obtained the land east of the Rhine, known in history as the East Frankish Kingdom; this was the beginning of Germany. Another son received the land west of the Meuse and the Rhone; this was known as the West Frankish Kingdom and included what is now France, Belgium, and the Netherlands. The third son took the long strip of land in between the other two territories. It included Italy and was called the Middle Kingdom.

To the inner divisions and internecine warfare, the Empire was attacked from the East by the Slavs and the Hungarians who used fast horses. From Scandinavia in the North came rugged Norsemen sailing speedy ships up the rivers, where they made landings in the Netherlands and France. Without mercy the Norsemen plundered and burned churches and monasteries while murdering many of the inhabitants. For three hundred years the people of God cried in Europe, "Lord, deliver us from the Norsemen!"

Also, there was the presence of the Arabs. Prior to the Islamic conquests, there was widespread commerce along the Mediterranean and into the Orient. Because of military success, the Arabs were able to curtail trade with the Orient and rule the southern and eastern shores of the Mediterranean. Money in Europe almost ceased to circulate. Gold coins were rare. To deal with the chaos of constant conflict and the shortage of money, a way of life emerged called feudalism whereby land became the main source of wealth.

Feudalism was a hierarchical system based on the holdings of lands. The kings of various kingdoms divided their territory among leading citizens, provided they remain loyal, shared in paying taxes, and provided military assistance upon request. Each of the subsequent princes divided his estate among lesser nobles, who in turn granted sections of land to still lesser tenants called vassals, who then contracted with fiefs who ruled over an estate or domain. This was his fiefdom. The peasants who worked the land were called serfs. Initially, grants of land were for one lifetime, but eventually the grants became hereditary and therefore more permanent.

The Church became part of the feudal system when pious people left land to churches or monasteries. In this way bishops, archbishops, abbots (heads of monasteries), and popes became landowners. Unfortunately, the emperors, who were at the top of the social hierarchy, looked upon the pope and other Church dignitaries as their vassals!

Dependency on Emperors

The development of feudalism had a direct bearing on the stability of the Church. Pope succeeded pope in breathtaking rapidity. Some were strangled, or died of starvation in the dungeons where they had been cast by their successors. To offer one example of the horrors of this period, there was the action of Stephen VI. In January, 897 he presided over what came to be called the "Cadaveric Synod." One of his predecessors, Formosus, was dug up from his grave, dressed in his papal robes, and paraded on the streets. Then, Formosus was tried, found guilty of a multitude of crimes, and mutilated. What remained of the body was thrown into the Tiber!

The Church had to endure this long period of shame and disgrace, because the Church was in bondage to the secular rulers. As one nobleman in Italy won a strategic victory, he would put the man of his choosing on the papal seat in Rome. Finally, John XII had enough and called for outside aid from Otto I, a strong ruler in Germany.

Otto I (912–973), king of the Germans, had been able to consolidate his land holdings while bringing the dukes of Germany under his will. Once in power, Otto I controlled the appointment of bishops and abbots through a process called *lay investiture*. Lay investiture took place when a non-authorized Church person, such as an emperor, bestowed a Church office upon someone, and invested him with the three symbols of spiritual authority: ring, staff, and keys. Between 1059 and 1122, a tremendous conflict emerged over this practice. From the reign of Nicholas II (Pope, 1059–1061), the popes made every effort[1] to reform the Church by freeing it from this plague, which often led to simony and sexual licentiousness.

When Otto I came to the assistance of John XII, the pope expressed his appreciation by crowning Otto emperor on February 2, 962. By this action, the Empire in the west was restored and was called the Holy Roman Empire. It continued to exist in association with Germany until 1806—when Napoleon brought that which was neither holy, nor Roman, nor an Empire, to a decisive end.

By recognizing Otto I as king of Germany, John XII wrote a new chapter in the history of the papacy. An old tradition of having only Italian popes was broken during this period. Otto III placed his tutor upon the papal throne in 999, Gerbert of Aurillac, formerly the archbishop of Rheims. Changing his name to Sylvester II, Gerbert was the first French pope and one of the most educated men of his time. As a prolific scholar and teacher he made a courageous but unsuccessful attempt to reform the papacy as well as the whole Church.

Simony: The Selling of the Papal Office

The depths of human depravity became manifest in the highest Church office, when an Italian noble family made Benedict IX pope in 1033. He was only twelve years old. As the years passed his undisciplined behavior moved the Crescenzio family, rivals of the Tuscom party, to drive him from Rome in 1045. Sylvester III (1000–1063) was then appointed pope. The appointment proved to be temporary because Benedict returned to Rome to resume the pontificate—only to become bored with it. So, he literally sold the office for one thousand pounds of silver to the man known as Gregory VI!

---

[1] "every effort"—the struggle reached its climax in 1075, when Gregory VII (Hildebrand) delivered an ultimatum to the emperor Henry IV. Henry resisted, but then was excommunicated. The conflict was finally resolved by a compromise in the *Concordat of Worms* in 1122, between Henry V and Callistus II. All this was yet to come (described in chapter 15).

News of this act of simony, the selling of a Church office for money, created a backlash of protest, which made Benedict decide to refuse to surrender the papal office after all! As a result, three men now claimed to be pope: Benedict IX, Sylvester III, and Gregory VI.

This matter was finally settled by Henry III of Germany. After an interview with Gregory VI, he gathered a council that deposed all three popes and named Clement II. The same council also passed ecclesiastical legislation against corrupt practices, particularly simony. Still, it was plain for all to see that the Church had gone into the world, and the world had come into the Church!

Map of the Holy Roman Empire

CHAPTER 12

A House Divided
A.D. 1054

The Eastern Church

In the year 1054, the Church of Jesus Christ was formally and forever divided. The Pope of Rome sent his messenger to lay the decree of excommunication upon the altar of St. Sophia in Constantinople. In retaliation, the patriarch of the East issued his own decree, excommunicating Rome and the churches submitting to the pope. In this manner, the Greek Eastern part of the Church, and the Latin Western part (with the majority of its members belonging to the Germanic race), separated from each other. Several factors had brought about this great division.

The Iconoclastic Controversy

An iconoclast is a person who destroys religious images or opposes their veneration. In the East in 726, Byzantine Ruler Leo III (c. 680–741; ruled, 717–741) had issued the first iconoclastic decree (forbidding the worship of images), largely because the Mohammedan's were charging Christians with being polytheistic. Leo was supported by the Patriarch of Constantinople and the higher clergy. However, many of the monks and common people opposed this decree. At Rome, Pope Gregory II denounced this imperial interference because the charges of idolatry did not really affect the Western Church, and because he believed that the secular political powers had no right to interfere in the affairs of the Church.

The controversy continued during the reign of Byzantine Emperor Constantine V (741–774). But during the reign of the Empress Irene, it concluded with a victory for image worship. Irene was born of a humble family in Athens. In 769 she married

Emperor Leo IV (750–780). After her husband's death she ruled as regent for her minor son, Constantine VI (771?–797). However, when Constantine did come of age to rule, Irene contested him for the throne. In the struggle, she had her own son imprisoned and blinded in 797.

Irene's rule was not contested seriously again until 802, when the patricians revolted and forced her into exile to the island of Lesvos. Still, while she reigned, Irene was able to influence the Church. A devoted worshipper of images, she called the Second Council of Nicea, which was the Seventh Ecumenical Council. Held in 787, it was decreed by this Council that images should be venerated but not worshipped.

During the reign of Leo V (813–820), the controversy broke out again, as the effort again was made to impose iconoclasm upon the Church. This time, the chief defender of iconodulism (or the use of images), was Theodore of Studion (759–826). He was born in Antioch, and educated there along with his friend and fellow-student, John Chrysostom.

The attempt to remove images from the Church failed once more in the reign of Theodora. Empress Theodora (810–862) was the second wife of Emperor Theophilus (829). On his death in 842, she was made regent for their son Michael III. As a devoted iconodule, Theodora called a Church Council in 843, which restored the worship of images and drove from office the iconoclasts. In the Greek Orthodox Church, this event is still celebrated in The Festive of Orthodoxy. In 858, the Empress herself was forced to retire to a convent. These constant attempts to rid the Church of images produced a deep and lasting rupture between Rome and Constantinople.

The Filioque Controversy

This doctrinal issue was also instrumental in separating the Church in the West from the Church in the East. The Latin (Western) theologians argued that the Holy Spirit proceeds from the Father *and* the Son; in Latin it is the word *filioque*. The Greek (Eastern) theologians said that the Holy Spirit proceeds only from the Father, leaving out the word *filioque*. Over that one word countless debates have been held, a multitude of books have been written, blood has been shed, and the Church has divided.[1]

---

[1] See the third paragraph of the Nicene Creed chapter 5.

The Authority Controversy

As the power of Rome grew, so did the authority of the office of bishop in Constantinople. Finally, there was an unwillingness on the part of the patriarch of Constantinople and the pope at Rome to be subservient to each other, and the Church divided.

Territorial Dispute

Because there was no sharp definition of the boundaries of the territories to be ruled by Rome and Constantinople, frequent struggles arose over administration of border areas, and the Church divided.

Cultural Differences

In the ceremonies of the Church, different practices became the custom in the East and in the West, and these customs were formulated into Church laws. For example, the marriage of priests became forbidden in the western church, while they were sanctioned in the East. In the western church, the adoration of statues was practiced, while the Greek churches embraced pictures as well as statues. In the communion service of the western churches, the wafer of unleavened bread was used, while common bread was used in the Greek communion. These cultural differences are still honored today, and the Church is still divided over them.

Political Differences

In the East, the Church had no real concerns with being subservient to the emperor, while the Western Church insisted upon (1) independence from the state and (2) the right of moral supervision of rulers of state. And so the Church divided.

The Western Church

Following the great ecclesiastical division in 1054, the Church in the West was to be found in Italy, France, the Netherlands, England, Germany, Austria, Denmark, Norway, Sweden, Ireland, Scotland, and Russia. In these nations the papacy would seek unity, peace, and stability. Unfortunately, this was not to be. The Church in the West would continue to experience constant upheaval as religious reformers met firm opposition from secular rulers who did not want to recognize any Church authority over them.

PART TWO
THE CHURCH IN THE MIDDLE AGES
A.D. 754—1517

CHAPTER 13

Monasticism and the Cluny Reforms
A.D. 1054

Asceticism

As the struggle for Church unity and papal authority was constant, so was the struggle for spiritual reality. In the quest for personal integrity many Christians embraced *asceticism*, which refers to extreme acts of self-denial. In the western Church the cloister[1] life developed inside the monasteries. The cloister life is the life that is designed to be hidden in God. To that end monks and nuns renounced all possession of earthly goods. They did not eat or drink more than was necessary. Many monks would eat nothing but bread and drank only water. Rigorous periods of fasting were followed. Using instruments of punishment, monks would flagellate themselves with whips, a rod, cords, or a stick in a vain attempt to rid themselves of unworthy thoughts. Monks and nuns did not marry, but devoted themselves to good works, prayer, reading of religious books, and meditation. In the Patristic tradition, celibacy was believed to be superior to marriage.

Unfortunately, the record reveals that the very place which was designed to become a sanctuary from sin, instead became a breeding place of debauchery. John Chrysostom had warned of this possibility noting, "Celibacy in itself is neither good nor bad, but becomes so from the disposition of those who practice it." All forms of immorality found freedom to express themselves, because of the isolation of the monasteries, the silence of those committing sin, and the inherent trust allowed between men and women who had come together in the name of Christ.

---

[1] Cloister (Latin: *claustra*; bar, bolt, bound). Refers to an open court in a monastery or cathedral surrounded by an arched walkway. This secluded area was intended primarily as a place for monks and clergy to walk in.

Reform at the Monastery of Cluny

Not all monks and nuns practiced ascetism or were hypocritical. There have always been faithful servants of the Lord who were sincere in their religious zeal. Some of these were Abbot Berno (c. 850–927) and his immediate successors, who founded a monastery in Cluny in eastern France in 910.

At Cluny, the Benedictine rules of ascetism were diligently enforced, and reforms were developed. For the next two hundred years, the Cluny reform movement spread to other monasteries as a means of genuine spiritual awakening and social reform. With the new reforms, emphasis was once more placed upon true religion, scholarship, and the cultivation of the arts. Over two thousand monastic establishments grew out of this effort. It was the Cluny movement that produced noteworthy men such as Hildebrand, who as pope became known as Gregory VII.

* * *

The Doctrine of Fasting

(1) Fasting refers to the voluntary abstention from food for religious purposes (Esth 4:3; Dan 6:18; Matt 15:32; Luke 2:37; Acts 14:23; 2 Cor 6:5).

(2) Fasting was common among God's people. While much fasting became ineffectual (Isa 58:3–9), a solemn fast could elicit the grace and mercy of God (Esth 4:15).

(3) Fasting was commonly accompanied by the refusal to drink wine or water or both. Fasting was also accompanied by:

- abstaining from work (Lev 16:29);
- not using a razor or touching the dead (Num 6:1ff);
- assembling (Num 29:7; Neh 9:1);
- pulling the hair on the head (Ezr 9:3);
- weeping (Jdgs 20:26);
- and mourning (2 Sam 1:12);
- presenting an offering (Lev 23:27; Jdgs 20:26; Jer 14:12);
- pouring out water (1 Sam 7:6);

- tearing of the clothes (2 Sam 1:11);
- putting on sackcloth (1 Kgs 21:27);
- covering oneself with ashes (Dan 9:3);
- refusing to talk (2 Sam 12:16f).

(4) In the early Church, *The Didache*[2] (1:3) urged fasting for one's enemies as a means of showing grace towards them (cp. Psa 35:13).

(5) People in the Bible fasted for a variety of reasons:

- when they were dedicated or separated unto the Lord (Num 6:1ff) for special service;
- in an act of worship (Jer 14:12);
- as an expression of sorrow (1 Chron 10:12);
- as a sign of repentance (1 Kgs 21:27–29);
- in order to seek the Lord's grace (Esth 4:15).

(6) Fasting, prayer, and the giving of alms were three acts of devotion that were highly respected in the early Church. They are often mentioned together (cp. Luke 5:33; 18:12; Acts 10:31).

(7) For a while, the early Church may have observed the fast on the Day of Atonement as the Law required (Lev 16:29ff). In *The Didache* (8:1), Christians were instructed to fast on Wednesdays and Fridays.

(8) Though the Law of Moses commanded only one fast on the Day of Atonement (Lev 16:29ff), other fasts were added to commemorate traumatic moments in Hebrew history, such as the siege of Jerusalem by Nebuchadnezzar and the murder of Gedaliah.

---

[2] Didache – *The Didache* ("The Teachings of the Apostles," or "The Teaching of the Lord through the Twelve Apostles") refers to a short manual of Church life and morals, written c. A.D. 150. The first part provides a series of prohibitions and warnings. The second part provides instructions as to baptism, fasts, prayer, and the Lord's Supper. It was discovered in 1873 and published in 1883.

CHAPTER 14

The Church Cries Out for Spiritual Reform
A.D. 1049–1073

The Cluny Reforms: A.D. 1049–1058

As a reaction to the appalling spiritual conditions in the Church during the tenth century, there took place a religious renewal. This time of spiritual awakening began with the founding of the monastery at Cluny. The objective was to bring spiritual vitality back to the clergy, the monk and the papacy.

To help reform and stabilize the papacy, the Cluny reformers enlisted the aid of German Emperor Henry III, who was the political leader of the Holy Roman Empire. Being a devout man, Henry III was willing to help advance the cause of Christ and bring about spiritual reform. In time he was able to place on the papal seat Clement II. Unfortunately, both Clement and the next pope after him, Benedict IX died within a year after taking office. Following the even shorter twenty four day papal reign of Damascus II, Henry III then appointed his cousin Bruno, Bishop of Toul (in north-eastern Franc), to be the pope. He would become known as Leo IX.

Pope Leo IX

Leo IX (Pope, 1049–1054) was a strong supporter of the Cluny spiritual renewal, reflected in the great change he made in the College of Cardinals. From the inception of the papacy, there had been cardinals in Rome. These men were leading bishops who served as special personal assistants and gave advice to the popes. When Leo IX became pope, he realized that this spiritual advisory cabinet consisted entirely of Rome's aristocratic families, who really controlled the papacy. These same families also contributed to the corruption of the papacy, and therefore were not sympathetic to the Cluny reform movement. So the first change Leo IX made was to find men who were spiritually-minded. The new cardinals came from various parts of the Church, which meant that Leo had individuals whom he could confide in and who had the best interest of others at heart.

To make other necessary reforms and ensure spiritual renewal, Leo IX traveled through France and Germany holding synods and demanding obedience to three principles. First, the priests were not to marry. Second, they were not to practice simony. Third, no one should obtain a Church office apart from the consensus of the clergy and the people (no lay investiture).

Despite these positive improvements, the administration of Leo IX was not without stress, for it was during his tenure that the two parts of the Church separated from each other. It was Leo IX who excommunicated the patriarch of Constantinople, Michael Cerularius, thereby creating the Greek Eastern Church, and the Latin (Roman or Western) Church.

Following the death of Leo IX in 1054, Emperor Henry III, appointed another German to the papacy, who took the name of Victor II. He would hold the office of the papacy for only two years, from 1055–1057. In 1056 Henry III died unexpectedly, creating a political opportunity for Victor II. He immediately moved to have Henry's son, a child of six, established as successor to the imperial throne. His mother Agnes would rule as empress until Henry IV came of age.

By involving himself in this political strategy, Victor II had created a dilemma for the Church. Whereas it had been successful in freeing itself from the Roman nobility due to the Cluny reforms, it was in danger of subjecting itself to the imperial favors of Germany. And now at the head of the Holy Roman Empire was not a strong ruler like Henry III, who could protect the papacy, but a weak woman regent named Agnes. For thinking reformers in Rome, it seemed that the stage was set for breaking the imperial bonds with all earthly rulers. Perhaps a climate could be created in which the papacy would protect itself, without being unduly influenced or submissive to either the nobility or imperial rulers.

Pope Stephen X

With these thoughts in mind and without consulting the Empress Agnes, the reformed party in control in Rome elected Stephen X as their new pope. Stephen wanted to be a strong and capable religious leader. To that end, he insisted that appointments to Church office must be made by the Church and not by lay investitures. By declaring this policy, Pope Stephen X was in effect weakening the power of the German emperor, who had been enhancing his own political prestige by appointing bishops favorable to himself.

Had Stephen tried to carry out the new policy he had announced, it would have resulted in a great conflict between pope and emperor, for no ruler would give up the right of lay investiture without strong opposition. But Stephen X did not bring the impending conflict to a confrontation. He acquiesced instead, by asking the regent mother (Empress Agnes) to approve his own ascension to the papal office. Her approval was granted. Soon thereafter Stephen died.

Following the death of this pope, the Roman nobility perceived a renewed opportunity to re-assert their power over the papacy. Within a week of Stephen's death, the nobility elected one of their own kind, a pope with the title Benedict X. Suddenly thrown into panic, the reform-minded cardinals fled Rome. It seemed as if the dark days of Benedict IX had returned. The Church needed help! It was to come, but from an unusual source.

Hildebrand: The Power behind the Throne

Within the Church structure was a capable man named Hilde-brand (c. 1021–1085), who had served Pope Leo IX as a sub-deacon in charge of the financial affairs of the papacy. In this hour of crisis, with the nobility of Rome trying to unduly influence the papacy, Hildebrand decided their movements should be challenged.

He did this by seeking out a man who was sympathetic to the Cluny reforms. Hildebrand selected as his candidate the bishop of Florence. Enlisting the support of the Duke of Tuscany and a portion of the people of Rome, Hildebrand appealed to the empress Agnes to recognize his candidate, as opposed to the one selected by the nobility. The Empress agreed. Her support allowed the reform-minded cardinals to come back to Rome from their flight to safety. When the cardinals met to select the next pope, Hildebrand's candidate was elected, and assumed the title Pope Nicholas II (Pope, 1058–1061), originally Gerard of Burgundy. While Nicholas II occupied the papal seat, therefore, the real power behind the throne was Hildebrand.

Movement toward Maturity: 1059–1073

A New Method for Electing a Pope

Hildebrand's later success in bringing about Church reform had its basis in a new method for electing the pope, which significantly strengthened the papacy. The new process was introduced after the papal administration of Nicholas II; it was formulated at the Second Lateran[1] Council (1059).

At this council, it was decided that the power of election of the pope was to rest with the cardinals who also held the title of bishop. The intent of this new method was to remove the election of the popes (and thus the control of the papacy), out of the hands of the Italian nobility, out of the hands of the emperors, and out of the hands of other religious leaders who were not reform-minded. Predictably, bishops in Germany and Lombardy, the nobility of Italy, and select government rulers did not like this new method; it would be challenged on all sides.

The first person duly elected under this new process was Anselm of Lucca, who as pope was known as Alexander II (d. 1073; Pope, 1061–1073). Because Alexander II was a reformer, he was opposed by the German bishops. They set up an anti-pope in Hororius II. In the contest that ensued, Hororius came close to being the victor! In the providence of God, however, the Cluny reforms would stand—due to an incident in Germany in 1062.

An archbishop of Cologne named Anno kidnapped the young Henry IV, and was made his guardian in the place of his mother, the empress Agnes. Being an ambitious man, Anno believed his own interests could be advanced by the Cluny reform party, so he displaced Hororius II and recognized Alexander II as the rightful pope. This established the new powers of the papacy.

Nevertheless the old temptations to become involved in worldly affairs would return, thus losing focus on spiritual issues. Very interested in politics, Alexander engaged in voluminous diplomatic correspondence and support of military activity. For example, when William Duke of Normandy was planning his conquest of England, Alexander gave his approval. He also sanctioned military action against the Muslims.

However, when he did engage in more pastoral matters, Alexander II was able to make two of the most powerful archbishops in Germany do penance, after confessing to the sin of simony. He also refused the request of Henry IV to divorce his queen, thereby upholding the sanctity of marriage. By enforcing spiritual decisions consistent with the cause of Christ, Alexander II strengthened the power of the papacy, thereby making it possible for principled men like Hildebrand to make further reforms.

---

[1] Lateran – there were five ecumenical councils held at the Lateran Palace of the popes in Rome. These councils were so called because in history the Laterani family once occupied the site.

The Hope of Hildebrand

Hildebrand was born in Tuscany, Italy, the son of poor parents. Although his early years are obscure, it is known that as a young Benedictine monk in the St. Mary's monastery at Rome, he was affected by the Cluny reforms. Hildebrand was respected for personal integrity, steadfastness to principle, and common sense. For many years in his pastoral ministry, "Monk Hildebrand" had directed pointed attacks against concubinage of the clergy, simony in the obtaining of ecclesiastical benefits, and lay investiture (Church appointments by secular rulers). His monastic life ended when his administrative abilities were recognized by higher Church officials. By 1046 he was an assistant to Pope Gregory VI.

During the following years of service at the center of papal power, Hildebrand saw the desperate need for religious reform. He discovered that secular rulers made regular appointments to ecclesiastical offices of individuals who were not morally or spiritually qualified, but who were willing to pay a high price for a place within the Church (simony). Hildebrand began working for change. His efforts would continue after Gregory VI, during the papal administrations of Leo IX, Victor II, Nicholas II, and Alexander II. Although he had denied himself the office of the papacy on several occasions, his words of wisdom were widely appreciated. His influence was far reaching: when he spoke, people listened. So finally, upon the death of Alexander II in 1073, Hildebrand himself received the unanimous support of the cardinals and was elected to the papacy as Gregory VII (Pope, 1073–1085).

Hildebrand's election was in a surprising manner, which circumvented the new reforms, almost undoing them as opponents of reform had tried to do without success. While Hildebrand was conducting the funeral services of Alexander II in the Basilica of St. John Lateran, the crowd was thinking of their next pope. The audience was filled with religious passion. A voice cried out for Hildebrand to be recognized as pope, and the crowd agreed. Swept up with emotion, the people literally carried Hildebrand to the Church of St. Peter! There he was consecrated and placed upon the papal throne. Though the cardinals had no part in this spontaneous selection (against the council decree of 1059), they later legalized Hildebrand's exaltation by formally electing him pope in the appointed way.

An ambitious and strong leader, Hildebrand (whose name literally means "brilliant flame") drew up his famous *Dictaus Papae*, outlining his vision for uniting all of the main elements of western Europe under Church control. He next moved to institute clerical reforms. No longer would Church offices be sold (simony), and the rules of celibacy would be enforced.

To ensure these things, Hildebrand issued two other general decrees: the reaffirmation of the supreme authority of papal decrees, and a final dissolution of all non-ecclesiastical investiture of Church office. Despite initial opposition to his actions, spiritually concerned members of the Church could hope that in Hildebrand further reforms would come.

CHAPTER 15

The Struggle for Independence from the State
A.D. 1073–1122

The Fight for Ultimate Authority

For both pope and emperor the right of investiture was critical. Ultimate power was at stake. If an emperor gave up the right to make Church appointments, he was seriously subverting his political authority. There was also the possibility of being deposed. If the pope did not have this right without question and without qualification, there could be no firm basis for clerical reform, and no holding of individuals accountable in an ecclesiastical court for their attitudes and actions within the body of Christ. The great conflict came to a head in the person of Pope Gregory VII (Hildebrand) and Henry IV.

Contesting the Church

The opening move in this great drama began in 1075 when Henry IV of Germany was believed by Pope Gregory VII to be at his weakest. In a bold move Gregory VII forbade investiture by layman. Although Henry was angered by the decision, he waited before responding. When he felt politically strong a few months later, Henry defied Gregory by conferring investiture upon three bishops. The world waited to see what Gregory would do next. In December, 1075, the answer came in a letter which counseled Henry to confess his wrong doing and to perform a proper penance with the promise of being absolved. The penance of Henry was to be reported back to Gregory.

"Therefore we counsel thy Highness that, if thou dost feel thyself guilty in this matter, thou do seek the advice of some canonical bishop with speedy confession. Who, with our permission enjoining on thee a proper penance for this fault, shall absolve thee and shall endeavor by letter to intimate to us truly, with thy consent, the measure of thy penitence."

The pope continued by listing the many sins of the emperor. He then reminded Henry IV that he was under the authority of Peter and his successors. Furthermore, Gregory argued that Henry deserved excommunication which meant that he should be cut off from membership in the Church and thus face a certain damnation. Henry was young, proud, determined and fresh with military victory. The more he read what Gregory had written the angrier he became. In this state of fury, Henry called a council of bishops which met in Worms on January 24, 1076. Upon orders from the king, the council declared that it no longer recognized Gregory VII as pope and sent a letter to that effect. The letter began: "Henry, king not through usurpation but through the holy ordination of God, to Hildebrand, at present not pope but false monk."

Implied in the letter is that Pope Gregory VII had taken the office by force and not by proper means (cf. 1 Pet 5:2). Henry ended his letter with the strongest condemnation of Gregory.

"I Henry, king by the grace of God, do say unto thee, together with all our bishops: Descend, descend, to be damned throughout the ages."

The assault upon his legitimacy to reign as pope and the attack on his personal character deeply offended Gregory. Most importantly, Henry was not to stand in ultimate judgment upon Gregory, but he upon Henry. Gregory chose February 14, 1076 as the date on which he would issue a solemn sentence deposing the emperor and excommunicating him. From the Lenten Synod at Rome the pope said:

> Therefore, confiding in this belief and for the honor and security of your Church, in the name of Almighty God, Father, Son and Holy Ghost, I withdraw, through your power and authority, from Henry the King, son of Henry the Emperor, who has risen against your Church with unheard of insolence, the rule over the whole Kingdom of the Germans and over Italy. And I release all Christians from the bonds of the oath that they have made or shall make to him; and I forbid any one to serve him as King. For it is fitting that he who strives to lessen the honor of the Church should himself lose the honor which belongs to him.

The next move was up to Henry and he wasted no time in making it. Henry chose to appeal to the people of Rome, and to that end sent a message urging the citizens in the strongest language to banish the "Monk Hildebrand" from their city. In like manner, Gregory sent a letter to the people of Germany telling them to choose someone else as their king unless Henry repented.

The outcome of this exchange of correspondence was that the people of Rome ignored the appeal of Henry, while the lords of Germany decided to honor the request of the Pope. The feudal lords were all too happy to have official papal sanction for continuing their disobedience to Henry, who had been ruling them in a capricious and arbitrary manner.

In October, 1076, the German nobility who opposed the king assembled at Tribur (modern Trebur, Germany). Some wanted to dispose the king; all wanted to humble him. The nobles decided that they would meet again in Augsburg on February 2, 1077, under the mediation of the pope. At that meeting Henry would be given a chance to repent and to clear himself of the many sins of which he was accused and to repent. If Henry had not freed himself from the papal ban of excommunication by that time, he was to forfeit the throne.

Henry knew that his situation was desperate and he had to do something drastic. He was willing to agree to anything to save himself and his reign. He would even repent. With little support in Germany, Henry decided to go to Italy to get out from under the ban (decree) of excommunication, and be restored to full Church membership by receiving absolution of his sins. With an entourage of only about fifty people, including his wife and infant son, Henry began his journey over the Swiss Alps during a harsh winter.

On the morning of January 25, 1077, with a blizzard raging, Henry climbed the hill to the castle of Canossa in northern Italy where Pope Gregory VII had come, and knocked at the outer gate. The gate was opened and Henry was allowed to pass through the gates of the first and second walls. There he was stopped to stand before the closed third gate.

All day long Henry fasted. Over his kingly garments he wore the garb of a penitent, which was a coarse woolen robe. He was bareheaded and barefooted. In this manner he stood in the courtyard in the cold and snow. Darkness descended and still the inner gate remained closed. The next morning Henry appeared again only to be forced to stand all the day long barefoot in the snow. By nightfall the gate remained shut and Henry returned to his lodging. The third morning dawned.

Henry arose and went to stand as a penitent in the courtyard of Canossa. The hours slowly moved by. Noon time came and nothing happened. Then the afternoon arrived. Finally, on the eve of January 27, 1077, the inner gate slowly opened; Henry was allowed to step inside. As Henry made his way into a large room, there sat at one end Hildebrand, an old man—once a poor boy but now powerful enough to humble a king. Before him stood the young and strong king dressed in the clothing of a penitent. With tears in his eyes, the emperor prostrated himself to the ground. He kissed the foot of the pope and begged for his forgiveness. The absolution was granted and the ban of excommunication was lifted, but not before Henry promised Gregory, with an oath, that he would behave better.

As dramatic as this encounter was, it would not be the end of the story nor of the struggle, for the people in Germany and Italy were confused and divided into warring camps. The opponents of Henry in Germany in 1077 went on to elect Rudolph of Swabia to be king. From 1078 to 1080 civil war ensued, until Rudolph was wounded in battle and bled to death.

Pope Gregory had tried to resolve the conflict but was told not to interfere. Rather than do that, in 1080, Gregory VII again put Henry under the ban. However, this time there would be no acts of repentance. Powerful cardinals had finally turned against the pope to support the king. This time it would be Henry who would humble the pope. In fact, he would drive Gregory from the papal chair. Henry did this by marching his army into Italy and placing on the papal throne the anti-pope Guibert (Clement III, 1084).

When Gregory heard the approaching hoof-beats of Henry's army, he fled into the castle of St. Angelo on the left bank of the Tiber River, and called for help to the Normans in southern Italy. They came to his aid, and Henry was forced to retreat. However, the Normans stayed in Rome to plunder it. The people blamed Gregory and drove him from the city and into exile. In Salerno, Gregory died in 1085, a broken man. His last words were: "I have loved righteousness and hated iniquity; therefore I died in exile."

A Compromising Compact

Despite all that Gregory VII was able to accomplish as pope, the struggle over investiture continued for thirty-five years until the *Concordat of Worms* resolved the issue in 1122. According to the terms reached between Emperor Henry V and Pope Calixtus II on September 23, Henry V would relinquish investiture by ring and staff, while permitting the free election of bishops. Calixtus agreed that all elections would be conducted before the emperor, who would retain the right to invest the elected ecclesiastic with the temporal prerogatives of the office.

Summary Timetable

    1046 Hildebrand becomes assistant to Pope Gregory VI
    1073 Hildebrand is made Pope Gregory VII
    1075 Gregory forbids lay investiture to Henry IV of Germany
    1/76 Henry no longer recognizes Gregory as pope
    2/76 Gregory excommunicates Henry
    10/76 German nobles side with the pope
    1/77 Henry repents and receives absolution
    78–80 Civil war in Germany
    1080 Gregory again excommunicates Henry
    1084 Henry marches on Rome and drives Gregory into exile
    1122 Concordat of Worms resolves controversy over lay investiture

* * *

THE DOCTRINE OF REPENTANCE[1]

(1) Gospel repentance does not belong to a Jewish dispensation[2] in the past, but is for men today as per Acts 17:30: "But God now commandeth all men everywhere to repent."

(2) There is nothing meritorious in a sinner's compliance with the righteous demand of God to repent.

---

[1] Extracted with modification from the writings of A.W. Pink (1886–1952): Pastor, itinerate Bible teacher, voluminous author of *Studies in the Scriptures* and many books including his well-known *The Sovereignty of God* and *The Attributes of God*, both available from Ichthus Publications. Born in Nottingham, England, immigrated to the U.S., and later returned to his homeland in 1934. More than 350 Pink tracts, booklets, and paperback titles are available from Chapel Library. The material in this section on Repentance is extracted from the *Studies in the Scriptures*. Chapel Library is reprinting this monthly expository digest and sending it without charge quarterly to subscribers in North America.

[2] dispensation – age; period.

(3) It is the gospel duty of man to repent (Prov 28:13; Isa 55:7).

(4) The necessity for Gospel repentance is rooted in the fact and consequences that the Law of God has been broken, for "by the law is the knowledge of sin" (Rom 3:20).

Here in part may lay a practical reason as to why repentance is no longer preached, practiced, or even understood by a large part of society today or by the Church. A new generation has arisen believing that the Law of God has no place in this "age of grace."

Can there be any wonder that our country and the nations of the Western world are in moral and spiritual chaos? A particular teaching in the Church has united with Humanism, Communism, and anarchy in a common contempt for the Law of God. Why should men have respect for human laws if they are taught that the Law of God has no rule and reign over their lives today?

In contrast to popular theology of recent origin, the Apostle Paul plainly affirms, "I had not known sin, but by the law" (Rom 7:7). The exceeding sinfulness of sin (Rom 7:13) is only exposed or made manifest when the Holy Spirit turns the light of God's Law upon our conscience and heart.

"Practical godliness consists in conformity of our heart and life to the Law of God, and in a sincere compliance with the Gospel of Christ" (A.W. Pink). This is not legalism. It is the antidote for anti-nomianism (or lawlessness), which pervades our society and our churches.

The requirements of the Law are summed up in the Word of Christ, "Thou shalt love the Lord thy God with all thine heart, and with all thy soul, and with all thy might" (Deut 6:5; Matt 22:37). Man is required to love God. The ground or reason for this love is because He is the Lord our God. The extent of this duty is to love God with *all the heart.*

Sin is failure to love God in this manner. Sin is saying, "I renounce God who made me; I disallow His right to govern me. I care not what He says to me, what commandments He has given, nor how He explains His Word: I prefer self-indulgence to His approval. I am indifferent to all He has done to and for me; His blessings and gifts move me not; ultimately I am going to be lord of myself." Sin is rebellion against the Majesty of heaven; it is to treat the Almighty with contempt.

(5) In contrast to sin, repentance results from a realization in the heart, wrought therein by the Holy Spirit, of the sinfulness of sin, of the awfulness of ignoring the

claims of God and defying His authority. It is therefore a deep hatred of sin, both an acknowledgment and a complete heart-forsaking of it before God. When we turn to God, we turn away from our sin. It is in this repentant faith that God will pardon us (cp. Lev 23:29; 1 Kgs 8:47–50). No change in dispensation has wrought any change in the character of the thrice holy God. His claims are ever the same.

(6) The Prophets taught repentance (Psa 32:3–5; Prov 29:13; Jer 4:4; Ezek 18:30–32; Hos 5:15; Joel 2:12–18).

(7) John the Baptist preached repentance (Matt 3:2; Luke 1:16–17).

(8) The Lord Jesus preached and illustrated repentance (Mark 1:15; Matt 5:3; Luke 4:18; 5:32; 13:3, 5; 15:17–20).

(9) When risen from the dead, Christ commissioned His servants "that repentance and remission of sins should be preached in his name among all nations" (Luke 24:47), and Acts 5:31 tells us that both repentance and forgiveness of sins were given to the Church.

(10) On the Day of Pentecost, Peter did not say that the people were to do nothing but "receive Christ by a decision" they make. Rather, he preached repentance, saying, "Repent ye therefore and be converted, that your sins may be blotted out!" (Acts 3:19).

(11) When Paul was converted and sent to preach the Gospel to the Gentiles, it was to "open their eyes and to turn them from darkness to light and from the power of Satan unto God, that they might receive forgiveness of sins" (Acts 26:20; cp. 20:21).

(12) Only to those who shut their eyes, stopped their ears, hardened their hearts, and were given up to destruction in the days of the Prophets (Isa 6:10), of Christ (Matt 13:15), and of the Apostles (Acts 28:27), would the sentence be, "Lest they should see with their eyes, hear with their ears, understand with their hearts, and be converted, and I should heal them" (Mark 4:12).

(13) The nature of true evangelical repentance should be clearly understood (Luke 13:3).

   a. Trembling beneath the preaching of God's Word is not re-pentance. Felix "trembled" (Acts 24:25), but he was not converted.
   b. Being almost persuaded is not repentance. Agrippa illustrates this (Acts 26:28; see also Matt 13:20–21). A person may be conscious of his evil doing and acknowledge the same without being converted, just as Pharaoh confessed his sins (Exod 10:16).
   c. Humbling ourselves beneath the mighty hand of God on occasion, is not repentance. A solemn example of this is Ahab, who was sorry he had killed Naboth (1 Kgs 21:27–29). Yet in the next chapter he again is rebelling against God.
   d. Confessing sins is not repentance. Thousands have gone forward to the "altar" or "mourners bench" and then backwards into the same sin.
   e. A person may even do works meet for repentance and yet remain impenitent, just as Judas confessed his sins to the priest, returned the money, but then committed suicide (Matt 27:3–5).
   f. Repentance is more than conviction of sin or fear of wrath to come. In Acts 2:37–38 men were already under such fear, but then still were commanded to repent. Their legal fear of punishment did not produce saving repentance, in which there is an evangelical judging of self, and a mourning over sin out of a sense of God's grace and goodness.

(14) What then is repentance? In the words of A. W. Pink (paraphrased): Repentance is a supernatural and inward revelation from God, giving deep consciousness of what I am in *His* sight, resulting in a bitter sorrow for sin, a hatred for sin, a turning away from or forsaking of sin. It is the discovery of God's high and righteous claims upon me, and of my lifelong failure to meet those claims. It is the recognition of the holiness and goodness of His Law, and my defiant insubordination thereto. It is the perception that God has the right to rule and govern me, and of my refusal to submit unto Him. It is the apprehension that He has dealt in goodness and kindness with me, and that I have repaid Him with evil, by having no concern for His honor and glory. It is the realization of His gracious patience with me, and how that instead of this melting my heart and causing me to yield loving obedience to Him, I have abused His forbearance by continuing a course of self-will.

Evangelical repentance is a heart apprehension of the exceeding sinfulness of sin. It is the recognition of the chief thing wherein I am blameworthy, namely, in having so miserably failed to render unto God that which is His rightful due.

True repentance is always accompanied by a deep longing and a sincere determination to forsake that course which is displeasing to God, out of a motive of love for Him. With what honesty could any man seek God's pardon while he continued to defy Him and to part not with that which He forbids? Would any king pardon a traitor, though he seemed ever so humble, if he saw that he would be a traitor still? True, God is infinitely more merciful than any human king, yet in the very passage where He first formally proclaimed His mercy, He at once added that He "will by no means clear the guilty" (Exod 34:5–7), i.e. guilty-hearted, those with false and disloyal hearts toward Himself, who would not be subject to Him in all things, and who decline to have their every thought brought into captivity to obedience unto Him (2 Cor 10:5).

God's mercy (Psa 130:4) is never exercised at the expense of His holiness. God never displays one of His attributes so as to dishonor another. To pity a thief, while continuing as a thief, would be folly, not wisdom. Well did the Puritan Thomas Goodwin[3] say, "Resolve either to leave every known sin and to submit to every known duty, or else never look to find mercy and favor with God" (cp. Deut 28:19–20).

(15) Biblical repentance presupposes several factors.

   a. It presupposes a recognition and acknowledgment of God's claims upon us as our Creator, Governor, Provider, and Protector. Thus repentance does presuppose that a supernatural enlightenment has been given by God (1 John 5:20).
   b. Biblical repentance presupposes a hearty approval of God's Law and a full consent to its righteous requirements. "The Law is holy, and the

---

[3] Thomas Goodwin (1600–1680) – born in Norfolk and educated at Cambridge, he became vicar of Holy Trinity Church, Cambridge. He became a Congregationalist in London in 1634. In 1639 persecution drove him to Holland, where he pastored a church at Arnheim. He returned to London and became a member of the Westminster Assembly, and leader of the Dissenting Brethren in it. In 1650 he was appointed president of Magdalen College, Oxford. He was a prominent member of the Savoy Assembly in 1658

commandment is holy, and just, and good" (Rom 7:12). It cannot be otherwise, for God is its Author.

c. Biblical repentance presupposes that the Law was never repealed.

1). Jesus said, "Think not that I am come to earth to destroy the Law, or the prophets: I am not come to destroy, but to fulfill (Matt 5:17–18).

2). Jesus condemned the Pharisees, because they pretended that their rules and regulations surpassed the Law (Matt 5:20).

3). That the Law of God was never to be repealed is taught in the Psalms (Psa 119:142, 144, 152, 160).

4). Christ did not die to *annul* the Law so that now it wholly ceases to be a rule of life to believers, but rather to *recover* His people unto a conformity thereto (Titus 2:11–13). Though men love their corruptions, God sitteth as king forever (Psa 29:10), and He will assert His crown rights (Luke 19:27).

5). Only a regenerated man can delight in the Law of God after the inward man (Rom 7:22).

6). By righteousness we establish the Law (Rom 3:31), that all the world might become guilty before God (Rom 1:18, cp. 3:19).

7). Without God's Law, there is no sin (Rom 5:13).

8). If the Law were repealed, what is the need to argue, as Paul does, that "by deeds of the law there shall no flesh be justified in his sight" (Rom 3:20)? It would have been sufficient to say that a repealed Law could neither justify nor condemn anyone. Instead, the Apostle shows that the Law requires a "patient continuance in well doing" and threatens "tribulation and anguish upon every soul of man that doeth evil" (Rom 2:5, 7).

9). The New Testament speaks in a uniform manner, teaching that those who have no saving interests in Christ's righteousness by faith are under the wrath of God and the curse of the Law, as though He had never died.

10). Christless sinners are really awakened by the Holy Spirit to see and feel what a dreadful state they are in: under the wrath of God and the curse of His Law (see Rom 7:9–11) because they have broken it! But this argument could not be made if the Law had been repealed.

11). God the Father, as the Governor of the world, gave the Law. God the Son magnified it (Isa 42:21) by expounding its purity, by obeying its precepts, and by enduring its penalty. God the Holy Spirit honors the Law by pressing upon the sinner its holy demands, and by using it as a schoolmaster to bring the soul to Christ (Gal 3:24). It is the special, secret, sovereign work of the Holy Spirit to impress the Law of God upon the hearts of those God draws to Himself (Heb 8:10), so that it becomes their very nature to love God with all their hearts, and so that they might serve Him in holiness and righteousness all the days of their lives without servile fear (Luke 1:74–75).

    d. True repentance presupposes an honest and broken-hearted acknowledgement of sin—our wicked failure to keep God's righteous Law.

(16) Unfortunately, it is this enforcing of the infinite glory of God, of His governmental supremacy, of His holy Law, of His righteous claims, of His demand for loving obedience, that is left out of much of the professing Church even today, due in large part to the excesses of "dispensational teaching."[4]

(17) There are three kinds of repentance spoken of in Scripture.

    a. The Repentance of *desperation* illustrated in the lives of Esau, Pharaoh, Ahithophel, and Judas.
    b. The Repentance of *reformation* such as was manifested by Ahab, and by the people of Nineveh under the preaching of Jonah.
    c. The Repentance of *salvation* (Acts 11:18; 2 Cor 7:10) based upon an evangelical conviction of sin.

        1). A legal conviction fears hell; evangelical repentance reveres God.
        2). A legal conviction dreads punishment, while evangelical repentance hates sin.
        3). Legal conviction informs the mind, while evangelical repentance melts the heart.
        4). Legal conviction excuses itself and claims the finished work of Christ as a basis to continue in sin, while evangelical repentance makes no excuses and has no reserves, but instead cries, "I have dishonored Thy name, grieved Thy Spirit, and abused Thy patience!"

---

[4] dispensational teaching – system of theology that divides the Word of God into arbitrary periods with supposed differences in the way God saves men from their sins. It proposes that the Old Testament saints were not a part of the Church of God, and that the Law has no bearing on the Christian as a guide to moral living.

(18) There is discernible fruit when repentance is genuine.

   a. There is a real hatred of sin as sin, not merely its consequences (Ezek 14:6; 20:43; Psa 119:104).
   b. There is a deep sorrow for sin (2 Cor 7:9–10; Matt 26:75; Lev 16:29; Joel 2:12–13; Gal 5:24).
   c. There is a confessing of sin (Pro 28:13; Psa 32:3–4).
   d. There is an actual turning away from sin, as an integral part of turning to God. It is not a separate "act or work," but part of saving faith.

* * *

Charles Spurgeon on Repentance

Repentance to be sure must be *entire*. Many will say, "Sir, I will renounce this sin and the other, but there are certain darling lusts which I must keep." O Sirs, in God's name let me entreat you: it is not the giving up of any one sin, nor fifty sins, that is true repentance; it is the *solemn renunciation of every sin*. If thou dost harbor one of these accursed vipers in thy heart, thy repentance is but a sham; if thou doest indulge in but one lust and dost give up every other, that one lust, like one leak in a ship, will sink thy soul. Think it not sufficient to give up thy outward vices; fancy it not enough to cut off the more corrupt sins of thy life—it is all or none which God demands. "Repent," says He, and He bids you repent. He means repent of all thy sins, otherwise He can never accept thy repentance as being real. He says, "Guild thee as thou wilt, O sinner, I abhor thee! Aye, make thyself gaudy, like the snake in its azure scales, I hate thee still, for I know thy venom, and I will flee from thee when thou comest to Me in thy most specious garb." All sin must be given up, or else you shall never have Christ; all transgression must be renounced, or else the gates of heaven must be barred against thee. Let us remember this, that repentance to be sincere, must be entire.

True repentance is a *turning of the heart*, as well as the life; it is the giving up of the whole soul to God to be His forever; it is a renunciation of the sins of the heart, as well as of the crimes of the life. Ah, dear hearers, let none of us fancy we have repented when we have only a false and fictitious repentance; let none of us take that to be the work of the Spirit which is only the work of poor human nature; let us not dream that we have savingly turned unto God, when perhaps we have only turned to ourselves; let us not think it is enough to have turned from vice to virtue. Let us remember it must be a turning of the whole soul to God, so as to be made anew in Christ Jesus; otherwise we have not met the requirements of the text.

Lastly upon this point, true repentance must be *perpetual*. It is not my turning to God during today that will be a proof that I am a true convert; it is forsaking my sins throughout the whole course of my life, until I sleep in the grave. You must not fancy that to be upright for a week will be a proof that you are saved; it is a perpetual abhorrence of evil. The change that God works is neither a transitory nor superficial one; not a cutting off the top of the weed, but an eradication of it; not the sweeping away of the dust of one day, but the taking away of that which is the cause of the dust.

You may today go home and pretend to pray; you may today be serious, tomorrow honest, and the next day you may pretend to be devout; but yet, if you return—as Scripture has it, like the dog to its vomit and like the sow to its wallowing in the mire (2 Pet. 2:22)—your repentance shall but sink you deeper into hell, instead of being a proof of divine grace in your heart.[5]

* * *

To learn by heart that which others say from the heart, to get the outline of a believer's own experience, this is a thing so simple that instead of wondering that there are hypocrites, I often marvel that there are not ten times more. And then again, the graces—the real graces within—are very easy to counterfeit. There is a repentance that needs to be repented of, and yet approaches near as possible to true repentance.

Does repentance make men hate sin? They who have a false repentance may detest some crimes. Does repentance make men resolve that they will not sin? So will this false repentance, for Balaam said: "If Balak would give me his house full of silver and gold, I cannot go beyond the word of the LORD my God" (Num 22:18). Does true repentance make men humble themselves? Yes, but so does false repentance, for Ahab humbled himself before God, and yet perished (1 Kgs 21:29). There is a line of distinction so fine that an eagle's eye hath not seen it; and only God Himself, and the soul that is enlightened by His Spirit, can tell whether our repentance be real or not.[6]

---

[5] From "Turn or Burn," Sermon 106, *New Park Street Pulpit*, vol. 2, page 417.
[6] From "Self-Delusion," Sermon 475, *Metropolitan Tabernacle Pulpit*, vol. 8, page 577.

CHAPTER 16

Killing in the Name of Christ: The Crusades
A.D. 1096–1291

Raising an Army of God

During His earthly ministry, Jesus promised that the kingdom of God would be firmly established (Matt 16:18). As the early Church moved East the promise of Jesus was fulfilled as the Church formulated the majestic foundational documents in the Creeds of the Ecumenical Councils. From the East the Church moved West to proclaim the good news of redeeming grace.

For more than a thousand years orthodox Christians were united in faith hope, and purpose. Though it was not without corruption and chaos, and was in need of cleaning and spiritual renewal, the visible Church was still essentially one.

That essential unity ended in 1054 when the Church divided into the Greek Eastern and the Latin Western Church. From that point on the dream for many was to see the Church reunited. Pope Gregory VII (Hildebrand) in particular longed to see the Church made whole. But it would not be easy, because many of its members were now under the rule of Mohammedanism (Islam).

Like Christianity, the faith of Islam arose in the East. With violent and bloody hands the Mohammedan Arabs drew their swords to hack their way through all opposition, to become the religious masters and political rulers of the East. They wrestled from the old Roman Eastern Empire the provinces of Syria, Palestine, Egypt, and North Africa. From Africa they moved through Spain and into the center of France. Only at Tours was the bloodthirsty appetite and quest for power of the Mohammedans stopped by Charles Martel "The Hammer." The year was 732.

As time moved forward and the centuries passed, the Arabs lost their political and military strength. They were supplanted by the Turks, who also followed the Islamic faith. By 1070 the Turks, had seized Palestine and Syria from the Arabs. They had invaded Asia Minor and were at the doorsteps of Constantinople. The remaining territory of the Eastern Empire and the Christian Church was threatened with being conquered. The Church in the East needed help—and found it in Gregory VII.

In 1073 Gregory VII (Hildebrand) became pope. Anxious to bind up the wounds that had separated the Church in 1054, Gregory also wanted to liberate his fellow Christians from the oppression of the Mohammedan Turks. The opportunity to do something came when the Emperor Alexius I, who ruled the Eastern Church, appealed to the pope in Rome for help. The promise was made that if help from the West came, an end would be put to the schism started by Patriarch Michael Cerularius.

Gregory was ready to provide assistance. He believed that a threefold objective could be reached all at once:

(1) the Eastern Church could be saved from the Muslims;
(2) the Eastern and Western Churches could be reunited;
(3) and, the universal rule of the papacy could be reestablished.

Gregory envisioned himself raising an army of Christian soldiers of God and, with himself leading the way, marching to free the captives in the Church for Christ. But the dream would never materialize, because Gregory soon found himself involved with the investiture conflict with Henry IV. All of his time and energies had to be spent dealing with domestic issues. Meanwhile, the fate of Christians in the East grew worse.

When the Mohammedans first conquered the Christian lands, they did not mind Christian pilgrims coming to their religious artifacts, because the travelers brought money. Tourism was a profitable business. But all this changed when the Seljuk Turks took the Holy Land away from the Arabs. The Seljuk Turks hated Christians because they were Christians. They did not want the money of the Christians, nor did they want the followers of Christ visiting any sacred places. Personal insults and injuries followed the Christian pilgrims. When reports of this reached the West, natural resentment set in. Hearts were inflamed to go to the East and retake the Holy Land for the Lord.

"God Wills It!"

Leading the way for military conquest was Pope Urban II (Pope, 1088–1099). In the fall of 1095 in Clermont, this tall, handsome, impressive man of oratorical skills assembled before him a large audience of eager warriors from France, the Netherlands, and Italy. He spoke of the life of Christ, reconstructing the Lord's birth, public ministry, arrest, crucifixion, death, and burial. Urban II recreated the travels of the Lord, making every place sacred that the Savior visited. This land, he said, must be reclaimed for Christ. All who were willing to fight would be rewarded. For one thing, their time in *purgatory* would be reduced.

Purgatory is an imaginary place of suffering, where Roman Catholics believe that all souls must first go for purification prior to entrance into heaven. This doctrine teaches that all men go to a "hell" of some sort, after which they will move on to heaven. Heaven can then be entered because the right has been earned through pain and suffering. The soul is purified. Instead of heaven being a provision of God based upon the free grace of the Gospel (the finished work of Christ on the cross, whereby we are washed clean by His blood, and which is embraced by faith in Christ), men have a part in their own salvation. Purgatory is therefore contrary to the teachings of the Bible (cp. Phi 1:21–23; Joh 14:1–4; Luk 23:39–43).

For those who might die in battle, Urban promised eternal life in heaven immediately. The vast assembly who heard Urban speak went wild with excitement. With one voice the multitude cried out, "God wills it! God wills it!"

Pleased with this response, Urban had red cloth cut up into strips which were sewn together in the forms of crosses. A cross was attached to the sleeve of every one who agreed to belong to the holy "cross" or "crusade." In this manner military expeditions were formed by the Christians of Western Europe, for the purpose of taking back by force from the Mohammedans the Holy Land and its sacred places. The vain pursuits of religious conquests for Christ were about to begin.

The First Crusade began in 1096 and met with great success. The Holy City was retaken in 1099, and The Kingdom of Jerusalem was established. Though the Kingdom was to last for eighty-eight years until 1187, it was by no means strong or spiritual.

More Military Adventures

Subsequent military adventures to Palestine were sent forth to strengthen the weak and vacillating Kingdom of Jerusalem. In the Second Crusade (1147), the king of

France and the emperor of the Holy Roman Empire led the armies, but the expedition was unsuccessful. The City of Peace was left in greater danger than ever. This is why Jerusalem was recaptured in 1187, by Saladin, Sultan of Egypt and Syria.

This led to the Third Crusade (1189–1192), known as the Crusade of the Three Kings. It was founded by Richard I (the Lion Hearted) of England, Philip of France, and the Emperor Frederick Barbarossa. The effort was a disaster. Barbarossa drowned while crossing a river in Cilicia; and Philip returned to France, leaving Richard I alone. After much fighting, all Richard could achieve was to gain a treaty with Saladin that allowed Christians to visit the Holy Sepulcher.

The Fourth Crusade began in 1201, under the leadership of Pope Innocent III (Pope, 1198–1216). He urged the capture of Egypt in order to use it as a base of operations against Palestine. When the army was finally assembled on the beaches, the discovery was made that it was without the shipping that Venice had agreed to supply. So another decision was made. The Crusaders would capture Constantinople to pay for provisions and transportation. A battle was fought and won. One Church-related result of this victory was that Pope Innocent III suddenly had control of both the Eastern Orthodox Church and the Eastern Empire. Not until 1261 would the Eastern Empire regain her independence from Rome.

As pope, Innocent III proved to be a powerful personality, as illustrated in his ability to humble royalty. Innocent humiliated Philip Augustus of France for example, by forcing him to take back the wife he had divorced, after she had appealed to the papacy for help. Shortly after this, in 1208, Innocent humbled King John of England, in a clash of wills over the appointment of a new arch-bishop of Canterbury. To have his way, Innocent used the interdict, which meant placing the whole country outside the grace of the Church. No church service could be officially held. The next year King John was excommunicated. His subjects were no longer required to obey him and he was deprived of his throne. The pope also invited Philip of France to invade England if John refused to humble himself. In 1213 John submitted to the pope, and England became a self-acknowledged slave of the papacy.

During this same period, Innocent interfered in the affairs of Germany by dictating the imperial succession there. Finally, Innocent convened the Fourth Lateran Council in 1215 to deal with practical concerns, one of which was making confession mandatory once a year for all laymen. The Council also considered the doctrinal issue of transubstantiation. This doctrine teaches the belief that the communion bread and wine become the actual body and blood of Christ.

Accordingly, the Roman Church teaches that the priests are able to perform an actual sacrifice of Christ every time the mass is said.

The Children's Crusade

Of all the major crusades, the most tragic was the attempt of the Children's Crusade. In 1212 a German youth named Nicholas proclaimed that God had ordained him to lead a crusade of children to the Holy Land. The idea captured the imagination of the children. Thirty thousand young people (including some girls dressed as boys), averaging twelve years of age, slipped away from their parents to follow Nicholas. As they marched from Cologne, down the Rhine and over the Alps, they sang:

> *Fair are the meadows,*
>   *Fairer still the woodlands,*
> *Robed in the pleasant garb of spring;*
>   *Jesus is fairer, Jesus is purer,*
> *He makes the grieving heart to sing.*

Many died of hunger. Some stragglers were devoured by wolves. Thieves mingled with the marchers and stole money, food, and clothing. The survivors reached Genoa in Italy only to discover that no ships would carry them to Palestine. Pope Innocent III told the children as kindly as possible to go home. Some did, but many stayed.

In France, in the same year of 1212, a twelve year old shepherd named Stephen came to Philip Augustus, and announced that Christ had appeared to him while tending his flock, and commanded him to lead a children's crusade to Palestine. The king ordered him to return home. Still, twenty thousand young people gathered to follow Stephen, wherever he would lead them. He chose to lead them across France to Marseille where, Stephen promised, the ocean would divide in a miraculous manner and they would walk to Palestine on dry ground. The ocean did not open like the Red Sea, but two ship owners did offer to take as many young people as possible to Palestine without charge. The children crowded into seven ships and sailed forth singing hymns of triumph. On the way two of the ships were wrecked off Sardina, with the death of all on board. The other children were brought to Tunisia or Egypt, where they were sold as slaves. The ship owners were hanged by the order of Frederick II.

The Results of the Crusades

The Crusades never accomplished the original purposes for which they were designed, despite two hundred years of conflict. However, the Crusades did change the world. A few results may be noted:

(1) the rise of towns;
(2) the destruction of feudalism;
(3) the decay of serfdom, and the rise of the middle class between lord and serf;
(4) the development of national monarchies;
(5) the rise of romantic literature;
(6) greater interest in international trade and commerce;
(7) increase of heretical teaching;
(8) increase of banking and shipping industry;
(9) increased hostility between Christianity and Islam;
(10) increased power of the papacy;
(11) increase in population and wealth of Palestine;
(12) protection of sacred places;
(13) a blockage of the Moslem aggressions on Europe;
(14) a better acquaintance of nations with one another;
(15) an increase of wealth for the Church, which bought lands or loaned money on them as security to the knights who went forth to fight in the name of Christ; and,
(16) the slaughter of thousands upon thousands, including Turkish women, children, and infants.

By the middle of the 1200s, the Crusades were over. The Turks would remain in ultimate control of Palestine until 1917, when Jerusalem was turned over to the British General Allenby on December 8, during World War I. While the Crusades may initially have been based upon good motives, no one seemed to be asking if such adventures were the will of God.

The Major Crusades

First Crusade (1095)	Fourth Crusade (1202–04)	Sixth Crusade (1228–29)
Second Crusade (1147–49)	Children's Crusade (1212)	Seventh Crusade (1248–54)
Third Crusade (1189–92)	Fifth Crusade (1217–21)	

CHAPTER 17

The Height of Earthly Power
A.D. 1198–1216

The Zenith of Earthly Glory

The Church of Jesus Christ rose to the height of earthly prestige and power under Innocent III. His papal administration lasted from 1198 to 1216. Well educated, Innocent had studied languages in Paris and law in Bologna. He was an eloquent speaker and singer. At the young age of twenty-nine he was made a cardinal, and at age thirty-seven was elected to the papacy. Innocent had exalted ideas about the office he held. Five factors guided his beliefs and behavior.

The Example of Pope Gregory VII. Even though Gregory's attempt to establish the power of the Church over the State ended in failure, his example was established for others to follow.

The "Donation of Constantine." This is a forged Roman imperial decree, purportedly from Emperor Constantine in the fourth century that transferred wealth and power over much of the Roman Empire to the bishop of Rome. The authenticity of this document was accepted for several centuries and was even used in the thirteenth century to furnish Innocent with a strong legal basis for claiming great papal power. However, the document was exposed in the fourteenth century by Lorenzo Valla as a forgery dating back only to the eighth-century, hundreds of years after the life of Constantine. However, by the time the truth emerged, Rome had already secured for herself an irrevocable place of power and influence.

The Crusades. These military adventures were inspired by the popes, who encouraged the kings and emperors to lead the soldiers into combat while obeying the pope. In this manner the pope gave the appearance of being the head of all Christendom.

The Principle of "Ratione Peccati." This Latin term means "by reason of sin." The popes tended to accept the political authority of the rulers, but they maintained that they, the popes, were supreme in the areas of religion and morality. However, since every political action has a moral side, the principle of *ratione peccati* gave the pope ultimate authority also in political matters. In this way the popes became dictators over kings and emperors.

Political Acumen. Being politically astute, Innocent knew how to assert his authority. In individual confrontations with rulers, he knew how to win. For example, when the emperor Frederick Barbarossa challenged the pope's authority in 1177, it was Frederick who finally knelt before the pope under the porch of the Cathedral of St. Mark in Venice. Spreading his cloak upon the pavement, Frederick knelt upon it and kissed the pope's foot. When Frederick arose, the pope gave him the kiss of peace. But it was not Frederick alone who became a vassal of the Church. One after another of the emperors and all the kings, lords, and princes of Europe acknowledged the pope as spiritual lord.

In addition to his political acumen, Innocent flexed his political power by reclaiming the patrimony of St. Peter, as the Papal States were called. This territory, located in the middle of the Italian peninsula, had been gradually diminished as succeeding popes made sacrifices of the land to the Holy Roman Emperor in exchange for protection. Now back under papal control, the boundaries would remain for the next six hundred years as Pope Innocent III had forged.

Beyond political acumen and the exercise of papal power, Innocent III attempted to bring about spiritual reform. In 1215 he held the fourth Lateran Council in Rome. The purpose of the council was to reform the church and recover the Holy Land.

Over fifteen hundred persons attended this Lateran Council, including the highest ranking clergy in Christendom. The patriarchs of Constantinople and Jerusalem were present, as were emissaries from Emperor Frederick, the kings of France, England, Aragon, Hungary, Jerusalem, and Cyprus. Representatives of the Italian cities came. A number of decisions were made.

(1) A new Crusade should be conducted. Pope Innocent III offered to lead this one in person.

(2) The teachings of the Waldensian and the Albigensian movements were condemned.

(3) Punishment of all unrepentant heretics was prescribed.

(4) The granting of indulgences should be restricted.

(5) Bishops were instructed to appoint competent men to preach the Gospel, and to provide free education for scholars too poor to pay.

(6) It was ordered that Jews and Saracens [nomadic people of the deserts between Syria and Arabia] should wear distinctive clothing.

(7) No Jews were to be allowed to hold public office that would give them any authority over Christians.

The year following the council Innocent III died.

Wealth and Wickedness

The continual need for reform in the Church was universally recognized. The Church had amassed enormous territory, power, and wealth. Illustrating the need for reform is a story associated with Innocent II and Thomas Aquinas. Entering the presence of Innocent II, before whom a large sum of money was spread out, the Pope observed, "You see, the Church is no longer in that age in which she said, 'Silver and gold have I none.'" "True, holy father," replied Aquinas; "neither can she any longer say to the lame, 'Rise up and walk'" (cf. Acts 3:2–8). For many people the Church was nothing but an easy and enjoyable way to live.

Not all who were identified with the Church abused the system. There were many devout individuals such as Bernard of Clairvaus (1090–1153) who wrote lovely hymns that are still sung today. "O Sacred Head, Now Wounded" was written by this devout monk. His motto has been embraced by countless Christians: "To know Jesus and Jesus Crucified." Bernard challenged popes and political princes about the depth of their Christian lives and challenged all of Christendom to seek mystical devotion. Said Bernard, "Spiritual life is like living water that springs up from the very depths of our own spiritual experience. In spiritual life everyone has to drink from his or her own well."

As monks and nuns took the efforts of spiritual renewal seriously they attracted others. Peter the Venerable, abbot of Cluny, said, "The innumerable multitude of monks covers almost all the lands. It fills the cities, castles, and fortified places. What a variety of garbs and customs in this army of the Lord which has taken an oath to live according to the rule, in the name of faith and charity!"

In Palestine three military monastic orders were established to care for the sick and to protect Christian pilgrims on their journeys to the sacred shrines. There were the Templars, the Hospitalers, and the Teutonic Knights. The Teutonic Knights had their headquarters in Acre until it fell in 1291. By 1226 they were found in Hungary and Prussia where they battled the Slavs and Tartars as they brought Christ to the Baltic lands. The order was dissolved when the Grand Master, Albert of Brandenburg became a Protestant during the Reformation.

The Mendicant Orders

Another important order of this time was the Dominican order. Dominic was a monk who had been born and schooled in Spain. His special burden seemed to be a desire to preach the gospel in order to bring back into the Church those who had withdrawn and were teaching other doctrines. At the Lateran Council of 1215 he received formal recognition for his order from Pope Innocent III. The Dominicans adopted the name of "Preaching Friars." The name speaks of their ideals. They were to preach as friars, a name derived from the word frater, or brother. However, these men were not monks. They were not to live in a cloister but in the midst of society.

In just four years time, this movement saw the establishment of sixty convents in eight provinces. The Dominicans adopted the vow of poverty for they were a mendicant order which means they begged for their needs.

Another important order of this time period was established by Francis of Assisi who was born in Italy in 1182. The son of a rich merchant, Francis abandoned himself to a life of licentiousness in his youth. At the age of twenty he became violently ill and was gloriously converted. Recovering his health, Francis devoted himself to a life of poverty and charity. Following his example, others joined him.

At the Lateran Council of 1215, Francis and his followers appealed to the pope for formal recognition of their order. The request was granted and the Minorites or Friars Minor (lesser) began their work. Francis insisted upon absolute poverty. If he saw anyone poorer than himself, he would try to give what he could. The brethren were to labor with their hands, but were not allowed to receive any wages for what they did. They were to "take no thought for the morrow" (Matt 6:34).

A man with a tender heart, Francis loved all of creation and was even known to preach to the birds. With his eloquence in preaching he persuaded many people to follow Christ. One result of the mendicant orders is that people were attracted to the Church because of the simplicity and sincerity of its followers who did good and not evil to men. Loving actions and attitudes conquered hearts. In the midst of good deeds, the mental life of the Church was also being stimulated. Many universities sprang up in Italy, Germany, France, and England. There were great teachers who emerged.

Teachers of the Church

In the midst of good deeds, the mental life of the Church was also being stimulated. Many universities sprang up in Italy, Germany, France, and England. From these, many great teachers emerged.

Anselm (1033–1109)

Born in Aosta, Italy, of a noble family, Anselm was educated at the abbey of St. Leger. His father wanted him to train to have a career in politics, but Anselm wanted to become a monk. In 1057 he left home and wandered in Burgundy, France, and Normandy before taking up residence in a Benedictine monastery at Bec, Normandy. There he took the monastic vows and began to teach. Later he became Abbot of Bec (1078–1093), and after that, the Archbishop of Canterbury.

As a teacher Anselm showed wisdom and compassion. Once, when a visiting abbot complained that he could not get the students to learn no matter how much he beat them, Anselm replied gently, "Have you tried not beating them?" A man of spiritual sensitivity, Anselm prayed, "Grant that I may taste by love what I apprehend by knowledge, that I may feel in my heart what I touch through the Spirit."

As a scholar, Anselm returned to the works of Augustine. As a theologian he wanted to prove and demonstrate the existence and attributes of God by an appeal to reason alone. With this objective in view, Anselm set forth the *Ontological Argument*, which contends that the existence of the idea of God necessarily implies the objective existence of God. However, Anselm always insisted that faith must precede reason: "I do not seek to understand in order that I may believe, but I believe in order to understand."

Anselm is also credited with the *Satisfaction Theory* of the atonement, which views God as the offended party and man as the offender. Only the One who is the God-man can provide satisfaction to the infinite God, which justice demands because of the penalty of sin. Anselm rejected the *Ransom Theory* of the atonement, whereby a lawsuit was settled between God and the devil. Because of his appeal to reason based upon faith rather than the traditions of men, Anselm is described as the founder of Scholasticism.

Peter Abelard (1079–1142)

Peter Abelard became a medieval French philosopher, teacher, and theologian. Born in Brittany, Abelard studied with some of the great teachers of his day, and then taught at Melun, Corbeil, and later at Paris. While in Paris, Abelard lived at the house of Fulbert, who was the canon[1] at Notre Dame. While living with Fulbert, Abelard fell deeply in love with his niece, Heloise. A son was born to her, although the couple was not married. Abelard offered to marry Heloise, but Fulbert was furious. He ordered Abelard castrated. Heloise entered into a convent, believing it was better to do this than to hamper Abelard's career in the Church. Abelard himself retired to the monastery of St. Denis. Despite these decisions, the couple continued to carry on a lifelong correspondence.

In 1121 Abelard was condemned by the Council of Soissons for heresy, and was forced to flee into exile. He found asylum in the distant monastery of St. Gildas in Brittany, where he stayed for ten years. He was abbot there until forced to leave by the monks. Returning to Paris, Abelard became popular with the students, but again faced new charges of heresy regarding the Trinity, from Norbert of Premontre and Bernard of Clairvaux. Again Abelard was condemned by the Church, this time at the Council of Sens in 1141.

Despite his philosophical speculations, Abelard is on record as saying "I do not wish to be a philosopher if it means resisting St. Paul; I do not wish to be Aristotle if it must separate me from Christ." Aristotle (Greek philosopher, 384–322 B.C.) was the master of a world-centered philosophy and of the rational scientific method, which dispensed with "God" and faith that was transcendental (i.e., abstract and altogether above this world). While Abelard did not dispense with God, he did give his life to his motto: "I understand so that I might believe [in God]." He gave his life to rationalism. It is to be noted that this motto is the reverse of that embraced by Augustine of Hippo and Anselm of Canterbury.

---

[1] canon – in this context: a clergyman who is on staff of a cathedral or collegiate church.

Peter the Lombard (c. 1095–c. 1164)

Peter the Lombard was an Italian theologian, bishop, and disciple of Abelard. Born at Novara, which was then in Lombardy, Peter studied at Bologna and afterwards in France. He taught at the cathedral school of Notre Dame in Paris, where he became an important figure in scholasticism and spokesperson for the Church. Peter may have been the first to contend that there are seven sacraments: baptism, confirmation, communion, anointing, matrimony, ordination, penance. This number was finally accepted by the Council of Florence in 1439. According to Peter, a sacrament is not only a symbol of divine grace, but a means of actually conveying divine grace.

A prolific writer, Peter produced commentaries on the Psalms, Job, and the Pauline Epistles. His most famous manuscript was *Libri Quatuar Sententiarum* (*"Four Books of Sentences"*), written between 1147 and 1150. This work is a summary of Catholic doctrine. Though he was once accused of heresy by his arch-enemy, Walter St. Victor, Peter was declared to be a faithful Christian by the Fourth Lateran Council, in 1215. When the Protestant Reformers came, they did not find the writings of Peter Lombard to be altogether disagreeable to their cause, because he had raised a number of important doctrinal questions in his book *Yes and No*.

Albertus Magnus (1193–1280)

Albertus Magnus was born in Bavaria. In 1223, as an adult, he entered the newly established Dominican Order in Padua, Italy. Albertus taught in several Dominican schools in Germany (1228–1245), in Paris (1245–1248), and then at Cologne (1248–1255), where he had Thomas Aquinas as a student. A profound scholar, Albertus mastered the thoughts of Aristotle while reading widely the works of Jewish thinkers, such as Gabirol and Maimonides. He also read the Arab philosophers: Averroes, Avicenna, and Algazel. In his reading and extensive writings (twenty-one volumes in all), Albertus was careful to acknowledge that many things could only be determined with certainty by revelation, because of the limitations of rational thought. Like other scholastic theologians, Albertus believed that human knowledge could be used to discover the divine mysteries of God.

Thomas Aquinas (1225–1274)

This distinguished medieval theologian and philosopher has had a tremendous impact upon the Church to the present hour. Born in the town of Aquino, Italy, about eighty miles southeast of Rome, Aquinas was a large man, which caused him to be mocked by his fellow students as a "dumb ox." However, he was not dumb but brilliant. Educated at the Universities of Naples, Paris, and Cologne, he entered the Dominican order of preachers.

Thomas is most criticized by Protestants for his attempt to synthesize Aristotelian philosophy and biblical theology, which led to a compromise of the doctrines of the sovereignty of God and the total depravity of man. In his defense, Thomas insisted that while theology is the "queen of science," philosophy is its servant and can establish what theology assumes: the existence of God and the immortality of the soul. Still, Protestants feared that Thomas leaned too much toward the autonomy of natural reason, which would disregard or diminish divine revelation.

Despite these things, Thomas Aquinas has contributed to the theological discussion by arguing for a natural theology and a natural law ethic. With respect to ethics, Aquinas made a distinction between eternal law, divine law, natural law, and human law. With respect to the existence of God, he formulated five ways of proving the existence of God, although he rejected the ontological argument formulated by Anselm of Canterbury. Nor did Thomas regard the existence of God as being self-evident to human beings, since they initially do not know enough about God to know that His existence is necessary.

In summary, Thomas argued from universal truths about nature to the cause of nature and its creator, God. His thinking today is still studied; it is both prevalent and profound.

John Duns Scotus (1266–1308)

John Duns Scotus was a medieval scholastic theologian. Because of his Scottish birth, he acquired the Latin nickname Scotus ("the Scot"). Scotus was educated to be a priest. He became a member of the Franciscan Order. Though he spent most of his career as a teacher at Oxford, Scotus taught also at Paris and Cologne.

Though in many areas Scotus agreed with Thomas Aquinas, he introduced distinct changes into the philosophy and theology that Thomas had set forth. Upon evaluating the five proofs by Thomas, Scotus argued that many assertions in theology are not philosophically demonstrable or even probable. He believed that God does not act out of logical necessity nor out of the inner necessity of His own nature. Since God does not act of necessity; God acts as He freely chooses.

In another area, in contrast to the rationalism of Thomas, Scotus suggested a "voluntarist" view of life, arguing that a choice by the will determines what a person does. Reason is merely an instrument to that end. Such an emphasis helped to drive a dramatic division between faith and reason, which eventually led to the decline of scholasticism itself.

Another contribution of Scotus was to teach the uniqueness of individuals. Aquinas had taught that a human being consists of a body and soul, with the soul comprising the essence of human nature. Scotus insisted on a third component, personal individualism. He believed that God purposely created individuals, not merely a universal human nature, which lineage and circumstances have made particular. Each person possesses an eternal individuality that has been granted both freedom and value.

Scotus also believed that Christ's incarnation would have occurred even if the Fall had not, a position with which Aquinas would not have agreed. Even more disturbing is the fact that Scotus was the first major Catholic theologian to argue for the Immaculate Conception of the Virgin Mary. This doctrine teaches that the mother of Christ was conceived in holiness without the pollution of original sin, even though she was born of two human parents. Thomas Aquinas, who died in 1274, had earlier rejected this whole notion. In December, 1854, Pope Pius IX (a Franciscan) declared that the doctrine of the Immaculate Conception was to be regarded as a divinely revealed fact and an official Catholic dogma.

Summary

Together, these men and others called Schoolmen, imparted the knowledge known as scholasticism. The emphasis on learning influenced other areas such as architecture and art. It was the medieval individuals who built the ornate cathedrals such as those in Milan, Italy; Rheims, France; and Cologne, Germany, perhaps the most elaborate and beautiful cathedral ever erected.

CHAPTER 18

The Passing of Power
A.D. 1294–1417

The Trouble with Taxes

Beginning with the reign of Boniface VIII (Pope, 1294–1303), a definite decline took place in the temporal power of the Church. One of the great conflicts that brought about the decline came over the matter of taxation. Philip the Fair, king of France, was determined to tax the clergy in his country. In a famous letter, *Clericos laicos*, the pope instructed the clergy not to pay their taxes. Philip responded by not allowing any French funds to be sent to Rome. In this way he would be able to keep the currency within the country at his discretion, and would cut off the pope receiving financial resources for the Church.

Boniface VIII responded to this act in 1302 by issuing a papal bull, which is an official pronouncement or declaration. The bull is so named because such a papal document is affixed a round leaden seal, called in Latin a *bulla*. In the bull *Unam Sanctam* (One holy), Boniface set forth his argument for ultimate authority in the matter in question, and what he proposed to do to King Philip and also to France. The result of this attempted ecclesiastical assertion of power proved disastrous. Both monarchs rejected the claims of Boniface and became hostile to Boniface.

Many years earlier, when Pope Gregory VII had placed the Emperor Henry IV under the ban, it had the desired effect of subduing the king. The same result would not happen with King Philip of France. The times had changed. Feudalism had fallen into decline, replaced with the rise of nationalism. The papal bull was perceived to be an attack not only on King Philip, but upon France herself. Boniface had failed to understand and appreciate this.

Knowing that he had popular support for resisting the ban, Philip decided to send two representatives with a band of soldiers to Anagni in Italy to arrest the pope. This was a mistake on Philip's part, for the soldiers did not use wisdom. They treated the Pontiff roughly, which caused the citizens of Anagni to come to the defense of the eighty-seven year old pope. Though Boniface was not arrested, he was badly shaken and his spirit was broken. A few days after he returned to Rome he died.

Still, Philip had won the victory for the States-General of France, composed of nobles, clergy, and the commoners. These all united to officially declare that in civil matters the pope had no authority, and that the king had no superior but God. The Church was learning afresh that it has no more power than what people are willing to give it.

Factors Contributing to Decline

To further humiliate the papacy, Philip was able to have the seat of power moved from Rome to Avignon in Provence, immediately adjacent to France. The year was 1309. For about seventy years the popes would rule from Avignon as the virtual prisoner of the French king. This period would become known as "the Babylonian Captivity" (1305–1377), because it lasted about the same length of time as the captivity of the Israelites in Babylon in Old Testament times (c. 586–516 B.C.). In addition to the political impotence caused by the Babylonian Captivity, at least seven other factors contributed to the decline of the power of the Church.

Intolerance. Feeling threatened with the rise of nationalism, the Church tried to keep its members subservient by the rigid enforcement of doctrine and practice. Heresy was to be rooted out and the faithful were to be encouraged to remain true to the Church. To accomplish these goals, the *Inquisition* was established under the guidance of the Dominican Order, which was known for having men of great learning. The harsh methods that were eventually used created tremendous opposition and dissent. The Church brought shame upon herself.

Greed. While they were living in Avignon, many of the popes maintained a very luxurious lifestyle, which cost a great deal of money. To obtain the money the popes openly resorted to simony and the selling of *indulgences*, which are documents that represent papal forgiveness of sin even prior to the sins being committed. Many people began to say that the pope was the Anti-Christ and the son of Satan.

Bureaucracy. The increasing cost of maintaining the hierarchy of the Church and the oppressive means of securing money for it also brought shame, loss of respect, and loss of power to the Church.

Immorality. There was an ever-increasing moral laxity among the clergy, especially during the fifteenth century. The lifestyle of monks and nuns and popes was an open scandal to the Savior.

Secularization. When morality declines in the Church, so does spirituality, which allows the Church to become more secularized. The world offered an alternative way of thinking and living to the Church: the *Renaissance.* Captured by the concepts of the Renaissance was Nicholas V (Pope, 1447–1455), who was a great lover of classical literature. He founded the Vatican Library.

The Renaissance was not just a rebirth of knowledge as the name implies, but a revitalization of the classical spirit with its rationalistic outlook on life. Ethics were once more viewed as being relative. Morality did not follow an unchangeable revealed standard. What was wrong in one culture or for one person might be just fine in another time and place. Also, the Renaissance saw the rise of the middle class with new wealth—which it chose to spend not on the Church, but upon itself and on art, literature, education, pleasure, and travel.

The Crusades. The military expeditions into foreign lands caused the eyes of many serfs in Europe to be opened. No longer could they be held in bondage through religious superstitions of the time. There were new ideas to embrace, and new ways of living and thinking. The East had met the West and changed it, by weakening the ties of many to the Church.

Church Division. Perhaps the thing that hurt the papacy more than anything else, including the Babylonian Captivity, was the *Papal Schism,* which was to last from 1378 to 1417.

The Papal Schism (1378–1417)

The Great Schism resulted when the French and Italian cardinals could not agree on ending the Babylonian Captivity. Because there was a division in the College of Cardinals, two popes were elected, one at Rome and one at Avignon. When the Council of Pisa tried to resolve the controversy in 1409, the result was the election of a third pope! Each one of these men anathematized and excommunicated one another, so that the Church as a whole was confused and disgusted.

Reform parties grew rapidly in the midst of this chaos. Leading the way in the quest for spiritual renewal were men such as John Huss (1369–1415) and John Wycliffe (1320–1384). Huss was a professor of philosophy at the University of Prague, who preached with great success in Bohemia as he called upon individuals to repent and believe. Wycliffe gathered around him a group of men, called Lollards, who helped change the Church in England and Scotland by preaching the doctrines of redeeming grace. The voice of the Reformers was beginning to be heard

At last, in 1417, the Council of Constance managed to elect an Italian cardinal pope, Martin V. The other three competing popes, weary with the social and political instability, gave Martin their support so that once more the Church in the West had one spiritual leader. The Great Schism was healed. But the wounds which were inflicted on the papacy were to prove to have far reaching repercussions.

CHAPTER 19

The Search for Sanctification
A.D. 1200–1517

The Return of Heresy

As people returned from the Crusades in the East to their lands in Western Europe, they brought much back with them, including some ancient heresies. One such doctrinal error was that of Manicheism. Although Augustine had effectively combated this teaching, driving it from the West, it had lingered on in the East. During the Crusades, the Manichean ideas filtered back into Western Europe through Bulgaria, along the newly established trade routes. In the town of Albi in southern France, the Manichean ideas flourished. Those who embraced them were called Albigenses or Cathari.

The Cathari were dualists in that they embraced the idea of a good god and a bad god. The visible world is the result of the evil god. In some manner the souls of men have been taken captive by this bad god, and are being held in bondage. They must be set free. This is done by emphasizing the spiritual over the material.

Rarely does heresy concentrate itself on only one point. Like an octopus with its many tentacles, heresy reaches out to touch other truths. Some of the Albigenses rejected the Old Testament, considering it to be the work of the evil god. Others accepted the Psalms and the prophets. All accepted the New Testament as the work of the good god. However, they did not believe its teachings in every part, especially concerning the body of Christ. Since all material things are evil, Christ could not have had a real body and He did not really die a real death. Thus the Cross held no respect or reverence for the Albigenses. In like manner, the sacraments were rejected because their elements are material. Church buildings were not allowed because they were built of material things. Feeling themselves superior to other professing Christians because of their spiritual knowledge, some of the Albigenses met resistance by the Church. The Fourth Lateran Council authorized the state to inflict punishment on religious dissenters and confiscate all the land and property of the Cathars. Resenting this rejection, they turned into a hostile group. To their credit the Cathars did believe that everyone should be able to read the Bible and made efforts to translate the Bible into the local language. Because of this, the Synod of Toulouse in 1229 condemned such translation and forbade lay people from owning a Bible.

The Followers of Peter Waldo

In contrast to the Albigenses were the followers of Peter Waldo. This wealthy merchant placed great emphasis on the Scripture. Taking the teachings of Christ regarding wealth literally, around 1176 Waldo sold all of his goods and gave his money to the poor. Then he translated portions of the Bible into the language of the people. Peter stressed preaching by laymen to include men and women. Sending out seventy disciples two by two, dressed in simple woolen garments and barefoot, Waldo encouraged the Gospel to be proclaimed in southern France, Italy, Spain, and the Rhine Valley. The Waldensians, as the disciples became known, fasted on Mondays, Wednesdays, and Fridays. They would not take an oath nor serve in the military. Peter taught that the Church was subject to error, and so rejected the doctrine of purgatory and the saying of prayers for the dead. The Church was not infallible, he argued. Though Peter Waldo had no intention of breaking with Rome, the pope excommunicated him and his followers.

Then Came the Inquisition

As the Church found itself powerless against the various movements it considered heretical, the decision was made by several councils to persecute the heretics. As a result of this decision, the Inquisition emerged, which was guided by the Dominican Friars. A person who was suspected or accused of heresy could be brought before this formal Church board. Once assembled, the trial followed established procedures.

Anyone discovered with heretical ideas would be instructed to recant (to deny the erroneous beliefs). If this happened, there was freedom to leave. If a person did not recant but held to a certain position, he was to be abandoned by the Church and turned over to the affairs of the civil government for the purpose of punishment. Officially, the Church did not shed blood. However, since the state was subject to the will of the Church at this time, the Church was not guiltless when punishment was administered. The most frequent form of chastisement was death by fire: the heretic was burned at the stake. Short of this, an alleged heretic could be tortured—until he confessed the error of his ways or died from the wounds inflicted.

Many Albigenses and Waldenses were murdered as a result of the methods and madness of the Inquisition. When the number of people being put to death in southern France grew too large for the Church to handle, the pope resorted to other methods such as calling the nobles to fight a "holy war" against their own countrymen. State persecution of dissenting professing Christians was authorized by Christians!

For twenty years blood flowed like water in southern France. The country was ravaged by civil war. The loveliest of France's provinces was turned into a scorched earth as the Albigenses were utterly destroyed, much to the delight of Pope Innocent III, who had encouraged their annihilation. The Waldenses found refuge in the high valleys of the Alps, where some of their descendants still live today. Of all the gatherings who broke away from the Roman Catholic Church during the Medieval Age, the Waldenses are the only group to have survived to the present time.

John Wycliffe, "The Morning Star of the Reformation"

Despite the torture inflicted upon individuals by the Inquisition, courageous souls still became champions in the search for personal and corporate sanctification. Two of the most important men that God ever raised up to criticize and cleanse the doctrine and government of the Roman Catholic Church were John Wycliffe and John Huss.

Wycliffe was born in England in 1320. After studying at the University of Oxford he later became a professor there. In 1378 he began to openly criticize the Church and the clergy. The Church was called into account for amassing tremendous wealth, while the clergy were chastised for their moral corruption. Wycliffe believed that the Church should return to poverty, simplicity, and holiness of life.

Moving into other areas, Wycliffe taught that the Bible should be the only rule of faith. It also should be placed into the hands of the common people. With this objective in mind, Wycliffe translated the Bible into the English language. Outraged at his teachings and his audacity to give the common people the Word of God, the

Church hunted Wycliffe—but could not hurt him because he was protected by the nobles. Wycliffe died in peace on December 31, 1384.

Those who followed the teachings of Wycliffe were called the Lollards (Dutch, "mumblers"). They too denounced the pope, opposed a corrupt clergy, practiced poverty, and acknowledged the Bible as the only standard of faith and practice. For these beliefs, the Lollards were branded as heretics. Many suffered as martyrs in the flames. Still, their movement lingered on until the time of the Reformation, for in other places other men were taking up the cause of Christ. One such man was named John Huss.

John Huss

In Bohemia, John Huss (b. 1369) was introduced to the teachings of Wycliffe and embraced them with a passion, despite the fact that he had been trained for the priesthood. Huss had become dean of the theological faculty at the University of Prague in the capitol of Bohemia, and later became the leader of the institution. Encouraged by the teachings of Wycliffe, John Huss began to preach with great boldness against the corruption of the clergy. He also taught many ideas which were later part of the main teachings of the Reformers during the Reformation, which were:

(1) God has predestined souls to salvation.
(2) There is a distinction between being *in* the Church and being *of* the Church.
(3) A person can be in the visible Church and yet not be a real member of the invisible true Church.
(4) Jesus Christ is the true leader of the universal Church and not the pope.
(5) The pope and cardinals are not necessary to the government of the Church.
(6) The selling of indulgences is an abomination to the Lord.

Because of these teachings, Pope John XXIII in Avignon excommunicated John Huss. Huss declared his excommunication to be null and void, and appealed from the pope to the Church Council. He wanted an ecclesiastical trial. In 1414 Huss thought that his chance to be heard in a fair trial would be realized when a general council assembled in Constance. The council had been called by the emperor Sigismund (1368–1437) for the purpose of putting an end to the Great Schism. Reforms were to be introduced and reformers would be heard.

Sigismund was emperor of the Holy Roman Empire from 1411–1437; king of Hungary, 1387–1437; and king of Bohemia, 1419–1437. Exercising his royal prerogative, Sigismund invited John Huss to attend the council under a safe conduct pass. Huss made the fatal mistake of trusting the sovereign, and accepted his invitation. A few weeks later, Huss found himself imprisoned by Pope John XXIII for heresy. After being left to suffer in prison for more than eight months, Huss was to be burned at the stake, despite an outpouring of public protest.

Without a chance to defend himself, Huss was brought from the dungeon to the cathedral in Constance, where on July 6, 1415, he was degraded before bishops and royalty. The Emperor Sigismund did not move to help him. The articles of clothing of Huss were removed piece by piece with an appropriate curse pronounced on each one. Then a paper cone picturing three hideous demons was placed upon his head. The cone bore the inscription, "The Heretic."

From the cathedral Huss was taken to a place before one of the gates of the city, where a high stake had been posted and surrounded with firewood. Huss was tied to the stake with cords which had been soaked in water, to make sure he was held securely when the flames rose up around him. A torch was put to the wood, and John Huss died for the sake of Jesus Christ. Then his followers were hunted down; Bohemia became engulfed in civil war. Despite these efforts of the Catholic Church to silence the voices of those calling for sanctification, the land of Huss would still know reform.

Wounded Healers

Between the years 1409 and 1449, three general Church councils were convened. The first was held in Pisa in 1409. The second was in Constance from 1414 to 1418. The third council was held in Basel and met from 1431 to 1449. The purpose for holding these councils was to heal the Great Schism, bring spiritual renewal to the Church, and suppress heresy and heretics.

The Council of Pisa did not have much success in meeting their stated objectives, but the Council of Constance did bring an end to the Great Schism by appointing Martin V to be the legitimate pope. It was this Council that condemned John Huss to death, while ordering the writings of John Wycliffe to be burned. In its foolish wisdom, the Council of Constance ordered that the body of Wycliffe should be exhumed and burned and his ashes poured into the River Swift. This was done.

When the Council of Basel met, one of its objectives was to return unity to the Church in Bohemia, where the bloody work of the Inquisition had failed to stop the followers of John Huss from carrying on his work. In 1436 an agreement with the Hussites was reached. There would be freedom of preaching, better attempts made to reform the clergy, and those Church members of Bohemia who so desired could partake of the bread and the wine in Holy Communion.

The Council of Basel was also able to make an agreement with representatives of the Eastern Church. In exchange for military assistance against the Islamic Turks, who were again threatening to destroy the Eastern Empire and Church, the Church in the East would accept the doctrines of the Western Church. Unfortunately for Rome, when reports of this agreement reached the East, there was violent opposition to such official acceptance. The representatives were denounced. Ten years later the Turks conquered Constantinople. All attempts to reunite the Eastern and Western churches would end.

The "Rebirth" of Learning

While the Church searched for sanctification and unity, the Renaissance surfaced to change the world. The word *renaissance* means "rebirth," and carries with it both a secular and religious meaning. It denotes an intellectual, aesthetic, and spiritual awakening. The Renaissance arrived in force—first in Italy with the power of a revolution. Its guiding principle was the need for a philosophy of secular humanism as opposed to a religious revival. This new emphasis was on the recognition of human and worldly values. These things were declared to have validity apart from theological considerations or ecclesiastical approval. Sin and grace were no longer the focal point of discussion. Rather, attention would be upon the natural man. It was argued that man, by his own powers, could expand the resources of knowledge and have very satisfying personal experiences. The Church was not needed. Formal religion could be relegated to the rubbish of history.

The Renaissance leaders appealed to the literature of classical antiquity to justify this conscious, but unashamed, new delight in life. They would teach people not to feel guilty nor to be apologetic for what was said or done. Man, not God and not the Church, would be the court of final appeal of what was right and what was wrong. From these philosophical tenets came several more distinctives of the Renaissance revolution.

(1) The ideal of liberty was exalted.

(2) There was a high degree of individualism, both in thought and in the conduct of one's private life.

(3) There was a more free exercise of criticism in regard to accepted ideas and existing institutions.

(4) There was the development of the spirit of experimentation and exploration.

(5) Creativity was stimulated.

(6) Sensuous beauty was loved for its own sake and the pleasures it produced.

(7) There was a more realistic attitude toward human and natural phenomena, so that the miraculous was constantly doubted. Scientific investigation was honored.

(8) The Christian moral code of conduct (which was considered oppressive and unattainable) would be modified or discarded for a new set of rules.

(9) The ideal of versatility was considered more admirable than specialization in one field of endeavor. Ideally, the Renaissance man was well rounded in his knowledge, culture, and tastes.

The effects of the Renaissance upon the Church were immediate.

(1) The Church lost prestige and control over the masses and especially over the intellectuals, even where its authority was not challenged.

(2) The Church hierarchy justified its own corruption. Bishops and cardinals adopted the pagan morality and sensuality of Renaissance philosophy, without adopting its intellectual processes. Apparently, free living was easier than free thinking!

(3) There developed new techniques of thought and criticism that, when used by wicked men, served to destroy the authority of the faith (which was once and for all delivered unto the saints). The Church should have been contending for the Bible, morality, miracles, and the divinity of Christ, instead of finding ways to explain faith away.

It is no wonder that the Reformers spent much of their time and efforts combating the influences of the Renaissance upon the people of God in particular, and upon society in general.

Savonarola

As the Church began to be affected by the Renaissance, a fiery monk named Savonarola stood up to oppose the intellectual and moral corruption he was witnessing. Girolamo Savonarola (1452–1498) became an itinerant preacher ministering in Florence, Italy. After the fulfillment of his prophetic utterance concerning the invasion of France by Charles VIII, he was able to lead a theocratic reform movement there. Initially, there was great change in outward morality. Encouraged by what he saw, Savonarola found freedom to speak out against the corruption of the Church and the authority of the pope. He preached salvation apart from the Church, but a reaction set in. Pope Alexander VI issued a formal condemnation of this Dominican monk. He was captured by a fanatical mob and condemned to be burned at the stake. He was hanged in 1498 and then his body was burned.

Educating Youth for Christ

Around 1350 there arose in the Netherlands and Germany another reform-minded movement characteristic of this time period. This movement was called "The Brethren of the Holy Life," or "The Brotherhood of the Common Life." It was founded by Gerard [Gregory] Groote (1340–1380). At thirty years of age, while still a distinguished professor of theology and philosophy in Cologne, Groote gave up honors and wealth to follow Christ. Though a gifted preacher, he was noted for his strong emphasis on the Christian education of youth. By establishing many Christian schools, Groote hoped to bring reform to the Church by means of education. His labors were not in vain, for among those who attended one of the schools of this movement in Magdeburg was Martin Luther.

Future Leaders

Other future luminaries were John of Wessel, Erasmus, and Thomas à Kempis.

Johann of Wessel (c. 1420–1489) was one of the leading thinkers of his day. He knew Greek and Hebrew and studied theology at Paris. From 1445 to 1456 he was a professor in the University of Erfurt in Germany. Forty-nine years later Martin Luther would receive his degree of Master of Arts from this same university. Wessel has been called "The Light of the World" because he denounced the doctrine of transubstantiation, attacked indulgences, taught the doctrine of justification by faith alone, and insisted that the elect are saved by grace alone. Declared Wessel, "Whom God wishes to save, He would save by giving him grace, even if all the priests should wish to damn and excommunicate him." Luther would later say of him, "If I had read the works of Wessel beforehand, it might well have seemed that I derived all my ideas from him."

The Catholic Church did not approve of Wessel's teaching, and, despite his old age, tried him for heresy before the archbishop of Mainz. Wessel recanted only to be cast into prison anyway, where he died in October, 1489.

Erasmus (1466–1536). One of Wessel's most famous students would fare better than Wessel despite his own criticisms of the Church. While Erasmus never did leave the Catholic structure, he was able and willing to use his great learning and agile pen to ridicule the ignorance of the monks and condemn the abuses of the Church which he saw. One of his most famous works is titled *In Praise of Folly.* Perhaps his most significant contribution to the Church was his publication of his 1516 Greek-Latin New Testament. Martin Luther used this book as the primary source text to translate the New Testament into German in 1522. William Tyndale used the work of Erasmus to translate the New Testament into English in 1526.

Thomas à Kempis. Another man of great influence who followed the spirit of the Brethren of the Common Life was Thomas à Kempis. Thomas lived in the Netherlands near the city of Zwolle. He is credited with writing *The Imitation of Christ,* one of the most famous books in the world. The spiritual counsel of this work is very simple: read the Bible and flee the vanities of this world. Such counsel was needed, for the world was about to change once more. Little did anyone realize it, but the western world was on the doorsteps of true reformation.

On the Doorsteps of the Reformation

For so many years, faithful Christians had pleaded and prayed for a divine outpouring of the Holy Spirit and a genuine reformation of the Church of Jesus Christ. Such a reformation would come.

(1) The Reformation would come in response to the prayers of the saints.

(2) The Reformation would come in honor of the blood that had been spilt by the martyrs.

(3) The Reformation would come because of the impetus for change integral to the Renaissance.

(4) The Reformation would come as an answer to the prayers of the early reformers.

(5) The Reformation would come because there was obvious corruption of the clergy.

(6) The Reformation would come because the power of the papacy was being diminished.

(7) The Reformation would come because of the rise of nationalism.

(8) But most of all, the Reformation would come because of a gracious and merciful God.

The Lord was about to shake up the world with the great and glorious doctrines of free grace. Millions would be swept into the kingdom of God, and the Christian community would be given some of the finest leaders and literature it would ever have!

SOLI DEO GLORIA,
To God Alone Be the Glory

Part Three

The Reformation and Its Aftermath

A.D. 1517—1648

CHAPTER 20

The Reformation Begins
A.D. 1517

The Reformation Era

Around noon time on October 31, 1517, Martin Luther (1483–1546) nailed his 95 theses to the old wooden door of the Castle Church at Wittenburg, Germany. There is a lovely story which says that Frederick, Elector of Saxony, had a dream on the previous night. He saw a monk writing on the Castle Church in letters large enough to be read by the Elector of Schweinitz more than twelve miles away, and with a pen that appeared to reach as far as Rome, where it unfastened the crown of the pope! Since this story cannot be traced back beyond 1591, it is probably a legend; but it satisfactorily pictures the early perception of many, that the simple act of a concerned monk would be used by God. It was the spark that ignited a series of events that ushered in a new age in world history, now known as The Reformation.

During this period, the power of Rome over the souls of individuals would be challenged. Individuals would rise to remove spiritual oppression and restore Christian liberty. Those who led the Reformation were people of faith and conviction. They had high intelligence and tremendous personal courage. Many died to preserve and protect the purity of the Gospel of grace.

The Reformation Era was an exciting and heroic epoch, as people followed their leaders despite all the dangers and sacrifices involved. And the Lord honored those who honored Him: the Reformation spread through Germany, Switzerland, France, the Netherlands, England, Scotland, Norway, and Sweden. God set His people free to worship Him "in spirit and in truth" (John 4:23).

The Day God Shook the World

There are specific dates in the history of the world that are of unique importance. The events that transpire on these dates are remembered often in the centuries that follow. October 31, 1517 is such a date. Martin Luther used that day to make his views about certain religious abuses known to the public. Luther felt this could best be done by holding a scholarly debate in the open. He decided to make a civic pronouncement of his theological position. The Lord honored that decision and used it to shake the world!

The seeds of change had already been sown by others. Politically, the power of the papacy was being challenged. In Portugal, Spain, France, and England, national states were seeking to rise. Emperors felt the restrictions of religion on their decisions, and they wanted more freedom from the Church. Elsewhere, the followers of Mohammed continued to move against the borders of the Holy Roman Empire. After conquering Constantinople and the Eastern Empire in 1453, Islamic armies marched across Eastern Europe until they arrived at the gates of Vienna in 1529. The world was rapidly changing, and religion was not exempted. When Constantinople was conquered by the Mohammedan Turks, the central power of the Eastern Orthodox Church was lost, and national churches soon emerged.

Other important things were happening. Christopher (literal meaning, "Christ-like") Columbus made his valiant voyage, which led to the discovery of the New World. This, in turn, allowed a Spanish empire in the West. Ferdinand Magellan circumnavigated the globe. Meanwhile, the Portuguese claimed territory in Brazil, Africa, and the Far East.

Also during this period, advances were being made in knowledge. The scientific legacy of the Middle Ages includes the Hindu numerals, the decimal system, the discovery of gunpowder, and the inventions of the eyeglass, the mariner's compass, and the pendulum clock. The invention of moveable type at Mayence on the Rhine in 1456 by Johann Gutenberg, ensured that learning would be widely encouraged and new ideas would be spread. It is significant that the first book printed by Gutenberg was 200 copies of Jerome's Vulgate Bible.[1] Later, printing presses would be used to bring the Scriptures to everyone through clear translations into common

---

[1] Vulgate Bible – late 4th-century Latin translation of the Bible. It was largely the work of Jerome, who was commissioned by Pope Damasus I in 382 to make a new revision of older Latin translations. By the 13th century this revision had come to be called the *versio vulgata*, that is, the "commonly used translation." It ultimately became the official Latin version of the Bible in the Roman Catholic Church.

languages that all could read. Once people were able to read the Bible for themselves, many would realize that the Catholic Church had become far removed from the ideals of the New Testament.

As the printing press made the Scriptures available to a wider audience, so it made people more aware of secular concepts. Humanism would come to enjoy a wide following as specific ideas were articulated. One belief that found popular appeal was the humanistic teaching that individuals could be made better by moral reformation, apart from religious instruction by the Church. It was also contended that the world itself could be improved by creative thinking on the part of man. To discover how, an appeal was made to the literature of the Classical Age of the Greeks. It seemed that the past would be the key to the future. However, in order to understand the past, the ancient languages of Greek and Hebrew had to be seriously studied once more. The irony is that this led secular scholars back to the Bible, because the old manuscripts had to be mastered.

To enhance this renewed interest in learning, universities arose to educate a larger number of people. The educational process helped to instill an objective spirit of inquiry into the mind. Individuals were encouraged to challenge established authority, and to think in critical terms. Some of those who were religiously inclined, began to think critically about the state of the Church. It did not take much of a discerning mind to realize that a great deal needed to be changed. There was sin in the sanctuary. The sins of the saints included *simony* (the selling of Church offices), ecclesiastical arrogance, immorality among members of the clergy, and the selling of salvation and sanctification through *indulgences*.

These and other abuses caused spiritual unrest to concerned souls, which only added to the disturbance of a society experiencing social and economic unrest. People desired more personal freedom, more money, and more opportunities to be individually creative. Multitudes were crowding into towns in a desperate attempt to flee the harsh life under feudalism. There were differing degrees of independence and serfdom among the peasantry of Europe, but for all, it was a very hard way of existence. Life on the land had a regular, monotonous, repetitive pattern. In autumn pigs were killed, and in the spring oxen were led out to plough. People wanted more.

Ecclesiastical Power over People

Though there was renewed emphasis on classical learning, though there was a movement towards humanistic thinking, though emperors wanted more political strength, and though people wanted more personal autonomy, the Church still held a powerful grip upon the hearts of its hearers. This was possible because of specific doctrinal teachings that caused individuals to have hope in the pope, and in his spiritual power. No matter how corrupt the clergy became, nor how many unusual non-biblical theological concepts were conceived, the Catholic Church was able to influence the thoughts of multitudes. Hearts still wanted to know the way to heaven.

A System of Sacraments

According to the Church in medieval times, entrance into heaven was based upon merit. In order to merit eternal life in the presence of God, there first had to be a cleansing by fire after death in a place called *purgatory*. In addition, there had to be evidence of having lived a worthy life. In order to help professing Christians live a worthy life of merit, which would reduce time spent in purgatory, the Church developed a system of *sacraments*.

The philosophical undergirding for sacraments is the recognition that man has a mind and a body. He is both physical and spiritual. In like manner, the world is experienced on two levels, the physical and the spiritual. It is obvious that God has ordained that man be touched and helped through material objects and visible means, in addition to faith. There is the fact of the *Incarnation*, in which God was manifested in the flesh in the person of Jesus Christ (John 1:1, 14).

Extending these biblical truths beyond the Bible, the Catholic Church began to teach about a number of other outward and visible signs. These signs, it said, were indicators of an inward and spiritual grace, given and ordained by Christ Himself, as a means by which individuals might receive heaven's blessings and be assured of eternal life. These signs of grace were called *sacraments*. In each sacrament there are certain elements that are constant, including the matter and the form. The grace or benefit of the sacrament is given objectively, but apprehended subjectively by "virtuous faith." Medieval tradition recognized seven sacraments.

BAPTISM. In the act of infant baptism, it is declared that original sin is removed, and the soul is incorporated into the Church. The error of baptismal regeneration was embraced by the Church (cp. 1 Pet 3:21)!

CONFIRMATION. The completion of baptism is confirmed by the laying on of hands. During this ceremony, it is believed that the Holy Spirit is conferred upon a person so that they are empowered to live out the ethics of the Christian life (cp. John 14:16–17; Acts 2:1–4).

PENANCE. Realizing that even Christians sin, the Church made provision for penance by confession of sins in the presence of a priest, who was able to declare God's forgiveness and absolve the soul of all transgressions. Outward acts were expected to be displayed by the penitent, manifesting contrition and faith (cp. 1 John 1:9; Mark 2:7).

HOLY EUCHARIST. In the taking of the Lord's Supper, the soul is strengthened and refreshed. Union with God is found by assimilation of Christ, who is believed to be literally present in the two elements: bread and fruit of the vine (cp. Matt 26:26–30; 1 Cor 11:23–30).

HOLY ORDERS. Select individuals are conferred with spiritual power and the privilege of ministry (cp. Rev 1:6; 1 Pet 2:9).

HOLY MATRIMONY. This outward ritual was designed to enhance a life-long monogamous union between a man and a woman. The benefits of marriage include grace to find help in life, companionship, enjoyment of the act of marriage, procreation, and the ability to maintain sexual honor (cp. Gen 2:24; Heb 13:4; Eph 5:25).

UNCTION. As the sick and dying were anointed with oil, a prayer for grace was offered (cp. Jas 5:14–15).

A Non-Salvation of Penance

Of particular importance was the sacrament of *penance*. Daily, people sinned, and daily they needed to know if they could be forgiven. The Church taught that the priest had the power to pardon sins, in the name of Christ, and to release any soul from the eternal punishment that is visited upon sin. However, those who received the sacrament of penance had to express contrition, after an honest confession to a priest. Then, there had to be satisfaction. The priest determined what satisfaction the erring penitent had to make, in order to display outwardly a heart of contrition. It was not uncommon for the priest to instruct the penitent to fast, recite a specific number of prayers, give alms to the poor, go on a pilgrimage, visit a shrine, or even take part in a religious crusade to the Holy Land. The focus of attention was upon *doing something* to merit the grace and goodness of God, rather than recognizing by faith what God had done and had given to us in Christ's completed sacrifice on the cross, apart from our own works (cp. Rom 5:1–2; Eph 2:8–9; Rom 8:28–29).

Indulgences

Although the system of penance was developed to assist concerned souls in finding comfort after sin, abuse and corruption emerged. The Kingdom of Christ found itself able to make money. Guilt-laden individuals were willing to pay for peace of mind and favor with God. The decision was made to allow a monetary gift to be given to the work of the Lord, through the Church. The impersonal contribution of money would replace outward forms of penitential acts of contrition. And so gold began to replace grace, and the congregation of the righteous became unrighteously greedy. In order to encourage more money to come into its coffers, the Church went so far as to provide the penitent an official document of *indulgence*, declaring that the power and pollution of sin was broken, and the soul was under no further obligation to perform acts of contrition as a penalty. The iniquity of selling indulgences had begun.

Supererogation

The theological justification for the granting of an indulgence was grounded in the concept of *works of supererogation*. Technically, such works went beyond the demands of God's law and earned a reward. It was believed that Jesus had lived a life of purity and holiness that went far beyond what was necessary to secure the salvation of sinners. Therefore, He must have stored up a rich treasury of merits in heaven that could be appropriated by others.

In like manner, the Church taught that the saints have stored up merits in heaven. Such a storehouse of spiritual treasure is needed because the Gospel comes to men demanding a certain measure of perfection (Matt 19:21). According to Catholic dogma, if the Rich Young Ruler (Matt 19:16–22) had honored the admonition of Christ, he would have performed the works of supererogation, and so would have merited great reward, leading to eternal life. [While the Rich Young Ruler failed in his spiritual obligations, others have not. There are saints who have sold their goods, given their wealth to the poor (or better yet, the Church), and by so doing have laid up treasure in heaven.] To continue the thought, a treasure necessitates a treasurer. As Christ's vicar on earth, the pope must be the one best qualified for this position. Based on this assumption, the Catholic Church began to teach that at his discretion, the pope could credit to a person's account whatsoever merits were needed to ensure salvation.

It is hard to believe that this speculative and scriptureless theology found a wide audience of acceptance, but it did. There was something about these concepts that appealed to Church leaders, and to their congregations. It appealed to the innate pride of self-effort present in all men. The common people were quick to perceive that it is much easier to buy an indulgence, than to endure the process of sanctification, involving the mortification[2] of fleshly desires. The people realized that it might be easier to pay money, in order to help a departed soul out of purgatory, than to pray a person into heaven.

As the common people liked the concept of indulgences, based upon superficial acts of repentance, so the Church leaders quickly grew to like the results of their religious thinking, because money began to pour into the coffers. But as the Church grew rich, its monetary appetite became insatiable. There is a wonderful legend associated with Thomas Aquinas (1225–1274). As the story goes, one day Thomas came upon Pope Gregory X counting coins after a worship service. "Look Thomas," cried the pope, "no longer can the Church say 'Silver and gold have I none.'" "And neither," replied Thomas, "can the Church say, 'Rise up and walk.'"

John Tetzel: A Master of Deceit

In the quest for more gold for the Church, official spokesmen were sent into the countries of Europe to raise money. One of the best of these "gospel hucksters" was a man named John Tetzel, an eloquent Dominican Friar. Legend has it that Tetzel would tell audiences, with a flair for the dramatic,

> "Whenever a coin in the coffer rings,
>   a soul from purgatory springs!"

John Tetzel did not realize that the day was soon coming when he would have to give an account for his actions. First Tetzel, and then the world, were about to hear of the holy displeasure Martin Luther possessed against all who were making merchandise of the Gospel.

A Man Named Martin

Martin Luther was born in Eisleben, Germany, on November 10, 1483, to devout parents, John and Margaret. His father valued education and made it possible,

---

[2] mortification – putting to death. See FGB 201, *Mortification*, from CHAPEL LIBRARY.

through hard work in the mining industry, for Martin to attend college in Erfurt. The University of Erfurt was the most celebrated in all Germany.

Luther arrived at this university in 1501, when he was eighteen years old. Two years later, while browsing in the school's library, Luther made an amazing discovery. As he opened books at random to learn the name of the author, his eye was attracted to one in particular. And as he read the title, his excitement only grew. It was a complete Bible, something almost unknown in those times. As Luther began to study the Scriptures, he was astonished that there was so much more than the select passages from the Gospels and Epistles that the Church allowed to be read on Sundays. Here was a volume the young student was determined to devour.

Always a brilliant scholar, Luther received a Master's degree in 1505. Wanting to please his parents, Luther next took up the study of law in the same university. However, six months later he suddenly changed his mind and entered the Augustinian monastery in Erfurt. The change in direction came because of a religious awakening Luther experienced one day when he was caught in the midst of a thunderstorm.

In the summer of 1505, Luther had decided to visit his parents who were living in Mansfeldt. The vacation proved to be stressful, and Luther returned to school. As he neared Erfurt, he was overtaken by a violent storm. The clouds clapped out thunder, and a tremendous lightening bolt flashed at his feet! Luther threw himself upon his knees believing that he was going to die. Sudden destruction, judgment, and eternity, with all their terrors, appeared before his eyes. Encompassed with the anguish and horror of death, Luther made a vow. If the Lord should deliver him from this danger, he would leave the world and devote himself entirely to God.

A Religious Awakening

When Luther's father learned that his son had given up the study of law, he was more than disappointed; he was outraged! Still, Martin withstood the pressure to reverse his decision about pursuing a religious life. Within six months, Luther had taken the vows of a monk. After studying theology, Luther was ordained a priest in 1507. The following year he was assigned a tutoring position in the University of Wittenburg. While there, Luther obtained the Bachelor of Bible degree in theology.

After one year in Wittenberg, Martin was transferred back to Erfurt, where he received his second degree in theology, after which he was given a prestigious teaching position. At the tender age of twenty-six years, Luther was appointed to teach the *Sentences of Peter Lombard*, the standard textbook of theology.

In the year 1510, Luther was provided an opportunity to travel to Rome as a companion to an older brother in the Augustinian Order. His heart was thrilled at the great privilege of making a holy pilgrimage. Once in Rome, Luther moved from place to place in religious excitement. "I remember," he wrote, "that when I went to Rome I ran about like a madman to all the churches, all the convents, all the places of note of any kind. I implicitly believed every tale about all of them that imposture had invented."

Luther climbed on his knees the Scala Santa, believed to be the stairs (transported from Jerusalem) which Jesus once climbed to reach Pilate's judgment hall. As he climbed the stairs, praying a *pater noster* on each step (a standard Catholic prayer), doubt crept into Luther's mind. When he came to the top step, he stood up and silently asked, "Who knows whether this is true?"

While many of his religious experiences in Rome were exciting, as Luther continued to tour the historic city, what he saw and heard shocked his spiritual sensitivity. There was open graft, corruption, and immorality. The holy city was not holy at all. Though he remained a loyal Catholic for the time, the seed was sown in Luther's mind that the Church needed radical reformation. After being in Rome, Luther was prepared to say, "If there is a hell, Rome is built over it."

Luther returned to Wittenberg to lecture on the Bible in the University. He taught and preached while continuing his personal pursuit of knowledge, until he received the degree of Doctor of Divinity.

In 1515, Luther began to speak in the parish church. While the parishioners heard him gladly, they did not know that Dr. Luther was still searching for his own personal salvation. Part of the search involved a life of strict asceticism. In a small cell in the tower of the Black Cloister (a residence for monks and nuns), Luther tried to earn salvation by good works. Cheerfully, he performed the most menial tasks. Happily, he prayed and fasted. With grim determination, Luther flogged himself until he fainted from the self-inflicted pain. Because of this religious ordeal, his body deteriorated until Luther looked like a skeleton. His cell remained unheated despite harsh winters. He maintained all night vigils and only rarely would he sleep on a mat for comfort.

Salvation in a Solitary Cell

And yet, despite all of his efforts, Luther was still burdened with a sense of shame and guilt. His soul was in the deepest depths of despair because, no matter how hard he tried, he knew he had not done enough to merit salvation. Later, looking back on this period of his life, Luther wrote the pope a letter and said, "I often endured an agony so hellish in violence, that if those spells had lasted a minute longer, I must have died then and there."

Finally, in matchless mercy, God sent comfort to Luther through several sources. One source was the spiritual writing of Bernard of Clairvaux (1090–1153). Bernard knew something about the free grace of Christ for salvation. A second source of spiritual help came from the kindness of the vicar of Luther's monastic order. Johann von Staupitz was able to temper and encourage his zealous monk during the days when Luther's religious zeal bordered upon madness. But most of all, there was the gift of the Holy Spirit. God was pleased to visit Luther with the gift of redeeming grace (John 3:7–8; Titus 3:5).

One day, toward the end of the year 1515, Luther was alone in his cell with a Bible. The Scriptures were opened to Paul's letter to the Romans. Luther's eyes rested upon verse seventeen in chapter one, which declares, "The just shall live by faith." Suddenly, the sunshine of radiant, Gospel truth broke through the dense clouds of spiritual darkness. "The just shall live by faith!" In a moment of divine illumination, Luther understood. He had been trying to earn salvation by works. But "the just shall live by *faith!*"

Romans 1:17 became to Luther the gates of Paradise. After years of trying to merit the merits of Christ, Luther was finally converted. Immediately, he cast himself upon Jesus Christ, and trusted in Him for salvation, forgiveness, and freedom from the power and pollution of sin (Acts 16:31).

Ninety-Five Theses

One can only imagine that instance of indescribable joy that came to Martin Luther in the small, cold cell of the Black Cloister in Wittenberg. In a moment of glory, Luther met the Master. He came to know Jesus Christ personally. His soul was suddenly filled with peace, hope, and joy unspeakable. He was a different person (2 Cor 5:17).

As a new creature in Christ Jesus, Luther began to see the Church in a new way. What he saw horrified him to the point that he could not keep quiet. An enemy had come and sown seeds of moral corruption in the Church of the living God (Matt 13:25)!

Luther soon discerned that most of the spiritual abuse in the Church could be traced to the system of penance and the selling of indulgences. He rightly perceived that precious souls, for whom Christ had died, were being deceived. Luther was determined to expose the putrid system he found, and hopefully, to change it for the better.

One day, after returning to his cell in the tower, Luther picked up his pen and recorded his views about indulgences in ninety-five theses, which are statements or propositions. It is not hard to imagine Luther writing rapidly, vigorously dipping his pen in the inkwell time and again in order to record as quickly as possible the words that burned in his breast. Having put his thoughts on paper, Luther looked over the statements one last time before descending the stairs that led him down to the massive oak doors of the Castle Church in Wittenberg. There he nailed his document for all to see. Little did Luther realize, as he turned away from the Church door, that he would be used of God to turn the world upside down (cp. Acts 17:6). He was only thirty-four years old.

When Luther nailed his theses[3] to the door of the Castle Church, he was not doing anything uncommon. That door served as a public place for gathering information at the University. By putting his document there, Luther was simply inviting a scholarly debate on the merits of his proposition. This was the custom of the period.

Initial Response to Luther

While Luther may have anticipated some general excitement, he had no comprehension that God would use something so small to ignite a religious bonfire that would consume the world (Zech 4:8–10). Within four weeks the Ninety-five Theses, which had been written in Latin, were translated into many languages, printed and carried with incredible speed to every country of Western Europe. People immediately wondered what would happen to Dr. Luther! And they also wondered what would happen to the selling of indulgences!

---

[3] his theses – the full text of Luther's *Ninety-five Theses* is available in the Study Guide.

A pro-Lutheran artist in 1617 shows Luther one hundred years earlier writing his *Ninety-five Theses* on the church door. Luther's pen pierces the ears of Pope Leo X, symbolized by the lion, and knocks the crown off the head of Charles V, emperor of the Holy Roman Empire. Further to the right, the Bible symbolically sheds light on Jesus in the clouds of heaven. The burning goose symbolizes the martyr John Hus, burned at the stake by the Council of Constance for his reforming ideas almost a hundred years earlier.

The archbishop of Mainz wanted to build a new cathedral with some of the proceeds from the sale of indulgences by Tetzel. He certainly did not like the frontal attack Luther had launched against a profitable "doctrine." With great indignation he sent a copy of the theses to Pope Leo X (1513–1521) in Rome. The pontiff was not happy at what he had to read. Many of the propositions challenged papal authority.

While the highest Church official in Rome considered how to deal with the exploding situation, Tetzel enlisted help to publish a set of "counter theses," defending the sale of indulgences. Other loyal Catholics took up the cause as well, such as the Dominican monk named Mazzolini. Mazzolini was serving as an inquisitor in Rome. He wrote a book condemning the conclusions of Luther, as did John Eck, a theology professor.

Having boldly issued a challenge to the Church regarding the selling of indulgences, Luther was forced to defend his position. It would not be easy spiritually, physically, or psychologically. Luther found himself almost alone. Friends he thought he could count on to agree with him, had withdrawn their support—deciding that he had been too rash.

The atmosphere was tense in April, 1518, when the monasteries associated with the Augustinian Order convened in Heidelberg. As expected, the Ninety-five theses soon became the major topic of discussion. When the convention was over, Luther was more encouraged. Though there had been some intense discussions, they all seemed to be friendly. Luther went back to Wittenberg to write a general answer to his critics in a book called *Resolutions*. Addressing it to the pope, Luther made a point by point defense of his propositions.

Upon receiving *Resolutions*, the Pope was discerning enough to realize the far reaching implications of Luther's arguments, if left unchallenged. For one thing, the immense income the Church received from the revenues indulgences produced would be severely curtailed. How then, would St. Peter's Cathedral at Rome be rebuilt, not to mention other costly projects?

Even more alarming, the theological foundation of Catholicism would be undermined. The Church had taught the people to believe that only the priest could administer the sacraments, which were the means of receiving God's grace. It was basic Catholic theology that, without the sacrament of penance, without absolution and indulgences, there could be no hope of salvation. How then were souls to be saved? Martin Luther would have to be answered. He had struck a severe blow to the foundation of the Roman Catholic Church.

CHAPTER 21

Upheaval!
A.D. 1518

A Saint is Summoned to Rome

In July, 1518, Pope Leo X discovered that the meeting of the Augustinian Order had not succeeded in silencing Luther from speaking out against indulgences. A summons was sent for Luther to appear in Rome. Such a summons was serious, for he easily could be charged with heresy in the sight of the Church. If convicted in Rome by the pope of being a heretic, Luther could be put to death by fire immediately.

In the providence of the Lord, Luther had a powerful friend and protector in Frederick the Wise, a devout Catholic. Frederick was a religious zealot, manifested in the fact that he had purchased more than five thousand relics from all over Christendom. Then, to house these artifacts, Frederick had built the Castle Church at Wittenburg, in the region of Saxony where he ruled.

Despite this religious passion for relics from the past and wanting to be loyal to Rome, Frederick was his own man. He could stand against those things he perceived to be wrong, and he believed the selling of indulgences to be wrong. Frederick had forbidden Tetzel to market indulgences in Saxony. Unfortunately, many of the citizens of Wittenburg did not agree with either Luther or Frederick on this matter. The people were willing to make the short journey to other towns where Tetzel appeared to buy indulgences. It was this foolish activity on the part of the people that prompted Luther to post his Ninety-five Theses on the Church door, as a protest against the indulgence sales.

In truth, there was another reason why Frederick opposed the sale of indulgences. He was interested in promoting a sense of nationalism. Frederick simply did not want to see local money from his country going into the treasury of the pope in Rome. He believed that the money could be better used to advance the work of the University of Wittenberg. And because Luther was its most prestigious and popular professor, Frederick decided to use all of his influence to have the papal summons against Luther dismissed.

Frederick was not without strong political power. At this time the emperor Maximilian I (b. 1459) was old and near death. He had ruled as emperor of the Holy Roman Empire since 1493. By 1519, it was obvious that a new emperor would have to be selected. There were three contestants for the crown: Charles, king of Spain; Francis, king of France; and Frederick, elector of Saxony.

Pope Leo X favored Frederick because he believed the ruler of Saxony would be the easiest to control. A war against the Turks was still being fought; the pope believed that the next ruler of Germany should support that effort. After listening to Frederick's arguments as to why Luther should not appear before him in Rome, Leo X canceled the papal summons. However, the pope had no intention of dismissing the case against the critical and troublesome monk.

Emissaries of the Pope

Leo knew that one of his legates (i.e., delegate), Cajetan, was traveling in Germany in order to attend a diet[1] in Augsburg. Leo sent Cajetan papal authority to order Luther to appear before him in Augsburg. The purpose was to hear Luther recant his charges against the Church. If Luther would not recant, he was to be arrested, bound, and sent to Rome for trial. Upon failure to arrest Luther, Cajetan was to place him and all his followers under the *ban*: denial of access to all the sacraments and priestly functions.

Once more Luther was in a precarious position. To go to Augsburg unrepentant would mean certain death. To deny his conscience would mean spiritual death. And this time Frederick the Wise of Saxony could not secure a cancellation of the papal order. What Frederick could do for Luther, however, was to obtain from the extremely ill emperor Maximilian a pass of safe conduct. Luther was to be guaranteed that he would not be harmed or arrested, regardless of the outcome of his appearance at his hearing.

---

[1] diet – national meeting of princes and powerful leaders.

With this understanding, Luther made the ill-fated journey to Augsburg. In October, 1518, he had three interviews with Cajetan. The discussions became fierce. Luther's friends counseled him to be calm and recant. But Luther refused to renounce those truths which had been taught to him by God. Finally, in the secret of the night, he left Augsburg.

Finding himself in the midst of a situation he could not control, Cajetan urged Leo X to settle the points in dispute by making an official pronouncement. The pope acted upon this counsel of expediency and issued a "bull" (Latin *bulla*, a seal; refers to any document with an official seal), that definite statements by certain monks against indulgences were heretical. Without being mentioned by name, Luther and the world knew that he was being regarded as a suspected heretic.

Miltitz and Eck

To press his papal authority, Leo X decided to arrest Luther. A special representative was sent into Germany to accomplish this difficult task. His name was Karl von Miltitz. The pope believed that Frederick would allow Miltitz to arrest Luther, since he was a close associate of Spalatin, the private secretary of the elector of Saxony. Furthermore, Miltitz was Frederick's own representative at the papal court in Rome. Now, Miltitz would return to Germany with a gift for his ruler. In a symbolic gesture, the pope sent Frederick the Wise an expensive golden rose as a token of papal love and goodwill. The fragrance of the flower suggested that Frederick honor the request of Rome, to withdraw support from Luther and allow his arrest.

Prior to an official meeting with Frederick, Karl von Miltitz asked for a private meeting with Luther and John Tetzel. Luther made himself available alone for this meeting. The result was surprising. Luther promised not to speak out against indulgences, if his opponents agreed not to speak out against him. He also agreed to put in writing any humility he felt in his heart, thereby expressing subordination to the pope.

Leo was so delighted with Luther's letter that on March 29, 1519 the pope corresponded with him using gracious language. An invitation was extended for him to visit Rome, at the pope's expense, and make his apologies personally at the papal court.

One can only speculate as to what might have happened had Luther made that special pilgrimage. It seemed that the theological differences between Luther and Rome were on the road to reconciliation. Then came the setback. The problem was that while Luther was willing to subdue his language, his fellow professors were not. In particular, there was Andreas Carlstadt, who was determined to debate Johann Eck (1486–1543), a German Roman Catholic theologian. Eck had originally supported the sale of indulgences, and issued a pamphlet against Luther's Ninety-Five Theses. Now Eck was at it again, answering Carlstadt's concerns with more counter theses in which he contended for papal supremacy.

Not to be left on the sidelines in his own University during a theological debate of monumental significance, Luther entered the fray by publishing twelve new theses. In the last one, Luther argued that the claim of papal authority over all the churches rested upon spurious historical ground. Using historical documents, Luther showed that the popes had been claiming supremacy for only four hundred years. Prior to that, for the first eleven centuries after Christ, no claim to supremacy existed.

Such an attack upon the authority of the pope was beyond belief. Once more Martin Luther had caused a sensation, and once more Dr. Eck was ready to challenge his conclusions. This time it was Luther who was challenged to a debate. The question would focus upon the supremacy of the pope.

In preparation for debate, Luther diligently studied canon law, which consisted of *Decretals*, the decisions of popes and general councils. Luther had been amazed to discover that many Decretals were forgeries. Armed with the verdict of the historical record and the truth of the Word of God, Luther was ready to face the challenge of Eck, at Leipzig on July 4, 1519.

The Leipzig Debate

The atmosphere at Frederick's palace, where the formal debate took place, was electrifying. Armed guards had been posted at every table, to keep the students from Wittenberg from fighting with the students from Leipzig.

As the debate began, it was obvious that both Luther and Eck were equal in verbal and intellectual abilities to their assigned roles. However, not being able to argue his own position based on its merits, Eck cleverly got Luther to concede that he agreed with some of the teachings of John Huss, who had been condemned by the Council of Constance. Luther said Huss had been condemned in an unrighteous manner. As soon as Luther was perceived as siding with an officially condemned heretic, the psychological advantage went to Eck. A wave of astonishment swept over the listening audience. Duke George of Saxony was heard to exclaim, "God help us; that is the pestilence!"[2]

Despite the psychological advantage going to Eck, Luther did win the strategic advantage, in that he based his arguments on fact, using the historical process. Luther pointed out that the Eastern Greek Church had never acknowledged the supremacy of the bishops of Rome. Yet, it was admitted by all, that the Eastern Church was Christian. The papacy faced a dilemma. How could the pope claim supremacy over all the churches, and yet a large part of the Church, recognized as Christian, not honor that claim? In addition, Luther noted that the great ecumenical councils of the early centuries did not teach the supremacy of the papacy.

Though the immediate impression might have been that the debate at Leipzig was won by Eck, important results went with Luther. He was far from being defeated. Following the Leipzig debate, the supporters of Luther grew. Among those who joined in Luther's cause was Martin Bucer (1491–1551). In time, Bucer would become a leading Reformer in the crucial German city of Strassburg, capital of the territory of Alsace. A man of great organizational skills, Bucer also possessed the ability to make new and complex thoughts understandable to common people. God would be pleased to use Bucer to mold the mind and heart of another Reformation leader, John Calvin.

Besides gaining more converts, a second result of the debate at Leipzig was that Luther's own thinking was solidified (Prov 27:17). His motive all along was to bring needed change to the Roman Catholic Church, not to leave it. But now Luther had publicly rejected the supremacy of the pope and the infallibility of the Church councils. The Leipzig debate crystallized the fact that irreconcilable differences existed between Luther and the Roman Catholic Church.

The Gathering Assault

Following the debate, Dr. Eck left for Rome to ask the pope to issue a bull excommunicating Luther. On June 15, 1520, the deed was done. Martin Luther was made to be a marked man, assigned to an eternity in hell by the very Church he had tried to serve so well. Rather than listen to Luther and deal with his areas of legitimate concern, the Church decided to excommunicate him and burn all of his writings.

---

[2] Kuiper, *The Church in History*, 173.

Weaving Scripture with a spirit of vindictiveness, the papal bull began with the words: "Arise, O Lord, and judge thy cause. A wild boar has invaded thy vineyard."[3]

With enormous courage Luther faced this new ordeal, manifesting a holy defiance (1 Tim 1:18), faith (Isa 54:17), and perhaps even a little bit of common coarseness. He called the papal decree, "the execrable bull of Anti-Christ."

Then, on December 10, 1520, Luther burned the document in public at the gates of Wittenberg. Gathered around him to witness this burning were University professors, students, and ordinary people from towns and villages. Into the fiery flames Luther also tossed copies of canon laws on which the Church of Rome relied for maintaining its authority over the souls of men. As Luther watched the papers turn into ashes, he knew that this was his final act of renunciation of the Roman Catholic Church. During one moment of thoughtfulness, Luther said, "As thou hast wasted the Holy One of God, so may the eternal flames waste thee."

Because the papal bull called upon the followers of Luther to recant their allegiance to him in public within sixty days or be treated as heretics, preparation had to be made to withstand the persecution that was sure to come. Luther began to publish three significant works. "To the Christian Nobility of Germany" was published first. This work was a clarion call to abolish the abuses which had been decreed by Rome. His *The Babylonian Captivity of the Church* was issued next. This work destroyed the Catholic belief that men could only be redeemed through the priest and the Roman system of sacramental salvation. Finally, the *Liberty of a Christian Man* summarized the privileges and obligations of the believer.

For Luther, the greatest privilege was to believe on the Lord Jesus Christ as personal Savior. The greatest obligation was to receive Him by grace through faith alone. Said Luther in May, 1520, in his pamphlet "On Good Works," "The noblest of all good works is to believe in Jesus Christ." Because of faith in Christ, good deeds would follow (Eph 6:5–9).

The Emperor Joins the Fray

While Luther defied the papal bull in the safety of Wittenberg under the protection of Frederick the Wise, Leo X was plotting his next move. In order to regain control of the situation, the pope felt he had to find a way to challenge and curb the growing

---

[3] Bainton, *Here I Stand: A Life of Martin Luther*, 156.

power of this troublesome monk. The decision was made to appeal to the new emperor, Charles, king of Spain.

Charles V, as he is known to history, was the heir to the domains of Austria and Spain. He had been elected Emperor of the Holy Roman Empire during the same period that the debate was raging in Leipzig. As king of Spain, Charles also had dominion over the Netherlands, a large section of Italy, and in theory, that part of the world discovered by Columbus. The sum of all this is that, as the elected emperor of Germany and Austria, Charles ruled over a larger portion of the earth than any man since Charlemagne.

It was to this powerful secular monarch that Pope Leo X appealed for help in handling the spiritual crisis created by Martin Luther. What Leo wanted was for Charles to help bring Luther to repentance, or to the place of physical execution. The pope knew that Charles was a devout Catholic who would not want to see the Church torn apart. Therefore, after much discussion, Charles was persuaded to summon Luther to appear for questioning before him in the city of Worms on the Rhine.

Luther received the royal summons with sadness. He knew he had to go to the Diet or Supreme Council of the German rulers. He was wanted by the papal court and by the royal crown. And so, on April 2, 1521, Luther started to go to the place where he was certain he would die. Prior to his departure, Luther had appealed to Melanchthon, a colleague at the University. "My dear brother," he said, "if I do not come back, if my enemies put me to death, you will go on teaching and standing fast in the truth; if you live, my death will matter little."

Though Luther was heavy of heart he was not afraid. "I will go to Worms," he declared, "though as many devils were aiming at me as tiles on the roof." Along the way, Luther was encouraged by the great crowds that came out to cheer him on. The roads were crowded with people who wanted to get a glimpse of the man who had created so much controversy within the kingdom of Christ. The journey continued until finally, at four o"clock in the afternoon of Wednesday, April 17, 1521, Luther arrived at the Diet of Worms. Just before he entered the conference hall, a well-known knight said to him, "My poor monk, my poor monk, you are on your way to make such a stand as I, and many of my knights, have never done in our toughest battle. If you are sure of the justice of your cause, then forward in the Name of God, and be of good courage, God will not forsake you."

Standing Resolute at the Diet of Worms

A dramatic scene unfolded. On a splendid royal throne sat Charles V, one of the most powerful of all men to have walked the face of the earth. The emperor was surrounded by his royal court with all of their pomp and pageantry. Also present were six electors of the empire and twenty-four dukes. To show their support for the crown and to display their hostility to Luther, were thirty archbishops, bishops, and abbots, seven ambassadors, and papal nuncios (official representatives from Pope Leo X). Before Charles stood the poor priest, dressed in the black robe of an Augustinian monk. Luther looked at Charles, and the king looked at Luther, for the first time. Both were young men. The king was twenty-one; Luther was thirty-seven.

In the royal room, a table had been placed with the many writings of Luther spread out. The audience grew silent as the Church official spoke. The Presiding Officer was none other than Dr. Johann von Eck! He had only two questions to ask: "(1) Are these your writings; and, (2) do you wish to retract them, or do you adhere to them and continue to assert them?" The official demanded a simple and plain answer.

Luther was surprised. He thought he had come to defend himself by debating the merits of his works. But there was to be no defense. There was to be no exchanging of ideas. Luther had been asked two questions. He had to respond on the spot.

Luther replied to the inquiry of the Church official. These were his writings. He would admit that. Did he wish to retract them? On that question, Luther asked for more time to respond. The secular members of the Diet consulted and agreed. Luther would be given more time. Court would reconvene twenty-four hours later. The general meeting was over for day one.

Upon casual reflection, it seems that the request by Luther to Charles V for more time, was a reasonable and innocent request. In retrospect, it was much more. It was nothing short of brilliance, for the simple request crystallized, and settled, an important issue that dealt with ultimate authority between Church and State.

For many years, the Church had been insisting that it had authority over the State. Secular powers should be submissive to papal powers. When the emperor and German princes granted Luther the requested delay, they were in effect demonstrating that they would not be submissive to Rome. The State was not going to be a tool in the hands of the papacy. The representatives from Rome might want an immediate recantation by Luther and no delay, but the State was willing to wait.

Luther would be granted additional time, and a message would be sent that the Church does not have ultimate authority over all others.

On the following day, Thursday, April 18, 1521, at the appointed hour, Luther returned to face Charles V and the princes of Germany. He had spent much of the night in prayer. He was ready to give the Diet an answer to the second question: whether or not he would denounce his own writings.

Once more the sweltering crowd in the room grew silent. Griped with emotion, from the depths of his soul, Luther answered the question formulated by Dr. Eck (Prov 16:1):

> Your Imperial Majesty and Your Lordships demand a simple answer. Here it is, plain and unvarnished. Unless I am convicted of error by the testimony of Scriptures or—since I put no trust in the unsupported authority of Pope or councils, since it is plain that they have often erred and often contradicted themselves—by manifest reasoning I stand convicted by the Scriptures to which I have appealed, and my conscience is taken captive by God's Word, *I cannot and will not recant anything,* for to act against our conscience is neither safe for us, nor open to us. On this I take my stand. I can do no other. God help me. Amen.[4]

With those words, Luther turned and started to leave the room. When a number of Spaniards began to cry out in anger at what they heard, German nobles and others formed a protective circle around Luther. He was escorted to safety as pandemonium erupted. Despite more appearances before the Diet over the next few days, it was apparent that there would be no reconciliation between Luther's ideas and the Catholic Church. Charles V was astonished; he told his courtiers that he "could not see how a single monk could be right, and the testimony of a thousand years of Christendom be wrong."

Kidnapped!

Amazingly enough, Luther was allowed to leave Worms. The promised safe-conduct would be honored. Luther could go back to Wittenberg, but he was ordered not to preach. During the night of April 26, 1521, Luther left Worms. Two days later, on April 28, Luther reached Frankfurt on the Main. On May 1, he resided at Hersfeld

---

[4] See *Documents of the Christian Church*, selected and edited by Henry Bettenson, second edition (Oxford University Press, London and New York, 1963).

where, despite orders to the contrary, he preached the Gospel. On May 2, he came to Eisenach where he preached on May 3, before riding on through the forest of Mohra. May 4 found Luther preaching once more, this time in the open air. In the evening his journey continued. Suddenly, in the midst of the forest, five riders with masks came upon Luther, lifted him out of the cart on which he was traveling, and rode off with him into the woods in the direction of Eisenach. Martin Luther had been kidnapped!

The "kidnapping" of Luther had been the idea of Luther's prince and friend, the elector Frederick of Saxony, whom he would never meet. Frederick had instructed those involved in this scheme to take Luther by "force" to the Wartburg Castle in Eisenach, Germany. Though Luther would stay here for ten months (May 4, 1521 to March 3, 1522), he would not be bored. During this period he rested, took walks in the forest, and produced the first translation of the New Testament into the German language!

There on one occasion, while looking for strawberries, Luther came across a hare being chased. He later remembered that moment in a sermon. "I saved alive a poor little hare, which I picked up, all trembling from its pursuers. After keeping it in my sleeve for some time, I set it down, and the creature was running off to secure its liberty—when the dogs getting scent of it, ran up, broke its leg, and then pitilessly killed it. The dogs were the Pope and Satan, destroying the souls that I seek to save, as I sought to save the poor little hare."

Finally, tired of being in isolation for ten months, Luther decided to return to Wittenberg in order to resume his place in the leadership of the movement for a Reformed Church. Luther found a dangerous situation. The German states were engaging in a religious civil war between the North and the South. The rulers of the South, led by Austria, were choosing to be loyal to Rome, while many states in the North became followers of Luther.

A Protestation

In 1529, a Diet was held at Speyer to reconcile the warring factions between the Lutherans and the Church of Rome. It was too little too late. Since the Catholic rulers were in the majority, they were able to condemn the doctrines articulated by Luther. In addition, Lutheranism was forbidden to be taught in those states where it had not been widely received. And even in those states that were already Lutheran, it was required that the Catholics should have religious freedom to advocate the teachings of the Catholic Church. It was to this unequal ruling that many Lutheran princes registered a formal "protestation" at the meeting of the Reichstag at Speyer. In this manner the term *Protestant* was born.

In the following year of 1530, a number of Protestant rulers convened in what was called the Schmalkald League. The Emperor Charles V needed their support against the Mohammedan Turks, who were threatening the very existence of Vienna. So religious freedom was granted to the princes in 1532, but the peace would be only temporary.

Duly alarmed and afraid of the spread of Protestantism, Catholics united to form the Holy League. Religious fighting broke out in 1546, the year Luther died. Despite initial losses, the Protestant forces were able to defeat the imperial forces in enough encounters to push them out of Germany. At the Diet of Augsburg in 1555, the struggle finally ended—provision was made for a permanent peace. Those who adhered to the *Augsburg Confession* were recognized as Protestants and given legal status and religious freedom. Despite this victory, the Catholics were able to keep a large part of the land, because the terms of agreement contained an ecclesiastical reservation. Any Catholic prince who became a Protestant faced the forfeiture of these estates.

CHAPTER 22

A New Way of Life for Luther & the Lutherans
A.D. 1525

A New Principle of Christian Liberty

The term *reformation* seems to be an appropriate word to apply to the sweeping changes that were taking place within the Roman Catholic Church during the days of Luther. The invisible "Church within the Church" (Rom 9:6) was being rediscovered, refined, and purified.[1] And in the providence of God, the changes did not stop there. People took reformation principles into their hearts and applied them to daily life at home, at work, and at play. Many of God's people discovered that life could be enjoyed because there was freedom to worship the Lord informally as well as formally (1Co 10:31). Luther himself discovered a zest for life that more than made up for years of asceticism. Said Luther, "Our loving God wills that we eat, drink, and be merry."

Luther approved of a variety of amusements, enjoyed a good game of chess, and loved music. "I seek and accept joy wherever I can find it. We now know, thank God, that we can be happy with a good conscience." While life was to be enjoyed, religious duties were not to be neglected but participated in most fully. If Luther was correct in his understanding of the Bible, then all believers are priests unto God and must serve as the same. In the service of the Lord there should be joy and freedom of expression. A guiding principle was that if the Bible did not prohibit something, or if no one was hurt, or if the conscience was not violated, then there was to be Christian liberty.

---

[1] See *The Invisible Church*, in chapter one of Part One.

Unfortunately, the practical implications of this principle were not understood nor agreed upon by all. As time passed, debates began to rage over particular acts of behavior. For example, many people who were departing from Catholicism wanted to divest themselves of physical reminders of the Church of Rome. Altars and images were removed from places of worship, sometimes by physical force. Other Protestants chose to keep the main altar, candles, and even some images of Christ. A place was protected for the use of religious art in worship.

Transubstantiation

As Luther continued to consider additional aspects of Catholic dogma, besides indulgences and the supremacy of the pope, attention was focused upon the doctrine of *transubstantiation*. According to the Catholic Church, the Lord's Supper is a sacrifice that requires a priest. When the priest blesses the elements of bread and wine, a miracle takes place: the elements become the actual and literal body and blood of Jesus! No matter how often this is done, no matter how many priests are involved, no matter how unworthy a priest may be, a change in substance (transubstantiation) takes place.

Because of the importance of this miracle, Catholic authorities decided that only the priest could drink the wine. It was feared that the parishioners (the laity) might drop some of the wine, thereby spilling the blood of Christ. The laity was trusted to properly eat the body of Christ, in the form of a wafer, but only after the priest placed the host upon the tongue of the worshipper.

Consubstantiation

Luther came to view the Lord's Supper in a way that radically departed from the official position of the Catholic Church. Luther denied that the Lord's Supper was a sacrifice that should be, or even could be, repeated over and over again, century after century, on a thousand different altars. Appealing to Scripture, Luther taught that Christ was offered once for all, as a substitutionary sacrifice, upon the cross of Calvary (Heb 9:28).

What Luther failed to do, in the view of later Reformers, was to distance himself far enough from the Catholic doctrine of transubstantiation. Luther taught that Christ's body is present in the *Eucharist* (Greek, thanksgiving). While this word is used in the New Testament to refer to prayer in general, the term had come to be applied to the Lord's Supper by the Catholic Church, because it was at the last supper, prior to His death, that Christ had "given thanks" (1 Cor 11:23–26).

Luther's teaching on the Lord's Supper has been designated by the term *consubstantiation*. According to Lutheran doctrine, the Lord's Supper is the means of receiving God's grace, by which Christ, in a unique and personal way, gives Himself to us. The Lord Jesus distributed the elements of bread and wine at the Last Supper as pledges of the assurance that sins would be forgiven. The believer receives these pledges from the hands of Christ in order to strengthen faith.

In the observance of the Lord's Supper, primary emphasis is not to be placed on the faith and love manifested by those who partake. Rather, attention is to be focused on the grace of God who manifested Himself in the Person and love of Christ. Finally, the Lord's Supper is to be considered a memorial of Christ, a testimony of faith, and an open expression of Christian fellowship in the unity of faith.

Desiring to return to the original observance of the institution, Luther taught that those who partake of the Lord's Supper should receive the cup as well as the bread (from the *Augsburg Confession*, Article X, XXII, and XXIV; and the *Formula of Concord*, Chapter VII). In the same way that Luther moved away from the Catholic teaching of transubstantiation, other reformers would soon distance themselves from Luther's doctrine of consubstantiation.

Spiritual Resources for the Righteous

As the Reformation continued, there was a desperate need for new scriptural material to guide the growth of the saints. Being a prolific writer, Luther was able to provide valuable literary resources. Using Erasmus' *Greek Testament* of 1516, the first printed Greek Testament, Luther translated the Scriptures into the language of the German people using a common vernacular. His work was widely welcomed for its simplicity and beauty. Luther believed that every person had the right and the responsibility to read, study, and interpret the Bible.

This basic concept was radically different from the Catholic Church, which believed that only church leaders and educated scholars with linguistic abilities had the necessary ability to understand the Bible properly. The Catholic Church took the position of being afraid that careless study of the Scriptures could lead to careless interpretation. Perhaps they were more afraid of losing control over the minds of individuals. "Knowledge is power" in the wisdom of man.

Because Luther was not afraid of an educated congregation, he did much to dispel the darkness of ignorance. Free primary and secondary schools were encouraged to be established throughout Germany. Luther's own *Shorter Catechism* was part of the core curriculum. In this small work, Luther was able to provide a doctrinal foundation for future generations to build upon. Luther also did much towards training the clergy for the work of the ministry.

In addition to Scripture translation and the Shorter Catechism, Luther encouraged the singing of new hymns, many of which he wrote himself. Perhaps his most enduring hymn is "A Mighty Fortress Is Our God":

> A mighty fortress is our God,
>   A bulwark never failing;
> Our helper He amid the flood,
>   Of mortal ills prevailing.

Always believing that there is only one true Church, Luther desired that a formal and official statement of faith be drafted and declared. Historically, this was not a new concept. In 1530, at the Diet of Augsburg, the document was presented and accepted. The statement of faith has become known as the *Augsburg Confession*.

No ancient creed of Christendom was replaced by this new expression of faith. The Lutheran Church embraced the Apostles' Creed, and the Creeds of Nicea and Chalcedon. What the *Augsburg Confession* did do was to incorporate the historical positions of faith of the Church and to amplify them.

Master Melanchthon

To assist Luther in his great work of "reforming" a Church in need, God provided him with a wonderful co-worker named Philip Melanchthon. Born in Brettan, Baden, in 1497, the son of George Schwartzerd, Philip was given the unusual name "Melanchthon" (Greek, black earth) by his great uncle John Reuchlin. An exceptionally brilliant student, Philip was graduated in 1511 at the age of fourteen. The next year he received a Master of Arts degree from Tubingen. When only twenty-one years old, he was appointed professor of Greek in Wittenburg. More degrees and honors would be conferred upon him in the years to come.

Perhaps his greatest privilege was that of working with Martin Luther. From the start, Melanchthon was a strong champion and capable defender of the doctrines of the Reformation. His scholarly presence and calming influence was manifested on a number of occasions. Not the least of these was the Diet of Augsburg in 1530, where the basic Lutheran statement of faith was formulated and accepted. It was Melanchthon who wrote an *Apology* in 1531 to explain this confession of faith to those in the Catholic Church who opposed it.

On a more practical level, Melanchthon was very useful in organizing schools, training the clergy, and publishing the vast body of literature that helped to guide the Reformation through the early years of the movement. He was a man who desired peace. When he died in 1560, Melanchthon was buried alongside his beloved friend, Martin Luther.

Luther at Home

Despite the tremendous burdens of daily leadership, Luther found time by the goodness of God to fall in love with a great lady of grace. Her name was Catherine Von Bora (1499–1552) and on June 27, 1525, she married Martin. He was forty-two and she was twenty-six. Luther liked to tease and say that he married his Katie to please his father, spite the devil, and anger the pope.

Defying a Catholic tradition that was three hundred years old, Luther correctly broke his vows of celibacy—as did Catherine, who was a former nun (1 Tim 4:1–3; Heb 13:4). She was a lady of good birth and reputation. Their marriage was pleasant. Later in life Luther would repeat on his own what he had been taught in his youth: "The greatest gift of God to man is a pious, kindly, God-fearing, home-loving wife." Together they would have six children.

As a father, Luther was stern but kind. "Punish if you must," he said, "but let the sugar-plum go with the rod." He composed songs for his children and sang them as he played the lute. The death of his daughter Magdalena at the age of fourteen brought his heart much sorrow. Like King David, Luther prayed day and night for her recovery, and then submitted her to God, saying, "I love her very much, but dear God, if it is Thy holy will to take her, I would gladly leave her with Thee." After a moment, Luther spoke to Magdalene, "Lena dear, my little daughter, thou wouldst love to remain here with thy father; art thou willing to go to that other Father?" And the child answered, "Yes, dear father, just as God wills." When Magdalena died, Luther wept many bitter tears for a long period. At her funeral he spoke to her one last time, saying, "Magdalena, you will rise and shine like the stars and the sun." Then he added, "How strange it is to know that she is at peace and all is well, and yet be so sorrowful."

A Faithful Servant

No great man or woman of God has ever been without critics, and Luther was no exception. During his lifetime, Luther knew what it was to pass through the fires of personal persecution. He experienced many of the perils associated with the cause of Christ. But through it all, Luther was faithful. "I bear upon me the malice of the whole world," he once said, "the hatred of the Emperor, of the Pope, and of all their retinue. Well, onward, in God's name!"

Perhaps Luther did not go far enough in some of his reforming practices and doctrine. Perhaps Luther should not have made the Church subordinate to the control of civil authorities. Perhaps Luther should not have been so intemperate in his remarks during the Peasant's War of 1525, when he called for mass executions of the mob. Certainly he could have co-operated more with the Swiss reformers, thereby presenting a stronger force of resistance against the power of Catholicism in various European states. And there is no doubt that at times he sang too much, ate too much, danced too much, and drank too much. God would hold Luther accountable for going to excess in enjoying some of the things of life, for the anti-Semitism that poured forth from Luther's lips and pen, and for the intolerance he displayed in later life.

It has been observed that Luther should never have grown old. By 1522, some said that he was acting worse than the popes. "I do not admit," he wrote, "that my doctrine can be judged by anyone, even by the angels. He who does not receive my doctrine cannot be saved." By 1529, he was again a little more temperate, though still advocating that even "unbelievers should be forced to obey the Ten Commandments, attend church, and outwardly conform," and heretics should be put to death. Fortunately, his bark was worse than his bite.

Without question, some of the reproof leveled against Luther has been justified. His great faults were as real as his many virtues. But Luther never claimed to be more than he was, a sinner saved by grace. There is no doubt that the day Luther died in Eisleben, Germany, February 18, 1546, multitudes of thankful souls welcomed him home to heaven, where he heard the words of his Lord saying to him, "Well done, thy good and faithful servant" (Matt 25:23). "Well done."

CHAPTER 23

The Reformation Reaches Beyond Germany
A.D. 1526

A Foundation for the Reformation

While Martin Luther worked diligently to fan the flames of spiritual renewal in the Church of Germany, the spirit of the Reformation spread beyond the borders of his native land. The general distinguishing principles of the Reformation may be identified.

A fundamental respect for the Scriptures and their primacy. For centuries the Catholic Church had diminished the importance of Scripture. The Bible was not believed to be sufficient for life, so the writings of men and the authority of Church councils were given equal or superior weight to the Word of God. The Scriptures virtually were withheld from the people, for it was not allowed to be translated into the vernacular of the common man. Very few people had even seen a copy of the Bible, let alone held one in their hands. The Reformers restored the Scripture to its rightful position. It was the Bible that was to determine the Church's doctrine, regulate its practice, and guide the daily conduct of the believer.

A religion based upon reason. The Church of Rome had introduced and advanced many illogical doctrines. And it had forced people to embrace them upon penalty of temporal punishment or eternal pain. There was the mystical doctrine of transubstantiation. There were the greedy and terribly misleading pretensions of papal indulgences. There was the supercilious supply of images in the hour of worship. The Reformers placed before the people of God a creed, a code of conduct, and a way of worship that did not outrage the rational nature of the mind.

A religion of personal piety. Catholicism did not encourage individuals to go directly and personally to God the Father. Between the heart of man and the heart of the God of heaven, both popes and councils had interjected their own authority. Before a soul burdened with sin could find divine forgiveness, the priest had to intervene to hear one's confession and then render absolution. No longer could a saint come boldly before the throne of grace. The Virgin Mary and departed saints were interjected, demanding needless mediation.

But with the mighty power of the Holy Spirit, the Reformers swept away all false barriers. They declared the right of private judgment. They proclaimed the Bible's universal priesthood of the believer with direct access to the throne room of God (1 Pet 2:5, 9; Rev 1:6; 20:6), and they emphasized personal responsibility (Jas 5:16). Each soul has the privilege of speaking directly to the Savior, the true source of salvation.

A spiritual religion. Because a multitude of outward ordinances and ceremonies had been imposed upon the people, the true spiritual nature of the faith had become obscured. The Reformers arose to emphasize an inward religious experience over external ecclesiastical rituals without reality. The Reformers replaced penance with penitence, works with faith, asceticism with true self-denial, celibacy with chastity, and the mass with real spiritual communion.

The rise of nationalism. Desiring to subjugate the world to itself, Rome made each nation subservient to an ecclesiastical hierarchy over which it presided. The Reformers protested against papal intervention into the internal affairs of individual countries, thereby denying religious independence.

At the Diet of Spires in 1526, it was decreed that in regard to religion "each state should live, govern, and behave itself as it should answer to God and the Emperor." From time to time, when he was not fighting perpetual wars outside his domain, Charles V, Emperor of the Holy Roman Empire, attempted to reverse the decree and bring everyone back to the Catholic faith, but national freedom of religion was reaffirmed at the Augsburg Diet in 1555. The rise of nationalism, encouraged by the Reformers, established the principle that Rome had no right to impose its ecclesiastical discipline, ritual, or creed upon other Christians outside its sphere of influence.

A Mixed Heritage

While establishing these general principles, the Reformers did accept the historic creeds of Nicea and Chalcedon, as well as the Augustinian doctrines of the necessity of inward grace and of justification by faith. What the Reformers rejected were the many false doctrines of Catholicism that were not found in the Bible, but are based instead primarily on traditions of the Roman Catholic Church. These included the supremacy of the pope, an exclusive priesthood, the worship of Mary as the mother of God and the queen of heaven, the worship of saints, the withholding of the cup of communion from the laity, indulgences, purgatory, prayers for the dead, monasticism, compulsory celibacy, obligatory confession, and the exclusive use of Latin in public worship.

Ulrich Zwingli

To lead the Reformation in Switzerland, God raised up men such as Ulrich Zwingli. Zwingli was born on January 1, 1484, in Wildhaus, a German-speaking region in Switzerland. A gifted student, Zwingli studied at Bern, Vienna, and Basel. After receiving the degree of Master of Arts in 1506, he was ordained a priest and served a parish at Glarus for ten years. In 1516, Zwingli moved to Einsiedeln, where he would remain for three years. As a scholar, Zwingli was able to study the classics in the original languages.

Unlike Luther, Zwingli never had a crisis of the soul. He studied the Gospel, was illuminated by the Holy Spirit (John 3:1–8), and preached what he studied, which meant that he also preached against what was not to be found in Scripture. In particular, in 1517, Zwingli began to oppose a false doctrine of Rome which taught that there was remission of sins for those who made a pilgrimage to a shrine of the Virgin Mary at Einsiedeln. The whole system of relics and Mariology was vigorously attacked as people were pointed to the true way of salvation in Christ: "the Lamb of God, which taketh away the sin of the world" (John 1:29). In 1518, Zwingli turned his considerable oratorical abilities to attacking indulgences.

By 1522, while serving as a priest in a large cathedral in Zurich, Zwingli finally broke with Rome. He removed images from the Church, abolished the Mass, reformed the school system, got married, and preached against celibacy. When opposition to his ministry became too great, the city council decided to hold public hearings. At the open meetings, Zwingli used the opportunity to present the *Sixty-seven Articles of Faith* which he had drafted. He managed to persuade the city leaders to endorse his reform efforts. Unfortunately, in 1529, civil war resulted between the Roman Catholics and the Protestants. In 1531, Zwingli was brutally killed in battle. Having been severely wounded in the leg by a spear, and with his helmet bashed in by a stone, Zwingli lay down to die. Eventually, he was struck through by an enemy's sword. His body was quartered. The individual limbs were mixed with excrement and burned. His ashes were scattered to the winds.

With the death of Zwingli at age 47, the Protestant cause suffered a setback. Their Christian Civic League was no match against the Catholic coalition that had also formed and made an alliance with Ferdinand of Austria. The importance of Zwingli's work in Switzerland cannot be overstated. Educated under the influence of Renaissance idealism, he recognized the need for nations to return to God, and so attempted political reforms as well as spiritual regeneration. His theology emphasized the sovereignty of God and the election to salvation of precious souls.

Zwingli also taught that the Lord's Supper held no special merit in the salvation of the elect, because it was merely a symbol or remembrance of the sacrificial, substitutionary work of Christ at Calvary. This position served to alienate Zwingli from Luther, who insisted that the body and blood of Christ are really present in the communion. All of this was discussed in October, 1529, when Luther and Zwingli held a conference at Marburg. Because the German and Swiss reformers could not agree, an opportunity was lost to form a spiritual alliance against the forces of the pope.

John Calvin

In the summer of 1536, a young author, age twenty-seven, arrived at Geneva to spend the night. With the exception of three years in exile, John Calvin would remain in Geneva for the rest of his life.

Calvin was born July 10, 1509, in a small town called Noyon, located in northern France near Paris. His father, Gerard, was financially prosperous. He enjoyed excellent political connections while serving as secretary to the bishop of Noyon, proctor (supervisor) in the cathedral, and fiscal procurator of the province. Calvin was introduced to the Catholic bureaucracy at age eleven when he was appointed to be a chaplain. It was an accepted practice to appoint a child to a church office, receive the salary, and then allow an adult priest to perform the actual work for a portion of the revenues. Though Calvin would stay in the Catholic Church structure for many years, he was never ordained to the priesthood.

Despite his father's comfortable position in life, Calvin knew sorrow at an early age when his mother died. His father married again. Young Calvin was sent to Paris to further his education before moving on to study law at Orleans. In 1531, he took his Bachelor of Laws degree.

Sometime during 1532 or 1533, Calvin became a true Christian. He says that his salvation experience was abrupt. While engaged in private study, God, by a sudden conversion, subdued his heart. Like Luther, Calvin had not found peace with God in absolutions, sacraments, penance, indulgences, or intercessory prayer.

While in Paris, Calvin became a religious refugee because of his known sympathies with the principles of the Protestant Reformation. Warned by friends that he was scheduled to be arrested, Calvin left Paris (January 1534) and found refuge in Angouleme. In May he returned to Noyon and resigned from the offices from which income had been helping to support him.

Calvin was arrested and thrown into prison for the cause of Christ. Upon release, Calvin was hunted from city to city (December 1534). Compelled to use assumed names, he taught small groups in quiet gatherings in various parts of Germany and Switzerland.

For awhile in 1535, Calvin found rest in Basel, Switzerland. By the grace of God, he was also able during this period to establish a friendship with Martin Bucer, the reformer of Strassburg who was a professor of theology at the university. It was at Basel, at age twenty-six, that Calvin formulated and published (1536) the first edition of his *Institutes of the Christian Religion*. The work was intended to be a catechism, whereby the fundamental teachings of the Protestant movement were set forth.

Upon reflection, Calvin became convinced that the book could also be useful in explaining to the Catholic ruler of France, Francis I (king, 1515–1547), that those who embraced the Reformation principles were not disloyal citizens. Protestants were not radicals nor revolutionaries, but firm believers in the Word of God. They deserved to be treated in a kinder manner. The Lord was pleased to use Calvin's work, which went through many editions until the last in 1559 (the final edition was three times the size of the first). *The Institutes of the Christian Religion* is considered by many to be the finest concise expression of evangelical faith. Concerned for his safety once more, Calvin decided to leave Basel and go to Strassburg in southwest Germany, where he could live quietly as a scholar. However, as Calvin passed through Geneva on the way to Strassburg, God had ordained that he would meet "William" Farel.

The Beliefs of Farel

Guillaume Farel (1489–1565) had first begun to hold regular Reformed worship services in Geneva in 1534. He was an experienced champion of the evangelical cause, having seen spiritual success in 1528 in Bern. Together with J. Hussgen (Oecolampadius), Farel was victorious during the Bern Disputation, a forum in which the city leaders decided to embrace the Protestant position. Bern then sponsored the work of Farel as he moved on to minister in Vaud, Neuchatel (1530), and Geneva.

Because of Farel's faithfulness, zeal, persuasive abilities, and anointment of the Holy Spirit, Geneva officially became Protestant in 1535. The city council then moved to legislate what it believed to be Christian ethics. Laws were enacted against drunkenness, gambling, dancing, dice, and many other moral vices. But the laws had little effect upon the personal lives of the people. Farel knew that a mighty man of God was needed to bring souls into conformity with the standards of the Gospel. The city needed a man of conviction, strength, and integrity. The city needed John Calvin!

Hearing that Calvin was in town for the night, Farel sought him out, much to Calvin's great surprise. He had entered Geneva as a stranger and had no idea that anyone knew he was there. Farel told Calvin what was on his heart. The city needed him. Calvin shook his head in disagreement at the implications. He was too young for an important leadership position. He knew nothing of the problems of Geneva. He was timid by nature and wanted to live the life of a scholar. He was not prepared for fierce, personal, and prolonged religious struggles. Calvin would go on to Strassburg where there was peace and safety. There he could study and write.

Farel listened to Calvin's comments and grew more intense. The discussion continued until Farel grew weary and angry. The forty-seven year-old man stopped talking and stood up. His beard fell upon his chest. His eyes were fiery as he looked at the youth twenty years his junior. Farel would speak one last time. He would speak as a prophet of God, and he would bring the wrath of heaven down upon the head of this obstinate young man. With coldness in his voice Farel said, "May God curse your studies if now in her time of need you refuse to lend your aid to His Church!" This was too much for Calvin. He was shaken. How could he refuse to help when such words were spoken? He would concede to the will of God as manifested through Farel. Calvin would stay in Geneva and the two men would become close friends in the work of the Lord. Geneva could be grateful that Farel had found for them a wonderful spiritual leader.

A Great Work in Geneva

When John Calvin made the monumental decision to stay in Geneva and work with Farel, he could not have imagined the fantastic future of tragedy and triumph that awaited him. The life of Calvin was in three distinct phases:

Phase I: First stay in Geneva	Aug 1536–Apr 1538
Phase II: Exiled in Strassburg	May 1538–Sep 1541
Phase III: Return to lead	Sep 1541–May 1564

The beginning of Calvin's ministry in Geneva was very humble. He was accepted by the Great Council (the civil ruling body in Geneva) and approved by the presbytery (the subordinate ruling body of the Church). With no other ordination he began his ministry on September 5, 1536, by preaching on the Epistles of St. Paul in the Church of St. Peter. But trouble began soon after that, when Calvin and Farel placed before the city council three proposals.

First, it was suggested that the Lord's Supper should be administered on a regular basis. Communion was to be closed in the sense that every person not living a godly life would be disciplined even to the point of excommunication. The minister of the Gospel would determine who was a fit communicant to receive the Lord's Supper. Calvin and Farel were shocked to find the people of Geneva giving themselves to dancing, gambling, drunkenness, and adultery. An entire district of the city, known as the Brothel Queen, was given to prostitutes. Farel and Calvin felt a moral obligation to hold people spiritually accountable for their sins.

Second, it was proposed that a catechism which Calvin had written should be adopted. The *third* proposal stated that every citizen should embrace as a standard the *Confession of Faith and Discipline* drafted by Farel. The objectives of Calvin and Farel were to make Geneva a true and righteous "city of God," while maintaining the autonomy of the Church from the state.

The Great Council of the city approved the proposals in November 1536. Anyone who openly transgressed the moral code was to be excommunicated and sent into exile. The order was given. In July 1537, all citizens were to gather at the Church of St. Peter and give their allegiance to the *Confession of Faith and Discipline*.

Anyone who displayed any form of Catholicism, such as carrying a rosary or sacred relic, or observing a saint's day, was subject to punishment. Gamblers were placed into the stocks. Known adulterers were paraded through the streets before being sent into exile.

Banished!

It was all too much. The people had grown to enjoy the lenient moral discipline they had found under Catholicism. Militant groups began to come together. The Patriots reorganized themselves. They had freed the city once from oppressive secular rules, they would free it again from these strangers in their midst, who wanted to make all men saints. Others, called Libertines or Liberals, desired liberty of conscience, morals, and worship. They joined with the Patriots and those who secretly remained Catholics. In the election of February 3, 1538, this new coalition won the majority in the Great Council. Now they were in a position to confront the zealous ministers of St. Peter.

Farel and Calvin rose to meet the challenge against their authority. They denounced the Council and refused to serve communion unless the Council members accepted Church discipline. The Council met and decided to banish the two ministers, which was done on April 23, 1538. They were ordered to leave the city within three days. The people rejoiced with public celebrations.

Farel returned to a pastoral ministry in Neuchatel. He would never go back to Geneva. Calvin traveled to Strassburg at the invitation of Martin Bucer, who had been won to the Reformation cause after listening to Luther during the great Leipzig Debate. After eighteen months of constant conflict in Geneva, Calvin was ready for the peace of Strassburg.

Here he would study and preach—and get married. He asked Farel and Bucer to help him find a wife with specific qualifications. "I am none of those insane lovers," wrote Calvin, "who, when once smitten with the fine figure of a woman, embrace also her faults. This only is the beauty which allures me: that she be chaste, obliging, not fastidious, economical, patient, and careful for my health." In 1540, with Farel officiating, Calvin married Idelette de Bure, a poor widow with several children. They had one child, a son, who died in infancy. When Idelette died in 1549, Calvin wrote of her with great love. He never remarried, but chose to live in marital loneliness during the last fifteen years of his life.

Life in Strassburg was a time of peace for Calvin, but also of much activity. There were a number of French Protestant refugees who had fled to Strassburg (in Germany) to escape the persecution they faced in France. Calvin would be a pastor to them. Calvin would also have the opportunity to meet many of the leading men of the Reformation, as he attended various conferences in Germany that had been called by the Holy Roman Emperor Charles V.

Charles V (ruler, 1519–1558) was determined to restore the unity in the body of Christ by bringing the Protestants and Catholics together again. If he were ever to revive the universal empire of Charlemagne, he must have peace in his immense kingdom. Charles was not only the Emperor of Germany, but the sovereign of Spain, Portugal, Austria, much of Italy, Burgundy, and the Netherlands. And he really wanted unity! But it was not to be. The differences of the Reformers were too great. Time could not be reversed, and the divisions could not healed. But some good did come out of the conferences. While Calvin and Luther never met, Calvin became friends with Melanchthon and other Lutheran leaders.

Return to Geneva

As Calvin enjoyed a more serene life in Strassburg, the situation in Geneva was deteriorating. The Catholic Church saw an opportunity to regain its lost influence. Cardinal Iacopo Sadoleto wrote the *Epistle to the Genevese* urging them to return to their Catholic faith (1539). It was a masterful document, full of diplomatic courtesies and theological exhortations.

The Great Council thanked the Cardinal for his letter, promised a response, and became concerned. Who could adequately respond to such a gifted representative of the Catholic Church? A number of citizens were already asking to be released from their oath to support the *Confession of Faith and Discipline*. Perhaps the city would return to Catholicism!

Calvin learned of the situation in Geneva and wrote a reply to the Cardinal. He would be just as diplomatic, and just as forceful, with his theological exhortations. He too regretted the division of the Church, but the corruptions were so great that reformation was needed. The papacy had been taken hostage by Anti-Christ! Reading Calvin's reply in Wittenberg, Martin Luther regarded it as an effective response. "I rejoice," he said, "that God raises up men who will . . . finish the war against Anti-Christ which I began."

Geneva would remain Protestant. The Great Council was impressed with what Calvin had accomplished with his letter, and they even wondered if perhaps they should not invite him to return. Good preaching had not replaced the messages of Farel and Calvin at St. Peters. People had no respect for their new pastors and so returned to gambling, drunkenness, street fighting, adultery, the singing of lewd songs, and running unclothed through the streets. The four magistrates who had led the original movement to banish Farel and Calvin had proven to be unworthy leaders. One was put to death for murder, another was charged with forgery, and a third with treason. The fourth died while trying to escape arrest.

Over a period of time, a majority of the members of the Great Council came to the conclusion that Calvin should be recalled. On May 1, 1541, his sentence of banishment and that of Farel were annulled. Calvin and Farel were declared to be honorable men after all. A delegation was sent to Strassburg to inform Calvin of that fact.

At first, Calvin was not impressed with the news. He enjoyed life in Germany and did not want to leave to return to a hostile environment. However, he would visit Geneva. When Calvin arrived, September 3, 1541, he received so many gifts, honors, apologies, and promises of co-operation that he felt compelled to stay and see what could be done for Christ.

The Rule of the Righteous

To assist him in the great work of guiding the city of Geneva and reforming it along biblical terms, Calvin formulated a new ecclesiastical code. On January 2, 1542, the Great Council ratified the set of rules for the governing of the Church. The leadership of the ministry would be invested in four offices: pastors, teachers, elders, and deacons. The pastors of Geneva would be recognized as "The Venerable Company." They would have the oversight of the Church and train candidates for the ministry.

This new Consistory (the local Church's ruling body) would have authority to demand obedience to the rules outlined in Calvin's manual of Church Order, and to discipline those who were slow in obedience. Discipline would vary from private warnings to public rebukes. Fines could be levied. "Should anyone come after the sermon has begun, let him be warned. If he does not amend, let him pay a fine of three sous." Heresy was punishable by death, as was witchcraft and striking a parent. Discipline was expected by all. No facet of life would go undisciplined or unexamined by the spiritual leaders. This examination included such things as the color of clothing that was worn, the length of hair, and how many dishes could be served at a meal.

Pharisaic or Pure Religion?

As might be expected, there were various reactions to the new policies and practices implemented in the name of Christ by the Consistory. Some idealized what was happening in Geneva and wanted to be part of it. From Wittenburg, Germany, in 1610, a Lutheran minister named Valentin Andreae wrote a glowing report of what he had seen and heard while visiting Geneva.

> When I was in Geneva, I observed something great that I shall remember and desire as long as I live. There is in that city not only the perfect institute of a perfect republic, but, as a special ornament, a moral discipline which makes weekly investigations into the conduct, and even the smallest transgressions, of the citizens . . . All cursing and swearing, gambling, luxury, strife, hatred, fraud, etc., are forbidden, while greater sins are hardly heard of. What a glorious ornament of the Christian religion is such a purity of morals! We must lament with tears that it is wanting with us [Germans] and almost totally neglected. If it were not for the difference of religion, I would have been chained to Geneva forever.

Not everyone was willing to give such glowing reports. Many felt they were chained to Geneva, but not because of their free will. As early as December 16, 1547, the tension in the city was so great that the Patriots and Libertines came to a meeting of the Great Council with weapons. They wanted, no, they demanded, an end to the power of the Consistory over the citizens. Angry words were exchanged. Suddenly Calvin entered into the room, faced the mad mob, and then, striking his breast, said, "If you want blood, there are still a few drops here; strike, then!" The bold invitation was almost acted upon as swords were drawn. But no one wanted to be the assassin. The moment of passion passed and Calvin was able to put down the revolt by the force of his personality and the grace of God, who gave him the courage and the words to speak in the hour of crisis.

Still, there was the problem of people appearing to obey rules and regulations of righteousness, but without true godliness. The records of the Great Council reflect a large number of children being born out of wedlock in a community of 20,000. There were many cases of children being abandoned, and of marriages being forced. Ecclesiastical sentences of death were being passed for witchcraft and heresy. Calvin's own son-in-law and step-daughter are listed among those condemned of adultery.

The single, darkest spot on the overall glorious record of the great reformer is Calvin's part in the case of Michael Servetus (1511–1553). Servetus was an extremely well-educated Spanish physician. He was also a heretic, from a Christian point of view, who was militant in his opposition to the historic Christian faith. Servetus denied the deity of Christ, the doctrine of the Trinity, and salvation by grace through faith alone. When he came back to Geneva after being sent away, Servetus was arrested, tried, found guilty, condemned as a heretic, and finally, on October 27, 1553, was burned to death on the hill of Champel, just south of Geneva. Even the gentle Melanchthon in a letter to Calvin expressed his thanks for the punishment of such a blasphemous man.

Calvin's Contributions

The influence of Calvin upon Geneva and the rest of the world is without measure. Out of every country in Europe, refugees from the persecution of Rome or inquirers in search of biblical truth made their way to see this great man of God, who was poor in health so much of his life. Calvin suffered over the years from severe headaches, gout, and asthma with hemorrhages of the lungs. He barely ate, fasted often, slept only six hours a day, refused to leave the city, was pure in his private life, and could not be bribed. Pope Pius IV once said of him, "The strength of that heretic consisted in this, that money never had the slightest charm for him. If I had such servants my dominion would extend from sea to sea." From Geneva, visitors carried home Calvin's truths to teach and his principles and practices to implement. Because these were rooted in Scripture, individual lives were changed, then nations, and then the world.

From Calvin people learned afresh the biblical doctrine of *predestination*. To "predestine" means to establish or arrange beforehand all that shall come to pass. It means to foreordain. God has predestined all things according to the counsel of His own good will (Rom 8:29; Eph 1:5, 11). Predestination takes into account not only what shall come to pass, but also the order in which events will take place. The doctrine incorporates: (1) which men will perform which deeds, (2) who is to be saved and who will not be saved, and (3) everything else! There are no "accidents" for the Christian, only incidents. All things, no matter how inconsequential or important, happen in accordance with the will of God, for the ultimate achievement of what He considers to be admirable (Rom 8:28).

As Calvin taught the doctrines of grace,[1] people listened and learned of a great and glorious God. They listened again as he spoke of the spiritual presence of Christ in the consecrated bread and wine, thereby avoiding Zwingli's position of communion being mere symbolism, and the Catholic's position of Christ's corporal presence.

In other areas, Calvin taught what he believed to be a proper mode of Church worship. Simplicity, he argued, should be followed instead of ceremony. The mind should be appealed to rather than the bodily senses. It was all right to combine liturgical order with freedom of expression.

Calvin taught the essential equality of ministers and the priesthood of all believers. He taught that laymen should be allowed to share in Church government through the institution of a plurality of elders. And he taught the spiritual independence of the Church from the state, although the Church should have a moral influence over secular rulers.[2]

---

[1] doctrines of grace – a name given to the system of theology usually known as Calvinism, which emphasizes that salvation is all of grace, by the merit of Christ alone, absolutely without any addition from the works of man, either in an unregenerate or regenerate state. See *The Doctrines of Grace in the Gospel of John*, available from Chapel Library.

[2] See *Calvin on Self-denial*, *Calvin on Prayer*, and *Calvin on The Mediator*, all abstracted from the *Institutes* and available from Chapel Library.

CHAPTER 24

Blood and Violence in the Body of Christ

A Spiritual Battle

One of the most shocking realities in the study of Church history is the amount of killing and the number of violent acts that professing Christians have perpetrated on one another and upon their enemies. While many people embraced Christianity and quietly lived out the ethics of the kingdom of God, in each succeeding century a scarlet thread of bloody violence was also woven into the fabric of faith by fallen humanity, struggling to implement high and noble ideals. This part of the story of the Church must not be ignored. It must not be glossed over. It must not be justified as being acceptable behavior because the Church was caught up in turbulent times of social upheaval.

The search for vindication for engaging in brutality, in the name of the Prince of Peace, only reveals the truth that the heart is deceitful above all things and desperately wicked (Jer 17:9). Violence begets violence. Unfortunately, more often than not, the origin of conflict cannot be identified so that balanced blame can be assessed. Once name-calling starts in the name of Christ, once persecutions are practiced, once fines for religious infractions are levied, once imprisonments are implemented, once burning and beheadings begin, an objective observer has trouble discovering the righteousness of anyone in the carnage that is left behind. The Church must recognize this dark side of itself and assess what is happening, even if the truth condemns (1 Pet 4:17).

In the search for the origin of violence (Jas 4:1), the Bible reveals that the affairs of man are part of the great angelic conflict. The Apostle Paul reminds the Church that, "we wrestle not against flesh and blood, but against principalities, against powers, against the rulers of the darkness of this world, against spiritual wickedness in high places" (Eph 6:12). The demonic servants of the devil do not want to see peace among men, and so there is a spiritual stirring up of trouble (2 Cor 11:15). The Scriptures are often taken and twisted by misguided souls who have not learned to handle properly the Word of Truth (2 Tim 2:15; 2 Pet 1:16). Error rides securely on the back of truth.

The Peasants Misunderstand

When Martin Luther defied the Church and challenged the Holy Roman Emperor without impunity, the dams of discipline and awe among the peasantry were broken. The news spread from serf to serf. Every man was a priest! There was freedom for the Christian man in the kingdom of Christ!

Other revolutionary ideas followed. The circulation of the New Testament by way of the invention of the printing press, helped to destroy political, as well as accepted religious, orthodoxy. Individuals could read for themselves that the practices of the Church were far removed from the teaching of Scriptures. The early Church shared and held all possessions in common. Christ had compassion for the poor and the oppressed. There was the promise of a new heaven and a new earth, in which righteousness dwells. It was not wrong to dream of a time when the "poor... would inherit the earth" (Matt 5:3, 5).

All of this was good and true. Society should be changed. Evil should be challenged. However, what was not true is that the Scriptures provided people the right to rebel, with hatred and murderous intent, against ordained authority (Rom 13:1; Matt 22:21). The peasants either did not, or chose not to, understand that Christ did not come to conquer this world with a sword. Rather, He came to conquer the hearts of men by dying on a cross!

Soon after the Reformation began in 1517, pamphlets began to appear in Germany with a common theme: revolt. It was argued that the peasants must arm themselves and revolt against the clergy and the state. Luther and the Reformers were not the cause of the willingness of the peasants to revolt, for they had just grievances. But the new principles of the Reformation, when misapplied, provided fuel for the flames of discontent.

Thomas Müntzer

Leaders of the peasants surfaced. One such man was Thomas Müntzer (c. 1490–1525). Müntzer, born at Stolberg, Germany, studied at Leipzig and Frankfurt "an der Oder." Though a student of medieval realism, he was well read in the Scriptures, knowing Greek and Hebrew. He also enjoyed reading the German mystics. With the help of Martin Luther, Müntzer was placed as a minister at Zwickau in 1520. However, he soon managed to alienate the artisans in the city, who wanted a greater role in government. He also managed to estrange those in government, who wanted to be free of ecclesiastical powers. By 1522, Müntzer had been asked to leave.

His travels finally brought him as parish priest to Allstedt in 1523, where he promoted liturgical reform by introducing German liturgies, psalms, and hymns. Müntzer preached the doctrine of salvation by grace through faith alone. But then he went beyond the Gospel to teach that military might should be used to convert the masses. In a sermon on Daniel 2, Müntzer insisted the dukes of Saxony use force in forming the Church, so that salvation could come to the common man, after which there would be a democratic theocracy established. When called upon to explain before the Weimar court just what all of this meant, Müntzer left Allstedt and went to Muhlhausen, Nuremberg, Basel, and then back to Muhlhausen.

During this time he had a change of heart as to the amount of power earthly princes should hold over people. Müntzer sided with the peasants in their open revolt against established authority. In the free city of Muhlhausen in Thuringia, Müntzer found people willing to follow him. Heinrich Pfeiffer, an ex-monk and coworker, had already aroused the passions of the people. Müntzer would exploit them.

On March 17, 1525, violence erupted. Armed followers of Pfeiffer and Müntzer successfully overtook the city. An "Eternal Council" was established to rule Muhlhausen. Monks were driven out of the cells, and the property of the Church was confiscated. But no communist commonwealth was ever established.

Instead, leading citizens of the town sent for imperial troops to regain control. Müntzer once more organized the peasants to resist the coming conflict. "Forward!" he cried; "forward while the fire is hot! Let your swords be ever warm with blood." But the brave words were not enough. The passion of the peasants was not enough. The city was retaken and the peasant revolt was crushed in Muhlhausen. Müntzer's body was not allowed to be buried; it was hung to rot on spikes. Those who had lived by the sword, died by the sword (Luke 21:24).

The Peasants' War Continues

In the weeks and months to follow, town after town became a battle-ground as The Peasants' Revolt grew in strength. Martin Luther saw his world literally going up in flames. The smell of death and destruction was in the air. From the press of Wittenburg, in the middle of May, 1525, Luther issued the pamphlet *Against the Robbing and Murdering Hordes of Peasants*. Luther was angry and did not conceal an ounce of his wrath. The vehemence of the pamphlet shocked prince and peasant alike. Siding with the imperiled princes, Luther wrote, "Any man against whom sedition can be proved is outside the law of God and the Empire, so that the first who can slay him is doing right and well." That was just the beginning of a verbal diatribe against the peasants, who were labeled with many unflattering terms.

The peasants were shocked. They felt betrayed. They thought Luther would understand. But Luther showed no mercy to them. Mercy, Luther insisted, was reserved to Christians in private acts of charity. The state must protect all the people and show no mercy. To allow the peasants to go unchallenged would be the end of civilization. Left to their passions and ignorance, the peasants would overturn all law, destroy government, demolish the means of production, and disrupt distribution of goods and services in Germany. They must be killed as mad dogs, said Luther, just as a mad dog will kill a man.

Many of the peasants felt that Luther and Lutheranism had justified their cause, aroused them to hope and action, and then deserted them in the hour of need. Some grew angry. Others grew bitter. Many returned to the Catholic Church. Some turned to alternative groups such as the Anabaptists.

The Anabaptists

Anabaptist was the name of contempt given to a portion of professing Christians in the sixteenth century who existed outside the Catholic Church, and who operated independently of the Reformation movement. The term "Anabaptist" simply refers to one who "baptizes again." Anabaptism was considered by its many critics to be a dangerous movement within the body of Christ. It was said to be full of heretical concepts and was known to have ruthless leaders. However, those who were attracted to the movement were impressed by the personal piety that was encouraged, the self-sacrifice that was evident, the hard work insisted upon, and the frugality that allowed others to be helped through acts of charity and kindness born of a communal spirit. In addition, no one was to be sued or taken to court, and no oaths were to be uttered.

Anabaptism began formally in Neustadgasse, Switzerland in 1525, when individuals formulated new ideas departing from those taught by the Reformer Huldreich Zwingli. Men such as Conrad Grebal (1498–1526) and Felix Manz (c. 1498–1527) were among those who proposed new and radical ideas. In his formative years, Grebal received a good education that included study in Basel, Vienna, and Paris. While living in Zurich, he embraced the ministry of Zwingli. With Felix Manz, Grebal joined with Zwingli in the study of the Greek New Testament. There was great excitement over the plans to continue to reform Zurich. Reformation had already begun in 1519.

But then a change took place among the men. Grebal and Manz came to believe that the Reformation leaders of the city of Zurich were not doing enough to advance the kingdom of God. They argued with Zwingli that neither prudence, nor fear of men, was pleasing to the Lord. More radical measures had to be taken, though in a non-violent way. Besides, there was no essential difference they could discern between having a Christian government and having a non-Christian government. It would be better for the Church and State to be separate. Other changes should also be made in order to have a Church based upon the New Testament pattern. For Grebal this meant a rejection of singing in public worship.

In addition, the emerging leaders of a counter movement within the Reformed circles had come to believe that the name "Christian" should not be applied to all people indiscriminately through a baptism at birth. The title of "Christian" should be reserved for those who had professed Christ as Lord and Savior and then were re-baptized (being first baptized as infants). Others agreed. In 1524, in communities just outside of Zurich, Wilhelm Reublin and Johannes Brotli were found to be preaching against the baptizing of infants. They were ordered to cease their teachings and not to gather groups together for worship.

Opposition to the Anabaptists

Because Zwingli himself opposed these new views and practices, conflict was inevitable. Fellowship with Grebal and Manz was broken. The small group of Anabaptists that they led in Zurich decided to take radical steps. First, they would meet in secret for Bible study, prayer, and communion. Second, they would re-baptize each other in order to establish the true Church once more on earth. Third, they would commission one another to become tireless ministers, missionaries, and shepherds, thereby building up the body of Christ on earth. Finally, they would expect and accept physical persecution, which they believed would shortly come. They would not use any earthly weapons to defend themselves against personal attacks, but rely upon the Lord for divine deliverance.

The persecution came. Many in that first group were put in prison. After a few months of trying to stay together despite hardships and secret meetings, the assembly disbanded. But the movement did not die; many of the new ideas had found a following. Grebal, who continued to preach outside of Zurich in other communities, enjoyed great success.

People could understand the concept of sinners being found in the midst of the saints, because of the indiscriminate policy of baptizing infants and confirming the unconverted. People could understand how it was possible for those who had grown up in the Church, to turn away from the teachings of Christ and live a life contrary to the Gospel, all the while feeling safe and secure. People could understand how others could be religious, but not righteous. People could understand how others could feel no need to change, because they believed they were already part of the Church of the redeemed. The ideas of the Anabaptists found fertile spiritual soil in which to grow.

Unfortunately for the Anabaptist movement, Grebal died of the plague in 1526, after suffering imprisonment for his beliefs. On January 5, 1527, Felix Manz, who had also found success in attracting followers, was publicly executed in Zurich by drowning. He had been charged with the crime of re-baptizing professing Christians. Manz became the first martyr of the Swiss Brethren.

The Movement Grows

As might be expected, the death of Felix Manz did not stop the rapid spread of the movement throughout Europe. Other leaders emerged in various places to carry on the causes of separating the Church from the State, and of re-baptizing those who professed faith in Christ. One such man in the south of Germany was Hans Denck (1500–1527).

Denck was born in Upper Bavaria into a well to do, God-fearing family which was able to give him a good education. From 1517–1519, Denck studied Latin, Greek, and Hebrew while reading the mystical and humanistic manuscripts that were available. In 1523, he was appointed headmaster of the reputable St. Sebald School in Nuremberg. But then Denck was expelled from Nuremberg on January 21, 1525.

He had been found to be too critical of Lutheran doctrine. Leaving behind a wife and child, Denck lived the life of a fugitive. He went to Augsburg, where he became an Anabaptist.

From city to city Denck moved, winning converts to the Anabaptist movement. The Strassburg Reformer Martin Bucer began to call him the "pope of the Anabaptists." Denck died of the plague in Basel in November 1527. Perhaps his most important legacy for the Anabaptist cause was that he baptized Hans Hutt (d. 1527), who would prove to be one of the most vigorous and successful of the Anabaptist leaders in Austria and Moravia. Hutt is credited with making more converts to Anabaptism in the south of Europe than all the other Anabaptists combined, thereby earning the title "Apostle of Austria."

Because the Anabaptist movement was new and diversified, strange practices and doctrines emerged in the name of spirituality. For example, because the Bible said that people must become as little children in order to enter the kingdom of heaven, some began to behave like little children in a literal manner. They played with toys, drooled, and babbled like babies. One Anabaptist from Thuringia claimed to be the Son of God. In addition to such nonsense, violence and bloodshed followed the Anabaptist movement for years to come.

Transformed by the Power of God

Fortunately, there is another side to the Anabaptist story. A change did come to this movement under the guidance of men such as Menno Simons. In 1524, Simons was priest at a Catholic Church in the province of Friesland. But there he began to question the doctrine of transubstantiation. The Scriptures were sought afresh. Church history was studied. The writings of Luther and other Reformers were read. Finally, in 1536, Simons left the Catholic Church and joined with the Frisian Anabaptists. A gifted speaker and organizer, Simons traveled widely and attracted many followers.

In time, others took to calling his converts *Mennonites*, a term which has survived to the present day. Menno preached the peace of God and the love of Christ, and these replaced militant passion. Industry, prosperity, and respect came to the Anabaptist movement. Today, direct descendants of Anabaptists number more than 730,000 in 57 countries. There are 21 distinct religious groups that claim to be able to trace their origins back to the Anabaptist movement, among them Mennonites, Amish, Hutterites, Mennonite Brethren, and Brethren in Christ. A radical movement was transformed to become the cornerstone for kindness and Christian charity, while the major Christian doctrines were embraced: God as Father, the deity of Christ, the true Church being a body of converted and baptized believers, the Bible as the infallible and authoritative Word of God, and the second coming of Christ. Once more, the grace of God had redeemed a part of the world (2 Cor 5:17).

CHAPTER 25

Reformation Faith is Found in France

The Need for Reform

As the Spirit of the Living God moved upon the hearts of people in Germany, so God was working in the lives of many in France. There was a growing desire for spiritual renewal. Over the years, people had begun to look at the Church with a more discerning eye. Some had become concerned because the papacy was completely under the domination of the French kings for about seventy years. This "Babylonian Captivity" (1309–1376) decreased the prestige of the Church.

Then there was the Great Schism (1378–1417) when the world had two popes; one in Rome and one in Avignon, France. The popes denounced and damned, excommunicated and anathematized[1] each other, in a desperate struggle for power and prestige. A Church council was held in Pisa in 1409 to end the Great Schism. Instead, things were only made worse when the current reigning popes were deposed and Alexander V was appointed to the office. Now the world had three popes—and a very perplexed Church!

The deplorable state of spiritual leadership manifested in the highest echelons of the visible Kingdom of Christ filtered down to corrupt the clergy and the laity. Sincere converts to Christ wanted nothing to do with the blatant expressions of sins that had become all too acceptable inside organized religion. Something had to be changed. Christians knew that Christ came to save His people from their sins (Matt 1:21). Jesus did not come to leave souls chained in the kingdom of darkness (2 Cor 5:17).

---

[1] anathematized – cursed.

Unless spiritual reformation came to the Church in France, radical groups would continue to survive—such as the Albigenses in the southern part of the country. The Albigenses were named after the town of Albi.

During part of their early history in the 11th through 13th centuries, the Albigenses embraced Manichean doctrines and practices. The predictable result was a mystical asceticism, based on the concept that matter is evil and light is the only good. As heretical as these concepts were, the Albigenses were ruthlessly persecuted for two other beliefs: their criticism of the clergy, and their teaching that they were the only true church. Rome would not tolerate such a rival concept, and sought to annihilate the Albigenses.

The Waldenses

Another radical group making their presence known in France was the Waldenses. Unlike the Albigenses, the Waldenses consisted of what amounted to be a Protestant community, which was Calvinistic in principle[2] prior to the Reformation.

The history of this people is clearly identified with Peter Waldo, who was converted in A.D. 1170. After giving up his goods to the poor and preaching a life of self-abnegation, Peter Waldo died in A.D. 1217. His hardy mountaineer followers survived to become known as "The Poor Men of Lyon." They had severe demands for membership: rejection of private property, a temperate way of living, separation of husband and wife, and a willingness to fast three days in the week.

On the positive side, in doctrine the Waldenses denounced indulgences, purgatory, and masses for the dead. They said that the sacraments were not effective when administered by unworthy priests. And they also insisted that the apostles, and not Peter Waldo, originated their beliefs and practices.

What attracted people to these radical groups was not so much their doctrinal distinctive, but the seriousness of a spiritual life with integrity. The Waldenses in particular gained a following because they embraced a simple and literal belief in the Bible. This belief gave a holy boldness to condemn the Church's lust of power and lust of money. The Waldenses lived a life of poverty that provided a feeling of moral superiority—and the right to speak against the Church's wealth, pride, and worldly pleasure. As preachers of apostolic purity, they rejected Rome and its papal claim.

---

[2] Calvinistic in principle – that is, they believed in the sovereign rule of God over all things in the affairs of men, that men are to live a holy life separate from the wickedness of worldly pleasures, and that the Bible is authoritative and literally true.

The Waldenses helped others to see the need for independence from Rome, in order to enjoy personal peace in the quest for Christian perfection.

Jacques d'E'taples Lefevre

The movement towards religious reform in some parts of France found hearts ready to receive the widening influence of more prominent spiritual leaders such as Lefevre, Luther, and Calvin.

Jacques Lefevre (Jacobus Stapulensis Faber, 1455–1536) was born in Picardy, France. After being trained as a humanist scholar, he settled in Paris as a teacher in the University (in 1492). With 300,000 people, Paris was one of the largest cities in Europe. Lefevre's fame spread widely, thereby attracting many students, including William Farel—who would help to lead the Reformation in Geneva and Neuchatel.

As an independent thinker, Lefevre was critical of the Church of Rome. He also openly proclaimed the doctrine of justification by faith. In 1512 Lefevre published his *Commentary on the Epistle to the Romans* in Latin. Other important works followed, each of which emphasized the free grace of a free Gospel. For such thoughts the Sorbonne, the school of theology that dominated the University of Paris, condemned Lefevre as a heretic. He fled to Strassburg in 1525. Margaret, the sister of King Francis I, heard of his plight and came to his rescue. She had read some of the Lutheran literature, and endorsed the attacks upon the immorality and greed of the clergy.

While Lefevre never severed his relationship with the Roman Catholic Church, he did influence the thinkers of the Reformation through his high regard for the Bible as the only true guide to eternal life, and by his view on the doctrine of the Lord's Supper. Lefevre believed that Christ is present in the Eucharist by His own good pleasure, and not because of any priestly transubstantiation of bread and wine.

Lefevre knew that these doctrines were unacceptable to Rome. He also knew that his views were divisive. Still, Lefevre longed for the unity of the Catholic Church and, like Erasmus (c. 1466–1536), would not leave it. He died at the age of eighty-seven in 1536.

Though Lefevre refused to be totally identified with the Reformation, there was no turning back. In the providence of the Lord, the works of Martin Luther and the leadership of men like John Calvin would guarantee that spiritual renewal in France continued. Though he had fled from France to Geneva for safety, Calvin was able to keep in close contact with developments in all parts of Europe. He was also able to maintain an extensive correspondence with Protestant ministers and missionaries in Catholic territories—including France.

The Death of Jean Leclerc

The Reformers knew that neither King Francis I nor the Sorbonne could halt the flow of Reformation ideas from crossing the Rhine and coming into France from Frankfurt, Strassburg, and Basel. The writings of the Reformers were anxiously desired by workingmen, who were willing to give their lives to be free of the doctrines of the Catholic Church. One such man was Jean Leclerc, a worker of wool in the town of Meaux. When Bishop Briconnet published on the doors of his church cathedral a bull of indulgences, Leclerc torn it down and put in its place a sign which said that the pope was Anti-Christ. Leclerc was arrested and punished by being branded on the forehead in 1525. Though he moved to Metz, unbridled zeal motivated Leclerc to smash religious images before a public procession could offer incense to religious idols of the Church. Leclerc was once more arrested. His right hand was cut off. His face was disfigured. His head was bound tight with a band of red hot iron. Before he could lose total consciousness, Leclerc was burned at the stake (1526). The Catholic Church grew more forceful in the persecution of opponents. Between 1526 and 1527, several more Protestants were executed for "blasphemy," which meant they denied Mary and that the departed saints had the power to intercede in prayer.

The Cruelty of a King

Watching all of this happen was Francis I (king, 1515–1547). For many years the king vacillated between tolerance for the Protestants in his kingdom, and the power of the Church. He knew that his sister was religiously inclined to show favor to the Protestants. But then, she did not have to depend upon the Church for funds and authority. In the end, Francis came down on the side of the Catholic Church. He may have been frightened by the Peasant's Revolt in Germany to allow too many Reformation ideas to flourish in France. The Protestant cause seemed to promote social unrest. He ordered it stamped out.

Between November 10, 1534 and May 5, 1535, twenty-four Protestants were taken to stakes in Paris and burned alive. This became too much even for the pope.

Paul III rebuked Francis for needless harshness, and ordered him to end the ill-treatment of his subjects.

Taking advantage of the reprieve, the Waldenses, quietly existing in some villages along the Durance River in Provence in 1530, began to correspond with Reformers in Germany and Switzerland. To their detriment, this activity was discovered and reported to Rome. A papal legate was sent to examine the situation. The Inquisition was established. The Waldenses appealed to Francis who ordered that the prosecution cease (1533). But Cardinal de Tournon was determined that the prosecution should not cease. He charged the Waldenses with treason against the government. He then persuaded the ever-vacillating King to sign a decree on January 1, 1545 that all of the Waldenses found guilty of heresy should be eliminated. Mass executions began. Blood flowed. In the one week of April 12–18, several villages were burned to the ground. In one village alone 800 men, women, and children were killed. In two months, the number killed rose to more than 3,000. Twenty-two of the thirty villages were destroyed. Seven hundred men were hanged. The Protestants in Switzerland and Germany heard of these horrors and vigorously protested. In contrast, Spain sent Francis messages of commendation, and the persecutions continued. A year later, a small Lutheran gathering was found in Meaux under the pastoral guidance of Pierre Leclerc, brother of the branded Jean. Eight had their tongues tore out; it was October 7, 1546.

The Gallic Confession of Faith

Despite these acts of violence, the Protestant Church continued to exist and grow in Lyons, Orleans, Reims, and in a multitude of other towns and cities. The true Church militant would yet be triumphant in France. By 1559, fully one-sixth of the population of France was considered to be Protestant. This is why a synod was allowed to be held in Paris in May of that year. At this synod a creed was adopted known as the *Gallic Confession*. The Confession had initially been prepared by John Calvin himself and his pupil, De Chandieu.

The Confession opens with an explanation to the King that it is from "The French subjects who wish to live in the purity of the Gospel of our Lord Jesus Christ." Then, in the *Forty Articles of Faith*, the ethics and beliefs of the French Church are set forth regarding God the Father, the Holy Scriptures, the Trinity, sin, salvation, justification, the sacraments, Church, government, and Christian duties.

Having been revised and approved by the Synod of Paris, this Confession was later delivered by Beza to Charles IX in 1561. It was then adopted by the Synod of La Rochelle in 1571 and solemnly sanctioned by Henry IV (reigned, 1589–1610). What a wonderful testimony this Gallic Confession is to the grace of God. The Protestant saints in France had been found faithful. They had paid the price. They had traveled a long, violent, and often bloody road. But then they were justly rewarded. The day came when Protestants were able to shout from the rooftops and openly confess their faith in the only Savior of souls, the Lord Jesus Christ. What greater privilege could any Christian want?

The Reformation Reaches the Netherlands

Many of the spiritual conditions that mandated a need for religious reform in Germany and France, could also be found in the Netherlands (Holland and Belgium together at that time), which was then controlled by Spain. The existence of absentee bishops, worldly clergymen, idle monks, and immoral priests necessitated Church reform. Erasmus wrote brilliant satires against the Catholic Church in such works as *The Praise of Folly* and *Familiar Colloquies*. Still, it would not be easy to accomplish ecclesiastical reform. In addition to the powerful hold of Catholic dogma upon the hearts of people, the conflicting ideas of the Reformers were present in the general population. Some people wanted to follow Luther, and others Zwingli. Still others were Anabaptists. Someone was needed to help bring order back to society.

Thoughtful heads turned toward Switzerland. Emerging Church leaders went to Geneva to learn from Calvin what principles and practices to implement. Among the many suggestions offered was to write a formal confession of faith. This suggestion was accepted, and in 1561 Guido de Bres drafted the *Belgic Confession*. It is also known as *The Netherlands Confession*, or the *Thirty-seven Articles*.

Two years later, the *Heidelberg Catechism* was published and became very popular. This Calvinist work had originally been written in 1562 by Zacharias Ursinus, a professor at the Heidelberg University, and Caspar Olevianus, the court minister at Heidelberg, at the insistence of the German Elector of the Palatinate, Frederick III "The Pious" (1559–1576). It was the desire of Frederick to use the catechism in schools in order to move his territories from Lutheranism to the Reformed faith and practice of Calvin and Zwingli.[3]

---

[3] Gradually the term *reformed* had come to be associated with them, and not with Luther.

The *Belgic Confession*, the *Heidelberg Catechism*, and the *Genevan Psalter*, translated by Dathenus, became the foundation documents for the Church in the Netherlands. A strong foundation of faith was needed, because formal Catholic opposition to the growing Protestant community continued. Charles V of Spain, and then his son Philip II (b. 1527; reigned 1556–1598), tried to stop the drive toward political freedom and Protestantism. A formal Inquisition was initiated in the Netherlands. At times, the persecution was so intense that any Protestant synod had to meet elsewhere, as one did in 1571 in Emden, in East Friesland near the border in Germany.

While the spiritual dream continued for a reformed Church, the physical sword of warfare was picked up and wielded to bring it all to pass. William of Orange organized armed resistance by Dutch patriots, who fought on land and sea, being aided by a navy supplied by Queen Elizabeth. At one point he saved the city of Amsterdam from Spanish siege, by breaking the North Sea dikes and flooding the surrounding approaches with water. Although William was assassinated in 1584, the battles continued, until finally the Dutch were able to force all foreigners to leave in 1609. In 1648, the *Peace of Westphalia* formally recognized the independence of the Netherlands and the official establishment of the Reformed Church.

CHAPTER 26

John Knox and the Scottish Reformation
A.D. 1513–1572

A Spark Ignites Scotland

The professing Church of Jesus Christ in Scotland needed a spiritual reformation as much as the Church in other parts of Europe. The clergy were greedy. A papal envoy at the dawn of the sixteenth century reported to the pope that the income of the Church in Scotland was more than all other income combined. The corrupt clergy encouraged the sins of the laity, which flourished in the absence of truth, accountability, and the fear of God.

There had been attempts at reform, but they met with great resistance. In 1433, Paul Crawar was convicted by the Church and burned at the stake for bringing into the country the doctrines of John Wycliffe and John Huss. In 1494, thirty of the followers of Huss were brought before the Bishop of Glasgow, and accused of speaking against all of the following: religious relics and images, the confession, the ordination of priests, their power to forgive sins, the doctrine of transubstantiation, purgatory, indulgences, masses for the dead, the celibacy of the priesthood, and the authority of the pope. Though the men retracted in fear, the truth could not be suppressed.

By 1523, the writings of Martin Luther had found their way into the country. A copy of Wycliffe's New Testament was translated into the Scottish language, to the delight of many and to the horror of Rome. Men like Patrick Hamilton, who preached the doctrine of justification by faith, were invited by James Beaton, Archbishop of St. Andrews, to come and defend their position. Hamilton did in 1528—and was burned to death for his efforts. Two other "professors," as the early

Reformers were called, were burned in 1534. In 1544, four men were hanged and a woman was drowned for their faith.

Because these incidents were few and separate from each other, there was little public outcry. Something more drastic had to happen to capture the minds and imagination of the masses. The hanging of George Wishart did just that. His death marked the first telling event of the Scottish Reformation.

During the 1540s, George Wishart was among those brave souls who traveled and preached the message of God's redeeming, sovereign grace. John Knox heard Wishart preach and joined his happy band, as a body guard able to wield a two-handed sword. For five weeks Knox traveled with Wishart. Then Wishart sent him away, because he knew that arrest was imminent.

Cardinal David Beaton, the new archbishop of St. Andrews, ordered the arrest to take place in January, 1546. After Wishart was found guilty of heresy, he was strangled and then his body burned on March 1. But it was too much. John Knox summarized the feelings of many when he wrote that George Wishart was, "a man of such graces as before him were never heard within this realm, yea, and are rare to be found yet in any man." His death would be avenged.

The Castilians and Their Capture

On May 29, 1546, a group of nobles and criminals forced their way into the Cardinal's palace bedroom where he was entertaining his mistress, Marion Ogilvy. Beaton pleaded that he should not be killed because he was a priest. John Leslie and Peter Carmichael were not impressed with that fact, and they stabbed him with their small daggers. The third assassin, James Melville, called upon the Cardinal to repent of the execution of Wishart; then he ran him through twice. With his dying breath Beaton cried out, "I am a priest, fye, fye. All is gone." His body was first disgraced and then thrown into the same dungeon which had not so long ago held George Wishart. "Now, because the weather was hot," Knox later wrote, "it was thought best, to keep him from stinking, to give him great salt enough . . . to await what courtesies his brethren the bishops could prepare for him. These things we write merrily." Knox approved of the murder; he believed that God used men as the instruments of His wrath and judgment.

The death of the Cardinal might have vindicated the execution of Wishart, but it also immediately launched a revolt against the Catholic policy that Beaton had made with the French. The Cardinal had negotiated a treaty with the French to keep the

Protestant English from coming into Scotland. Opposed to this policy were the patriots who were known as *Castilians*. Because Knox was sympathetic to the Castilians, he too became a wanted man.

Following the murder of Cardinal Beaton, the Castilians fled to the castle of St. Andrews on the coast of Scotland. Knox went to be with the band of warriors. Everyone there believed that Henry VIII would send forces to rescue and protect them, since they were Protestant and sympathetic to his rule. But Henry sent no help. Instead, in July, a French fleet sailed up and bombarded St. Andrews Castle. After four weeks, those inside the castle were overpowered and imprisoned as galley slaves. John Knox was among those taken captive.

Life as a Galley Slave

A typical French galley ship of this period was between 100 feet and 150 feet long, 30 feet wide, and stood about 6 feet above the water line. It was not seaworthy in rough weather; in cold weather the ships would dock. About 150 galley slaves rowed, six to the oar. The 25 oars, about 45 feet long, passed through the sides of the ship. When not involved with other duties on board a sailing vessel, the slaves were chained to the oars. There they sat in uncomfortable uniforms—consisting of a coarse brown tunic, a vest, two shirts, and two pairs of canvas trousers. There was a red cap for the head but no shoes for the feet. Under the watchful eye of the comite (the captain of the guards), the prisoners worked with the threat of the whip of the souscomites (guards in the galley) not far away.

At 33 years of age and in good health, John Knox survived this nineteen month ordeal, and even managed to express some acts of passive defiance. On one occasion he was exhorted to take communion. A little statue of Mary was passed among the crew members to be kissed. When no one was watching, Knox threw the statue overboard. He wrote that no one tried to force anyone to submit to "idolatry" after that.

Though no English forces had prevented their capture, the English government took a great interest in the plight of the galley prisoners, and sought their release. It may have been at the request of King Edward VI that Knox and his fellow prisoners were freed from the galley *Notre Dame* in February 1549.

Marriage and an Unusual Mother-in-law

With gratitude in his heart, Knox made his way to England, where he became a Protestant clergyman. Knox was placed as the minister in Berwick-on-Tweed. It was there that he first befriended forty-five year old Elizabeth Bowes, who had five sons, ten daughters, and a Catholic husband.

Under the preaching of Knox, Mrs. Bowes was converted to the Protestant faith. She was very pleased when her fifth daughter Marjory (Margaret), agreed in 1553 to become the wife of the pastor who had led her back to Christ. In contrast, her husband Richard was not at all happy with the proposed marriage. But there was nothing that could be done. The wedding finally took place around 1555, when John Knox was about fifty years old.

The situation became more complicated when Mrs. Bowes left her husband in 1556, in order to live with Marjory and John in Geneva, where the couple had moved. Four years later, Marjory died (1560). Though Knox remarried, Mrs. Bowes remained with him and his new bride. While no unethical behavior was ever discovered, this unusual arrangement provided his critics with material to use in slanderous comments. Knox remained silent and maintained his relationship with Mrs. Bowes.

Because he was so close to his mother-in-law, Knox was able to confide in her freely. The ardent reformer was acutely aware of his own faults and failures. While preaching to others, Knox believed he was preaching to himself.

> Although I never lack the presence and plain image of my own wretched infirmity, yet seeing that sin so manifestly abounds in all estates, I am compelled to thunder out the threatening of God against the obstinate rebels. In doing whereof—albeit, as God knoweth, I am no malicious nor obstinate sinner—I sometimes am wounded, knowing myself to be criminal and guilty ... in all things ... that I reprehend in others. Judge not, mother, that I write these things, debasing myself otherwise than I am. No, I am worse than my pen can express.[1]

The "Black Rubric"

While the future of marriage and unusual family relations awaited Knox, the immediate relationship with the English congregation of Berwick had deteriorated

---

[1] Letter to Mrs. Elizabeth Bowes, June 1553.

in 1549, despite his obvious abilities to preach. By all accounts, the sermons of Knox were electrifying. After calmly exegeting a biblical passage for half an hour, he was prone to make personal application. At that point he would become "active and vigorous" according to one hearer. "He made me so to grew [quake] and tremble, that I could not hold pen to write."

There was fire in the soul of this man. There was a religious and patriotic passion that burned in his breast. Knox could not, and would not, keep quiet—especially about controversial subjects. For example, in 1550 Knox was called upon to defend his attacks upon the Catholic mass before Tunstall, the bishop of Durham. Fearing controversy, the bishop reassigned Knox to the south of England. There, Knox began to preach against the Anabaptists. Then he found fault with the liturgy in the *Book of Common Prayer* (1552), for it required those receiving communion to kneel while partaking of the elements.

Knox was opposed to people kneeling for communion. He taught that a rubric (a bold heading) should be included in the *Book of Common Prayer*, stating that kneeling did not mean belief in "the bodily presence of Christ in the elements." This became known as the "black rubric." Knox's criticism of the *Book of Common Prayer* alienated even Archbishop Cranmer. But Knox did not care. He would preach the truth as he understood it, and suffer the consequences for his faith.

Mary Tudor

The doctrinal concerns of Knox were compounded by political considerations when King Edward VI (b. 1537), son of Henry VIII and Jane Seymour, died on July 6, 1553 at the tender age of sixteen. His half sister Mary Tudor, a devout Roman Catholic, was crowned Queen by Stephen Gardiner, Bishop of Winchester and a valued advisor. Mary was determined to return the Church of England to Rome, even if it meant official religious persecution of the Protestants. Because of this she is often called "Bloody Mary."

"Bloody Mary" caused the Church of England to hold Latin services once more, while forbidding Protestant doctrine and worship. Next, she married a Catholic, Philip II of Spain. The marriage proved to be a disaster: Philip returned to Spain, and there were no children.

Meanwhile, with Mary's approval, Gardiner began to prosecute Protestants as heretics. The first Protestant execution was that of John Rogers in February, 1555. Rogers was guilty of translating the Scriptures into the language of the people.

Other Reformers followed him to heaven. When Hugh Latimer and Nicholas Ridley disputed with Roman Catholic theologians on the doctrine of the Mass, they were placed in the Tower of London. After being tried for heresy, they were burned at the stake on October 16, 1555. When the bonfire was finally lit, Latimer called out: "Be of good comfort, Master Ridley, and play the man. We shall this day light such a candle by God's grace in England as, I trust, shall never be put out!" It is said that Latimer died quickly while Ridley suffered slowly and with great pain. Foreseeing that such persecutions would take place, Knox had fled England to become a refugee in Dieppe, France, in January of 1554.

Compliments for Calvin

Safely on the mainland, Knox wrote many open letters exhorting the Protestants to stand firm. He then went to Geneva in 1554, where he came under the strong influence of John Calvin. His heart was stirred at what might be when the Church was able to righteously influence the government. Knox described Geneva as "the most perfect school of Christ that ever was on earth since the days of the Apostles."

From Geneva, Knox received a call to minister to the English refugee congregation in Frankfurt. Calvin encouraged Knox to accept the German pastorate, which he did. However, once more his confrontational spirit was manifested when a number of the English refugees in Frankfurt wanted to use the English *Book of Common Prayer* in the hour of worship. Knox refused. When a compromise order of service could not be reached, Knox was ordered by the city authorities not to preach. Disgusted, Knox left Frankfurt and returned to Geneva, where he became the co-pastor of a small English congregation of some two hundred souls.

Meanwhile, in Scotland, the Reformation efforts continued. The work was made more difficult because after the death of James V in 1542, Scotland was ruled by his wife, Mary of Guise. Mary, of noble French birth, was sympathetic to the Catholic faith. Her daughter, also named Mary, was sent to France to be educated and married to the Dauphin. In light of these things, it was obvious to some of the Church leaders that the presence of Knox was needed for ultimate success against Catholicism. In August, 1555, Knox returned to Scotland and spent nine months preaching in the newly emerging Protestant congregations in Edinburgh, Dundee, St. Andrews, Brechin, and Perth. His popularity caused the Catholic bishops to become alarmed. In May, 1556, he was summoned to Edinburgh to face spurious legal proceedings.

Although the summons was cancelled by Queen Mary of Guise, Knox felt compelled to leave the country and return to Geneva. Here, he believed he would be left alone. But it was not to be. Many of the Protestants in Scotland still wanted Knox to lead them, and he in turn wanted to bring reform to the Church. Beyond that, Knox wanted to reform the government of the land as well.

A Political Mistake

Knox believed that political and religious reform could best be done if women were not allowed to rule. Appealing to select Scriptures and the early church fathers, Knox published a pamphlet in 1558 against all female monarchies in general, and the rule of Catholic Mary Tudor in particular. The title of the pamphlet was *The First Blast of the Trumpet against the Monstrous Regiment of Women*. It was a political mistake, as Knox later conceded, saying "My *First Blast* hath blown from me all my friends in England." Now numbered among his most bitter enemies was the Protestant Queen, Elizabeth I, who had suddenly been elevated to the English throne.

Banished from England by the new Queen, Knox set sail for Scotland. In May, 1559, he arrived ready to preach. Within days, he spoke at Perth against the sin of idolatry. After the service, a riot erupted. Altars were destroyed, images were demolished, and houses of worship were burned. The regent Queen Mary of Guise threatened to deploy troops to restore the peace. Both Protestant and Catholics began to take up arms and stake out territories. Mary entered Perth only to be met with resistance. Deciding that she could not win the battle, Mary signed a truce on May 29, 1559.

Knox, savoring the taste of victory, left Perth and moved on to St. Andrews. There, he again preached against "all monuments of idolatry," much to the dismay of many. Predictably, social unrest followed. Catholic churches were entered, images were taken by force and destroyed before the eyes of the Catholic clergy.

It was all too much for the delicate Queen, who really had no real heart for religious hatred and bloodshed. Extremely ill, Mary of Guise fled to Leith, and tried to delay the victorious and rampaging Protestants with negotiations, until help could arrive from France. While she waited, the Protestants moved to win their own political and military support from Elizabeth of England. Soon, an English fleet in the Firth of Forth (a narrow bay surrounded by mountains) blocked any landing of French troops to help Mary. Having returned to the castle of Edinburgh, she wanted the nightmare of civil and religious unrest to end. Knowing the end of her illness was near, she kissed her retinue one by one—and then laid down to die. On June 10, 1560, the Queen was dead.

Her troops had been left in the city blockaded and starving, and they soon surrendered. A measure of peace finally was made possible when the *Treaty of Edinburgh* was signed on July 6, 1560. According to the terms of the agreement, all foreign troops were to leave Scotland—except 120 French troops. In addition, the long absent Mary (1542–1587), daughter of Mary of Guise and James V, was to be allowed to return to the country and acknowledged as Queen of Scots (reigned, 1561–1569). However, she and her husband Francis II were to relinquish all claim to the English crown. Moreover, she was not to make war or peace without the consent of the Estates (the ruling nobility).

Spiritual Victory in Scotland

By these and other restraints, the nobles and the Scottish Reformers won strategic political and religious victories over the returning Queen. The Protestant Church moved to take immediate advantage of the situation. Under the leadership of Knox and with the approval of Parliament, a Confession of Faith was adopted. In August, 1560, the legal acts were passed by Parliament to do away with the Mass on pain of corporal punishment, dispense with the jurisdiction of the pope, and repeal any and all laws which did not conform to the Reformed faith. The *First Book of Discipline* was offered to the General Assembly when the national church met in December, 1560. Later, in 1564, the *Book of Common Order* would be accepted as the official worship book of the country.

Taking personal advantage of the triumph of the Protestant faith, the nobility of Scotland denounced purgatory as a myth, and then claimed that the Catholic Church had taken their ancestral land by fraud. Perhaps the land should be returned? A vote taken by Parliament mandated that restitution should be made. Most of the ecclesiastical property acquired by the Catholic Church was soon restored to those laity landowners who were Protestant.

Death of the "Thundering Scot"

Despite the civil unrest that the country had endured, despite the posturing for position and power, and the obvious temptation for the new leaders to retaliate in kind for past grievances, the Scottish reformation probably shed the least blood and lasted longer than any reformed movement in other countries. Solidifying the Protestant position in Scotland was helped in large part because Mary Queen of Scots was not a wise ruler. She alienated important Church leaders such as John Knox, and also the moderate elements of society, who probably would have honored her right to rule regardless of her religious views. Then, by claiming to be the true heir to the English throne, Mary angered Elizabeth, who began to view her as a rival. Next, Mary alarmed the Protestants of England, who feared a return to Catholicism if Mary ever found the military power to invade England. A way had to be found to eliminate Mary Queen of Scots. It would not be difficult.

Mary's ultimate doom began when she married Henry Darnley, who also laid claim to the throne of England. After he was blown up in a house where he was staying, Mary married the man who was suspected of the murder, the Earl of Bothwell. The people of Scotland were outraged, and Mary was deposed. Fleeing to England, she was arrested and kept as a political prisoner by Elizabeth. In the end, Mary was executed at Fotheringay. Mary Queen of Scots died because she would not stop giving her consent to Catholic plots to overthrow Queen Elizabeth.

Meanwhile, the triumphs of Protestantism that John Knox was involved with had taken their own toll. Even victory has its price. Knox had grown old in the struggle, feeble in body, and perhaps a little more reflective. Near the end of life he wrote, "I know that many have complained much and loudly, and do still complain of my too great severity, but God knows my mind was always free from hatred to the persons of those against whom I denounced the heavy judgments of God." On November 9, 1572, John Knox preached for the last time. Five days later, the "thundering Scot" was dead. He was absent from the body and face to face with the Lord.

CHAPTER 27

Reformation Comes to England
A.D. 1558–1603

The "Morning Star" of the Reformation

It is a sign of sovereign grace whenever a nation enjoys a divine visitation. England was once favored by God in a special way. Under four successive rulers, the Reformation brought radical changes to the Church in the country. The reigns of Henry VIII (1509–1547), Edward VI (1547–1553), "Bloody Mary" (1553–1558), and Elizabeth I (1558–1603) would be largely remembered for their relationship with the Church and with the leaders of the Reformation. Yet it was John Wycliffe (1320–1384), the "morning star of the Reformation," who was instrumental in paving the way for later generations to be receptive to theologial change.

Born in Yorkshire and graduated from Oxford, Wycliffe had dared to boldly challenge the authority of the pope. He criticized the sale of indulgences, by denying that such non-spiritual transactions had power to release a person from punishment in purgatory. Wycliffe did not stop there. Having received a doctorate of theology (1372), he did not hesitate to deny the reality of transubstantiation. He declared that the bread and wine do not change into the actual body and blood of Christ during Communion.

The pope rebuked Wycliffe and urged Oxford University to dismiss the radical professor. The request was denied. Wycliffe was free to pursue his studies and other projects—such as translating the Scriptures from Latin into English. The New Testament was completed around 1380, and the Old Testament in 1382. The Church authorities were outraged that Wycliffe had made the Scriptures available to all. They felt that the Scriptures in the hands of the common man would lead to misinterpretations and doctrinal abuses. When the Council of Constance met,

Wycliffe was condemned as a heretic, even though he had died. His body was ordered to be dug up, his bones burned, and his ashes thrown into the Swift River.

But the desecration of his corpse did not matter. The ideas of Wycliffe had found fertile soil in which to grow. His work would live on after him, reflected in the fact that one of his associates, John Purvey (c. 1353–1428), produced a revision of the Wycliffe Bible in 1388. Like Able, John Wycliffe, being dead, yet lived (Heb 11:4).

The Powerful Prayer of a Dying Professor

The desire of John Wycliffe to place a copy of the Bible into the hands of every person burned brightly in the hearts of others, such as William Tyndale (c. 1494–1536). A Hebrew and Greek scholar from Oxford University, Tyndale was willing to challenge the Catholic belief that only the clergy were qualified to read and correctly understand the Scriptures. Said Tyndale, "If God spare my life, ere many years, I will cause a boy that driveth the plough to know more of the Scripture than thou dost." God spared the life of Tyndale long enough for His servant to complete the translation of the New Testament in 1525. During the next five years, fifteen thousand copies in six editions were smuggled into England from Hamburg, Germany, where Tyndale had fled in order to work. His final revision of the Bible appeared in 1535. In that same year, Tyndale was found and arrested. Brought before an ecclesiastical court, he was unjustly judged to be a heretic, and was sentenced to die. In Antwerp, on October 6, 1536, Tyndale was strangled and burnt at the stake. Allowed to speak one last time, William Tyndale cried out to heaven, "Lord, open the King of England's eyes."

A Potentially Splendid Sovereign

One of the great privileges in the study of history is the opportunity to see clearly the sovereign hand of Almighty God over the affairs of men. God can take all things, including the pride and arrogance of man, and make them serve His own purpose—as He did in the life of Henry VIII, son of Henry VII and Elizabeth of York. Born in the year 1491 at Greenwich, Henry was brought up as the crown prince, following the premature death of his elder brother, Arthur.

It was obvious to many that Henry would one day make a splendid king. He had an abundance of natural gifts: tremendous intelligence, physical beauty, athletic ability, a sense of humor, charming manners, tolerance, and the capacity to show clemency. There was great excitement throughout England in 1509, when the announcement was made that Henry VIII was king of England at the young age of eighteen. Here was a young man to admire because, according to Sir Thomas More, he "has more learning than any English monarch ever possessed before him." The only question to be answered was what Henry would do with his kingdom.

The Cardinal of the King

Realizing his need for guidance in affairs of State, young Henry found in Thomas Wolsey someone to rely upon. Wolsey was only three years older than Henry, and was a priest. Born at Ipswich of humble parents, Wolsey had risen to the attention of the royal court through his intellectual achievements at Oxford. He knew how to get along with others, while manifesting an ability for management and negotiation. Wolsey served Henry VII as a diplomat. Now, he would serve his son with tremendous success. Each political victory brought Wolsey more rewards and more royal power, all at the pleasure of Henry. As long as Wolsey made decisions that enhanced the power of the king, Henry was inclined to give him much leeway.

Weaving a Tangled Web

The legal power Wolsey held translated into spiritual power. He was made a Cardinal, and desired to have the papacy as well, which he openly sought in 1521 and again in 1523. While Wolsey longed for the papal robes, the Protestants had to be dealt with, and reform had to come to the clergy. Wolsey was very much aware of ecclesiastical corruptions. But after some initial policies were passed, Wolsey lost interest in monastic reforms.

Nor was he overly concerned with the Protestant movement. With the English Reformers, Wolsey decided to try and persuade them to be quiet—rather than to persecute them. He did hire a secret guard to report on suspected heresy, to examine the prevailing literature, and to report on who should be arrested. But there he stopped. No heretic was ever burned at the stake because of his orders—Wolsey showed surprising restraint. When Hugh Latimer denounced the sins of the priests, the bishop of Ely asked Wolsey to silence him. Instead, Wolsey gave Latimer license to preach in any Church in the country.

Meanwhile, the Cardinal's foreign policy began to collapse. Though allied with Charles V of Spain, the war with France (1522), which Wolsey had allowed England to engage in, proved to be a disaster in both money and men. The check and balance of power among nations, which Wolsey had tried to establish, was ruined when Charles not only defeated the forces of France, but captured Rome and the Pope in 1527. Unless the continent was to be ruled by Charles, something had to be done. England had to switch sides and fight against her own ally. So in January, 1528, England joined France in war against Charles.

A Questionable Marriage

To make diplomatic matters worse for Wolsey, Charles was the nephew of Catherine of Aragon, from whom Henry VIII had decided to get a divorce. In addition, Pope Clement VII, who alone had the ecclesiastical power to grant Henry a divorce, was being held captive by Charles.

Catherine of Aragon was the daughter of Ferdinand and Isabella. She had come to England in 1501, at the age of sixteen, to be married to Arthur, aged fifteen, the eldest son of Henry VII. The marriage ceremony took place on November 14. Arthur died on April 2, 1502. The great question that emerged was whether or not the marriage had been consummated by the young couple. The Spanish ambassador sent "proof" to Ferdinand that the marriage had been consummated; Catherine denied everything.

Henry VII was in a dilemma. He did not want the tremendous dowry that Catherine had brought with her to go back to the coffers of Spain, nor did he want a powerful alliance with Ferdinand to be broken. Appealing to the Scriptures (Deut 25:5), the English monarch proposed that Catherine marry Prince Henry, though she was his elder by six years.

Not everyone in the Church agreed that such a union should or could take place along biblical grounds. Nevertheless, Pope Julius II granted a special dispensation in 1503, and a legal marriage was made formal. The bridegroom was only twelve. In 1505 Prince Henry asked to have the marriage annulled, but his father prevailed upon him not to do that. In 1509, six weeks after Henry VIII's accession to the throne, the marriage was celebrated in public. Catherine of Aragon was Queen of England, for a while.

A Sovereign Wants a Son

The marriage was not to last, for Catherine could not give Henry what he wanted above all else: a son and a male heir to the throne. Desperately, Catherine tried. On

January 31, 1510, she bore her first child, who died at birth. A year later she bore a son, but in a few weeks the child also was dead. A second and third son also expired soon after birth (1513, 1514). Henry began to think of a divorce, or better yet for him, an annulment. Catherine tried again, and in 1516 she gave birth to the future Queen Mary. In 1518, Catherine delivered yet another baby, stillborn. Meanwhile, at age two, the young princess Mary was betrothed to the dauphin of France. If Henry had no son, his daughter Mary would inherit the English throne, and her husband, the future king of France, would become the king of England. Never! Never! Henry would not think of that. He must have a son. Catherine must not deny him a divorce. Nor must the Church!

By now, Henry had grown weary of Catherine. His lustful, roving eyes fell upon Elizabeth Blount, whom he took as his first mistress (1518). She gave him a son in 1519. Henry made him Duke of Richmond and Somerset, and considered making him a successor to the throne. Then he found another mistress, Mary Boleyn (1524), who had a charming sister named Anne. Henry was first infatuated, and then obsessed with Anne. He must have her as wife. No doubt she could give him an heir. By March, 1527, Henry had set in motion the process for having his marriage to Catherine annulled. Cardinal Wolsey assured him that a papal annulment easily could be attained. How wrong he was.

The final story of Henry's divorce from Catherine is sordid and filled with great sadness. The Queen did not deserve to be treated in the way she was. Indeed, she expressed herself on this matter on June 21, 1529. Having been granted an audience with the king, Catherine cast herself on her knees before him, and pleaded that their marriage last. She reminded him of her efforts to bear children. She had endured his extra marital affairs. She had been a good and faithful wife in the eyes of the law and in the sight of God. Henry picked her up from the floor and assured her that she was not to blame. But he would have a son!

The Pope Says, 'No'

Cardinal Wolsey was doing everything he could to secure for Henry the annulment desired. The main problem was that the pope was still a prisoner in the hands of Charles V of Spain, and Charles did not like how his aunt was being treated. There would be no annulment given by the Catholic Church, and Henry must obey the ruling of Rome. Perhaps Charles thought that he could help make Henry remain a good Catholic. After all, in 1521, Henry had written a tract against Martin Luther,

The Assertion of the Seven Sacraments, and received from Pope Leo X the title "Defender of the Faith."

But if Charles or the pope thought they could contain the proud monarch of England, they were wrong. Henry was furious. He was angry at the pope, and he was outraged at the political and spiritual power Charles V of Spain held. He was upset at Catherine for not giving him a divorce. And he was livid at Cardinal Wolsey for not being able to do anything within the Church. Did not anyone have an idea of what to do next? Thomas Cranmer, the Archbishop of Canterbury, did.

The Supremacy of the King

Aware of the mood of the nation in religious matters, Cranmer knew that the time was ripe for a break with Rome. He shrewdly suggested that the matter of a divorce be submitted to the leading universities of England and the continent. In this manner, Henry VIII found men willing to give him biblical sanction for obtaining a divorce. The next steps were both logical and audacious. Henry halted the transfer of financial resources from going to the pope, and then he had Parliament declare him to be the head of the Church of England (1534). The law which passed was called the *Act of Supremacy*. The provision was made that the king, not the pope, was the head of the Church of England.

An annulment was then pronounced by Archbishop Cranmer. Henry VIII was finally free to marry his mistress. A royal marriage took place; Anne was already pregnant. The result of this unholy union was a daughter, Elizabeth. Anne did not live to see her daughter reign. She was beheaded on a charge of adultery in 1536. Other wives followed. There was Jane Seymour, who gave birth to Edward; Anne of Cleves, whom Henry divorced soon after the marriage; Catherine Howard, who was beheaded within a year on the charge of adultery; and Catherine Parr, who outlived the monarch.

While Henry was making a mockery out of Christian marriage, others were beginning to mock him, or so Henry thought. One thing was certain: not everyone was willing to accept Henry as the supreme head of the Church. As the Reformers had rejected the ultimate authority of the pope, so they consistently rejected the attempt of one man to be made the head of the Church. In his arrogance, Henry had another law passed, the *Law of Treason and Heresy*. This law made a heretic of anyone who did not embrace the doctrines of the Catholic Church, and who did not acknowledge the king as the head of the Church in England. The penalty for violation of these laws was death. Soon, both Catholics and Protestants were being executed for not bending their knees or will to Henry, including Sir Thomas More, Lord Chancellor of England. More had been very zealous in causing many English Lutherans to be burned at the stake. Now he was the one who would not acknowledge (1) the legitimacy of Henry's divorce from Catherine, and (2) the king as head of the Church. On July 1, 1535, Sir Thomas More was beheaded.

Flickering Hope

When Henry died in 1547, many were not sorry to see him depart. Devout Christians wanted him to go and receive his own just reward. Henry had left behind a new Church structure, but he had made no provision for a Protestant theology. He only changed the political head of the Church. Henry also left behind a legacy of brutality and violence, while never moving too far from Catholic dogma. So there was much work to be done if the Church in England was truly going to be reformed. Still, the sins of a king served the true Sovereign of the Universe, for the suffering saints in England would yet produce much spiritual fruit.

When Henry VIII died in 1547, his son Edward VI (1547–1553) succeeded him to the throne. Because he was but a nine year old child, his uncle, the Duke of Somerset, was made regent. Somerset and his government were supportive of the Reformation. Changes were allowed to be made in the doctrine and form of worship in the Church of England. In 1549, Parliament passed the *Act of Uniformity*, which made the use of the *Book of Common Prayer* mandatory in the services of the Church. It is also called the *First Prayer Book of Edward VI*. A communion table took the place of the altar, and the preaching of the Word was honored. A new creed was formulated by Thomas Cranmer, the first Protestant archbishop of Canterbury. With the help of other theologians, including John Knox, the Church of England adopted the *Forty-two Articles*. All of these reforms moved the Church of England away from the Church of Rome.

"Bloody Mary"

But the Reformed measures were to be challenged. When he was only sixteen years old, Edward died unexpectedly of tuberculosis (1553). His half-sister Mary ascended to the throne of England. Mary (ruled, 1553–1558) was a devout Catholic and proceeded to undo twenty-five years of blood and sacrifice. Reformation leaders were arrested or removed from office. The Catholic form of worship authorized by Henry VIII was implemented again.

Many Protestants feared for their lives and fled to the continent. There was good reason to run and hide. In the year 1555 alone, seventy-five people were burnt to death for their beliefs. Even Thomas Cranmer, the Archbishop of Canterbury who had helped secure the separation of the Church of England from the jurisdiction of Rome, did not escape persecution. Late in 1555 he was excommunicated in Rome. Cardinal Pole was appointed to take the vacated office.

Mary was determined that Cranmer be put to death, even though he had renounced Protestantism publicly by signing a statement to that effect. Nevertheless, the Queen wanted his execution, and the date was set for March 21, 1556. Just before he was to die, Cranmer renounced his renunciation. He was sorry he had denied the Protestant faith. Then, in a dramatic gesture, Cranmer put into the flames the hand that had signed the denial. He kept the hand there until it was burned to a shrivel. Then, overcome by the flames, his body scorched, Cranmer died a martyr's death.

Mary continued to persecute the Protestants until the day of her death, November 17, 1558. She had needlessly destroyed the lives of over three hundred people by causing them to be burned at the stake. She is worthy of her graceless name, "Bloody Mary."

Hope Springs Eternal

The death of Mary brought her half sister, Elizabeth, to the throne of England. Elizabeth I (ruled, 1558–1603) was sympathetic to the Protestant position. Persecution came to an end, as did the threat of a Spanish invasion. Elizabeth would remain single and rule alone. More importantly, she would allow religious reforms to take place. For example, despite strong opposition, Parliament passed a second *Supremacy Act* on April 29, 1559, making the sovereign of the land the head of the Church of England. Then, once more, the government rejected all papal authority. The *Second Prayer Book of Edward VI* was revised. Finally, after a slight change was made in 1563, the *Forty-two Articles*, which are basically Lutheran in point of view, were reduced in number to *Thirty-nine Articles* and adopted. All of these provisions are known as the *Elizabethan Settlement*. The pope had hoped that Elizabeth would return to the fold. When she did not, her papal excommunication was decreed in 1570.

Elizabeth's reign was not without religious conflict. The Puritans opposed the Queen's propensity for liturgy, and she opposed their demand for the removal of bishops, which in theory was a direct challenge to a hereditary monarch. "No bishop, no king," she reasoned.

Also opposed to Elizabeth were the Independents, or Congregationalists, who emerged during her reign. They believed in separation of Church and State and resisted the hierarchical authority of the Church of England. The Baptists arose to object to infant baptism. They believed in baptism by immersion after a profession of faith. Despite these relative minor religious skirmishes with the Crown, the Protestant faith would thrive in England—and grow in power to influence all of Europe.

CHAPTER 28

Counter Reformation and Continuing Conflict
A.D. 1545–1563

The Religious Zeal of Ximenes

There is a temptation in the study of Church history to present an unbalanced view. Those who favor the Protestant position tend to present the body of material that makes the Protestants look best. Those who would favor the Catholic position want their point of view to prevail. Even the cults have their own religious historians, to make sure that the past is written in a certain way that is favorable to their cause.

While it is impossible not to be affected by one's doctrinal beliefs, culture, and religious affinity, any attempt at some objectivity leads to the conclusion that some people can be found in the most difficult places, and in the most trying of circumstances, attempting to do the will of God as they understand it should be done, regardless of how we might label their general position.

In the Catholic Church, prior to the official Reformation period that broke out in Germany under the influence of Martin Luther, there were sincere reformers in various countries. In Spain, there was Ximenes, a Franciscan monk, who desperately wanted the Church to become better and more pure.

Ximenes ministered during the dark days of the reign of Queen Isabella I (1451–1504) and her husband Ferdinand II of Aragon, who sponsored the Inquisition. While the Inquisition itself was cruelty incarnate, through the reform work of Ximenes, a part of the Church knew something about spiritual renewal—a generation before Martin Luther began the Reformation in Germany.

Initially placed in charge of several monasteries because of his special organizational and leadership skills, Ximenes began to correct blatant spiritual abuses such as the buying of Church offices. By attacking the papal sale of indulgences, he earned the enmity of the pope. However, Ximenes was protected by Queen Isabella and was able to continue his work. He enforced strict discipline in the monasteries under his care. New schools were established for the study of theology, so that the people could have an educated clergy. High moral standards were demanded of the priests. Any individual who did not comply with an ethical code of conduct was removed from office.

While Ximenes brought about external change, essential internal concerns that involved the heart of the Church were not challenged. Like many good men, Ximenes had a zeal for God, but not according to biblical knowledge. The pope was still looked to as the head of the Church, the sacraments remained, and the worship of idols was not abolished.

Realizing the Need for Reform

Because men like Ximenes did not go far enough in correcting internal corruption and doctrinal abuses in Catholic theology, the Protestant Reformation had to happen. When it finally came, the Catholic Church knew a response was needed. There were too many people leaving the Catholic Church. Some of the best and brightest, some of the most sensitive and spiritual, and some of the most gifted men and women were not going to stay in a social structure that allowed abuses to go unchallenged and uncorrected. It was obvious that the Catholic Church had to set its house in order. Furthermore, the Catholic Church had to find a better way than torture to motivate its members to be as zealous as the Protestants were for their cause. Even the most devout Catholic could not condone forever the use of the Inquisition.

The Nightmare Years

First established by Gregory IX (pope, 1227–1241), the purpose of the Inquisition (*inquirere*: Inquisition) was to inquire into the spread of teachings which were officially opposed to the faith of the Church. All Catholics suspected of heresy could be called before the local tribunal, where punishment could be rendered. It was sincerely believed that spiritual infidelity had to be corrected in order for the soul to be saved. By original design, the Inquisition was not to be a means to impose the Christian faith upon Jews, Muslims, or non-Catholics at large. Rather, the Inquisition was to be used to secure the salvation, coercion, and punishment of the disciples of Christ. In the sixteenth century, the Inquisition found ardent supporters to protect the Catholic faith, especially in Italy and Spain. Cardinal Giovanni Caraffa, Ignatius Loyola, and Charles V united to urge the restoration of the Inquisition. Pope Paul III agreed (1542) and appointed Caraffa, with five other cardinals, to reorganize the Inquisition. Authority was to be granted to specific clergy throughout the Christian world, to do whatever was necessary to keep souls in the Church. The Inquisitors, Local and General, were usually selected from among the members of the Franciscan and Dominican Orders, with the latter being preferred for their alleged knowledge of Scripture. Specific rules were established:

(1) When the faith is in question, there must be no delay, but on the slightest suspicion rigorous measures must be taken with all speed.
(2) No consideration is to be shown to any prince or prelate, however high his station.
(3) Extreme severity is rather to be exercised against those who attempt to shield themselves under the protection of any potentate. Only he who makes plenary confession should be treated with gentleness and fatherly compassion.
(4) No man must debase himself by showing toleration toward heretics of any kind, above all toward Calvinists.

When Caraffa became Paul IV (pope, 1555–1559), the Inquisition began in earnest, horrifying Catholic and Protestant alike. Cardinal Seripando wrote, "the Inquisition acquired such a reputation that from no other judgment seat on earth were more horrible and fearful sentences to be expected." Once the members of the Inquisition went to work, no one was safe, and nothing was sacred. Books were burned—including Bible translations. In 1559, Paul IV published the first papal Index. It listed all the forbidden books, including forty-eight heretical editions of the Bible. Sixty-one printers and publishers were put under the ban of excommunication. No book was to be read without a Church *imprimatur* (meaning, "let it be printed").

As certain books were no longer safe to be read, words were no longer safe to be spoken. Men who had been pillars of the Church were arrested on the slightest suspicion of a careless comment. The mad Pontiff pursued his victims. "Even if my own father were a heretic," he vowed, "I would gather the wood to burn him." No one doubted the truthfulness of the statement. And so, the bones of Church members were broken. Limbs were stretched. The most barbaric methods of torture the depraved minds of men could conceive were used. Blood flowed freely.

By the grace of God, Paul IV died after only four years of an unrighteous rule. Rome celebrated his death with four days of uninhibited joy. Crowds tore down the statue of the pope, dragged it through the streets, and threw it into the Tiber River. The buildings of the Inquisition were burned, the prisoners set free, and all documents were destroyed.

The Council of Trent

While members of the Inquisition were doing deeds of unspeakable darkness in the name of the Light of the World (John 1:4–8), in the little city of Trent in the mountains of northern Italy, a Church council was meeting. Paul III (pope, 1534–1549) had initially summoned the council, which would meet sporadically from 1545 to 1563. Twenty-five sessions would be held. The purpose of the Council was to reflect the Protestant initiative and formulate a confession of faith. A catechism was also adopted. When its work was completed, some obvious Church abuses were corrected by the Council, but the supremacy of the papacy, and the whole system of salvation by works, still stood as foundational truths. In addition, the Council embraced the validity of believing that the seven sacraments could bestow merit on the Christian. Furthermore, tradition was to be valued as much as the Bible, the fourteen apocryphal books of the Old Testament were to be included in the sacred canon of Scripture, purgatory did exist, and there was value in the invocation of saints, images, relics, and indulgences. Point by point the Protestants would continue to resist these basic Catholic beliefs as having no Scriptural support. The battle for the hearts and minds of millions throughout the world would continue in earnest.

The Cruelty of Charles V

In this ongoing struggle for the minds of men, the Catholic Church had always had a powerful ally in the emperor of the Holy Roman Empire, Charles V. Immediately after the Diet of Worms, the king vowed "To root out heresy, I shall stake my crown and my life." He was serious. After defeating the armies of France, turning back the Muslim Suleiman at Vienna, and withstanding Barbarossa in the Mediterranean, Charles was free to "root out" Protestant "heretics" who disagreed with the Catholic traditions.

In 1546, a new wave of persecution began. Protestants were burned to death as heretics in Italy, Spain, France, England, and Scotland. The Lutherans of Germany were grievously afflicted, while in the Netherlands the saints fell victim to the Spanish Inquisition. More than 18,000 were slaughtered.

Charles was able to viciously suppress the work of the Protestants until he suffered a political setback. One of his closest supporters, Maurice of Saxony, turned against him. Charles could have been captured and held a prisoner, but he was allowed to escape. When asked why he let the king flee, Maurice said, "I did not have a cage good enough for such a fine bird."

By 1555, Charles was forced to sign the *Peace of Augsburg*. The hurting was halted. According to the terms of the treaty, each prince of a territory would have the right to choose whether his kingdom would be Lutheran or Catholic. In this choice, the common people would have no voice. They would have to accept the religion of their ruler.

On September 28, 1556, Charles V, Emperor of Germany, king of Spain, and lord of the Netherlands made his way to Spain, where he would remain until his death on September 21, 1558. It did not help the cause of the Catholic Church that Charles was becoming senile. Perhaps some taint of insanity was inherited from his mother's blood.

In the final years of life, Charles was without mercy. He recommended vicious penalties to "cut out the root" of heresy. He regretted more than ever having let Luther escape him at Worms. By royal command, no woman was to be allowed within two bowshots of the monastery walls where he was staying, which was a monastery in name only. Charles had turned it into a palace. Changing his will, Charles ordered that 30,000 Masses be said for him after his death. Such royal instructions could be commanded because of a religious system that denies the simplicity of the Scriptures, which teach, "it is appointed unto men once to die, but after this the judgment" (Heb 9:27). Today is the day of salvation. "Today if ye will hear his voice, harden not your hearts" (Heb 3:15). Charles never understood that salvation does not come by Masses being said, or the sacraments being honored. Salvation is by grace through faith alone in the Person and work of Jesus Christ dying a substitutionary death at Calvary. "Neither is there salvation in any other: for there is none other name under heaven given among men, whereby we must be saved" (Acts 4:12).

The Power of Passionate People

Though Charles proved in the end to be counter-productive to the goals of the Counter-Reformation, the Catholic Church looked upon other sincere men with better hope. Some of the more earnest Catholic reformers were Teresa de Cepeda, Ignatius Loyola, and Francis Xavier.

Teresa de Cepeda (1515–1582) was the daughter of a Castilian knight of Avila, who read to his family each day from the lives of the saints. Her mother, a chronic invalid, enjoyed having read aloud romantic stories of chivalry. Teresa would vacillate between idyllic love and Church martyrdom. At ten she told everyone she was going to become a nun. Four years later Teresa had become a beautiful young woman with many admirers. It was only natural that she fall in love with one of them, but then Teresa became afraid. Her heart was divided between the world and the Church, and a choice had to be made. At age sixteen, Teresa became an Augustinian nun.

As the years passed, Teresa grew disappointed with the external behavior of those she found in the convents. Her own spiritual life was filled with visions of heaven. On one occasion, Teresa thought an "exceedingly beautiful angel" pierced her heart several times with "a long dart of gold," tipped with fire. "So real was the pain that I was forced to moan aloud, yet it was so surpassingly sweet that I would not wish to be delivered from it. No delight of life can give more content. As the angel withdrew the dart, he left me all burning with a great love of God." Such visions would continue throughout her life.

Teresa wanted others to know spiritual joy. But in order for that to happen, reform had to take place. A new convent had to be established with behavior conducive to Christian conduct. Despite opposition, Teresa would know success. In 1562, on a narrow street in Avila, the new convent of St. Joseph was opened. Eventually Teresa would establish seventeen convents, all of which would be obedient to the strict, Carmelite rule emphasizing asceticism, self-discipline, and prayer—in a loving and cheerful manner.

A gifted administrator and writer of mystical experiences, Teresa published her *Autobiography* in 1562. Respected in life, Teresa was revered in death. Claims were made that her body never decayed, and miracles took place at her tomb. An appeal was made to the pope to beatify her. *Beatification* (Latin *beatus*, blessed, and *facere*, to make or do) is the formal papal assurance that a deceased person, having lived a holy and heroic life, deserves to be called "blessed," and is therefore enjoying heaven without the pains of passing through purgatory. This was done in 1614. Eight years later Teresa was exalted and pronounced to be a patron saint of Spain. The only other person having received this honor was the Apostle James.

Ignatius of Loyola (1491–1556) was born into a powerful and wealthy Basque family living in the province of Guipuzcoa (Spain). Little could anyone imagine the impact Inigo Lopez de Onaz y de Loyola would have upon the world. Trained to be a soldier, Ignatius suffered a severe wound while fighting the French armies at Pamplona, capital of Navarre, a territory claimed by Spain. His leg was shattered by a cannon ball (May 20, 1521).

The victorious French were kind to their captives. Ignatius was put on a stretcher and his bones were set. But his bones were wrongly set. They had to be broken again and reset. The second operation was horrendous. A stump of bone stuck out from the leg. A third operation was performed to set the bones straight. This procedure was more successful, but it left one leg shorter than the other. A long, tortuous period of convalescence began.

During this time, Ignatius asked for books to read. He was given a copy of the *Life of Christ* by Ludolfus. A powerful spiritual awakening took place in the heart of Ignatius. One day Ignatius rose from his bed of affliction, knelt, and dedicated his life to being a soldier unto death of Christ, the Virgin Mary, and the Church.

While the spiritual journeys of Ignatius took him to many parts of the world, he chose to exist as an extreme ascetic. The once handsome, wealthy, and attractive aristocrat abused his body, to the point that his hair fell out, his beard was unkempt, his face became haggard, and his clothes rotted off his back. There was an intensity about the man that attracted others. He believed he knew how to advance the cause of Christ: individuals must become soldiers of the cross through rigid discipline and holy obedience.

For Ignatius, this meant slavish subservience to the Church. He and his followers would do whatever task the Church asked, no matter how menial or humiliating it might be. Out of this vision for spiritual soldiers came a core group of committed Catholics. They were formally recognized by Paul III (pope, 1534-1549) when he issued a papal bull establishing the *Regimini militantis ecclesiae*, "For the rule of the Church Militant," the Society of Jesus (the Jesuits), September 27, 1540. Valuing not only holy obedience but also education, the Jesuits sent its dedicated missionaries to Europe, India, China, Japan, and the New World.

Francis Xavier (1506–1552) was the youngest child of a Basque official, Juan de Yasu, and his wife Maria. Though a large portion of the family wealth was lost during border disputes between France and Spain, enough money remained to allow Francis to study law and theology at the University of Paris. While in Paris, he met Ignatius of Loyola and became one of his most loyal supporters. Ordained a priest in Venice (1537), Francis began a life of dedicated service.

His travels took him to the large Portuguese settlement of Goa (India), which was the source of a profitable spice trade. In Goa, Francis founded a missionary college. He also helped to defend the native Indians against foreign abuse. In 1545, Francis traveled to Malacca in the Malay Peninsula, and to the Molucca Islands, which are today part of Indonesia. From there he prepared to go to Japan (1549), where he successfully established a Christian community. He was the first to preach the Gospel of Christ to the Japanese.

He returned to Goa in 1552, desiring to explore the empire of China. While trying to gain an entrance to China, Francis died on Shangchuan Island, off the southern coast of the mainland. Francis has justly been criticized for displaying an intolerance of oriental religions, using the Inquisition in Goa, and using governmental policies to pressure people into becoming Catholics. However, Francis has also been praised for a life of devotion to the Church, resulting in the bringing of over 700,000 people into the Catholic Church. Believing that the good he did outweighed the bad, the Catholic Church canonized him in 1622.

The contributions of these people to the Catholic cause greatly enhanced Church unity. The Council of Trent also helped to bring an end to further Catholic divisions—by establishing a sense of unity through a creed, a catechism, and a sense of stability.

A Fragmented Faith

Meanwhile, the Protestant community was not so united. It continued to fragment for a number of reasons, none of them noble.

(1) One major cause for Protestant division was the lack of a central government with ecclesiastical control. The movement was not helped by its own teaching in this matter, which held suspect central power in the Church or State. While the privileges of the universal priesthood of the believer were exalted, in practical terms this teaching served to undermine the authority of ministers in the local assembly, and the power of the corporate Church.

(2) Another difficulty was that in some nations, a class division arose. When Martin Luther took a firm stand against the populace in the Peasant's War of 1525, the lower classes felt betrayed. Many in this segment of society turned against Luther and the Reformation, and returned to the Catholic Church. The movement was then confined to the middle and upper classes of society in Germany.

The rise of the Anabaptists did nothing initially to advance the cause of the Reformation. Many of the early Anabaptists were religious zealots. People felt that not only the Church was threatened by the Anabaptists, but so was all social and political order in nations. The Catholic Church took advantage of this innate fear to teach that the Reformation as a whole was disruptive to society and should not be supported.

(3) As the Protestants divided along class lines, so there was a tendency to divide along educational lines. To be a devout follower of Luther, Zwingli, and Calvin required prayerful study and careful thinking. While the Reformation leaders appealed to the mind, the Catholic Church continued to appeal to the emotions and senses of the general populace. There was pomp and ceremony, pageantry and programs, mystery and majesty seen physically in elaborate ceremonies in the Catholic Church. For many, the contrast between that and the bareness of the Protestant Church was too much. Catholicism promised salvation while Protestant sermons demanded the heart be constantly searched for the root of righteousness. In Protestant theology there was a constant emphasis upon sin, salvation, sanctification, and eternal damnation. It was just easier not to have to think so much about so many serious topics. It was easier to be a Catholic!

(4) The Protestant movement fragmented even more when its own foundational doctrine was abused. The essential teaching of the Reformation was that "justification is by faith alone apart from human works or merits." A careless thinker might assume that good works are not associated with salvation. If that is true, then it does not matter how one lives. Therefore, why not live life as one pleases while singing, "Free from the Law, O happy condition; sin as you please for there is remission!"

By embracing a system of salvation built upon "easy believism," people persuaded themselves that sin was not something to be taken seriously. Grace and love would cover a multitude of sin. The Catholic Church was quick to point out that a belief in salvation apart from works would tend to justify a life of unrestrained liberty (see Romans 6 for Paul's answer).

In addition to the abuse of doctrine, the division of doctrine brought a disruption of fellowship. Lutherans did not feel that they could have open fellowship with Calvinists.

(5) Finally, geography played a role in dividing the Protestant Church. While France, Scotland, and the Netherlands enjoyed a common unity by embracing the creeds of Calvinism, they were geographically apart. Physical fellowship among the various churches was difficult to achieve because of natural barriers.

Despite the fragmentation of the Protestant movement, the central work of calling individuals to Christ continued. In many ways the message was communicated that life is short, death is certain, eternity is real. There is a hell to shun, a heaven to gain, a God to fear, and a Savior to love. Like a mighty army, the Church of the Living Lord marched on. It had been bruised and bloodied on the spiritual field of battle, but never defeated. The Church was fragmented, but not faithless. It was divided, but not disloyal to the divine command to take the Gospel to every nation (Matt 28:19–20):

> Go ye therefore, and teach all nations, baptizing them in the name of the Father, and of the Son, and of the Holy Ghost: Teaching them to observe all things whatsoever I have commanded you: and, lo, I am with you always, even unto the end of the world. Amen.

CHAPTER 29

The Reformation in England Continues
A.D. 1647

More Purity for the Church in England

As the principles of the Reformation continued to change individuals, they in turn changed society. Unfortunately, cultural change can produce tension, unrest, and conflict. In the seventeenth century, England found herself in the midst of great social disharmony. The social turmoil came, in part, because the Elizabethan Settlement of 1563 did not resolve the continuing concerns expressed by the *Puritans*, the movement that sought to be totally biblically pure toward God and set apart from men's ways.

The Elizabethan Settlement is a term used to describe the position of the Church of England near the beginning of the reign of Queen Elizabeth (1558–1603), as established by the *Act of Supremacy* and the *Act of Uniformity*. In a cautious manner, the first act defined the authority of the State in the Church, while the second established the required use of the *Book of Common Prayer*.

In 1558, when Elizabeth succeeded "Bloody Mary" Tudor (1516–1558) to the throne of England, she discovered that many Protestants had returned from religious exile enamored with the concepts advocated by the great French reformer, John Calvin (1509–1564).

By using the Acts of Supremacy and Uniformity, the new Queen sought to avoid any more Church controversy. But her desires were not realized. There were those who wanted to see the Church of England completely divested of any reflections from Rome. Specific demands were being made by the Puritans: a sincere and spiritually-minded pastor, able to preach, was to be placed in every parish; there were to be no distinguishing clerical garments; no one should kneel at the Lord's Supper;

rings were not to be exchanged at weddings; and the use of signing of the cross at baptism must cease (the Roman Catholic movement of the hand in the shape of a cross).

These acts were objected to because of the symbolism associated with them. The clerical garments reminded the Puritans of the priests in the Catholic Church—and of the power they once wielded. The kneeling at communion was considered to be an acceptance of the Catholic belief of the physical presence of Christ as taught in the doctrine of transubstantiation. The exchanging of rings at weddings reminded the Puritans of the Catholic dogma of marriage being a sacrament, rather than a social institution to be honored by all. The signing of the cross at baptism was believed to be a superstition without any corresponding spiritual meaning. Therefore, it should not be used.

As the Puritans considered these things, they thought of other practices that would make the Church of England more distinct from the Catholic Church, and therefore more holy and pure. In each parish, elders should be appointed to exercise Church discipline; the office of Bishop should be done away with; local assemblies should have the right to select their own ministers; and all ministers were to be considered equal. A Presbyterian form of Church government (with local church autonomy) should replace the Episcopalian form (with a hierarchy of central authority).

The Authority of God's Word

The Puritans wanted these reforms because they were convinced that the Word of God directed the way the Christian life should be lived, and the way the local Church should be administered. This emphasis on the Bible, instead of tradition or human reason, became the main source of authority for the Puritans. They wanted to be a people of the Book. They wanted to be holy. They wanted a renewed emphasis upon strict morality. Going to the theater, playing cards, and dancing were frowned upon and preached against. Honoring the Sabbath was mandatory. There should to be a distinct separation between Church and State.

Thomas Cartwright

One prominent leader of the Puritan movement was Thomas Cartwright (b. 1535). A graduate of Cambridge, Cartwright spoke out openly against corruption in the

Catholic Church. As a result, he was driven from his teaching position at St. John's College when the Catholic Queen, Mary Tudor, ascended the throne in 1553.

As Cartwright exposed moral and doctrinal corruption in the Catholic Church, so he spoke against spiritual pollution in the Church of England, to the dismay of the Protestant Queen Elizabeth. Cartwright's reward for his honesty was removal from the teaching profession to which he had returned. He was decreed guilty of declaring that the Church of England had forsaken certain practices of the New Testament, and was banished from the country.

While living as a religious exile in Geneva, Switzerland, Cartwright was able to meet Theodore Beza, the Protestant leader who had replaced John Calvin upon his death. Desiring to return to England, Cartwright went home, but found he could not stay; he would not keep silent. After issuing a pamphlet, *Admonition to the Parliament* (1572), alleging there to be unworthy officials in the Church of England, Cartwright was once more compelled to leave the country.

Still, he spoke what was on his heart, always trying to purify the Church of England, spiritually and structurally. In the place of an Episcopal form of government, Cartwright argued for a Presbyterian type, in which local churches united to form a *synod*, or assembly, while recognizing the autonomy of each Church. Cartwright's concepts of Church government were widely received by other Puritan leaders. He died in 1603.

The Independents

Frustrated with the slow pace of reforming the Church of England, some concerned Christians decided to separate in dissent. They would leave the Church of England to create a new religious work, becoming known as *Separatists* or Dissenters. From this movement would come the *Congregationalists*, or Independents, stressing the freedom of the local assembly to select ministers, maintain Church autonomy, and worship without formal rituals.

Persecution of the Puritans

Despite their noble intentions to purify the Church of England, the Puritans found themselves afflicted by the Crown for their beliefs. For almost forty years after the death of Queen Elizabeth (d. 1603), the Puritans were persecuted directly and indirectly. There was public ridicule and private slander. The Puritans were subject to fines and imprisonments. Perhaps it was only natural that they allied themselves with those who politically opposed King Charles I (1600–1649). The Puritans longed for a legal forum to alter their harsh treatment, and advance their own agenda. In 1640, they found what their hearts desired. In that year the "Long Parliament" met, after an eleven year absence of convening. The Parliament was so named because it was determined not to disband, even if the Crown commanded its dismissal.

In the Long Parliament, the Presbyterian Puritans found themselves in the majority. They realized that they were now in a position to take revenge on past injustices. Two leading opponents of the Puritans had been the Earl of Strafford and William Laud. The king had made Laud bishop of London in 1628 and Archbishop of Canterbury in 1633. Under his leadership, many Puritans fled to America. Once the Puritans gained political power, Strafford and Laud were brought to trial, condemned, and executed—by beheading.

King Charles I

Meanwhile, relations between Parliament and King Charles continued to deteriorate. It was inevitable that there be tension because Charles, the younger son of King James I, believed in the concept of "the divine right of kings." This worldview held that God Himself made kings and not men. Therefore, while men and Parliaments might give counsel to the king, his word was ultimate law. Legally, the king could do no wrong. Therefore, any movement to remove a king, or even curtail his power, was a violation of natural rights and divine law.

Succeeding his father to the throne in 1625, Charles could not bear the concept of having limitations placed upon his royal commands. If Parliament would not do what Charles wanted, he would rule without them. The king did rule from 1629 to 1639 without Parliament. However, needing funds to fight the Scots, Charles summoned the English Parliament in 1640. Renewed confrontations came.

Alarmed by arbitrary actions taken by the Parliament, and its growing popularity with the people, Charles decided to arrest five members who were opposed to his reign. Armed soldiers were sent to seize select members who spoke against the Crown, but the House of Commons moved to protect their leaders. Willing to use military might to suppress this open rebellion, in 1642 the king left London, raised the royal flag at Nottingham, and engaged the country in civil war.

The People and Parliament Challenge the Crown

Initially, the majority of the nobles and country gentlemen supported the king. As capable horsemen they were known as Cavaliers. Opposing the king, and supporting the side of Parliament, were shopkeepers, small farmers, and entrepreneurs. These opponents of the Crown became known as Roundheads, because they cut their hair very short—the shape of the round head could be seen.

When the hostilities began, the king's forces were victorious for a very simple reason: the general population was not trained in the art of war. A wealthy farmer, elected to the House of Commons in 1628, said plainly that, "A set of poor tapsters [those who repaired pots and pans] and town apprentices cannot fight men of honor successfully." Oliver Cromwell (1599–1658) was right. The army raised by Parliament to fight the forces of the king, needed to be trained in a professional manner. Perhaps Cromwell could help, and he would.

Cromwell began by forming a new regiment, the Ironsides. The men who served in this regiment were never defeated on the field of battle. Seriously devout in their personal life, they did not swear or drink, and they charged their enemies singing psalms. Later, an army of twenty-one thousand men, patterned after the Ironsides, was created. The New Model Army also consisted of God-fearing soldiers who sang psalms, studied the Bible, and prayed when they were not fighting.

Supported by the Scots, the Ironsides defeated the king's army at Marston Moor (1644), and at Naseby (1645). Charles was compelled to surrender in 1646. However, ever the politician, while in custody Charles led the Scots to believe that, if they joined his side and invaded England, he would support their desire for a Presbyterian form of Church government. The Scots believed the word of the king and, on August 20, 1648, invaded England. Unfortunately for them, they were soundly routed by Cromwell's forces at Preston. The Model Army was now supreme in England.

This allowed "Pride's Purge" to take place on December 6, 1648. In the early morning hours, Colonel Thomas Pride and his soldiers seized the House of Commons by force. They barred or expelled 140 Royalist and Presbyterian members. Forty members who resisted the coup were sent to jail. Oliver Cromwell supported this use of physical force, which left what was called the "Rump Parliament." Charles I was arrested, brought to trial, and found guilty of being a tyrant, traitor, and murderer.

His trial began on January 19, 1649. An impromptu panel of judges convened in Westminster Hall. Soldiers stood guard. The galleries spilled over with spectators. Charles was seated in the midst of this chaotic assembly, alone. John Bradshaw acted as the presiding officer. The charges against the King were read, and he was instructed to answer. Charles did answer. He insisted that the court had no right to try him. Nor did it represent the people of England. Furthermore, the Rump Parliament was more of a tyrant than he. From the galleries the people cried out, "God save the King!" Bradshaw grew fearful. Four nobles stepped forward and offered to die in the King's place; this would not be allowed. The death sentence was pronounced and signed by fifty-nine judges, including Oliver Cromwell.

On January 30, 1649, Charles I walked from St. James Palace to the steps of the high scaffold erected in front of the royal palace of Whitehall in London. Before the great multitude that had gathered to witness the bloody spectacle, Charles was beheaded. The king went to his execution with personal dignity. The dark deed was done with one strike of the sharp ax. The executioner held the severed head up high—the crowd could see the death of their sovereign. One eyewitness wrote, "There was such a groan by the thousands then present, as I never heard before and desire I may never hear again." Later, many more would regret what had been done. Following the demise of Charles I, an alleged autobiography was published, *The Royal Image*, which won him renewed respect posthumously. The time would come when the people of England desired a restored monarchy. Until then, the Great Rebellion would continue. A strong military man would guide the country.

A "Lord Protector"

With the death of the king, Oliver Cromwell was the undisputed leader of the nation. Though he did refuse to be crowned king, Cromwell was willing to serve as "Lord Protector" of England from 1653 to his death on September 3, 1658. As a national leader, Cromwell made several important contributions. Perhaps the most important was establishment of peace in England, Scotland, and Ireland after ten years of violent civil conflict.

With civil peace in the land, the opportunity came for Cromwell to renew diplomatic relationships with many European countries. He strengthened the army, built up the naval forces, and restored respect for England's voice in world affairs. Finally, Cromwell established the principle of freedom of worship. Individuals could be *non-conformist:* they could refuse to submit to the established Church of England.

They could also avoid the Presbyterian form of Church government preferred by Parliament. Cromwell himself was an independent Congregationalist. He believed that local assemblies should be able to choose their own pastors, and enjoy their own order of worship.

Cromwell condemned the disruptive acts of such organizations as the Society of Friends and the Fifth Monarchy Men. Individuals belonging to these societies would interrupt traditional Church services, in order to advance their own agendas. Having studied the book of Daniel, the Fifth Monarchists believed that Jesus Christ was about to come to England and establish His Kingdom (the Fifth Monarchy—the execution of Charles I was the end of the fourth monarchy). In a month, perhaps a year, only two at the most, Christ would come to reign. In sermons, pamphlets, and planned acts of insurrection, the Fifth Monarchists shared their own view of millenial certainties.

While Cromwell contained the zeal of these religious enthusiasts, he did allow members of the Jewish community to live without opposition in England. However, with members of the Catholic faith, and with members of the Anglican Church, Cromwell was not so gracious. Severe restrictions were placed upon their acts of worship.

An Assembly of Saints

While the Civil War raged in England between Parliament and the king, changes were made in the Anglican Church. In 1643, the episcopal form of government was abolished by Parliament. A new structure was requested. It would be formulated by an assembly of one hundred twenty-one clergymen (the "divines") and thirty laymen: 10 members of the House of Lords and 20 members of the House of Commons. This Westminster Assembly of Divines met at Westminster Abbey in London.

Most of those who were present when the Assembly convened in 1643, were Presbyterian Puritans. Eight Scottish commissioners were allowed to be part of the gathering, in appreciation for their aid in fighting the king. While the Scottish representatives had no official role in the proceedings, their presence remained influential. The Assembly held 1,163 sessions between July 1, 1643, and February 22, 1649. A quorum of 40 members was required.

As work proceeded, a *Directory of Worship* was prepared to replace the Episcopal prayer book. In addition, a new confession of faith was drafted for the Church of

England. This *Westminster Confession* was the last of the great Protestant creeds of the Reformation era. Work on the Confession began in July, 1645, and continued, with interruptions, until its completion in December, 1646.

The Confession is a summary of major Christian beliefs in 33 chapters. Orthodox biblical theology permeates the Confession, with emphasis on the covenant relationships between God and man. The Confession was presented to both Houses of Parliament in 1647, under the title: *The Humble Advice of the Assembly of Divines, Quotations and Texts of Scripture Annexed Presented by Them Lately to Both Houses of Parliament.*

Though the Confession was only used briefly by the Church of England, it was adopted for common use in 1647 by the General Assembly of the Church of Scotland. The *Savoy Declaration* of 1658 of the English Congregationalists, and the *London Baptist Confession* of 1677,[1] both incorporated large parts of the *Westminster Confession*. Today, this document remains an authoritative statement of faith in many Presbyterian churches.

To help explain the Confession, a *Larger Catechism* was prepared by the Westminster Assembly, to be used by ministers in the pulpit for public teaching. A *Shorter Catechism* was published for instructing the youth.

The Restoration and Its Persecutions

The success of the Puritans in reforming the Church of England did not last. When Oliver Cromwell died in 1658, his son Richard, took the reigns of political power. Because Richard did not have the leadership skills or the political stature of his father, he ruled for only two years (1658–1660), and earned the humiliating nickname "Tumble Down Dick." Richard's demise paved the way for Charles II of the House of Stuart to be restored to the English throne of his father (Charles I) in 1660.

As the restored Stuart king of England, Charles II (1660–1685) issued a general pardon to all who had fought against his father in the great Civil War, but he did not mean it. By May, 1662, Parliament was once more controlled by Anglican members, sympathetic to the Episcopal Church. It passed a new Act of Uniformity, and printed a new Prayer Book, reversing the changes made by the previous, more Puritan, Parliament. The new laws were called the *Clarendon Code* after the politician who proposed them. One measure of the Clarendon Code was an *Act of Uniformity*

---

[1] London Baptist Confession of 1677 – adopted in 1677; first published in 1689.

(1662), which required all clergy to give "their unfeigned consent and assent" to everything that was in the *Book of Common Prayer*. Any form of Church service, other than that officially prescribed therein, was prohibited.

When over 2,000 Presbyterian ministers of the Gospel could not in good conscience subscribe to the *Act of Uniformity*, they were driven from their pulpits, reduced to poverty in many cases, and forced to hide as fugitives. In 1665 the *Five Mile Act* was passed, forbidding these ejected ministers to come within five miles of a city or town. The *Five Mile Act* was designed to deprive them of the power to earn a living of any sort. These Puritan Dissenters were persecuted in earnest in both Scotland and England. The Covenanters, as the Protestants in Scotland were called, were hunted like wild animals. They were chased by bloodhounds to the sound of bugle calls. Many were hanged or drowned. But these measures did not succeed, for the Lord knows how to take care of His own (Psalm 1). The bravery of these men remains to this day.

John Bunyan and John Milton

Among those who suffered for their faith was John Bunyan (1628–1688). Born at Elstow, Bedfordshire, Bunyan came to faith after he overheard some godly women talking about a life of grace. Bunyan realized that he knew nothing about such a religious experience, but he would like to know.

Moving to Bedford in 1653. Bunyan united with an Independent congregation. By 1657, he was preaching the Gospel of redeeming grace with great success. He had already begun a writing career. His first pamphlet was a tract against the Quakers entitled *Some Gospel Truths Opened*. This was followed by *A Vindication of Some Gospel Truths Opened*. His third work was on the parable of the rich man and Lazarus entitled *Sighs from Hell, or the Groans of a Damned Soul* (1658).

Bunyan continued to write and to preach as a *Non-conformist*—someone outside the official structure of the Church of England. In 1660 official persecution against the Non-conformists was renewed. Bunyan, caught up in the new cycle of violence, was arrested and imprisoned. As stressful as the circumstances were, his imprisonment was not as severe as it could have been. There were no prohibitions on visitors, and there were periods of parole.

While in prison Bunyan wrote his spiritual autobiography, *Grace Abounding to the Chief of Sinners*. This was followed in 1663 with *Christian Behavior*. Next came *The Holy City* (1665) to reveal the symbolism of the heavenly city described in

Revelation. Bunyan's greatest and most enduring work, *The Pilgrim's Progress*, was published in 1678.

As a prolific writer, all of the works of Bunyan were designed to help build-up the Christian's faith. In August of 1688, Bunyan rode through a heavy rain on his way to preach in London. Within a few days, he developed a violent fever and died. He was buried in Bunhill Fields, London.

Another Puritan, a man with unusual intellectual and literary gifts, was John Milton (1608–1674). As a young man, Milton enjoyed an exceptional education, with the opportunity to travel widely. In addition to English, Milton was fluent in Latin, Italian, Greek, Hebrew, and Aramaic, with a working knowledge of French and Spanish.

When the English Civil War began, Parliament invited Milton to serve as a chief apologist for the government. While the years in the service of the government were exciting and eventful, Milton's private life was filled with sorrow. His first two wives died bearing children. A son and a daughter also died in infancy, although three other children survived. Then, at the age of forty-seven, Milton went almost totally blind.

Marrying a third time, Milton settled down to live a quiet life until his death in 1674. During these twilight years (1660–1674), Milton wrote some of his greatest works, including the epic *Paradise Lost* (1667), setting forth the story of man's creation and fall. *Paradise Regained* depicted the temptation of Jesus and His victory over Satan. *Samson Agonistes* (1671) set forth the trials and tribulations of the biblical hero, Samson.

Return England to Catholicism?

While men like Bunyan continued to strengthen the spiritual life of Independent congregations, others were convinced that England should return to the Catholic Church. During his life Charles II vacillated between unbelief and Catholicism. On his deathbed in 1685, the king finally professed faith in the doctrines of the Romans Catholic Church. His brother James II ascended the throne without any moments of uncertainty. James II was a devout Catholic with a religious and political agenda of returning England to Catholicism. He found an ally in this objective in Louis XIV, king of France.

In the providence of God, William III (1650–1702) of the Netherlands emerged as a protector of the Protestant faith against the Catholic king, Louis XIV of France. His wife, Mary (b. 1662), was the daughter of the Catholic English king, James II. In fear and anguish, English Protestants appealed for help to William III of Orange, governor of the Netherlands (1672–1702). He readily responded. At the head of an army, William crossed the sea from Holland in 1688 and defeated the forces of James—who was forced into exile. William and Mary were crowned king and queen of England. William would reign from 1689–1702. Mary, recognized as a British joint sovereign, died in 1694.

In 1689, James made an earnest attempt to regain the English throne. Support was found in southern Ireland when he landed there with a French army. The people in Northern Ireland were Protestant, and chose to unite with William as "Orangemen" (an informal title which continues to this day). In 1690, the decisive battle of the Boyne took place. King James II, who had been watching the battle from a discrete distance, saw his army defeated, and he fled to France. William's victory allowed Holland, England, and America to continue to embrace the Protestant faith.

During the reign of William and Mary, religious toleration was given to all Protestant Dissenters: Presbyterians, Congregationalists, Baptists, and Quakers. The Catholics were placed on the defensive in England. *The Toleration Act* of 1689 allowed freedom of worship to those who were willing to: (1) pledge allegiance to William and Mary; (2) denounce the authority of the pope; (3) renounce transubstantiation and the mass; (4) forsake the invocation of the Virgin and saints; and (5) embrace the doctrinal portions of the *Thirty-nine Articles*.

A Summary of the *Thirty-Nine Articles*

The *Thirty-nine Articles*, formulated in the Canterbury Convocation of the Church of England in 1563, were a restatement of the *Forty-two Articles* set forth in 1552. The *Thirty-nine Articles* were used to support statutory law passed by Parliament in 1571. All ministers in the Anglican Church were required to acquiesce to them—or face penalties, persecution, and imprisonment. The historical effect of the *Articles* was to bring uniformity to the Church of England.

Articles 1 to 5 declare the historic faith of the creeds of Christendom concerning the Trinity, emphasizing the Person and work of the Lord Jesus Christ.

Articles 6 to 8 affirm the Scriptures as containing "all things necessary to salvation." The ancient creeds are "to be received and believed: for they may be proved by most certain warrants of Holy Scripture."

Articles 9 to 18 deal with the subject of personal religion. The orthodox doctrine of the Reformation is presented concerning free-will, grace, justification, predestination, and good works.

Articles 19 to 36 are concerned with the nature, constitution, structure, order, and authority of the Church. The sacraments are discussed. There is total rejection of purgatory.

In Article 28 the Catholic view of the Lord's Supper is renounced, as well as the Zwinglian interpretation. The doctrine is insisted upon that there is a real partaking of Christ, whose body is received in a heavenly and a spiritual manner by faith.

Articles 37 to 39 concern the national Church and its relation to the State. It is in this section that member churches of the Anglican community have had to make the most changes, in order to conform with changing political realities.

The Puritan Legacy

While the Puritans were not able to hold onto parliament or eliminate the state church permanently, they were such men of God in their personal lives that many of them were enabled by the Lord to write clear, deep, and blessed Christian books. In the last 50 years, Banner of Truth Press has begun to republish these, and in turn the books have stimulated a revival of interest in the "pure doctrines" of the Reformation. Some of the authors include the following.

Richard Baxter (1615–1691) was one of England's most respected and renowned preachers in an era of great ministers. He was one of the foremost spokesmen of the Puritan party within the Church of England. Baxter is the author of more than 160 works, including *The Saints' Everlasting Rest* (based on Hebrews 4:9). Those who would live a "heavenly life upon earth" are warned not to live in known sin, fellowship with the ungodly, argue over non-essential matters of Christian doctrine and conduct, or manifest a spirit of pride.

Thomas Goodwin (1600–1679). His parents devoted him to the Lord and to the work of the ministry when he was a child. Their desire to honor the Lord was not in vain. Gifted with intellectual abilities, Goodwin was admitted to Christ's College at the age of 13. After his conversion, Goodwin was appointed to the lectureship at Trinity Church, Cambridge, but resigned in 1634 for non-conformity. After pastoring in Holland, he returned to London. Thomas Goodwin was one of the divines at the Assembly of Westminster. His works have been reprinted in 12 volumes.

John Owen (1616–1683). Born at Stadhampton, Oxfordshire, John Owen was educated in the classics and theology before being ordained a minister in the Anglican Church. Dissatisfied with the changes mandated by Archbishop William Laud, Owen left that structure to become a leading theologian of the Congregational churches. When civil war broke out in the nation, Oliver Cromwell made Owen his chaplain during his military campaigns in Ireland and Scotland (1649–1651). A prolific writer and scholar, some of his greatest works are *The Display of Arminianism* (1642), *Doctrine of Justification by Faith* (1677), and *The Death of Deaths in the Death of Christ*.

Thomas Manton (1620–1677). In 1640 at the age of twenty, Thomas Manton was ordained deacon in the Anglican Church by the bishop of Exeter, even though the official minimum age was twenty-three. His life would be spent serving the Lord. Manton knew great success as a public orator; crowds would gather to hear him preach. But he also knew suffering through imprisonment, being jailed for six months after departing from the State Church. With others Manton drew up the *Fundamentals of Religion* (1658)—all the while trying to reach an accommodation with the bishops. His many Puritan works include commentaries on *James* (1651) and *Jude* (1658). Thomas Manton was a beloved minister of the Gospel and respected by conformists and non-conformists alike.

Steven Charnock (1628–1680). Charnock was acknowledged during his lifetime to be a Puritan preacher of sincere convictions, wisdom, and great learning. His fame as a theologian was widely appreciated and manifested in his various works: *A Discourse on Divine Providence*, *Discourses on Christ Crucified*, *Discourses on Regeneration, the Lord's Supper, and Other Subjects*, and *Discourses upon the Existence and Attributes of God* (1682)—which has become a classic.

CHAPTER 30

The Rise of New Expressions of Religion

A Fight without a Reasonable Finish

Born in a religious belief that "the just shall live by faith," the Reformation era ended in a social blood bath that included political, economic, and social considerations. Once more, the world was changed through three decades of physical violence (1618–1648). This *Thirty Years' War* would eventually involve most of the countries of western Europe, though it was fought mainly in Germany. At first, the struggle was basically a religious contest between Catholics and Protestants. In time, other factors changed its character. For example, Sweden and France entered the conflict to control the growing power of the Holy Roman Empire and its ruling family.

Armed struggles began in Bohemia after years of verbal conflict between Catholics and Calvinistic Protestants. In 1618 the Bohemians rejected the rule of the newly elected Catholic Emperor Ferdinand II (1578–1637), and elected the Protestant Calvinist, Elector Frederick V (1596–1632) of Germany. The predictable result was open civil war.

The Thirty Years' War can be divided into four distinct parts. In Part I (1618–1623), the Catholic armies were victorious over the Protestant forces in Bohemia, Moravia, and Austria. Frederick was completely defeated at the Battle of White Mountain (1620), deprived of his electorate (1623), and sent into exile until his death. His wife Elizabeth, daughter of James I, King of England, went into exile with him. They had been married in 1613.

In Part II (1623–1629), the battle ground shifted in Europe. Initially led by Christian IV of Denmark, the Catholics again defeated the Protestant armies. On

August 26, 1626, at Lutter am Barenberge, Germany, the main body of the Protestant army was routed. Towns and villages were pillaged in the aftermath.

In Part III (1630–1632), the various Catholic coalitions disintegrated. This allowed the zealous Lutheran, Gustavus Adolphus of Sweden, the "Lion of the North," to lead the Protestant forces to victory. He gave his life in the effort.

In Part IV (1632–1648), the war engaged all of Europe, as nation after nation struggled for power and political advantages.

Finally, the war was brought to an end by the *Peace of Westphalia*, signed at Munster on October 24, 1648. Switzerland and the Dutch Republic (the Netherlands) were established as independent states. The Holy Roman Empire and the Hapsburgs (Germany) were weakened. France emerged as the chief power on the Continent. Catholicism, Calvinism, and Lutheranism were all recognized as legitimate religions. Each prince or ruler was allowed to determine which religion he and his region would embrace. The religion of the prince would be the religion of the people.

A Tree of Life

Despite the political and religious wars, the roots of the Reformation produced a mighty spiritual tree with strong branches, which received nourishment to produce a variety of spiritual fruits (cp. Rev 22:2). In England, the common people and those who served in the House of Commons, could freely eat from the Tree of Life. One member of the House of Commons, Sir Walter Mildmay, founder of Emmanuel College in the city of Cambridge, had prayed that this would happen. It is reported that Queen Elizabeth had said to him: "Sir Walter, I hear you have erected a Puritan foundation."

"No, Madam," he replied, "far be it from me to countenance anything contrary to your established laws; but I have set an acorn, which when it becomes an oak, God alone knows what will be the fruit thereof."

Besides Walter Mildmay, there were other men under the early Stuarts to influence English Puritanism, such as William Perkins (1558–1602). His conversion to Christ came by a chance remark. One day as he was walking down the streets of Cambridge, he overheard a woman warn her child to "beware of drunken Perkins." His heart was smitten with sin by Almighty God. Shortly thereafter, "drunken Perkins' could be found preaching the Gospel of redeeming grace. He gave up the bottle for the Bible. In the years that followed, multitudes heard him gladly. He has been called "the Calvin of England."

Richard Sibbes (1577–1635) was another Cambridge Puritan who was used in a mighty way by God. Crowds gathered to hear him preach. Someone wrote, "Of this blest man, let this just praise be given: heaven was in him, before he was in heaven."

As people gathered to hear the Gospel, none presented it more clearly than Thomas Goodwin (1600–1679). Goodwin came to faith when he was nineteen years old. One day the Spirit of the Lord moved him to ride on horseback 35 miles, from Cambridge to Dedham, Essex, to listen to the preaching of the Puritan John Rogers, whereupon he was converted. Rogers was preaching against the sin of neglecting the Word of God. Suddenly, he began to personify the Lord. Another Puritan, John Howe (1630–1705), describes the scene and the sermon:

> "Well, I have trusted you so long with my Bible [preached Rogers], but you have slighted it; it lies in such and such houses all covered with dust and cobwebs. You care not to look into it. Do you use my Bible so? Then you shall have my Bible no longer."
>
> Next he takes up the Bible from its cushion, and seemed as if he were going away with it, and carrying it from them; but immediately he turns again, and personates the people to God, falls down on his knees, cries and pleads most earnestly,
>
> "Lord, whatsoever Thou doest to us, take not Thy Bible from us; kill our children, burn our houses, destroy our goods; only spare us Thy Bible, only take not away Thy Bible."
>
> And then he personates God again to the people: "Say you so? Well, I will try you a little longer; and here is my Bible for you. I will see how you will use it, whether you will practice it more, and live more according to it."

A Man of Conscience without Conviction

The Congregationalists, or Independents, reflect another sturdy branch of the Reformation tree. In doctrine they remained Calvinistic. In Church government, there were distinct changes. Radical changes in Church government in England were advocated vigorously by Robert Browne (c. 1550–1633), who was greatly influenced by Puritan theology. Graduated in 1572 from Corpus Christi College, Cambridge, Browne taught school. When he began to preach near Cambridge, Browne was confronted by Anglican Church officials. Refusing to accept an episcopal license, he and Robert Harrison established a separatist congregation in Norwich. This bold adventure brought persecution. Browne was put in prison.

After being released, he and a large portion of his congregation fled to Middleburg in the Netherlands (1582) to avoid future acts of religious hostility. It was in Middleburg that Browne wrote *A Treatise of Reformation without Tarrying for Any*. In this work, Browne argued that the authority of civil magistrates did not extend to doctrine, worship, or discipline in the Church. Jesus Christ rules over His people; and not the pope, nor the bishops, nor the king of England. The resurrected Christ guides His flock, through the power of the Holy Spirit, and the Word of Truth as contained in the Scriptures.

While many others began to find some of Browne's arguments persuasive, he personally did not have the courage to continue to live out the implications of his own initial convictions. He returned to England in 1585 because his congregation had become disruptive and divisive. While remaining sympathetic to the Puritan cause, by 1591 Browne was willing to become the rector of a local parish church. He had found a way in his own heart to be reconciled to the Church of England. Browne lived in relative obscurity until he was arrested for striking a policeman. He died in prison.

While Browne did not finally follow the practices of the principles he articulated, his concepts of separation between Church and State, with the Church being obedient to Christ, influenced later generations of believers in England and America. Others would implement his ideas concerning the autonomy of the local Church, the right for the local assembly to elect its own pastors and officers, and consideration by the whole congregation of important matters related to the Church.

A Burst of Anger and a New Bible

While the Separatist congregations struggled to survive, the Puritans continued to make efforts in reforming the Church of England. High hopes were held that James I, the new king, would help. James ascended the throne in 1603 following the death of Elizabeth I. He was the son of Mary, Queen of Scots by Lord Darnley, her second husband.

Though James had been reared a Presbyterian, he immediately embraced the Anglican principles and practices. In gratitude, the bishops and arch-bishops gladly paid him homage, and in time were well rewarded.

Prior to his official coronation, the Puritans had already presented the new King with a petition of reform signed by a thousand ministers. This *Millenary Petition*, as it became known, asked for the immediate removal of specific clergymen who still embraced practices that were associated with Catholicism.

In 1604, James decided to call a Church conference to discuss the issues involved. Bishops and Puritans gathered to debate in Hampton Court, London. The king, acting as chairman, threatened to "make the Puritans conform or else harry them out of the land." The proceedings came to a sudden halt when one of the Puritans used an unfortunate word. He referred to the gathering as a "synod," a word associated with Presbyterianism. James I broke out in anger.

"If," he said, "you aim at a Scottish Presbytery, it agrees as well with a monarchy as God and the devil! No bishop, no king." The Church conference was over. The King correctly perceived that if the presbyters could replace bishops, he himself could soon be driven off the throne by popular demand.

Following the conference, three hundred Puritan ministers were soon driven from the Church of England. One good thing did come of the Hampton Court conference: a decision to begin the translation for a new English Bible. The king wanted the popular Geneva Bible to be replaced because it had marginal notes, written by Separatists and Independents, that opposed the best interest of the monarchy. In 1611 the Authorized Version was published.

There were two Addresses placed in the forefront of the Authorized Version. The first Address honored King James I and Queen Elizabeth I, who is spoken of as "that bright Occidental [Western] Star." The king is referred to as the "most dread Sovereign, which Almighty God, the Father of all mercies, bestowed upon us the people of England, when first He sent Your Majesty's Royal Person to rule and reign over us."

The second Address, *The Epistle Dedicatory*, denounces both Catholics and Puritans. A complaint is registered against those "Popish Persons" who desire to keep the people in ignorance and darkness by denying them the Scriptures in their own language. The Puritans are alluded to as being "self-conceited brethren who run their own ways and give liking unto nothing but what is framed by themselves, and hammered on their anvil." There was one other significant result of the Hampton Court conference. Many of the Separatists left England for Holland—with the dream of finding ultimate freedom of worship in a place called America.

A Short Chronology of Two Congregations

In 1602, there emerged a distinct part of the Separatist movement that would become known as "Baptist." An early prominent leader of this period was John Smyth (c. 1560–1612), a former minister in the Church of England. Smyth had been ordained in 1594 by the Bishop of Lincoln, and was elected a Fellow at Christ's College. Being attracted first to the Puritans, and then to the principles of the Separatists, Smyth became the leader of a Separatist congregation in Gainsborough.

The Lord blessed and soon a second congregation was meeting in the home of William Brewster at Scrooby. In 1604 James Robinson, also a former minister of the Church of England, became the pastor of the people in Scrooby.

While the Scrooby congregation was growing, the Gainsborough assembly knew the pains of persecution. In 1607 the people, still led by John Smyth, sought religious refuge in Amsterdam. In 1609 the Scrooby congregation, under the combined leadership of Robinson and Brewster, relocated in Leyden in the Netherlands.

The peace that the Separatists enjoyed in the Netherlands allowed time for spiritual growth, and the formulation of far-reaching evangelistic objectives. A portion of the Gainsborough congregation felt led of the Lord to return to England in either 1611 or 1612, and established the first permanent Baptist Church in England. The Baptist movement would continue to grow. By 1644, seven congregations could be identified as "Baptistic." By 1649 John Myles and Thomas Proud could be sent forth by the London Baptists to preach the Gospel in Wales.

Distinctive Baptist Beliefs

One of the reasons for the growth of Baptist congregations was the movement's distinctives. The Baptists did not recognize sacraments per se, as did many other Christians. They believed in two ordinances, the Lord's Supper, and the baptism of professing believers. Early Baptists preferred to be baptized in "living waters," or water that flows in a river or a stream. In the Baptist Church government, the congregation ruled. It had total autonomy; it could call a pastor and dismiss him. There were no bishops or superintendents in the Baptist structure. No group had any governmental power over other individual congregations.

Initially, Baptists embraced the doctrine of particular (definite) redemption, as set forth in 1644 in the *London Confession*, and in the 1689 *Confession of Faith*.[1] Chapter 11 of the *Confession*, "Of Justification," Paragraph 3, states the following about particular recemption.

> Christ, by His obedience and death, did full discharge the debt of all those that are justified; and did, by the sacrifice of Himself in the blood of His cross, undergoing in their stead the penalty due unto them, make a proper, real, and full satisfaction to God's justice in their behalf; yet, inasmuch as He was given by the Father for them, and His obedience and satisfaction accepted in their stead, and both freely, not for anything in them, their justification is only of free grace, that both the exact justice and rich grace of God might be glorified in justification of the sinner (Heb 10:14; 1 Pet 1:18–19; Isa 53:5–6; Rom 8:32; 2 Cor 5:21; Rom 3:26; Eph 1:6–7; 2:7).

Charles Haddon Spurgeon (1834–1892), a London Baptist minister, has clearly articulated this belief.

> We are often told that we limit the atonement of Christ, because we say that Christ has not made a satisfaction for all men, or all men would be saved. Now, our reply to this is, that, on the other hand, our opponents limit it: we do not. The Arminians say, "Christ died for all men." Ask them what they mean by it. Did Christ die so as to secure the salvation of all men? They say, "No, certainly not." We ask them the next question. "Did Christ die so as to secure the salvation of any man in particular?" "No. Christ has died that any man may be saved if [he does this or that . . .]," and then follows certain conditions of salvation. Now, who is it that limits the death of Christ? Why, you! You say that Christ did not die so as infallibly to secure the salvation of anybody. We beg your pardon, when you say we limit Christ's death; we say, "No, my dear sir, it is you that do it." We say Christ so died that he infallibly secured the salvation of a multitude that no man can number, who through Christ's death not only may be saved, but *are* saved and cannot by any possibility run the hazard of being anything but saved. You are welcome to your atonement; you may keep it. We will never renounce ours for the sake of it.

---

[1] *London Baptist Confession of Faith of 1689* – one of the great historical confessions in continuous worldwide up to the present day; study guides available at www.ichthuspublications.com.

In political matters, the Baptists believed in a separation between Church and State. Though the king and Parliament had legitimate powers, they had no power over Church matters. During the Civil Wars and the *Interregnum* (1630–1660), between King Charles I and Parliament, the concept of a separation between Church and State caused many people to join the Congregationalists in general, and especially the Baptist movement.

The Savoy Synod

To maintain the growth they enjoyed, an assembly of Congregational leaders met in the Savoy Palace in London on September 29, 1658. The Synod adopted a *Declaration of Faith and Order Honored and Practiced in the Congregational Churches*. Based largely on the Calvinistic *Westminster Confession*, the *Savoy Declaration* included a section on "The Institution of Churches and the Order Appointed in Them by Jesus Christ." It advocated the Congregational form of Church government.

CHAPTER 31

The Changes in the Church Continue
A.D. 1618

Contending for the Faith

The Bible teaches that there is a faith "which was once delivered unto the saints" (Jude 1:3). There is a body of truth that has been discerned in each generation of believers as being non-negotiable. Cardinal doctrines of Christendom include the virgin birth, the deity of Christ, His true humanity, His substitutionary death at Calvary, His burial, His resurrection, His ascension into heaven, His Second Advent, and salvation by grace through faith alone. These truths, no person can deny and remain in the sphere of true saving faith. These truths form the fabric of the Christian faith that clothes all those who come to Christ.

While good Christian people might prefer different forms of Church government, and desire different modes of baptism, the cardinal doctrines, which are essential to salvation, must be embraced, lest there be a falling away from the truth into error, false teaching, heresy, and eternal judgment. The historic creeds of Christendom summarize the biblical boundaries, beyond which orthodox Christians dare not go. Unfortunately, within the Church, professing Christians[1] have come in to break through biblical boundaries. When one generation begins by challenging Christianity's historic beliefs, then later generations will go further by denying them.

Changing the Faith

One person that changed the historic beliefs of many within the Protestant Church, was James (Jacobus) Arminius. Arminius was born in the Netherlands at Oudewater,

---

[1] professing Christians – those who take the name of Christ without necessarily having been born again.

near Utrecht (1560). His father died around the time of his birth. Then, in the early years of childhood, the Spaniards came and destroyed his hometown. His family perished. Kind Dutch neighbors took Arminius into their home and provided for his needs.

Recognized as a capable student, Arminius was enrolled as the twelfth student at the new University of Leyden (1576). Here, for the first time on public record, he used his Latinized name, Jacobus Arminius, instead of his given name at birth, Jacob Harmenszoon. As expected, Arminius enjoyed academic excellence.

After completing his studies at Leyden, Arminius continued his education at the Geneva Academy (1582), which was headed by Theodore Beza, the successor to John Calvin. In 1588, Arminius was ordained a minister of the Gospel. He became a pastor of the Reformed Church in Amsterdam. In 1590 Arminius married a prosperous merchant's daughter, which gave him contact with the prominent members of society. As a minister, Jacobus was eloquent, educated, and enlightened. His sermons attracted large audiences, not only for their clear content, but for the controversy they created.

According to Arminius, the orthodox Reformation faith (commonly now termed "Calvinism") was wrong. (1) God did not extend His saving grace only to those whom He predestines to salvation, but to all men. (2) Nor is the will of man so bound in sin that he has no ability to act for good, but rather he is able to take a step toward God out of a spark of good within. (3) Nor does God sovereignly choose (elect) some men for salvation, out of all who receive the just condemnation for their sin, but rather God has elected those whom He has foreseen will believe. (4) Nor is man totally disabled by sin to merit favor with God; (5) nor is he fully depraved.

By 1592 Arminius had been formally accused of Pelagianism (a fifth century controversy which emphasized the freedom of man's will), and departure from the two reformed creeds: the *Belgic Confession* and the *Heidelberg Catechism*. Accusations of departing from the faith would continue to follow him until his death in 1609.

During his life, Arminius had asked for a Church council to be called to discuss afresh the concepts of predestination, election, and reprobation. Nine years after his death, such a council was finally held.

The Synod of Dort

When the Synod of Dort met, from November 13, 1618 to May 9, 1619, delegates from the Reformed Churches in the Netherlands, England, Germany, and

Switzerland attended. The teachings of Arminius were considered, but they were unanimously rejected and condemned. The established Calvinistic Reformed doctrines were affirmed in the *Canons of Dort*.[2]

Those who defend Jacobus Arminius from the condemnation of the Synod of Dort, make a distinction between the man and the message his followers manifested. It is a valid point. The views of Arminius were never systematically set forth until the year following his death, when his followers issued a declaration called *The Remonstrance* (1610).

It is doubtful that Arminius himself would have openly endorsed the positions that have become associated with his name. His thinking was more subtle. His language was more cautious. The writings of Arminius himself are so carefully worded that Moses Stuart (1831) found it possible to argue that Arminius was not an Arminian (i.e., that Arminius would not hold to the modern views associated with his name). However, in the end, the charge is valid that Arminius had an indirect role in denying accepted Protestant biblical truths, such as the depravity of man, the bondage of the will to sin, and the election of some souls unto salvation from the judgment all deserve.

If Arminius was by nature a gentle man in presenting his views and cautious in his comments, then at least it is true that the implications of his thinking inflamed, with combative religious zeal, the young ministers whom he had trained for the ministry. Forty-five of them signed *The Remonstrance*, which systematically set forth five points that came to be called *Arminianism*. And the whole church was soon caught up with theological controversy. Arminius is not without historical accountability. He did plant the seed that has proven to be a great challenge to the Church for the souls of men.

Those who continued to interpret the Scriptures according to the historic teachings of the Reformation, formulated a response to each of the five points—and these have come to be known as the five points of *Calvinism*. A brief summary of the direct conflict between the historic Reformation teaching and Arminianism may be stated as follows.

---

[2] *Canons of Dort* – reprinted by and available from Chapel Library.

CALVINISM	ARMINIANISM
Election is unconditional.	Election and condemnation (reprobation) are conditioned upon the foreseen faith or unbelief of man, not upon the sovereign choice of Almighty God.
The atonement is limited to the elect. A definite redemption was made.	The atonement was made for all, but only believers enjoy its benefits.
Man is depraved as far as any ability to have a part in his salvation, or to merit the merits of Christ.	Man, unaided by the Holy Spirit, is unable to come to God. However, the will of man is involved in salvation.
Grace is irresistible.	Grace can be resisted.
The saints will persevere in the faith, being kept by the power of God. Their salvation is certain.	The doctrine of the final perseverance of all the converted is still open to discussion. At least, Christians can "backslide" into not only occasional sin, but even lifestyles of habitual sin—and still be saved on the basis of their "decision to receive Christ."

Though Arminian theology was officially condemned at the Synod of Dort, its influence did not go away. It was accepted by multitudes in the Anglican Church, and by many in the dissenting denominations, including the Baptists and the Methodists. Arminian theology continues to be widely accepted in much of Christendom.

"Something" in the Soul

While the Church reconsidered its fundamental beliefs, a man by the name of George Fox (1624–1691) introduced new behavior for Christians to practice. Fox was the son of a weaver. He himself became a shoemaker.

A deeply religious man, Fox was hungry for sincerity in religion and a spiritual visitation from God. When he was nineteen years old, Fox was invited by Church members to a party. What he saw sickened him. Those who professed to be Christians could not be distinguished from the world.

As Fox meditated on the spiritual state of society and the Church, new ideas began to formulate in his mind. Fox came to believe that all men possessed something he called the "Inner Light." According to Fox, the Bible, which guides conduct, is a closed Book unless the mind is illuminated by the Spirit. The good news is that the Spirit has something to work with, because within each person is something that tells him what is right and what is wrong. That something in the soul will draw the heart from the false to the true, from the low to the high, and from the impure to the pure. That something is "Christ's Light" or divine illumination. Christ's Light gives illumination to the mind and heart. It also gives life and power, peace and joy. Here is the "Seed of God."

While disregarding all existing churches, creeds, and doctrine, while showing little appreciation for formal theological training or professional ministers, and while rejecting all outward sacraments, George Fox presented his views to the Christian community. He found a following. In 1654 there were sixty Quakers. Four years later there were thirty-thousand Quakers. Many people were attracted to a simple way of worshipping. Others welcomed meditation instead of formal study. Still others, who had lost respect for professional ministers, believed that their own opinions really were equally valid on religious matters.

Those who followed Fox were called *Quakers*. The origin of this term is uncertain. It may be that the term arose on an occasion in court at Derby in 1650. Fox had been convicted for blasphemy. When the judge spoke a word of ridicule, Fox responded by exhorting the magistrate to "tremble at the Word of the Lord." Another possibility is that the term "Quaker" was a name of derision. The opponents of Fox discovered that he and his followers "quaked" with emotion in their plain meetinghouses when they thought they had been visited by God. Whatever the origin of the word, it was resented. Fox and his followers wanted to be called "Friends," for Jesus said, "I have called you friends" (John 15:15).

When the Society of Friends met, they sat down and waited in silence for the Spirit of the Living God to come. There was no pulpit. There were no musical instruments; there was only silence. If the Spirit did not lead some man or woman to speak, everyone left after a determined length of time.

Doctrinally, the Friends stressed the "priesthood of all believers." They did not believe in taking oaths, going to war, or retaliating when persecuted. They believed that kindness will produce kindness. They believed that the same Inner Spirit which guided them in the meeting-house would guide them in their daily lives. The Friends believed that all people have dignity. Despite persecution, the Society of Friends survived the perils of their day to grow numerically as an organization.

Part Four

The Church in the Modern Age

A.D. 1648—Present

CHAPTER 32

The Continued Growth of Mysticism

Gnosticism Again!

As the seventeenth century progressed, cold orthodoxy continued to give way to mysticism. As noted, a large segment of European society was attracted to the Quakers, who stressed the work of the Holy Spirit. It was exciting for them to be told that the revelation of the "Inner Light" was superior to the Holy Scriptures, though not contrary to it. It was thrilling for some to hear that the Holy Spirit speaks to all—so that special scriptural training and ordained ministers of the Gospel were not necessary to personal growth or spiritual understanding of the Bible. It was revolutionary to consider the concept that formal worship might be an abomination to the Lord. It was daring to reject the sacraments, and renounce oaths, while refusing to serve in the military. The Quakers promoted mysticism, as did the Swedish scientist Emmanuel Swedenborg (1688–1772), whose followers founded the New Jerusalem Church.

As a man of science, Swedenborg was recognized as one of the leading thinkers of his day. Many wonderful inventions resulted from his research—including the designs for a submarine and a machine that could fly. Though brilliant in physics, music, astronomy, and natural history, Swedenborg is best remembered for his interest in religion. In 1743, Swedenborg insisted that he was able to communicate with the souls of the departed spirits and with the angelic hosts. He claimed that he had been shown the secrets of the universe. Such alleged superior knowledge led him to spiritualize the Bible (1 Cor 8:1). The things he then taught had similarities to Gnosticism, an early heresy in the Church (see Part 1, chapter 3).

The basic teaching of Gnosticism (Greek, *gnosis*, knowledge) was that matter is essentially evil and spirit is essentially good. The Gnostics would argue that since God is spirit, He would not touch anything that is material. Therefore God did not create the world. What God did do, according to the Gnostics, was to put forth a series of emanations of concentric circles. Think of a child throwing a small pebble into a pond of water: concentric circles are formed in small waves. The Gnostics declared that each divine emanation of God moved further and further from Him until one of these emanations at last touched matter. And that emanation was the Creator of the world. Cerinthus, one of the leaders of the Gnostics, said that "the world was created, not by God, but by a certain power far separate from Him, and far distant from that Power who is over the universe, and ignorant of the God who is over all." By the time John wrote His Gospel, some of the Gnostics were teaching that Jesus Christ was one of the emanations from God. They said that Jesus was not truly God.

Other Gnostics held that Jesus had no real body. They said that he was a phantom without real flesh and blood. They would never have said, "The Word was made flesh" (John 1:14). Saint Augustine tells how he read a great deal in the writings of the philosophers of his day. But he said, "'The Word was made flesh, and dwelt among us,' I did not read there."

John who had known Jesus, John who had touched Him, John who had leaned upon His breast and heard the thumping of the heart of heaven, was grieved with those who taught that Jesus only appeared to be human. He declared that anyone who denied that Jesus was come in the flesh was moved by the spirit of Anti-Christ (1 John 4:3). Emmanuel Swedenborg denied that Jesus was truly God in the flesh.

He was hostile not only to the doctrine of the Trinity, but also to the doctrine of salvation by grace through faith alone. Swedenborg believed that God imputed righteousness to individuals according to His own sovereign choice, including those who have never repented of their sins. Armed with such mystical musings, the followers of Emmanuel Swedenborg were able to establish churches in Sweden, England, Germany, and America.

Reaction to Rationalization of Roman Theology

Inside the Church of Rome there was also a reaction to the sterile rationalization of the Christian life. A mystical movement arose known as Quietism, which taught that God will visit with any person whose soul is fully surrendered to Him. If the heart is passive, there will be an imputation of the divine light from God. When the heavenly visitation comes, the soul will enjoy an intimate communion with God. Three leading writers of Quietism were Michael Molinos (1640–1697), a Spanish theologian; Madame Guyon (1648–1717) of France; and Francis Fenelon (1651–1715), a French minister and archbishop.

Elsewhere, a Dutch theologian, Cornelius Otto Jansen (1585–1638), founder of Jansenism, reacted to Catholic dogma being made lifeless. This bishop of Ypres in the Southern Netherlands (today Belgium) turned the eyes of the Church of Rome back to the basic teachings of Augustine, in order to emphasize holiness of life and the necessity of divine grace for regeneration. Many who were serious about their souls, and concerned about proper Christian conduct and character, were attracted to Jansenism. The center of the movement was established at a nunnery in Port Royal near Paris.

Roman Catholic Rejection of Reform

Fearful of losing their own sphere of influence, the Jesuits vigorously opposed the Jansenists. In 1710 the buildings of Port Royal were torched and destroyed. Alarmed with such militant behavior, in 1773 Clement XIV (pope, 1769–1774) disbanded the Order of Jesuits. However, when Pius VII (pope, 1800–1823) restored the order in 1814, the Jesuits were able to grow again in stature by influencing Catholic dogma and enhancing the power of the papal throne. During the Vatican Council of 1870, it was the Jesuits who encouraged the doctrine of the infallibility of the pope to be proclaimed. This teaching states that in matters of religion, when the pope speaks in an official capacity (*ex cathedra*), he cannot err. Prior to this the Catholic Church theologians had always insisted that general councils are supreme over the popes.

The strengthening of the papal power was needed because of such novel teaching as the one introduced in 1854 by Pius IX (pope, 1846–1878). Pius proclaimed the dogma of the Immaculate Conception of the Virgin Mary. The belief that Mary was free of original sin (cp. Rom 3:10, 23; 6:23) did not originate with Pius. However, he used this pronouncement, also inspired by the Jesuits, to challenge the nineteenth century spirit of skepticism.

In November, 1950, the power to speak *ex cathedra* (Latin, "from the chair") was again put to use when Pius XII (pope, 1939–1958) proclaimed the Assumption of Mary to be a true Catholic doctrine. Devout followers of the Catholic faith would be taught to believe that Mary did not die. Rather, her body and soul were taken up to heaven in the same manner as that of Jesus Christ (Acts 1:9). No scriptural evidence can be offered for this teaching.

Lutheran Pietism

Mysticism came to the Lutheran Church in the seventeenth century in the form of Pietism. It would not remain only in the Lutheran Church, but would cross cultural, language, and political boundaries to influence many facets of Christendom including the Puritans. Cotton Mather, for example, carried on correspondence from America with Pietist leaders in Europe.

Pietism emphasized the need for a personal work of regeneration, followed by a life of consistent Christian living, manifested with the love of God. Good works were to be considered a sign of salvation. Private study of the Bible was unimportant. Formal titles were avoided. Common nouns such as "brother," "sister," and "pastor" were introduced as nouns of address.

The Pietists considered themselves to be a continuation of the Reformation within the churches of the Reformation. They encouraged the concept of the creation of conventicles, or cell groups, thereby forming little churches within the Church. Visual aides were important; biblical themes were painted in beautiful and detailed works of art. Religious books contained symbolic pictures with words of moral exhortation.

The father of Pietism was the German born Philipp Jacob Spener (1635–1705). He believed that there was more to the Christian life than what the Lutheran Church had come to expect, which was not much. The Church seemed to be satisfied if the people could remember any portion of their catechism, attended the stated services, and received the sacraments. Nothing was ever said about personal regeneration or an inner work of divine grace. Many of the ministers did not appear to be converted. Open drunkenness and immorality was not censured in the assembly of the saints. After reading a copy of *True Christianity* by the German mystic Johann Arndt, Spener knew that there had to be a better way to live out the ethics of the kingdom of heaven.

August Francke (1663–1727) agreed. After being truly converted to Christ in 1687, at the age of twenty-four, Francke joined the Pietist movement. Interested in education, he founded a university at Halle (Germany) as a center of Pietism. A man of enormous energy and with great organizational skills, Francke established a school for poor children (1695). He also raised up a home for orphans. All of this and more was done without personal wealth. Francke believed that his heavenly Father could supply all of his needs through the power of prayer. Francke was right. In miraculous ways, God opened the windows of heaven and poured out a blessing. Money came from every part of Germany when Francke and others prayed.

The Unity of the Brethren

While new religious movements continued to emerge, old ones managed to find new spiritual life—illustrated in the Hussites. Despite severe persecution, the followers of John Huss (d. 1415) of Bohemia (today the Slovak Republic) survived. In 1457 they had embraced the name *Unitas Fratrum* ("Unity of the Brethren"). During the early days of the Reformation led by Martin Luther, the "Bohemian Brethren," as they were commonly called, enjoyed a membership of 200,000 and met to worship in over four-hundred churches. However, during the Counter Reformation period of the Catholic Church and the Thirty Years' War (1618–1648), this facet of the Christian faith was almost destroyed. Comenius (1592–1670) called those who remained the "Hidden Seed."

In the providence of the Lord, a young Lutheran count named Nikolaus Ludwig Von Zinzendorf emerged to help revitalize the *Unitas Fratrum*. Born in Dresden, Germany, in 1700, Zinzendorf enjoyed a life of luxury. His devout father was a high court official. At an early age, Nikolaus was drawn to the Savior. One day he came upon a picture of Christ suffering at Calvary. The words beneath the portrait burned their way into his heart, "This I did for you. What do you do for me?" Zinzendorf wanted to do something for Christ. He wanted to win souls to the Savior. But first he must honor his parents (Exod 20:12). He must study law at Wittenburg University (1716–1719) and become a civil servant of the government of Saxony. While Zinzendorf honored his parents, he longed for a way to be of better use for the Master. Finally the opportunity came in 1720, when he received a portion of his inheritance. Zinzendorf purchased from his grandmother a large estate located seventy miles east of Dresden, and called it Berthelsdorf.

At the urging of a humble Pietist carpenter named Christian David, Count Zinzendorf permitted the Hidden Seed to gather on his Berthelsdorf estate. Two families arrived in 1722. Five years later, several hundred Brethren had gathered to live in a community which they called Herrnhut, the "Lord's Lodge."

Caught up in the religious excitement which he witnessed on his own property, Zinzendorf resigned all civil duties to live in the midst of the Brethren. Taking advantage of his legal training, Zinzendorf was able to guide the emerging community in establishing spiritual rules of conduct without violating any of the civil laws of Saxony. The Lord blessed and the community of saints grew larger. When people arrived from the province of Moravia, located next to Bohemia, a new name was given to the community, the Moravians. Officially, the Moravian Church was formally organized on August 13, 1727, following a communion service at Herrnhut. The power of the Holy Spirit was present in a special way.

As a guiding influence in the assembly of the Brethren, Zinzendorf manifested both spiritual strength and weakness. His love for Christ gave way at times to very sentimental thoughts of the Lord. But Zinzendorf taught believers to be faithful soldiers of the Cross. Christians were to go forth and conquer the nations of the world by making disciples (Matt 28:19–20). Missionaries were sent to Africa, Asia, Greenland, Lapland, and North America. One faithful servant in North America was David Zeisberger. For sixty-three years he ministered to the American Indians. Such dedication is precious. And so it was that the Moravians, under the spiritual guidance of the Pietist Count Nikolaus Ludwig Von Zinzendorf, fanned the flames of Protestant missionary work.

* * *

A Concise Catechism on Conversion[1]

1. ***Question.*** What is sin?

Answer. Sin is any want[2] of conformity to the Law of God, or transgression of it. "Sin is a transgression of the law" (1 John 3:4).

Commentary. Of sin in general: (1) Sin is a violation or transgression. The Latin word, *transgredior*, to transgress, signifies to go beyond one's bounds. The moral law is to keep us within the bounds of duty. Sin is going beyond our bounds. (2) Sin is evil. It is a defiling thing. Sin is not only a defection, but a pollution. It is to the soul as rust is to gold, as a stain to beauty. It makes the soul red with guilt, and black with filth (note Isa 30:22; 1 Kgs 8:38; Zec 3:3). (3) Sin is grieving God's Spirit. "Grieve not the Holy Spirit of God" (Eph 4:30). (4) Sin is a disease. "The whole head is sick" (Isa 1:5). Some are sick with pride, others with lust, others with envy.

---

[1] Extracted from *A Body of Divinity* by Rev. Thomas Watson (1620–1686) with editorial observations by Stanford E. Murrell.

[2] want – lack.

Editorial Observation. The Bible teaches that "all have sinned, and come short of the glory of God" (Rom 3:23). "As it is written, there is none righteous, no not one" (Rom 3:10; Psa 14:1–3). As a result of sin, each person has received the penalty of sin, which is physical death in time and spiritual death in eternity. "For the wages of sin is death" (Rom 6:23; cp. Rev 20:6). That is the bad news. The "good news," the Gospel, is that there is hope. "For God so loved the world, that he gave his only begotten Son, that whosoever believeth in him should not perish, but have everlasting life" (John 3:16). Paul teaches that "God commendeth his love toward us, in that, while we were yet sinners, Christ died for us" (Rom 5:8). So there is a way of salvation. It has been graciously provided in the Person and work of Jesus Christ at Calvary. Individuals can be saved from the power and the pollution of sin. Those who are guilty can yet be declared righteous in the eyes of the Law. Individuals can still be justified in the sight of God by faith.

2. *Question.* What is justifying faith?

Answer. True justifying faith consists in three things:

(1) Self-renunciation. Faith is going out of one's self, being taken off from our own merits, and seeing we have no righteousness of our own. "Not having mine own righteousness" (Phil 3:9).

(2) Reliance. The soul casts itself upon Jesus Christ; faith rests on Christ's person. Faith believes the promise; but that which faith rests upon in the promise is the Person of Christ: therefore the spouse is said to "lean upon her Beloved" (Song 8:5). Faith is described to be "believing on the name of the Son of God" (1 John 3:23), that is, on His person. Faith rests on Christ's person, "as he was crucified." It glories in the cross of Christ (Gal 6:14).

(3) Appropriation, or applying Christ to ourselves. A medicine, though it be ever so effectual, if not applied, will do no good; though the plaster be made of Christ's own blood, it will not heal unless applied by faith; the blood of God, without faith in God, will not save. This applying of Christ is called receiving Him (John 1:12). The hand receiving the gold, enriches; so the hand of faith, receiving Christ's golden merits with salvation, enriches us.

Editorial Observation. At this point, it is possible for a conscientious seeking sinner to despair upon hearing the Gospel. If justifying faith involves self-renunciation, reliance upon the person of Christ, and the appropriation of Christ, there is concern—for the honest heart realizes that it has no innate ability to perform this spiritual good work. What can be done?

3. *Question.* How is faith wrought [produced]?

Answer. By the blessed Spirit; who is called the "Spirit of grace," because He is the spring of all grace (Zec 12:10). Faith is the chief work which the Spirit of God works in a man's heart. In making the world God did but speak a word, but in working faith He puts forth His arm (Luke 1:51). The Spirit's working faith is called the "exceeding greatness" of God's power (Eph 1:19). What a power was put forth in raising Christ from the grave, when such a tombstone lay upon Him as "the sins of all the world"—yet He was raised up by the Spirit! The same power is put forth by the Spirit of God in working faith. The Spirit irradiates the mind, and subdues the will. The will is like a garrison that holds out against God; the Spirit with sweet violence conquers, or rather changes it, making the sinner willing to have Christ upon any terms—to be ruled by Him as well as saved by Him.

Editorial Observation. While many talk about the free will of man, the Bible teaches about the *freed* will of man. The natural man is born with his will enslaved to sin. He is "dead in trespasses and sins" (Eph 2:1). The will of the natural man is enslaved to "the lusts of the flesh" (Eph 2:3). Jesus Christ must come and set the captive free in a sovereign way (Matt 1:21; Luke 4:18), so that it can be said for all eternity that the soul is born again (John 23:3), "not of blood, nor of the will of the flesh, nor of the will of man, but of God" (John 1:13). While some may boast of free will, the heart of the redeemed glories in the free grace of a free Gospel of our great God and our Savior, Jesus Christ (2 Pet 1:1), who has *freed* the wicked heart from the power and pollution of sin.

It is imperative that each person examine themselves to see if they are within the sphere of true saving faith (2 Cor 13:5). It is possible to be religious, but not regenerated. It is possible to be baptized, without ever having truly believed on the Lord Jesus Christ for salvation and the forgiveness of sin (Acts 16:31; cp. Acts 8:35–38). It is possible for a person to grow up in the Church without being converted (John 3:10). Therefore, "give diligence to make your calling and election sure" (2 Pet 1:10). If you have never made your own calling and election sure, why not do that right now?

> The word is nigh thee, even in thy mouth, and in thy heart: that is, the word of faith, which we preach; [so] that if thou shalt confess with thy mouth the Lord Jesus, and shalt believe in thine heart that God hath raised him from the dead, thou shalt be saved. For with the heart man believeth unto righteousness; and with the mouth confession is made unto salvation. For the scripture saith, Whosoever believeth on him shall not be ashamed (Rom 10:8–10).

If God grants you faith to believe and converts you, please write to the publisher and share what God has done in this hour of grace (Luke 15:10). And "the Lord shall count, when he writeth up the people, that this man was born there" (Psa 87:6).

CHAPTER 33

The Boundaries of Acceptable Beliefs

The Sin of Socinianism

The Quakers, Quietist, Pietists, and Moravians challenged the boundaries of orthodox beliefs and behavior. But other religious groups emerged that made no pretension to preserving the faith of the church. Among these new bodies, none was bolder than the *Socinians* (2 Pet 2:1). Two Italian Roman Catholics, Laelius Socinus and his nephew Faustus Socinus (1539–1604), were responsible for promoting doctrinal error that destroyed cardinal truths held by that Church. The weapon of destruction was political discretion. Laelius Socinus did not openly defy the Catholic Church. Rather, he raised clever questions that were difficult to answer, much like Lucifer questioned Eve (Gen 3:1).

The most private manuscripts containing the true thoughts of Laelius were passed on to his nephew Faustus, who was studying theology at Basel, Switzerland. More bold than his uncle, Faustus went to Poland and, in 1579, began to publish heretical views on the Trinity. In 1605, the *Racovian Catechism* was published in Rakow, Poland. In this document, the deity of Christ was denied. Jesus was declared to be a good man, but only a man. His death at Calvary could not, and did not, atone for the sins of anyone. Nor is man enslaved to sin and unable to do good. The disciples of Faustus Socinus were so filled with spiritual defiance against the Lord Jesus Christ that they inscribed on their leader's tomb a taunt: "Lofty Babylon lies prostrate. Luther destroyed its roof, Calvin its walls, but Socinus its foundations." The meaning was clear. The Catholic Church in particular and Christianity in general had found a formidable enemy of the Cross (Phil 3:18).

The Ugliness of Unitarianism

Those in England who decided to embrace Socinianism were known as Unitarians. As faithless followers of Christ were to be found in the Catholic Church (Jude 1:4), so such men were found in the Episcopal Church of England. Theophilus Lindsey cleverly argued with Anglican Church officials that subscription to the doctrinal statement, the *Thirty-nine Articles*, should not be mandatory for ministers. He piously pretended that fidelity to the Bible should be the only criteria of doctrinal purity. In this way, ministers who secretly embraced Socinian theology, could keep their livelihood while not affirming the deity of Christ—for the Scriptures were open to interpretation.

When Parliament was asked to consider the concerns of Lindsey, his petition was rejected. This forced Lindsey to withdraw from the Episcopal Church in 1774 to establish a Unitarian Church in London. However, in 1779 Parliament reversed itself. The *Toleration Acts* were amended so that all who denied the Trinity could remain in the established Church of England!

The Spiritual Madness of Modernism

English Unitarianism became the forerunner of Modernism in the nineteenth and twentieth centuries. The Modernists emerged to deny the supernatural. They did not believe in biblical miracles, the virgin birth of Christ, His deity, or His substitutionary work at Calvary. The Modernists exalted reason to the point that they denied the Lord's resurrection and ascension into heaven. They had no hope of a Second Advent (Heb 9:28). The inerrancy (i.e., without the possibility of error) of the Bible was rejected. The sad reality is that many, if not most, Protestant Churches today are influenced by Modernism. A lesson is learned. The evil that some men do, does not die with them—it lives on. But there will be a payday, someday, for men like Laelius and Faustus Socinus, and Theophilus Lindsey—who helped to destroy in many the Gospel of redeeming grace (2 Cor 5:10).

The Message of Two Methodists

"The best of all, God is with us."—John Wesley

While the Enemy sowed tares in the Lord's vineyard (Matt 13:24–25), the Gospel continued to triumph—though not always in a predictable manner. The great orthodox doctrines of grace were not valued by all within the Church. Arminian theology emerged to exert a mighty influence over nations, especially in England and America. Two great champions of this theology were John and Charles Wesley. John Wesley was the fifteenth child born to Samuel Wesley and his remarkable wife Susanna Annesley. Charles, next to last, was the eighteenth to be born.

Reared in a godly home, John (b. 1703) had a sense of destiny fostered by a fire in 1709. Late one night, his father's parsonage at Epworth began to burn. John was literally snatched from the blazing inferno by a neighbor, who stood on the shoulders of another man to rescue the seven year old child. John's mother told him often that he was a "brand plucked" from the burning (Zec 3:2). He had been spared to serve the Savior.

For John, coming to know Christ in a personal way would not prove easy. Despite an excellent education and diligent involvement with the Holy Club, which he and Charles started at Oxford, John did not know anything about true saving faith. He who had mastered seven languages did not know the language of heaven. He who read the Scriptures daily and longed for practical holiness, knew nothing of positional sanctification. He who went to the American colony of Georgia with Governor Oglethorpe to preach the Gospel (1735) to the heathen, had the heart of the same, by his own honest testimony!

In 1737, filled with spiritual desperation, John sought counsel from Peter Boehler, a Moravian. Unusual advice was given. John was to preach the Gospel until he received faith, and then he was to preach the Gospel because he had faith. So John continued to study and preach and dwell on the meaning of salvation. His search was not in vain (John 7:17). According to God's wonderful, matchless grace, on May 24, 1738, John Wesley, already ordained as a minister of the Anglican Church, was converted to Christ. His "heart was strangely warmed" as he listened to the reading of Martin Luther's commentary on the book of Romans. John Wesley received faith. Now he would preach faith because he had it.

Wesley preached until his dying day in 1791. The Lord blessed with unusual physical strength, and the salvation of many souls. By the time of his death, Wesley had ridden more than 250,000 miles on horseback. He had preached more than 40,000 sermons to tens of thousands in the open air. He had published 5,000 works, and established a religious following numbering 79,000 in England and 40,000 in America. Though small in stature, five feet three inches tall and one hundred twenty-eight pounds, Wesley was strong in the Spirit of the Lord. He once said, "I look upon all the world as my parish." With his brilliant organizational skills, the "Father of the

Methodists" gave the world the enduring message of redeeming love, as did his brother Charles.

Charles Wesley (1707–1788) used music to illuminate the divine message John preached so well. Of the 6,500 hymns that he composed, the Church still sings many of them—such as *O for a Thousand Tongues*:

> "O for a thousand tongues to sing
>   My great Redeemer's praise;
> The glories of my God and King,
>   The triumphs of His grace."

Charles turned down a worldly fortune to gain the greater glory and crown of eternal life. He is rightly remembered as the "Poet of the Evangelical Revival."

(Selected Dates in the Life of John Wesley)

1703 Birth of John Wesley (Charles 1707).
1709 Rescued from a fire at Epworth Rectory.
1720 Admitted to Oxford.
1727 Is assistant pastor of Wroote, Lincs.
1729 Returns to Oxford, assumes leadership of the Holy Club.
1735 His father, Samuel, dies. John and Charles leave for America.
1737 An unsuccessful romance with Sophie Hopkey; leaves America.
1738 John Wesley is converted on Wednesday, May 23, at sea.
1739 Preaches in the open air for the first time.
1740 Separates from the Moravians.
1741 Preaches in South Wales for the first time.
1742 Preaches in the north of England for the first time with Charles. An orphanage and Sunday school are established.
1744 First Methodist Conference is held.
1747 Makes the first of forty-two trips to preach in Ireland.
1751 John is married to Mrs. Vazeille. Makes the first of twenty-two trips to preach in Scotland.
1755 John separates from his wife.
1768 A Methodist Chapel is opened in New York. Founding of Lady Huntington's College of Trevecca.

1776 John Wesley publishes *A Calm Address to Our American Colonies*, advocating loyalty to England.

1784 John Wesley formally ordains Thomas Coke and others for ministry in America, leads to a final separation with the Anglican Church, whose position is that "ordination is separation".

1791 On March 2, John Wesley dies (Charles, 1788).

John Wesley's Rule for Christian Living

> "Do all the good you can,
>   By all the means you can,
> In all the ways you can,
>   In all the places you can,
> At all the times you can,
>   To all the people you can,
> As long as ever you can!"

The Very Interesting Edward Irving

While the Anglican Church struggled with its response to the Methodists, independent movements continued to multiply with dramatic distinctives among themselves. One of the more interesting groups was led by Edward Irving, a former Presbyterian minister.

Irving was born on August 4, 1792, in Annan, Scotland. Blessed with natural intelligence, Irving entered Edinburgh University when he was thirteen years old. He received a Master of Arts degree in April, 1809, at age sixteen, and was licensed as a Presbyterian minister at age twenty-three. After serving four years as assistant pastor in Glasgow, in 1822 and thirty years old, Irving became pastor of the Caledonian (Presbyterian) Chapel at Hatton Garden in London. His fame as a great orator spread throughout the entire region.

While enjoying a popular public ministry, Irving was aware that there was a revival of interest in *pre-millennialism*. This system of belief teaches that Jesus Christ will one day return to earth to set up a kingdom in Jerusalem, which will last a thousand years (a millennium). From a rebuilt Temple, Christ will sit on the ancient throne of David and rule the nations of the world.

His own interest in pre-millennialism led Irving to the discovery of Manuel de Lacunza's book, *The Coming of Messiah in Glory and Majesty* (1812), written under the pen name Juan Josafat Ben-Ezra. Lacunza believed that the coming Anti-Christ would not be a person but a corrupted Roman Catholic priesthood. By 1826 Irving had translated this Spanish work into English.

In addition to prophecy, Irving also came to believe, as early as 1828, that the spiritual gifts of the apostles, used in Acts, belonged to the Church of all ages. If the gifts of speaking in tongues, prophesying, and healing the sick were not being used, it was because of lack of faith. Combining these two major thoughts—millenarianism and miracles—Irving began to write in a prolific manner that the coming of Christ was imminent, and that the Lord's coming would be proceeded by an outpouring of the apostolic gifts.

Irving, who has been called "the Father of Modern Pentecostalism," was not surprised to learn that a charismatic revival had broken out in some small towns in western Scotland. A delegation from his congregation was sent to investigate. The glowing report of spiritual renewal that was brought back to the local church created great excitement. Throughout the autumn of 1830, prayer vigils began to be held in London to seek an outpouring of the Spirit—to be manifested by the ability to speak in tongues.

One such meeting was held in the home of J. B. Cardale, the leader of the delegation to Scotland. There was a measure of success as the first known case of speaking in tongues in London was recorded. The person who spoke in tongues on April 20, 1831, was Cardale's wife. According to the interpretation given, this is what she said: "The Lord will speak to His people; the Lord hasteneth His Coming; the Lord cometh." Excitement of the imminent coming of Christ was enhanced. There is no record that the "spirit" by which Mrs. Cardale spoke and prophesied was ever tested (cp. 1 John 4:1, 1 Cor 14:34).

In places where the teaching of Irving was embraced, speaking in tongues and prophesying became regular features. Tongues were spoken in the Regent Square Church until concerned Trustees of the Church filed a formal complaint against Irving with the Presbytery of London. A trial was deemed necessary. On April 26, 1832, the first ecclesiastical trial of Edward Irving began. Irving was found guilty of violating the order of services allowed by the Presbyterian structure, and was removed from his church.

On Sunday morning, May 6, 1832, the Trustees locked Irving and a large part of the congregation out of the building. Undaunted, Irving and his people began to meet in a building in Gray's Inn Road, thereby creating The Catholic Apostolic Church. After some time, twelve members of his "church" were formally recognized as "apostles." These were believed to be instruments of the Holy Spirit with all the authority of the Twelve ordained by Christ. The last of these latter day apostles died in 1901.

Although Irving himself never prophesied nor spoke in tongues, he was deposed from the ministry altogether by his hometown presbytery of Annan. The reason was his teaching that when Christ became incarnate, He fully assumed sinful nature, so that His sinless life depended on the power of the Holy Spirit, not on an innately sinless human nature. This heretical teaching denying the *impeccability of Christ*, was exposed during a second ecclesiastical trial, which took place March 13, 1833. On December 7, 1834, Edward Irving died and was buried in a crypt in Glasgow Cathedral. He was 42 years old.

The Pentecostal Movement saw no real further progress until 1901, in Kansas City, Kansas USA. Then and there the modern day charismatic movement had its beginnings. In October of 1900, a former Methodist minister named Charles F. Parham had opened a Bible college in Topeka, Kansas. He believed that sanctification was a second work of grace, whereby all inbred sin was destroyed. Just before Christmas, Parham asked his students to study the Bible and learn what the evidence was for being baptized with the Holy Spirit. He would come back for their answers in three days. Upon his return, he was astonished to discover that all forty students had come to the same conclusion: speaking with other tongues was the indisputable proof that the blessing of Pentecost had come. This, of course, was in spite of the fact that Augustine, Luther, Calvin, Whitefield, Wesley, Spurgeon, and the host of others had not in 1900 years reached any such conclusion! The young people began actively to seek a "baptism" with the Holy Spirit manifested by speaking in tongues.

On January 1, 1901, the group found what it was seeking; something happened. Miss Agnes Ozman began to speak in tongues, after Parham had laid hands on her. Soon, other students began to speak in tongues also, and Parham joined them. The modern Pentecostal revival had begun; and from this beginning has circled the globe! However, we must ask the question: Is it of God? If it were to be real, its practice would have to match the Scriptures. But a careful study of Acts 2, 8, 10, 11,

19, and 1 Corinthians 12—14 will find no parallel between that which prevails in the modern movement and the Word of Truth. Moreover, the Word points to a diminishing of emphasis of tongues throughout Acts, where it was a manifestation of the Spirit for that period only while the New Testament Scriptures were being compiled. Any who are involved with the movement are earnestly entreated: *please* carefully study the Scriptures mentioned above. Seek Christ in humility, and the Spirit will teach the heart and mind through His Word.[1]

The Impeccability of Christ

1. In the year A.D. 451 the Council of Chalcedon met and formulated the faith of the Church respecting the person of Christ, and declared Him "to be acknowledged in two natures, inconfusedly, unchangeable, indivisible, inseparably; the distinction of the natures being in no wise taken away by the union, but rather the property of each nature being preserved, and concurring in one Person and one Subsistence, not parted or divided into two persons."

2. The great truth enunciated is that the eternal Son of God took upon Himself our humanity, and not that the man Jesus acquired divinity.

3. Fierce controversy has raged around the subject. Did the Lord's deity render sin impossible, and consequently make His temptations unreal? The following argument is set forth: "If sin was impossible to Christ, then His temptation by Satan was a meaningless display, and His victory a mere delusion, and His coronation a shadow (Phil 2:6)."

4. One charitable answer to this theological problem is that, "We may say it was impossible Jesus would sin. We dare not say it was impossible He could not sin."

5. While this response would please many, for others it does not do justice to either the Scriptures or to the person of Christ. It is a matter of record that once the concept is embraced that Jesus could sin, the temptation comes to teach and believe that He did sin.

6. Historically, the church has argued that Jesus was free both from hereditary depravity and from actual sin. This is shown:

    a. by His never offering a sacrifice.

---

[1] For biblical evidence of sign gift cessation, see *Spirit of Truth*, available from Chapel Library.

  b. by His never praying for forgiveness. Jesus frequently went up to the Temple, but He never offered a sacrifice. He prayed "Father, forgive them" (Luk 23:34); but He never prayed "Father, forgive Me."
  c. by His teaching that all but He needed the new birth. Jesus said "Ye must be born again" (John 3:7); but the words indicated that He personally had no such need. Jesus not only yielded to God's will when made known to Him, but He sought it: "I seek not mine own will, but the will of him that sent me" (John 5:30). It was not personal experience of sin, but perfect resistance to it that made Jesus fit to deliver us from sin.
  d. by His challenging all to convict Him of a single sin. "Therefore also that *holy* thing which shall be born of thee shall be called the Son of God" (Luke 1:35). "Which of you convinceth me of sin? And if I say the truth, why do ye not believe me?" (John 8:46). "Hereafter I will not talk much with you: for the prince of this world cometh, and hath nothing in me" (John 14:30). There was not the slightest evil inclination upon which His temptations could lay hold.

7. But if in Christ there was no sin, or tendency to sin, how could He be tempted? The answer is that Jesus was tempted in the same way that Adam was tempted—which is susceptibility to all the forms of innocent desire. To these desires temptations may appeal. Sin consists not in these desires, but in the gratification of them out of God's order, and contrary to God's will (Jas 1:13–15). So Satan appealed to our Lord's desire for food, for applause, and for power (Matt 4:1–11). All temptation must be addressed either to desire or fear; so Christ "was in all points tempted like as we are" (Heb 4:15). The first temptation, in the wilderness, was addressed to desire; the second, in the garden, was addressed to fear. Satan, after the first, "departed from him for a season" (Luke 4:13); but he returned in Gethsemane—"the prince of the world cometh: and he hath nothing in me" (John 14:30)—if possible to deter Jesus from His work, by rousing within Him vast and agonizing fear with which His holy soul was moved, yet He was "without sin" (Heb 4:15).

8. To press the point of the impeccability of Christ more closely, we ascribe to Christ not only natural integrity, but also moral integrity, or moral perfection, that is, *sinlessness*. This means not merely that Christ could avoid sinning, and did actually

avoid it, but also that it was impossible for Him to sin because of the essential bond between the human and the divine natures.

9. The sinlessness of Christ is clearly testified to in the following passages:

> Luke 1:35, "And the angel answered and said unto her, The Holy Ghost shall come upon thee, and the power of the Highest shall overshadow thee: therefore also that *holy* thing which shall be born of thee shall be called the Son of God."
>
> John 8:46, "Which of you convinceth me of sin? And if I say the truth, why do ye not believe me?"
>
> John 14:30, "Hereafter I will not talk much with you: for the prince of this world cometh, and *hath nothing in me*."
>
> 2 Corinthians 5:21, "For he hath made him to be sin for us, *who knew no sin*; that we might be made the righteousness of God in him."
>
> Hebrews 4:15, "For we have not an high priest which cannot be touched with the feeling of our infirmities; but was in all points tempted like as we are, *yet without sin*."
>
> Hebrews 9:14, "How much more shall the blood of Christ, who through the eternal Spirit offered himself *without spot* to God, purge your conscience from dead works to serve the living God?"
>
> 1 Peter 2:22, "Who *did no sin*, neither was guile found in his mouth."
>
> 1 John 3:5, "And ye know that he was manifested to take away our sins; and in him *is no sin*."

10. While Christ was made to be sin judicially, yet ethically He was free from both hereditary depravity and actual sin.

11. Part of the problem for those who do not embrace the impeccability of Christ is the tendency to believe that Jesus is but a man; yet at the same time they feel the constraint to ascribe to Him the value of God, or to claim divinity for Him in virtue of the immanence of God in Him, or of the indwelling Holy Spirit. Again, this does not do justice to the truth of the two natures in Christ: He is both divine and human in one Person forever. Amen!

CHAPTER 34

"*This is the Gospel!*"
A.D. 1714–1770

"I have put my soul, as a blank, into the hands of Jesus Christ my Redeemer, and desired him to write upon it what he pleases. I know it will be His own image."

—George Whitefield

Wesley and Whitefield

While John Wesley labored to advance the cause of Christ in England, the Lord raised up George Whitefield (pronounced WIT-field) to fan the flames of revival fire in England and in America. In many ways Wesley and Whitefield were similar. Both were graduates of Oxford. Both had belonged to the Holy Club. Both were ministers in the Anglican Church. Both engaged in open air preaching despite the opposition of the Anglican clergy. Both went into the by-ways to compel men to be saved (Luke 14:23). Both suffered bodily attacks for the cause of Christ. Once Whitefield was stoned until nearly dead; Wesley had rotten fruit thrown upon him. Both were dynamic preachers. Both had a zeal for the salvation of souls. Whitefield, in particular, was very intense and impassioned in his preaching. One observer wrote, "I could hardly bear such unreserved use of tears." Whitefield defended the tears by saying, "You blame me for weeping, but how can I help it when you will not weep for yourselves, though your immortal souls are on the verge of destruction?"

Despite the similarities, Wesley and Whitefield were radically different in theology. Wesley was an *Arminian*, while Whitefield embraced Puritan *Calvinism*, considered by most the orthodox faith of the Reformation up until that time. In March, 1739, Wesley decided to attack the Calvinistic position of grace. He first preached and then published a sermon entitled *"Free Grace."* Wesley justified his actions as being the will of God on the basis of having cast lots (cp. Acts 1:26; Prov 16:33), a practice which he later renounced. In December 1740, George Whitefield graciously but firmly responded to John Wesley in a thirty-one page pamphlet.[1]

While the theological debate continued, so did the parallel work of winning souls to Christ. Wesley's "United Societies" brought many people into the kingdom of heaven, as did Whitefield's "Calvinistic Methodist" societies. By 1755 the two brothers in Christ had reached "an agreement to differ."

Within his lifetime (1714–1770), Whitefield preached an estimated 18,000 times, and addressed as many as 10,000,000 people face to face. His American friend, Benjamin Franklin, once estimated that Whitefield, without any artificial means of amplification, was heard by more than 30,000 people in a single gathering. It was a privileged generation that heard George Whitefield preach the Gospel of redeeming grace. He reminded people of the life and death of Jesus Christ. "Behold, what man could not do, Jesus Christ, the Son of His Father's love, undertakes to do for him." Thus, "The Lord Jesus Christ is our righteousness ... This, this is Gospel, this is the only way of finding acceptance with God!"

The Danger of Deism

One personal friend of George Whitefield, who did not accept the Gospel, was Benjamin Franklin. Like many men of his day, Franklin was a deist. *Deism* (Latin *deus*, god) emerged from the writings of Lord Herbert Cherbury as an important rationalistic movement in England, before being embraced in the American colonies as well. Deism argued for a belief in one God, as divine creator of the universe. However, "God" was detached from the world and made no revelations to it. Neither His personal presence nor His revelations were needed, because God had so ordained the universe that it operated according to established natural laws.

Deism argued that, like a well organized time clock, the universe is a mechanism that functions on its own. God had "wound it up" and left it to run by itself. Therefore, logically, miracles are to be denied and theological concepts, like the atoning work of Christ and the regenerating work of the Holy Spirit, are to be rejected. The Bible is not unique and the supernatural is silly superstition. All that is needed is for the *lumen naturae*, the light of nature, to function. The light of nature is reason. Man must rely solely upon his own reason!

---

[1] "Whitefield's Letter to Wesley" is reprinted by and available from Ichthus Publications.

Lord Herbert of Cherbury (1583–1648), "the father of Deism," found other influential men to advance the basic tenets of Deism. One was Matthew Tindal, author of *Christianity as Old as the Creation; or the Gospel a Republication of the Religion of Nature* (1730). This work has often been called "the Deist's Bible." The word soon spread; a receptive audience was found in France, Germany, the Netherlands, and America.

With Deism, the hearts of people who wanted to reject the Lord and His anointed (Psa 2:1–4), could still maintain the semblance of being religious—for Deism taught its own version of ethical behavior. The morality of Deism is one that is practical, not spiritual. For example, Benjamin Franklin said that "Honesty is the best policy." By this Franklin meant that people should be honest because it is practical—and it *pays* to be honest. This type of thinking is far different from the concept that people should be honest because the Creator has instructed His creation to live in an honest manner (Exod 20:1–17; Rom 12:17; 1 Tim 2:2; Heb 13:18).

The Rise of the Age of Reason

In trying to determine the causes for the rise of rationalism, the following factors should be considered.

1. *The emphasis on emotionalism* by many mystical movements. An imbalance was created when this happened. A doctrinal basis of faith and action was neglected. One result was the failure of the Church to meet the intellectual needs of many thinking people in society with legitimate questions (cp. Isa 1:18). Theology was no longer considered to be the "Queen of Sciences."

2. *Theology began to be divorced from philosophy* in the universities of Europe. During the Middle Ages philosophy and theology had been united in a system known as Scholasticism. A dramatic distinction between the two allowed the development of natural reason unguided by divine illumination.

3. *Scientific discoveries*, wrongly interpreted, seemed to support the mechanical view of the universe embraced by Deism. When Copernicus (1473–1543) revealed that the earth revolved around the sun, the true center of the galaxy, the faith of multitudes was undermined. Christians had been taught for centuries that the earth (and therefore man) was the center of the universe. If the Church could be wrong on this important point, perhaps it was wrong on other things as well. The Church would have been wiser to teach that God is the center of the universe (Acts 17:28).

Esteem for Deism was enhanced when Galileo (1546–1642) turned his telescope on the heavens and supported the view of Copernicus regarding the solar system. Then, Descartes (1596–1650) and Isaac Newton (1642–1727) advanced the theory of a universe governed by natural law. Francis Bacon (1561–1626) developed the so called "scientific method"—demanding facts not faith, observation and repetition, not subjective religion.

The irony in the discovery of many of the major scientific facts is that they came because of historic Christian beliefs. Isaac Newton was a devout Christian. He began his scientific investigations because he believed that the God of the Universe was logical and could be known. What the deists dared to do was to take Christian discoveries of truth and reinterpret them so that the creature, not the Creator, was glorified. When carnal knowledge dismissed God, and then united itself to what the senses could determine and discern, the result was a rationalistic, naturalistic, materialistic understanding of life. Divine revelation was made subordinate to human reason (cp. Col 2:8).

4. *The emergence of a new social philosophy.* According to John Locke (1632–1704), just as there are natural laws to govern the universe, so there are certain natural rights that should guide society. Voltaire (1694–1778) and Rousseau (1712–1778) agreed with the basic pre-suppositional thinking of Locke. They began to write, sometimes seriously but more often with wit and satire, in order to make the thoughts of Locke palatable to the general public. With multitudes of others, Thomas Jefferson read their writings and was impressed. When the opportunity came, Jefferson incorporated the social theories of Locke into many of his own writings, including the United States of America's *Declaration of Independence* (1776). It says in part, "We hold these truths to be self-evident, that all men are created equal, that they are endowed by their Creator with certain inalienable Rights, that among these are Life, Liberty, and the pursuit of Happiness."

Since the "rights" of man could be discovered and applied to reconstruct society, men (not the Bible) could also construct what is proper conduct for people. In order for this to happen, the "rubbish" of the past had to be disregarded. The Church in particular had to be challenged, changed, or if necessary destroyed, if society was to progress. Such was the thinking of the Deists. In this way, the eighteenth century Age of Reason came to challenge the seventeenth century Age of Orthodoxy. A great spiritual battle took place for the souls of men and the fate of nations.

Three Parties of Anglicans (Mid-1700s–Mid-1800s)

In the midst of the conflict (Eph 6:12), the Church of Jesus Christ was not united. The assembly of the saints was not prepared for the tidal wave of spiritual destruction that swept over it in the form of Deism. The fragmentation of the Christian community is reflected in part by the threefold division discovered in the Anglican Church (cp. 1 Cor 1:10–13).

1. One part of this Church wanted to maintain the principles and practices which had been produced by the Reformation. There was a genuine love for and appreciation of the Calvinistic doctrines of sovereign grace. Those who embraced these beliefs wanted to remain in the Anglican Church and form the *"Low Church"* or *Evangelical* party.

2. When it appeared that the influence of the Evangelical party was gaining too much ground, a number of church leaders became concerned. It was felt that a way had to be found to preserve a more traditional religious heritage (stemming from the rituals of Catholicism), and so the *"High Church"* party emerged.

However, things did not go according to plan. Instead of remaining a natural bridge between the Protestants and the Catholics, the High Church party within the Anglican structure found many members wanting to return to Catholicism. People were being carried away by the rhetoric of such men as John Keble, who preached a memorable sermon in Oxford called *"The National Apostasy."* A new movement, the Oxford Movement, was born, and grew on the strength of religious tracts.

Initially, the tracts were to be written to justify the doctrines and practices of the High Church party, while opposing the changes desired by the Low Church party. But the result was that the tracts, written mainly by John Henry Newman, began to sound more Catholic in tone. Finally, the bishop of Oxford ordered their distribution to be stopped. For many it was too late. On October 9, 1845, John Henry Newman formally joined the Catholic Church. His example led thousands of others back to the Catholic fold. And even those who did not return to Rome, but remained Anglican, did so with strong Catholic overtones in both doctrine and practice.

3. In addition to the zeal of the Low Church party, and the confusion caused by the High Church party as to the true nature and beliefs of the Anglican Church, there emerged also the *Broad Church* party. This party believed that the Anglican Church should be a State Church. For this to happen, there must be a broad view taken so that no creed would be held with binding force. Everyone should be able to believe as they pleased.

Attack on "Saving Faith"

In this atmosphere, John Glas began to redefine the orthodox idea about saving faith. He was a minister of the Church of Scotland near Dundee in the 1720s, and a Calvinist. But he became uneasy about requiring ministers to accept documents such as *The Westminster Confession*. He believed it was sufficient for a man to say that he "believed" the Scriptures, but not to submit to the "words of men." And he began to redefine "saving faith" in terms of the intellect only: to "believe" with the mind.[2] For these teachings, he was deposed by the Church of Scotland in 1733. He then formed an Independent church of his own.

His son-in-law was Robert Sandeman, who much more aggressively promoted these new views. He reacted to Wesley and Whitefield's emphasis on repentance, will, and the corresponding emotions. He disdained Isaac Watts, Philip Doddridge, Thomas Boston, and Ralph Erskine—notable Puritans of the time. He regarded John Wesley as "the most dangerous man that had ever appeared in the Church!" By the 1780s in both Scotland and England, there were many churches teaching this view, which had come to be called *Sandemanianism*. Archibald Maclean, a former member of Glas' church, had spread it among the Baptist churches in Wales also.

Sandemanianism caused great trouble in the regions where it was taught, but was adequately dealt with at the time by Daniel Rowland, William Williams, Andrew Fuller, and Thomas Scot. However, it is important today for its significant influence on a very large part of the evangelical Church, because, as many have come to favor Arminianism over Calvinism, so they have also embraced Sandemanianism—although often unaware of its deviation from historical orthodoxy.

Exactly why have many called Sandemanianism a heresy?—because it fundamentally redefines the nature of saving faith! In Sandeman's own words: "the whole benefit of this event [Christ's death and resurrection] is conveyed to men only by the Apostolic report concerning it...Everyone who understands this report to be true, or is persuaded that the event actually happened...is justified." Principle Macleod responded that it was "in a way, a return to the Roman Catholic teaching, which is that all you have to do is to believe and accept the teaching of the Church. You accept that with your mind, and that is all that is necessary." Andrew Fuller said of Sandeman: "they will not have even a 'hearty persuasion,' but emphasize only a notional belief."

---

[2] believe – The *Confession* often makes use of the word "trust" in its full meaning: putting faith into full active dependency upon God.

The historical view of "saving faith," on the other hand, was "repent [from sin] and believe" (Mark 1:15)—all as an unmerited gift of God by grace, all bound up in great love and great humility. Sandeman equated grief over and repentance from sin as a "work" not to be added to "naked" belief of the intellect, and he frowned on all emotions. He used Romans 4:5 and John 5:1 as proof texts, but chose to redefine "heart" in Romans 10:9-10 as "mind only," whereas in fact the Scripture uses "heart" to refer to the center of personality—the mind, will, and emotions—as in Acts 8:37. And the Scriptures repeatedly point to a submitting of man's will to God, as in John 5:38–40, Matthew 6:10 and 7:21, 1 Peter 4:2, and 1 John 2:17. Finally, William Williams summarized it well: "Love is the greatest thing in religion, and if that is forgotten, nothing can take place." [3]

The Plymouth Brethren

Another group to emerge during this time of reaction against the sterility in the Anglican Church was *The Brethren*. The Brethren enjoyed a natural leader in the person of John Nelson Darby, who had been a minister near Plymouth, England.

John Darby was born on November 18, 1800, in London England. He entered Trinity College (Dublin, Ireland) in 1815 when he was fourteen. Four years later Darby was graduated with a law degree. Turning to religion, Darby became a deacon in the Anglican Church (1825). In 1826 he was ordained a priest and served in that capacity in County Wicklow, located south of Dublin. Concerned with the formality of the official services he was called upon to conduct, Darby began to hold informal home worship services. Out of these gatherings came the Brethren movement. Faith in Christ and love to the brethren was declared to be the only holy bond of spiritual union.

While that claim was made, there were other things which certainly helped to solidify the new movement. The Brethren came to believe that since every believer is a priest before God, there should be no ordained ministers. All creeds were to be opposed. Since the Holy Spirit guides all believers, and unites them in a common faith, worship should be conducted according to the apostolic example. Finally, formal religious structures and denominations must be rejected. The Brethren teachings found fertile soil in the souls of many. In Ireland and western England

---

[3] This synopsis and all quotations are from *The Puritans* by D. M. Lloyd-Jones, 1987, The Banner of Truth Trust, pp. 170–90.

organized assemblies were established. Brethren churches could be found in Switzerland, France, Germany, Canada, and the United States.

As Brethren churches grew, so did their doctrinal distinctives. Of particular interest were the prophetic teachings. Like Edward Irving, John Darby introduced the Christian community to concepts that had never before been considered by the Church in eighteen hundred years of existence. His views cannot be found in any of the historic creeds of Christendom.

Darby's new thoughts began to be taught after he had a terrible accident in 1827. A horse threw him against a door post. During a long convalescence, Darby enjoyed plenty of time to meditate upon the Bible. The result was that he formulated new views in the area of *eschatology* (end-time events). Darby came to believe that the "rapture" of the Church (taken from 1 Thess 4:16) was to be a separate phase of the Second Coming of the Lord, preceding Christ's actual return. In fact, it was to be another coming of Christ.

In opposition to this, one should consider the Scriptural statements: Jesus Christ returns the second time for *all* who believe (Heb 9:28), and Christians will be caught up to meet (greet) the Lord in the air. Such a greeting of the coming Christ is only proper. The word for "meet" is *apantesis* and means a friendly encounter. This word is used in Matthew 25:1:6 and Acts 28:14–16. In both places the concept is that people went out to "meet" someone in order to escort that person to the very place they were coming to. Christians will one day rise to meet the coming King of kings as He returns the second time for all who believe.

Darby's view of a "rapture" of the Church has been integrated with the *pre-millennial* interpretation of the end-times: Christ returns to establish a literal earthly kingdom, where He rules for a literal thousand years. This is an alternative interpretation to the one second coming in judgment embodied in the two historic views: (1) *post-millenial* where Christ establishes and rules the kingdoms of the earth through His presence in the hearts of leaders who are Christians, then He returns in judgment at the end, and (2) *amillennial,* or better, realized or fulfilled millenial according to promise: Christ's kingdom is in the hearts of men, and He returns in judgment at the end.

For Darby, the solution to the dilemma between a new system of belief and the historic interpretations of the Scriptures was very simple. The collective teaching of the Church had been wrong on its view of the second coming of Christ for almost two thousand years! He alone had the answer. The truth, according to Darby, is that when the Lord is greeted by His Bride, He will turn around in mid-air and go back to heaven (the "rapture"). Then later, the Lord will come again to the earth (after what has come to be called a seven year tribulation period). What John Nelson Darby began to teach was a third coming of Christ interposed between the other two: First Advent, Rapture, then (several years later) the Second Advent!

As this notion was expounded upon, more and more prophetic details were added to his overall view. For many orthodox Christians, the new teachings of John Darby were a movement away from the simplicity of the established biblical boundaries: that Jesus Christ will one day return in like manner as He went away (Acts 1:11).

Preaching the Gospel to Every Creature

While the Protestant Church struggled for personal purity and doctrinal faithfulness in Europe, efforts to spread "faith" around the globe were not neglected by either the Protestant or the Catholic communities. The Catholic Church found men of inspiration to carry their faith to new cultures, reflected in the dedication of Francis Xavier (1506–1552). Xavier ministered in Goa, India (1542–1549) before going to Japan, where his work gained many converts for Catholicism. In 1552, while seeking entrance into mainland China, Xavier died.

More converts flowed into the Catholic Church through Spanish missionaries working in the Philippines, South and Central America, and Mexico. In Canada, French speaking Jesuit priests established a Catholic Church in the province of Quebec before moving into the region of the Great Lakes. From there, missions were established along the Mississippi River all the way down to Louisiana. Then, spreading East and West, the Catholic Church founded missions in Florida, and along the coastline of California.

Undergirding the missionary activity of the Catholic Church was a fundamental desire to keep as much of Christendom as possible under the authority of the bishop of Rome, and thus under a centralized papal control. To that end, new missionary efforts took place in Ceylon, Japan, India, China, Korea, Cuba, Africa, Mongolia, Australia, the islands of the Pacific, and in North America.

The Protestants also went forth into all the world, and with the Gospel. Led by individuals such as the German Pietist August Francke (1663–1727), those who had a heart for the souls of men went forth into the fields that are white unto harvest (John 4:35). Christian Schwartz labored for Christ in India from 1750 until his death in 1798. The Baptists found a missionary champion with world vision in William Carey (1761–1834). Ministering for twenty years in India, Carey and his family faced years of poverty. Carey was challenged by frequent bouts of malaria and dysentery, the death of three children, and mental illness in loved ones.

Through all the sorrows and sufferings, William Carey never wavered. His passion for souls led to the conception of an idea of holding a world missionary conference. Carey wanted the meeting to be held at the Cape of Good Hope in 1810. Unfortunately, the proposal was considered ridiculous by the leading religious figures of his day. This idea was 100 years ahead of its time. But the seed was planted, and in 1910 it bore fruit—a World Missionary Conference was held in Edinburgh, Scotland.

Often referred to as "The Father of Modern Missions," William Carey inspired thousands of men and women to surrender all, in order to win others to Christ by having faith in God. In one of his sermons he cried, "Expect great things! Attempt great things!" Indeed, William Carey expected great things from God, and he attempted great things for God. One of his greatest achievements was the translation of the Bible into some twenty-six languages of India. Another achievement that can be directly attributed to his efforts was the founding of the Baptist Missionary Society at Kettering, England (1792).

The full impact of the life of William Carey and the wonderful things he did can only be revealed in eternity. When his journey on earth was drawing to an end, Carey felt he had done so little for the cause of Christ. Inscribed on the stone slab of his tomb is this simple epitaph: "A wretched, poor, and helpless worm; on Thy kind arms I fall." The Lord is always pleased with such faith and humility (Heb 10:38; 11:1; Luke 7:9; Matt 9:29).

The Work Continues

William Carey was followed in India by the Anglican Henry Martyn and Alexander Duff from the Church of Scotland. Elsewhere, Samuel Marsden (1764–1838) labored for more than forty years in a pioneer work in Australia, New Zealand, and the islands in the Pacific. The London Missionary Society sent Robert Morrison (1782–1834) to open the doors in China. Robert and Mary Moffat (1795–1883; 1795–1871) and David Livingstone (1813–1873) ministered to souls in darkest Africa, and caused others to want to do the same in life and in death. When Peter Cameron Scott, founder of the Africa Inland Mission, read the inscription on

Livingstone's tomb in Westminster Abbey, he was inspired to return to the work. On the tomb were the words of Jesus, "Other sheep I have which are not of this fold; them also I must bring" (John 10:16).

Morrison labored to produce a Chinese dictionary and translation of the Scriptures. The work of later missionaries was made much easier because of his successes. Moffat translated the Bible into the major tribal languages of the natives of South Africa, while Livingstone opened up Central Africa. In 1865 James Hudson Taylor (1832–1905) founded the China Inland Mission to promote faith missions in a co-operative effort among the different denominations. He refused to make personal needs known, relying instead on God alone to meet all his needs. Then there was Adoniram Judson (1788–1850),[4] whose self-sacrifice in taking the Gospel to Burma is noteworthy in all of Christendom. Enduring great hardship, he made a Burmese dictionary and translated the Bible, while serving the people. The Burmese emperor said of him: "We care nothing for his Bible, nothing for his Christ; but his scars are irresistible!"

Joining England and Scotland in sending out missionaries during the nineteenth century were the Basel Evangelical Missionary Society, and the Danish Missionary Society (founded, 1821). In 1824, both the Berlin Missionary Society and the Paris Missionary Society were established to proclaim the glorious Gospel of Jesus Christ.

---

[4] See *Adoniram Judson and the Missionary Call* and *Ann Judson*, both available from Chapel Library.

CHAPTER 35

Christianity Comes to the New World

Christ in the Colonies

On May 4, 1493, a remarkable event took place. Alexander VI (pope, 1492–1503) decided to settle a political dispute between two Catholic nations: Spain and Portugal. The issue concerned territorial possessions. When Columbus returned from his first voyage across the ocean, Portugal believed its own commercial ambitions would be limited to only Africa and the Far East. To prevent open conflict between two Catholic monarchies, guided by Solomon-like wisdom, Alexander issued a *papal bull* (official binding proclamation of the pope), which was to put an end to the area of concerns. Spheres of domination were agreed upon when a Demarcation Line was drawn. This line ran due north and south (about 300 miles) west of the Azores and Cape Verde Islands. All new lands lying east of this Demarcation Line were to be considered the possession of Portugal; all those to the west would belong to Spain. Because the Portuguese were not happy with this decision, in 1494 the *Treaty of Tordesillas* was signed with a new line of demarcation, sanctioned by Julius II in 1506 (pope, 1503–1513). The new line was about 1,110 miles west of the Cape Verde Islands. In this way Brazil became a Portuguese possession.

With renewed vigor these strongly Catholic nations set out to manifest their presence in new domains. They met with tremendous success. Prior to the founding of any other European colonies, the Spaniards established settlements in Mexico, the West Indies, Central America, and South America. Before the end of the century, two major universities were flourishing. The University of Mexico was founded in 1551 and the University of Lima in 1557. At Santo Domingo, in 1512, a bishopric was established, with another one in Cuba in 1522.

In 1565 the Spaniards founded St. Augustine, Florida, USA, after first driving out some French Protestants who had come there for religious freedom. The admiral of the French fleet, De Coligny, and 141 others were massacred. On each person's body, the Spanish commander attached a placard explaining why they were hung: "Not as Frenchmen but as heretics."

The Protestant Presence

While the Catholic Church solidified its presence in the New World, the Protestant Church also came to North America. In 1607 English settlers brought with them the traditions of the Episcopal (Anglican) Church. Some colonies during the colonial period recognized the Episcopal Church officially as the Established or State Church. The Anglican Church was established in South Carolina in 1706, Georgia in 1758, and North Carolina in 1765.

Joining the Protestant community in America were the Non-conformists. King James I of England had once promised to "harry them out of the land." Fleeing political persecution and seeking a place to worship freely, a small band of "Pilgrims" sailed from Plymouth in England on the Mayflower. They believed they were traveling towards a new Promised Land.

Drifting off course, the Mayflower landed along the desolate coast of Cape Cod, Massachusetts, November 11, 1620. Small search parties were sent out to explore the area. Finally, December 21, 1620, the Pilgrims stepped on shore. They put their foot on a solid rock, and they prayed. Heads were bowed as hearts were lifted in gratitude to God for the safe journey. Divine guidance was asked for the days to come. The Pilgrims realized that they had to face a harsh future. Still, they would stay. And they would survive the starving winter without losing faith. On Sunday, January 21, 1621, led by William Brewster, the Pilgrims conducted their first public worship in a crude structure at New Plymouth. But it would not be the last public service, for in the years to come many more people would arrive in the New World. Up and down the eastern coastline of North America, permanent settlements would be founded.

In 1628 English Puritans established the Massachusetts Bay Colony at Salem, Massachusetts. By 1640 almost 20,000 colonists were living in the vicinity. In the area of religion, most of them wanted to maintain the traditions of the Church of England. However, the Bay colonists were willing to accept the guidance and influence of the Plymouth colonists as to Church government in the New World. As a result, the congregational form of self-government was adopted. Within ten years, 33 assemblies existed in Massachusetts alone.

In other communities, different churches and forms of ecclesiastical government would be preferred:

Episcopal	Jamestown, VA; Salem and Boston, MA; Charleston, SC; Savannah, GA
Congregational	Plymouth, MA
Catholic	Baltimore and St. Mary, MD; St. Augustine, FL
Dutch Reformed	Albany and New Amsterdam, NY; Camden, NJ
Baptist	Providence, RI
Quaker	Philadelphia, PA
Moravian	Bethlehem, PA
Mennonite	Lancaster and Germantown, PA

Desiring Christ for their children, the colonists established schools of higher education, based soundly on the Bible. In 1636 the foundation was laid for Harvard College at Cambridge, Massachusetts, named after a wealthy Christian benefactor. In 1701, a college was started in Connecticut named Yale, also in honor of a generous donor. The Lord used the business prosperity He had granted to some to benefit all of society.

The Dutch Reformed Church

The English flow of settlers to the New World encouraged other nationalities to come. In 1623 the Dutch were able to establish two trading posts in strategic locations. One was placed on the Upper River in Albany, New York. The other trading post was set up near Camden, on the Delaware River in New Jersey. Peter Minuit (1580–1638) became the first governor of the New Netherlands. In 1664, when Peter Stuyvesant (1592–1672) was governor, the colony was captured by the English and renamed New York.

Despite the territorial and political maneuvering between the British and the Dutch, by 1628 the First Dutch Reformed Church was able to be established under the pastoral leadership of Rev. John Michaelius. It is no small measure of God's great mercy that just four years after the Synod of Dort was held, the doctrines of sovereign grace were being proclaimed in America.

When John Van Mekelenburg arrived in the New Netherlands, his passion for souls led him to learn the language of the Mohawks. He wanted to preach the death, burial, and resurrection of Christ to the Native Americans. Mekelenburg is considered to be the first Protestant missionary to the Indians.

Birth of the Baptists

"It is the will and command of God that ... consciences and worship be granted to all men in all nations and countries."—Roger Williams

The Congregational Church was the Established or State Church in the Massachusetts Bay Colony. But a young English minister arrived in Boston in 1631 who thought this was a mistake. Roger Williams (c. 1603–1683) believed in the separation of Church and State. Though ordained by the Church of England (1629), Williams had been influenced by the thinking of the Puritans on this matter. Others also should be convinced of the wisdom of separating the Church and State. Roger Williams would tell his concerns to the congregation in America.

When Williams finally voiced his views from the pulpit as minister of the Congregational Church in Salem (1634), the opposition was immediate. Called before the General Court (1635), Williams was told to leave the colony within six weeks. After discovering that his health was poor, permission was granted to leave in the spring. But he must not preach on the separation of Church and State! Nor was he to preach against infant baptism, or for baptism of believers by immersion. He was to be silent on those issues that caused controversy. But Roger Williams was determined to preach his convictions. After resigning as minister of the Salem Church, he began to hold services in his house for those agreed with his position. Angered by his persistency, the General Court ordered Williams to leave the Bay Colony immediately, leaving behind his wife and two children, into the freezing snow-covered forest. He must go; he was too dangerous a man.

For fourteen weeks Roger Williams managed to survive during the dead of winter. In the providence of the Lord, the Narragansett Indians found him and took him in. Williams was no stranger to this Indian tribe. Several years before, while a young pastor of the Pilgrim Church at Plymouth, Williams had taken the time to learn the language of the Narragansett. He had also opposed the taking of land from any native Indian population without fair payment. Knowing him to be a good man and champion for their causes, the Indians helped Roger Williams survive.

The following summer (June 1636), Williams was allowed to purchase from the Indians a section of ground at the mouth of the Mohassuck River. When people from Salem discovered this, they journeyed to be with their beloved but disgraced minister. The town of Providence was founded. Going to England, Roger Williams was able to secure a charter for the Providence Plantation, thereby establishing a new colony called Rhode Island (1643). The charter was reaffirmed in 1651.

Williams served as president of the colony (1654–1657). Meanwhile, the Bay Colony tried to destroy the seeds of discussion that Roger Williams had sown. Of particular concern was the teaching that believer's should be baptised as adults, following an open confession of an inward work of grace. In 1644 a law was passed that associated his ideas, in a negative way, with the Anabaptist movement of Europe.

> For as much as experience has plentifully and often proved that since the first arising of the Ana-Baptists, about a hundred years since, they have been incendiaries of commonwealth and the infectors of persons in main matters, and the troublers of churches in all places where they have been, and that they who have held the baptizing of infants unlawful have usually held other errors or heresies together therewith ...

Henceforth, there were to be no more re-baptisms (adult immersions upon public profession of faith)!

While laws were being passed in the Bay Colony to try to reverse the teaching of Roger Williams, in Providence the church was being firmly established. Mr. Holliman, a former member of the Salem congregation, accepted the teaching of professing believer's baptism by immersion as the proper time and mode, and administered this ritual by re-baptizing Roger Williams. Williams in turn re-baptized Holliman and ten others. The first Baptist Church in America became a reality.

Other Baptist distinctives would also be freely taught and practiced in Rhode Island. These included the separation between Church and State, the elimination of Church membership as a requirement for voting, and allowing liberty of conscience in worship. Rhode Island would host the first Jewish synagogue, and allow one of the first Quaker meeting houses to be established.

As word spread of the work in Providence, Rhode Island, Baptist churches appeared within the various colonies and flourished. By 1707 the first Baptist Association in America could be formed as representatives from five Baptist churches met in Philadelphia. By 1742, a Confession of Faith was adopted with special emphasis being placed on the Calvinistic doctrines of sovereign grace. The Baptist Church in America had grown up spiritually. It now had capable leadership, a distinct organizational structure, definite principles to practice, and a creed to confess. When he died on March 15, 1683, Roger Williams knew that he had left a great legacy to an emerging new nation. He had bestowed two precious principles to posterity: in America there would be the separation of Church and State, and there would be freedom of worship.

Catholicism in the Colonies

In 1632, King Charles I of England gave two gifts to George Calvert, a recent convert to Catholicism. The first was a title, Lord Baltimore. The second gift to George Calvert and his descendants was the territory around Chesapeake Bay. In gratitude for his generosity, Lord Baltimore named the territory "Maryland" after Mary, the king's wife.

Soon after receiving his gifts, George Calvert died. He was succeeded by his son Cecil Calvert. Assuming the title left by his father, this second Lord Baltimore initiated the settlement of the territory his family had received. He named the first settlement St. Mary in honor of the mother of Christ.

In the process of settling the colony, Lord Baltimore faced a practical problem. Not many Catholics in England wanted to make the difficult journey to Maryland. Protestants were willing to face the difficulties, provided there would be freedom of religion. As a matter of political expediency, if not personal conviction, Lord Baltimore agreed to allow freedom of religion. The only exception would be for those who denied the Trinity. If such a person were found in the colony, they would face death and the forfeiture of their property.

In 1649, at the request of Lord Baltimore, the Maryland Assembly passed the *Act of Toleration*. The document was destined to become important in the development of religious life in the New World. When the Baltimore family lost control of their colony, the territory returned to the control of the Crown in 1692. The Church of England was officially declared to be its established religion. Nevertheless, freedom of religion would continue to be honored. As tolerance had been shown to the Protestants, so tolerance would be shown to the Catholic community.

The Courage of the Quakers

Ten years after George Fox began his ministry in England, Quaker missionaries desired to come to America. The first two Quakers were women, Mary Fisher and Ann Austin. News of their pending arrival in Boston in 1656 preceded them. Time was provided for the Puritan clergy of the city to rally opposition. The women were arrested as they got off the boat and taken to prison for five weeks, where they shared indignities and depredations. At the end of this ordeal the two ladies were put on another boat heading out to sea.

But it was all to no avail. Their ship was not far out of sight when another vessel arrived in Boston harbor with eight other Quakers. There was no stopping their presence, no matter how the colonies tried. Laws were passed in 1661 by the Massachusetts colony preventing Quakers from entering. Any Quaker that returned after being banished faced the penalty of death. Still, the Quakers continued to come to America until finally, their quiet, courageous spirit found a resting place in 1681—when Pennsylvania was granted to William Penn. Peace and safety came to those who wanted all men to be Friends.

Religious Diversity

As William Penn welcomed Quakers to Pennsylvania, so he welcomed all other religious groups as well—Lutherans, Moravians, and Mennonites found a haven of rest in "The Keystone State." The first German Reformed Church was established in 1710 at Germantown, ten miles north of Philadelphia. Germantown itself had been settled in 1683 when thirteen German Mennonite families came to America. Later, a large number of Swiss Mennonites settled in Lancaster County. When the Swiss Reformed settlers arrived in the area, they were welcomed, as were the German Lutherans.

Then there were the German Baptists, who first appeared in 1719. Partly in humor, the other colonists gave them the name Dunkers, which comes from the German word *tunken*, meaning "to dip." The Dunkers were able to organize a church in 1723. In many ways the Dunkers were like the Quakers and the Mennonites. They dressed in a simple manner and practiced a congregational form of Church government. Like the Mennonites they practiced a threefold immersion in the name of the Father, Son, and Holy Spirit. One of the most significant Dunkers of the colonial period was Christopher Sower, the first German printer in America. The

Sower Bible, published in 1743, was the first Bible printed in America in a European language other than English.

When the Moravians arrived in 1740, they settled on 5,000 acres along the Delaware River. They wanted to work with the Indians and the poorer German settlers scattered in Pennsylvania. In 1741 Count Zinzendorf visited the colony. On Christmas Eve he named the Moravian settlement Bethlehem (lit. "house of bread"), in token of his "fervent desire and ardent hope that here the true bread of life might be broken for all who hungered."

The man who enabled Presbyterianism to be firmly established in America was Francis Makemie. In 1683 he came to eastern Maryland to preach in the Scotch Irish communities there, before moving on into Virginia and the Carolinas. In 1710 David Evans arose to preach among the Welsh settlers in Virginia. Because the Spirit of the living God was upon his life, he was used to bring many souls to Christ.

One important event for the Presbyterians in America was the passing of the *Adoption Act* by the Synod of 1729. This required all Presbyterian ministers in the New World to embrace without reservations the *Westminster Confession*. Presbyterian beliefs and practices were to influence the development of the country in many important ways.

Because the Methodist movement did not start in earnest in England until 1739, Methodism was a little slow in showing itself in America. The Methodists arrived first in the person of Philip Embury in 1766. Then came Robert Strawbridge who ministered in Maryland. In 1771 John Wesley made the fortunate decision to send Francis Ashbury (1745–1816) over from England to advance the cause of Christ. Before his death, Ashbury was able to see the Methodist Church in America grow from 15,000 in 1771 to over 200,000. He traveled about 4,000 miles a year on horseback, and preached over 20,000 sermons in his lifetime. Revival fires followed Ashbury and other Methodist ministers.

And so it was that, in a wonderful way, America proved that people of different persuasions could live, work, and worship in the same country, without plunging society into religious civil wars. The established State churches gradually gave way to true religious freedom. At one time, these State churches had included the following:

Anglican Georgia, Virginia, North Carolina, South Carolina, Maryland, New York City and the surrounding counties.

Congregational Massachusetts, Maine, Connecticut, and New Hampshire.

No state church New Jersey, Pennsylvania, Delaware, and Rhode Island.

Reasons America Does Not Have a State Church

The absence of an official state church in the United States may be due to several considerations.

The wide variety of emigration to the colonies after 1690. There were Huguenots and Quakers. There were 200,000 Germans of Lutheran and Reformed persuasion. There were Pietists, and Presbyterians of Scotch-Irish descent from Northern Ireland. By 1760 there were more than 2,500,000 people in the colonies, a third of which were born outside the American colonies. This great diversity discouraged the establishment of an official state church over all the colonies.

The effect of the proprietary colonies also hindered the establishing of a State Church. The desire to make a colony successful demanded co-operation of people from all walks of life and religious persuasions.

The great revivals in the colonies discouraged the preferring of one state church over another. Denominational lines are always transcended when the love of God and the grace of Christ are manifested.

A spirit of rugged individualism, which the American experience encouraged, does not blend well with the spirit of institutionalism, which an established religion demands. There were many people who did not belong to any church due to the westward movement of the frontier. The number of churches needed could not keep pace with the growing population moving west.

Philosophical societies arose to challenge formal religion and hinder the establishing of a state church. John Locke in his *Letters on Toleration* (1689–1706) argued persuasively for the separation of church and state, as did men like Thomas Jefferson. When given the opportunity, they wove their religious biases into the fabric of the documents they wrote on behalf of the country.

The Anglican Church offended many when the Society for the Propagation of the Gospel agitated for the appointment of a bishop. There was great resentment from the Congregational and Presbyterian churches, who had come to America to escape this very thing in England. If the English Parliament could appoint a bishop, if Parliament could establish a religion in the colonies, then it could also impose excessive taxes and other repressive law—against people who were looking for more freedoms, not more legislation.

One by one, all the colonies, territories, and states passed legislation separating the state from the church. The Congregational Church was the last to be separated from the state. This happened in New Hampshire in 1817, in Connecticut in 1818, and in Massachusetts in 1833.

CHAPTER 36

Religious Revivals in the United States
A.D. 1741–1859

"I did not come to tickle your ears; no, but I came to touch your hearts."
—George Whitefield

"They who come to Christ come to a banqueting-house where they may rest, and where they may feast."

—Jonathan Edwards

A Great Awakening (1741–1744)

The greatest manifestations of divine grace in the history of the Church are those times when the Lord visits His people in a mighty way. When the sins of secular humanism, Deism, and Rationalism tried to steal the hearts of millions, God used the power of His own Word to frustrate the work of the Wicked One (Matt 13:19, 38). Souls were snatched from the jaws of self-destruction by powerful preachers of righteousness. Among those most effective was Theodore Jacob Frelinghuysen (1691–1748), a former minister in the Netherlands. Frelinghuysen arrived in America to pastor a Dutch Reformed Church in New Jersey located along the Raritan River (c. 1720–1747). The need for a personal relationship with the living Lord was emphasized. The truth was proclaimed that a genuine Christian has a converted heart—evidenced by conviction of sin, repentance, and renewal by the Holy Spirit.

Frelinghuysen also insisted that converts show some evidence of salvation prior to receiving Communion. He addressed his congregation in plain words:

> Much loved hearers, who have so often been at the Lord's table, do you know that the unconverted may not approach? Have you with the utmost care

> examined whether you be born again? . . . Reflect, therefore, upon...and remember, that though morally and outwardly religious, if you still be unregenerate and destitute of spiritual life, you have no warrant for an approach to the table of grace.

God honored the faithful proclamation of His Word and the administration of Church discipline. A sense of spiritual renewal began to spread beyond the valley of the Raritan.

As the Lord used Theodore Frelinghuysen, so He poured out His Spirit upon other ministers of the Gospel—such as William Tennent, a minister of a Presbyterian assembly in Neshaminy, Pennsylvania (c. 1727). The father of four sons, Tennent had built a log cabin on his land to be used as a schoolhouse. His objective was to train his sons for the work of the ministry. When other men heard of Tennent's "Log College," as the humble structure became known, they asked to be trained as well. At least fifteen students received instructions in Latin, Greek, Hebrew, logic, theology, and personal work in evangelism. The Lord blessed and a revival broke out. Like a spreading forest fire out of control, spiritual renewal spread among the Presbyterians from Long Island to Virginia.

Jonathan Edwards

God continued to manifest Himself in Massachusetts by preparing a special person named Jonathan Edwards to be a mighty instrument in His hands. Edwards was born in 1703 in East Windsor, Connecticut, the son of a minister of the Congregational Church. Possessing a brilliant mind, Edwards was graduated from Yale at seventeen. After several more years of study and preparation, he was appointed minister of the Congregational Church in Northampton in central Massachusetts.

In December of 1734, Edwards began to preach on the doctrine of justification. His primary objective was to respond to the rise of Arminianism, which was being accepted in New England. Edwards proclaimed that salvation was of the Lord. Sinners were to flee from the wrath of God. They were to run to Christ and take refuge in His substitutionary death.

The illuminating power of the Holy Spirit fell upon the people who heard the sermons. A tremendous change came over the town and church. A sense of the presence of God prevailed in the community. Hardly a person could be found, regardless of their age, who was not concerned about the way of salvation. Before the year was out, three hundred precious souls professed to be converted.

The revival fires continued to spread in various parts of New England. By 1740, mass conversions were being reported. Between 25,000 and 50,000 new members were added to the churches out of a total population of 300,000.

Physical manifestations of strong emotions often attended the church services. When Edwards preached at Enfield, Connecticut, on July 8, 1741, he had to pause while the people wept and cried out in terror upon hearing about "Sinners in the Hands of an Angry God," his most famous sermon.[1] The religious awakening could not be attributed to any theatrics on the part of Edwards. One observer wrote, "He scarcely gestured or even moved; and he made no attempt by the elegance of his style, or the beauty of his pictures, to gratify the taste and fascinate the imagination." What Edwards did do was to convince his audience "with overwhelming weight of argument, and with such intensity of feeling."

George Whitefield

While Edwards was limited in his ability to travel and preach, George Whitefield was not. Born in Gloucester, England, December 16, 1714, Whitefield grew up working in the family tavern. Recognized as a capable student, Whitefield was allowed to enroll at Oxford University, where he became a guiding force in the Holy Club. Despite his religious inclination, Whitefield did not consider himself regenerated by the Holy Spirit until 1736. He was ordained a minister in the Church of England.

Being open to the leading of the Lord, Whitefield believed that God would have him minister also in America. From 1738–1770, he made seven preaching tours to America. So powerful was Whitefield's preaching that the mere mention of his name stirred great excitement. Men would drop their plows in the field to go listen to him speak. Store owners would close their shops. Prayer meetings would spontaneously arise. Thousands would gather in the open field with their faces turned towards heaven. Sometimes Whitefield would speak to as many as 20,000 people in one gathering as souls were swept into the kingdom.

His eloquence was memorable. Once, when preaching on eternity, he invited his listeners to imagine heaven.

---

[1] *Sinners in the Hands of an Angry God* – available from Ichthus Publications.

> Lift up your hearts frequently towards the mansions of eternal bliss, and with an eye of faith, like the great St. Stephen, see the heavens open, and the Son of Man with His glorious retinue of departed saints sitting and solacing themselves in eternal joys, and with unspeakable comfort looking back on their past sufferings and self-denials, as so many glorious means which exalted them to such a crown. Hark! Methinks I hear them chanting their everlasting hallelujahs, and spending an eternal day in echoing forth triumphant songs of joy. And do you not long, my brethren, to join this heavenly choir?

When Whitefield died on September 30, 1770 in Newburyport, Massachusetts, his body was laid to rest under the pulpit of the Old South Presbyterian Church.

Almost as suddenly as it came, the revival fire burned out. Between 1744–1748 Edwards himself lamented that his own church in Northhampton appeared to be once more spiritually dead. Not a single soul was converted to Christ in all that time. Edwards believed that one cause for the spiritual decline was blatant unbelief among the clergy represented in Boston by the minister Charles Chauncy. Congregational ministers in New England and Reformed ministers in New York argued over the value of the revival. Even the Presbyterians seemed to be confused as to how the sensational revival should be viewed. These "Old Lights," as the clergymen became known, first grieved and then quenched the Spirit of God (Eph 4:30; 1 Thess 5:19). It is a biblical truth that God will not stay savingly active where He is not wanted (Ezek 10:1–22).

Do It Again, Lord; Do It Again!

By the year 1800, many Christians knew that another spiritual revival was needed in America. Atheistic books like *The Age of Reason*, written by Thomas Paine, had led a generation to boldly dismiss the Christian faith. There were terrible consequences. Timothy Dwight, the grandson of Jonathan Edwards and president of Yale College, described the condition of New England during the days of the American Revolution.

> The profanation of the Sabbath . . . profaness of language, drunkenness, gambling, and lewdness, were exceedingly increased; and what is less commonly remarked, but is not less mischievous than any of them, a light, vain method of thinking concerning sacred things—a cold, contemptuous indifference toward every moral and religious subject.

These same vices and more were equally prevalent on the western frontier. Nearly a million people had made their way West by the turn of the century. They had settled in the Blue Ridge in Virginia, in Kentucky, Tennessee, the Northwest, and in Indian Territory. After Thomas Jefferson made the Louisiana Purchase, new emphasis was given to the West. A sense of "Manifest Destiny" materialized. Many people were convinced that God had determined that America would be settled from "sea to shining sea." It was the destiny of the nation to be big, bold, beautiful, and bounded together by a common culture and language. Of course, the Indians had to be dealt with, as well as the African slaves.

The Shame of Slavery

Slavery had always posed a problem for conscientious Christian thinkers and moral reformers in England and America. It is an anomaly that Thomas Jefferson could write "that all men are created equal" while being a slave owner. Though the Founding Fathers of America fought for political and personal freedoms, most managed to avoid setting their own slaves free.

In a spirit of compromise between conflicting ideas, provision had been made at the Constitutional Convention in Philadelphia that the slave trade would come to an end, but not before 1808. Georgia and the Carolinas would have it no other way. Those who wanted slavery to end would have to wait. What is shameful is that the enslaving of other humans was prolonged and justified by many professing Christians on biblical grounds. In the words of one Baptist minister, slavery existed "as an institution of God."

Specific arguments were made in defense of this "Peculiar Institution," as it was euphemistically called in the South. Abraham, the "father of faith," owned slaves without being reprimanded by the Lord (Gen 21:9–10). The same was true of other patriarchs. The Ten Commandments mention slavery twice without condemnation (Exod 20:10, 17). Slavery was prevalent in the ancient world, yet Jesus never spoke against it, and other such arguments.

But there is one passage in the New Testament that no slave trader could ever preach from in defense of the indefensible. The passage is 1 Timothy 1:10. In this text, "slave traders" (lit. "men-stealers") are specifically condemned. They are listed among those who are not righteous. The word translated "men-stealers" in the Authorized Version is *andrapodistes*; it refers to an enslaver, as one who brings men to his feet.

Before slavery was constitutionally prohibited with the passing of the Thirteenth Amendment (February 1, 1865; ratified, December 18, 1865), there would be untold suffering, a bloody Civil War, and a gaping wound made in the body of Christ. Baptists, Presbyterians, and Methodists would debate and divide over this issue. New denominations would be formed. Christians in the South who defended the literal words of the Bible, would increasingly insist on a strict and narrow interpretation of the Scriptures. Those in the North who opposed slavery would increasingly emphasize the spiritual and ethical principles of the Bible—such as love for one's brother, manifested in social concern and action.

In 1800 the future of slavery was still in question. What was not in question was that slavery was a contributing factor of moral decline where practiced. There was a need for another work of divine grace.

The Second Great Awakening (c. 1791–1835)

About the year 1799, a revival of religion could be sensed in the country. People began to take a renewed interest in spiritual matters. Something wonderful and mysterious was happening. One Presbyterian minister wrote, "We have heard from different parts the glad tidings of the outpourings of the Spirit, and of times of refreshing from the presence of the Lord ... From the east, from the west, and from the south, have these joyful tidings reached our ears." God had not forgotten His people. The work of Edwards, Wesley, and Whitefield was emerging once more. Unlike the First Great Awakening, this second season of spiritual vitality would last longer (c. 1791–1835), and come in distinct phases both West and East.

In the West, great spiritual attention became focused on the camp meetings conducted by the Presbyterian minister James McGready (c. 1762–1817). After years of fearless preaching to rugged pioneer families, the manifestation of God fell like fire from heaven on McGready's preaching (note 2 Chr 7:1). It all began in June, 1800. Almost five hundred people had gathered from the three congregations McGready pastored in Muddy River, Red River, and Gasper River in Logan County, Kentucky. The camp meeting was to last for several days. On the final day "a mighty effusion of [God's] Spirit" came upon the people, "and the floor was soon covered with the slain; their screams for mercy pierced the heavens."

Excited by the events, McGready and five ministers who had joined him planned for a camp meeting to be held in July at Gasper River. They were not prepared for what happened next. No one was. As many as 8,000 people showed up. Some had traveled as far as 100 miles to attend. Services were held for three days. McGready recalled what happened.

> The power of God seemed to shake the whole assembly. Towards the close of the sermon [by William McGee, a Presbyterian pastor], the cries of the distressed arose almost as loud as his voice... Here awakening and converting work was to be found in every part of the multitude; and even some things strangely and wonderfully new to me.

There were to be more expressions of revival through the activity of Barton W. Stone (1772–1844), pastor of Presbyterian churches at Cane Ridge and Concord, northeast of Lexington, Kentucky. In August, 1801, between 10,000 and 25,000 souls showed up from as far as Ohio and Tennessee. Lexington, the largest town in Kentucky, had less than 1,800 citizens. Only God could have brought His people together in this manner.

In the East, the longing for spiritual renewal found a leader in Timothy Dwight. With great tact and clear biblical arguments, he challenged the students of Yale College to consider becoming true disciples of Christ. Early in the spring of 1802 two students were convicted of their sins and came to faith in Jesus Christ as personal Savior. Soon, other students were gathering for prayer and worship. Out of a total of 160 enrollments, 80 rose up to follow Christ. In succeeding years (1808, 1813, 1815), revivals also came.

A Contrast of Two Christian Evangelists

"Holiness to the Lord seemed to be inscribed on all the exercises of my mind."
—Charles G. Finney

One popular Connecticut minister in the early years of the 1800s was Asahel Nettleton (1783–1844). The Lord honored his work with as many as 30,000 converts. His meetings were characterized by a quiet and solemn dignity, and thus were in great contrast to a more dynamic personality named Charles Grandison Finney (1792–1875), a man whom Nettleton would severely criticize.

Beginning in the town of Western, New York, in October 1825, Finney began one of the most extensive evangelistic campaigns that America had ever seen. Great crowds gathered to hear him preach in Wilmington, Philadelphia, New York City, Rochester, and many other places. A multitude of new professions were made. As the fame of Finney grew, so did the criticism surrounding his "new" methods. The new methods included praying for the salvation of people by name, permitting women to pray and give their personal testimonies, the "altar call" (inviting people to come forward at meetings, even putting emotional pressure upon them to do so), encouraging Church members to invite their friends and neighbors in the community, and holding special services for several days and even weeks.

In addition to different techniques of evangelism, Finney also introduced new theological concepts. Of particular importance was his view that revival was not a miraculous act of God but a simple use of human "techniques." If people did the right things, revival was certain to come. His thoughts were published in *Lectures on Revival of Religion* (1835). Finney also taught the doctrines of entire consecration, sinless perfection in this life, freedom of the will, moral responsibility, and the ability of Christians to fall from grace (i.e., lose their salvation, an integral part of original Arminianism). He encouraged people to become involved in social reform. An English worker named George Williams was inspired to do just that. After being converted by reading the writings of Finney, in 1844 he started the Young Men's Christian Association (YMCA).

Despite the obvious good that Finney accomplished in his lifetime, discerning pastors were alarmed that Finney was changing American religion from a God-centered to a man-centered religion. Nevertheless, as president and professor in the Oberlin School in Ohio, Finney was able to influence future Holiness and Pentecostal movements and leaders. Credited with the conversions of about 500,000 people, Finney found faithful followers who promoted both his methods and his message.

A Third Great Awakening (1857–1859)

By 1840 vital religious life in America was once more ebbing away. Sensational teachings began to replace spiritual stability. One radical group, the Millerites, had widely advertised that Christ would return to earth between March 21, 1843 and March 21, 1844. When the Lord did not appear according to schedule (note Acts 1:7), William Miller, the leader of the sect, reset the date for October 22, 1844. Those who trusted him as a student of the Bible were disappointed. Some were outraged. Others who had watched the sad spectacle of date setting, openly mocked (2 Pet 3:3–4).

Besides having to deal with the wide dissemination of false prophecies, Americans had other worries. On October 10, 1857, the New York stock market crashed. A financial panic occurred as businesses everywhere shut down. Major money institutions like the Bank of Pennsylvania in Philadelphia failed. Other banks soon closed. Railroads derailed into bankruptcy. Financial chaos was everywhere; and a civil war seemed imminent over state's rights, slavery, and other questions. Concern for the state of the nation and the sterility of the Church caused an outpouring of prayer by individual Christians. In 1857 Jeremiah Lanphier, a 48-year-old businessman, began to hold noon prayer meetings at North Dutch Church on Fulton Street in New York.

Soon record crowds were gathering to pray. Within six months 10,000 people were gathering daily for prayer throughout the state of New York. The New York Times reported that the popular pastor, Dr. Henry Ward Beecher was leading 3,000 people in daily devotions at the Burton Theater. As the news traveled, other major cities such as Philadelphia, Albany, Boston, Chicago, began to hold similar noon-day prayer meetings. The rules were simple: (1) a meeting was to begin and end on time, (2) no one should speak or pray for very long, five minutes at the most, (3) no more than two consecutive prayers or exhortations were to be offered, (4) no controversial points were to be discussed.

Those who attended the prayer meetings were impressed that there was no fanaticism, hysteria, or behavior that was unseemly. There was only an impulse to pray. One man noted, "The general impression seemed to be, 'We have had instruction until we are hardened; it is now time for us to pray.'" There was a great over reaching attitude that God was being called upon and glorified. It has been estimated that there were at least 500,000 conversions to Christ in the United States during this period. In 1859 the influence of the revival spread to the British Isles. It was ignited there in the ministry of Evan Roberts. The glory of God was filling the earth!

For a brief period from 1904 to 1908, God was pleased to use Evan John Roberts (1878–1951) and associated ministers, including Evan Hopkins, to bring spiritual renewal to His people in Wales. It has been estimated that at least 100,000 souls came to Christ during these days of divine visitation. This former blacksmith apprentice knew the power of God upon his life. He opened his heart to the Lord while studying for ministry in the Calvinist Methodist Church at the Minister's Training College at Newcastle Emlyn. Roberts followed in the footsteps of

Christmas Evans (1766–1838), another Welsh preacher that enjoyed a season of dynamic preaching with heavenly power. Christmas Evans was known as the "Welsh Bunyan," for he could make the large audiences roar with laughter and then move them to break forth into tears of repentance.

The renewed interest in the things of God, which had come during revival, was given a solid foundation in the work of such men as Robert Louis Dabney (1820–1898). Born in Virginia, Dabney was graduated from Union Theological Seminary in Virginia in 1846. A strong leader in the Presbyterian Church, Dabney fought to preserve conservative doctrinal orthodoxy against the attempts of James Woodrow of Columbia Seminary and others to revise it. Dabney also defended the Southern position in the Civil War. His major works included *Defense of Virginia and the South* (1867) and *Syllabus and Notes of the Course of Systematic and Polemic Theology* (1871).

CHAPTER 37

Counterfeit Religions to Christian Revivals
A.D. 1844

Ellen G. White and Seventh-Day Adventism

The Non-Advent of Christ

Christianity has always struggled with men and women who depart from the teachings of the Bible to establish their own opinions in the minds of many (note John 1:9–10). Because of the adulation invested in these charismatic and clever religious leaders, the structures built up around them are rightly called *cults*.[1] During the 1800s, the central western part of New York State produced two very influential cultic leaders: William Miller and Joseph Smith.

William Miller (1782–1849) was born in Pittsfield, Massachusetts. He was a farmer in New York, and then a captain during the War of 1812. In 1816, he was converted from Deism and started to study the Bible. Of particular interest to Miller were the prophetic passages of Daniel and Revelation. After fourteen years of study, he was convinced that he knew the approximate time and date of the Lord's Second Coming (Advent). To Miller, it was simple: the 2,300 days of Daniel 8:14 were counted as year-days, starting in 457 B.C. If properly calculated, the Lord would return within twelve months of March, 1843.

Having been licensed to preach by a Baptist church in 1833, Miller began to share his views in public congregations. When his messages were well received by an excited, if biblically uninformed, listening audience, Miller published (1836) his thoughts under the title *Evidence from Scripture and History of the Second Coming of Christ, about the Year 1843*. When the Lord did not return by March 1844, Miller

---

[1] cults – (Latin *cultus:* care, adoration) groups with devoted followers of unorthodox doctrines or practices.

recalculated his figures—and showed that the Lord would return on October 22, 1844. But there was no Advent on that date either.

Despite being discredited by these failed predictions, William Miller was able to keep followers. He organized them into a "church" in 1845 and served as their first president. Unity lasted only until 1846, when a division took place. One part, led by Mrs. Ellen G. White, began to call themselves the Seventh-Day Adventists. The separation took place over the question of the Jewish Sabbath, as well as the meaning of the sanctuary in Daniel chapter 8. Mrs. White had some very unusual ideas of her own.

A Modern Day Prophetess?

Ellen Gould White was born in 1827 at Gorham, Maine (d. 1915). At age ten, Ellen was accidentally struck by a rock; this put her into a coma for three weeks. Though she survived the ordeal, the next six years were spent in recuperation. In 1840, Ellen went to an evangelistic meeting conducted by William Miller. She was amazed by what she heard, and she believed. When the Lord did not appear as predicted, she and four other women began to hold a prayer meeting. One day, Ellen had a vision of being transported into heaven—where she was told that the Lord's Second Advent could not take place until the whole world had been evangelized according to Matthew 28:19–20. Christians must get busy.

Ellen Gould would do her part. She would marry and spread the Gospel according to the Advent faith, much of which she was about to create from her fertile imagination. On August 30, 1846, Ellen married the Reverend James White. He had been ordained a minister in the Adventist movement in 1843.

In 1846, when a portion of the Adventist movement separated from the main body, Ellen G. White emerged as a modern day prophetess. Of particular concern to ministers of the historic Christian faith were her new teachings in specific areas: the atonement; Satan being a sin-bearer; Christ having a sinful, fallen nature; soul-sleep; and the Sabbath.

In the movement to find a following of her own, Mrs. White began to deny the biblical doctrine of the atoning sacrifice of Christ as the only means of salvation. Said Mrs. White,

> The ministration of the priests throughout the year in the first apartment of the sanctuary [*Ed.:* which is in heaven, not on earth] ... represents the work

of ministration upon which Christ entered at His ascension ... For eighteen centuries this work of ministration continued in the first apartment of the sanctuary. The blood of Christ, pleaded in behalf of penitent believers, secured their pardon and acceptance with the Father, yet their sins still remained upon the books of record.[2]

Conservative ministers were shocked at such new doctrines. Is it really possible that sins can be pardoned and yet still be on the books (note Rom 5:1–2; 8:1)? Mrs. White was not through denying the finality of the work of Christ on the Cross—even though Christ had cried out "It is finished!" (John 19:30). Again, Mrs. White wrote:

As in typical service [Ed.: i.e., the Old Testament sacrifices] there was a work of atonement at the close of the year, so before Christ's work of redemption of men is completed, there is a work of atonement for the removal of sin from the sanctuary. This is the service which began when the 2,300 days end [Ed.: 1844 is in view here]. At that time, as foretold by Daniel the prophet, our high priest entered the most holy to perform the last division of His solemn work to cleanse the sanctuary ... In the new covenant the sins of the repentant are by faith placed upon Christ, and transferred, in fact, to the heavenly sanctuary ... So the actual cleansing of the heavenly [sanctuary] is to be accomplished by the removal, or blotting out, of the sins which are there recorded. But before this can be accomplished, there must be an examination of the books of record to determine who, through repentance of sin and faith in Christ, are entitled to the benefits of His atonement. The cleansing of the sanctuary therefore involves a work of investigation, a work of judgment. Those who followed in the light of the prophetic word saw that, instead of coming to the earth at the termination of the 2,300 day in 1844, Christ then entered into the most holy place of the heavenly, to perform the closing work of atonement preparatory to His coming.[3]

Mrs. White assumed that there is a sanctuary in heaven, there is sin in heaven, that the sanctuary serves as a kind of "mediator" and bears the sins of many for the present, and this cleansing and investigating to see who is worthy of the benefits of the atonement began in 1844 (cp. Eph 2:8–9; Rom 1:17).

---

[2] Ellen Gould White, *The Great Controversy*.
[3] Ibid.

In another area, Mrs. White declared that Satan was a joint sin-bearer, and the vicarious substitute of the sinner. According to Mrs. White,

> When Christ, by virtue of His own blood, removes the sins of His people from the heavenly sanctuary at the close of His ministration, He will place them upon Satan, who in the execution of the judgment must bear the final penalty. The scapegoat was sent into a land not inhabited, never to come again into the Congregation of Israel. So will Satan be forever banished from the presence of God and His people and he will be blotted from existence in the final destruction of sin and the sinner.[4]

Not only is the doctrine of justification by faith set aside by this teaching, but Satan's vicarious suffering in bearing away the sins of the people of God into a land of utter annihilation replaces the substitutionary work of Christ at Calvary (see 2Pe 2:1). Any number of Scriptures refute a Satanic work of co-redemption by speaking of the precious blood of Christ and what He accomplished (Lev 17:11; 1 Pet 1:19; 2:24; Col 1:20; Eph 2:13; John 3:18; Rom 8:1; 3:24; 1 John 1:7).

A third doctrine that Mrs. White and her followers advocated by departing from the historic Christian faith was that Jesus had a fallen, sinful nature.

> The idea that Christ was born of an immaculate or sinless mother [*Ed.*: this is Roman Catholic doctrine, not an evangelical Protestant doctrine], inherited no tendencies to sin, and for this reason did not sin, removes Him from the realm of a fallen world, and from the very place where help is needed. On His human side, Christ inherited just what every child of Adam inherits—a sinful nature. On the divine side, from His very conception He was begotten and born of the Spirit. And all this was done to place mankind on vantage ground, and to demonstrate that in the same way everyone who is "born of the Spirit" may gain like victories over sin in his own sinful flesh. Thus each one is to overcome as Christ overcame (Rev 3:21). Without this birth there can be no victory over temptation, and no salvation from sin (cp. Joh 3:3–7).[5]

In contrast to this teaching of Mrs. White, the Bible says that Christians are partakers of God's holiness (Heb 12:10), and that Christ and God are one (John 10:30). Jesus could not be both "holy" and "undefiled" and at the same time a

---

[4] Ibid.
[5] abstracted from *Bible Readings for the Home Circle*, 1915 edition.

partaker of a fallen nature, inheriting what sinners inherit, and be without sin (Heb 7:26; 4:15). Jesus said, "The prince of this world cometh, and hath nothing in me" (John 14:30). The Bible says that "In him [Christ] is no sin" (1 John 3:5).

A fourth teaching of Mrs. White was that the saints do not go to be with the Lord upon death. Rather, there is a soul-sleep.

> Upon the fundamental error of natural immortality rests the doctrine of consciousness in death, a doctrine like eternal torment, opposed to the teachings of the Scriptures, to the dictates of reason, and to our feelings of humanity. The theory of eternal punishment is one of the false doctrines that constitute the wine of the abominations of Babylon.

With this teaching Mrs. White dismissed all the passages in the Bible that teach otherwise. Paul said in 2 Corinthians 5:6, "Being of good cheer, therefore always and knowing that being at home in the body, we are away from home from the Lord" (author's literal translation; see also Luke 16:19–31; 23:43).

Another area of concern is Mrs. White's teaching on the Sabbath. Mrs. White claimed that she had a vision in which she was taken to heaven and shown the sanctuary and its appointments. Jesus Himself raised the cover of the ark, and she beheld the tables of stone on which the Ten Commandments were written. Mrs. White was amazed as she saw the Fourth Commandment in the very center of the ten precepts, with a soft halo of light encircling it. Mrs. White began to teach that Christians, being still under the Law of Moses, are bound to keep the "least of its precepts," and therefore must keep the Sabbath. It was soon argued that in A.D. 364, at the Council of Laodicea, the Roman Catholic Church changed the Sabbath (on the Seventh day) to Sunday (the First day). Neither the Scriptures nor history will bear such assertions out.

Why the Christian Sabbath is the First Day of the Week[6]

1. The Lord's Day of the Christian at once upholds the abiding principles of rest and worship for which the Jewish Sabbath was instituted, and is a remembrance of His resurrection from the dead on the first day of the week.

---

[6] Compiled from the writings of J. Oswald Sanders (1902–1992) – Sanders was general director of China Inland Mission and Overseas Missionary Fellowship in the 1950s and 1960s. He authored more than forty books on the Christian life. He became an elder statesman and worldwide conference speaker from his retirement until his death. Born in Invercargill, New Zealand.

2. Reasons for observing the First Day (Sunday) for worship. We observe the Lord's Day, the first day of the week, not because we must, but because we may—out of love for Him and not from legal constraint.

    a. It was on the first day that Jesus rose from the dead (John 20:1).

    b. It was foreshadowed in the Feast of Firstfruits (Lev 23:15–16), a festival which typified the resurrection of the Lord, which was followed after fifty days by the Feast of Pentecost, typical of the descent of the Holy Spirit.

    c. It was on the first day that Jesus met His people after His resurrection (Luke 24:13–31; John 20:19). He met with them again a week later (John 20:26). Thus the Lord's day was born.

    d. It was on the first day that the Holy Spirit descended to constitute the New Testament Church.

    e. It was on the first day that the rite of Christian baptism was first observed (Acts 2:41).

    f. It was on the first day that the New Testament Church met for worship (Acts 20:7; Rev 1:10).

    g. It was on the first day believers were exhorted to make their offerings (1 Cor 16:2).

    h. It was on the first day that Christians met to observe the Lord's Supper which had superseded the Passover Feast.

Joseph Smith and Mormonism

"No Man Knows My History"

Ellen G. White was not the only person in America having visions. So was the elusive Mr. Smith. At the young age of 38, Joseph Smith, first president of the Church of Jesus Christ of Latter Day Saints, died from the guns of assassins. In his death, Joseph Smith became a martyr for his cause and a man of mystique. In just a few short years he had established one of the most unusual cults of all.

Smith was born December 23, 1805 in Sharon, Windsor County, Vermont, the fourth of ten children. He was destined to be reared in ignorance and poverty under the guidance of a superstitious father who liked to search for buried treasure. When Joseph was ten the family moved to Palmyra, New York, where pious controversy was present. Later, Smith would testify that the religious arguments greatly troubled him. He wondered which church to join. He claimed that one night, God the Father and God the Son appeared to him offering divine guidance. In 1819 another divine visitation took place. This time Smith was told not to join any of the denominations. More visions would follow.

On September 22, 1823, when Joseph was eighteen, an angel named Moroni led him to some golden tablets buried in a stone box in the "Hill Cumorah" four miles from Palmyra. On these tablets, fastened together with gold rings, was the history of ancient America. The history had been recorded in "reformed-Egyptian characters (*sic*)" and then buried in A.D. 420. This ancient "language" was able to be translated because of some special eye glasses that had also been left. The glasses were two crystals set in a silver bow. Using these "Urim and Thummim," as Smith called them, he translated and then published *The Book of Mormon* (1830).

The actual translation took place behind a curtain. Smith dictated the work to Martin Harris who sat on one side of the drawn drapery. When Harris tired of writing, Smith would let Oliver Cowdery act as the writer. The result of all this labor was a very unusual story of the people of North America. Once the translation was completed, Smith took the golden tablets back to the hill where he had first found them. The angel Moroni came and carried the plates away, along with the special spectacles.

One very remarkable result of the translation by Smith of the "reformed-Egyptian" plates is that large portions give a faithful rendering of the Bible in the King James Version (1611)! The practical problem of course is that the "translation" contains modern phrases and ideas that would not have been known to its alleged author in A.D. 420.

As entertaining as this notion is, more probable is the fact that the manuscript which Smith, Harris, and Cowdery worked with was really a historical novel written by Solomon Spaulding, a Presbyterian minister who died at Conneaut, Ohio in 1816—before the novel could be published. There is evidence that the novel was discovered by a Sidney Rigdon in the printing office of Patterson and Lamdin of Pittsburgh, Pennsylvania. Rigdon may have wanted to publish it for financial gain. What is more certain is that in Joseph Smith a ready accomplice was found, who had the imagination to add passages of Scripture to the text. Also added were theories from the tales of the Italian mystic, Abbot Joachim of Flora (d. 1202), founder of a religious sect in the thirteenth century called The Order of Flora. From the ancient title of Joachim's main works, printed posthumously as *The Everlasting Gospel* (1254), came a new phrase to be applied to the Mormon "revelation."

Following the publication of *The Book of Mormon*, Smith humbly referred to himself as "seer, translator, prophet, apostle of Jesus Christ, and elder of the Church." In this spirit (which hardly reflected Christ's meekness and lowliness), on April 6, 1830, he formally founded the Church of Jesus Christ of Latter Day Saints. Six members were present to bear witness that the Lord's own apostles, Peter, James, and John, had previously conferred upon Joseph Smith and Oliver Cowdery the Melchizedek priesthood, which priesthood was superior to the one held by Aaron.

As word spread of a latter day Prophet sent from God to restore the true Church, based upon the writing of a new "Bible," curiosity alone caused some to listen to this exceptionally brazen man and his message. Being a charismatic leader and possessing many natural gifts, not the least of which was a vivid imagination, Smith attracted a following who gave generously to his cause.

With new financial resources available, Smith was able to establish a base of operation in Kirtland, Ohio. However, when the Mormon owned Safety Bank in Kirtland failed in 1838, Smith fled to Missouri—where he was soon arrested. Joseph was allowed to escape, after bribing his jailers, provided that he move on to Illinois.

Once established in Illinois, Smith was joined by his followers. Together they settled at Commerce, on the Mississippi River, and changed the name of the town to Nauvoo. Smith appointed himself major, commander of the Nauvoo Legion (a state militia unit whose uniforms he designed personally), and in February, 1844, announced that he would run for president of the United States.

When a group of local residents, joined by dissatisfied Mormons, printed accounts that ridiculed his presidential ambitions, denounced polygamy, and were critical of his leadership, Smith ordered the presses to be destroyed, which was done by militant Mormons. On the charge of destruction of property, Smith was arrested—as were his brother Hyrum and John Taylor. The three men were placed in a jail in Carthage, Illinois. The confinement was neither safe nor secure. On June 27, 1844, a mob broke into the prison and killed both Hyrum and Joseph Smith. John Taylor survived the assassins to become the third president of the Latter-day Saints.

While Mormons regarded Joseph Smith as a prophet of God who restored the true church, those within the true Christian Church regarded him as a false prophet, who denied or changed the major teachings of Christ, while living a shameful and licentious life based on plural "marriages." Though Smith publicly acknowledged only one wife, Emma Hale (m. 1827), who bore him nine children, his polygamous wives numbered as many as twenty-four. When Emma objected to her husband's immoral behavior, Smith responded by giving her a revelation from God: "And let Mine handmaid, Emma Smith, receive all those that have been given unto My servant Joseph, and who are virtuous and pure before Me" (*Doctrines and Covenants*, Sect. 132). Emma was not amused, nor did she ever recognize any other woman as being legally married to Joseph Smith.

Three works set forth Mormon beliefs and practices: *The Book of Mormon*, and two lesser works combined in one volume, *Doctrine and Covenants* and *The Pearl of Great Price*. To conservative Christians, the numerous teachings of Mormonism are almost too offensive to Christ to mention. A sample will suffice. (These points are extracted in part from among the following sources: "*What the Mormons Think of Christ*," Missions Office of the Church of Jesus Christ of Latter-Day Saints, Salt Lake City; *The Book of Mormon*; and *Doctrine and Covenants*.)

The Doctrines of Mormonism

Mormonism teaches God is an exalted man, once a man on earth as we are now, ever changing and advancing but never absolutely perfect. "God himself was once as we are now, and is an exalted man, and sits enthroned in yonder heavens: it is the first principle of the gospel to know that he was once a man like us; yea, that God the Father of us all dwelt on an earth, the same as Jesus Christ himself did."

Mormonism once taught that Adam is the Father of all, the Prince of all, and the Ancient of Days. Adam was God (see *Brigham Young's Journal of Discourses*, Vol. I, p. 50).

Mormonism teaches that all people live in a pre-mortal estate before they are born into this world; all were born in the pre-mortal existence as the spirit children of the Father, i.e., God the Father, an exalted man, with his heavenly wife (or wives) produces spirit children. What humans provide are bodies for the pre-existing spirits produced by a heavenly sexual union.

Jesus Christ is not the eternal God, very God of very God. Rather, He is the first begotten of the spirit children of the Father (*Doctrine and Covenants* 93:21–23).

Jesus, after His resurrection appeared to people in North America (*The Book of Mormon*, Ether 3:14, 16; 2 Nephi 11:7–11; Ether 12:39).

Mormonism teaches that through Joseph Smith alone, the perfect knowledge of Jesus Christ was returned to the earth. With the restoration of the Gospel of Christ through the Prophet Smith came the true and holy priesthood of God—the authority from God to administer the ordinances of salvation.

The Way West

The premature death of Joseph Smith brought forth a capable but ruthless leader in the person of Brigham Young. His ruthlessness would be manifested in the Mountain Meadow Massacre (1857). When a group of immigrants on their way from Arkansas to California would not unite with the Mormons, they were kept from leaving by being slaughtered. In 1877, Mormon John D. Lee was executed for his part in the massacre.

One of the first things Young did following the death of Joseph Smith was to continue to try and convince the public that Smith and the *The Book of Mormon* really were a new work of God. Said Young, "Every Spirit that confesseth that Joseph is a prophet, and that *The Book of Mormon* is true, is of God, and every Spirit that does not is of Antichrist!" While a powerful personality in his own right, Brigham Young had a lot to gain by continuing the work of Joseph Smith.

Young had first joined the Mormons when the followers of the Prophet had their headquarters in Kirtland, Ohio (1831–1837). Soon after joining the movement, Young became one of the "Twelve Apostles." It was under his leadership that the Mormons would move west for the Valley of the Great Salt Lake. A master organizer and ruthless controller of minds, Brigham Young guided the Mormons until his death in 1877. He left behind an estate worth over a half million dollars, seventeen wives, and fifty-six children.

Charles Taze Russell and Jehovah's Witnesses

"False Prophets and Promises"

Like Ellen G. White, "Pastor" Charles Taze Russell was influenced by the teachings of William Miller, one of the originators of the Second Adventist movement. Russell was born in Allegheny, Pennsylvania on February 16, 1852. Though religiously inclined, by the age of seventeen Russell was a skeptic. Of particular concern to him was the biblical doctrine of hell. Russell hated the very thought of a place of eternal torment. He wanted nothing to do with a God who would punish souls for all eternity.

In 1870, Russell was exposed to the ministry of Miller. Despite the failure of date setting, Miller was able to give Charles two things he needed: the ability theologically to deny the reality of hell, and a renewed interest in eschatology.

Without being much of an original thinker, Russell managed to build a religious movement by denying the historic doctrines of Christianity. He and his followers of various names (Millennial Dawnists, International Bible Students, Russellites), denied the Trinity, the deity of Christ, His physical resurrection from the dead, the literal second coming, and eternal judgment of the wicked. They taught a second opportunity for all to be saved in the millennium, while insisting on the annihilation of the wicked. The sufficiency of Christ's atonement was ridiculed. Human government was considered to be one of the three allies of Satan. The other two were the teachings of denominational churches, and the suppression of business!

A gifted public speaker, Russell was able to attract large crowds to hear his lectures on the second coming of Christ. By 1872, in Pittsburgh, Pennsylvania, Russell was able to organize his ministry. On December 18, 1884, Zion's Watch Tower Tract Society became a publishing auxiliary work of the Association. *The Millennial Dawn* flooded the religious markets in America and in Europe.

By 1886, Russell had crystallized his thinking enough to print *The Divine Plan of the Ages*, which suggested that in the year 1914 the world would witness Armageddon. This last great battle would precede the dawning of Christ's thousand year rule on a renewed earth. Russell also taught that the "end times" began in 1799, and that Christ had returned "spiritually" in October, 1874. Later these dates changed. It was decided that Christ entered into His kingly office sometime in April, 1878.

When World War I broke out in Europe, it seemed that Russell was a prophet. However, Armageddon did not materialize and Jesus did not come. After a legal separation from his wife in 1906, and the failure of his prophecies in 1914 and again in 1915, Russell died on October 31, 1916.

A New Leader of the Movement

"Judge" Joseph Franklin Rutherford (1869–1942) emerged as the new leader of the movement. He would revitalize the energy of the movement by making popular the slogan "Millions now living will never die." In 1931 he would rename the ministry Jehovah's Witnesses. Prior to that, Rutherford picked up where Russell left off and began making false predictions. He decided that Armageddon would be in 1918, and then 1925. Hope did not die when both prophecies failed. The Beth Sarim (lit. "house of princes") was purchased in San Diego, California in 1929 to have a place for the coming "princes of the earth" to live. It was believed that the resurrected Old Testament saints would want a nice place to reside, when they arose to take charge of God's new world order. There is no doubt that King David, Samson, and Joseph would have liked the luxury of Beth Sarim.

The predictive impulse did not stop with the death of "Judge" Rutherford. In 1966 Frederick Franz published his *Life Everlasting in the Freedom of the Sons of God*. He taught that "the seventh period of a thousand years of human history will begin in the fall of 1975 C.E." (Christian Era). The word was spread that Jesus was coming again. In 1974 many Witnesses believed so much that they sold their homes. Once more a false prophecy had disappointed many.

A Time for Terminology

Like all religious organizations, the Jehovah's Witnesses have specific words with special meanings.

- AWAKE!—the name of a Watchtower periodical that is used to introduce the public to the teachings of Jehovah's Witnesses.
- GOATS—a reference to everyone who is not part of the Association of Jehovah's Witnesses. The Goats will be judged by the Lord according to Matthew 25:31–46.
- SHEEP—also known as the GREAT CROWD, is the name given to the majority of Witnesses who will not live in heaven but will enjoy a paradise on Earth after the Lord returns.
- JEHOVAH—the special and only proper name given to the LORD.
- KINGDOM HALL—the local assembly hall of Jehovah's Witnesses. Here they meet for worship and training.
- LITTLE FLOCK—also called the "144,000" or the "Anointed Class." This elite group of Witnesses will live in heaven with Christ and reign with Him.
- MICHAEL—the archangel, is really the man Jesus Christ. He is Jehovah's first creation.
- NEW WORLD TRANSLATION—the official "biblical" translation of the Scriptures (pub. 1961). Its wording is deliberately and incorrectly

"translated" in such a way as to support Watchtower theology, most notably to remove any direct reference to Jesus as God (see, for example, John 1:1).

- THE WATCHTOWER—publication is designed to be a manual of instruction for its own members.

Jehovah's Witnesses (JW) vs. the Word of God (WOG)

Doctrine of God

JW: The doctrine of the Trinity is a doctrine originated by Satan.
    WOG: Deut 6:4; Phil 2:11 cp. John 5:18 and Acts 5:3–4, 9
JW: Christ was the first created being of Jehovah God.
    WOG: John 8:58; cp. Rev 1:7–18 with Isa 44:6
JW: Jesus was really the archangel Michael incarnate.
    WOG: Heb 1:1–14
JW: Christ arose from the dead as a spirit person.
    WOG: Luke 24:39; John 20:20, 25, 27; 20:1–9
JW: The Holy Spirit is not a Person but an active force.
    WOG: John 14:16–17, 26; Acts 5:3–4

The Doctrine of Man

JW: The soul cannot be separated from the body. When the body dies, the soul dies.
    WOG: Luke 16:19–31; 23:39–43; 2Co 5:5–8; Phil 1:19–24
JW: Satan originated the concept of the immortality of the soul.
    WOG: Eccl 12:7; 2 Cor 5:1, 6–8
JW: Because there is no existence of the soul after death, all Jehovah's Witnesses can be recreated to inhabit His kingdom.
    WOG: 1 Kgs 17:17–24; Luke 7:11–17 cp. Luke 24:36–43; Phi 3:20–21; 1 Cor 15:39–54

The Doctrine of Salvation

JW: The death of Christ only purchased the earthly life and blessings which Adam lost.
    WOG: Eph 1:3–14.
JW: The death of Christ did not save anyone. It only provided an opportunity for a person to gain eternal life through good works.

WOG: 1 Pet 3:18; Eph 2:8–9; 1 John 5:11–13; John 6:39; 10:28–29

JW: The blood of Christ at the Cross will only be applied to 144,000 special Witnesses.

WOG: 1 Tim 2:5–6; 1 John 2:2; 2 Cor 5:15; Heb 2:9

JW: The way of salvation is through personal Bible study, being a member of the Association, being baptized as a Jehovah's Witness, and doing good works such as preaching and spreading the news of God's coming kingdom.

WOG: Acts 4:10–12; 10:42–43; Rom 3:21–24

JW: There is no hell.

WOG: Rev 20:11–15; Matt 13:41, 49–50; Mark 9:47–48

Mary Baker Eddy and Christian Science

"No Pain for the People of God"

THE LIFE AND TIMES OF MARY BAKER: KEY DATES

1821	Born in New Hampshire, raised a Congregationalist.
1843	Marries George W. Glover; he dies six months later.
1853	Marries a dentist, Daniel M. Patterson.
1862	Meets Phineas Quimby.
1866	Discovers the "divine law of life".
1873	Divorces her husband on grounds of desertion.
1875	Forms her first society at Lynn, Massachusetts.
1875	Publishes her textbook, *Science and Health* with Key to the Scriptures
1877	Marries Asa G. Eddy.
1879	Establishes the Church of Christ, Scientist.
1892	Organization is moved to Boston where the "Mother Church" founds the Massachusetts Metaphysical College.
1895	Manual of the Mother Church is published.
1908	At age 87, establishes the *Christian Science Monitor*.
1910	Mary Baker Eddy dies at the age of 89, despite still teaching that "Sickness and death are non-existent."

The Man from Maine

In 1910 Mary Baker Glover Patterson Eddy died. Over 100,000 people around the world mourned her passage, believing her to be a prophetess of God. Mrs. Eddy was an amazing woman. Her journey towards fame and fortune began in 1862 when she heard of a blacksmith in Portland, Maine with unique methods of helping the sick. Mary had been sick for most her life with a spinal weakness. She was tired of the pain. Perhaps Phineas Quimby could help through his practice of hypnotism. Quimby himself was a follower of the Frenchman Charles Poyen, a noted mesmerist.

As Mary listened to the philosophy of Quimby and watched him practice hypnosis, she became excited. Quimby really could help many who were sick. He was so certain that sickness was basically the result of negative thoughts. It was "scientifically" proven. The ill could be cured by thinking positive thoughts. The work of the man from Maine was summarized into a system of belief called "Christian Science" according to the *Quimby Manuscripts*.

Mind over Matter

Without giving him proper credit, Mary first adopted and then transformed the beliefs and practices of Phineas Quimby, after claiming she had been shown by supernatural revelation the Divine Law of Life. The dawning of the Divine Law came to her in 1866. Mary would later claim that she was meditating on Matthew 9:2 when she suddenly experienced complete healing from injuries resulting from a fall. Now it was all very simple. "Nothing is real and eternal, nothing is spirit, but God and His ideal; evil has no reality." There is no sickness or sin, sorrow or death. Deny them and they cease to exist.

Shortly after her cure, Mary opened a healing center where she could openly advocate that the "Principle of all harmonies Mind-action" to be God, who is the "Eternal Mind," the source of all being. Mrs. Eddy could also explain that matter does not exist, disease is the product of wrong thoughts or errors of the mortal mind, and spiritual power is found through the teachings of Christian Science.

To guide people through the esoteric maze of nebulous words and phrases she was now articulating, Mrs. Eddy published a "Bible" called *Science and Health with the Key to the Scriptures*. Mrs. Eddy was so pleased with her own writings that she decided to elevate her textbook to a divine status. In 1901 she wrote, "I should blush to write of *Science and Health with the Key to the Scriptures*, as I have, were it of human origin, and I apart from God, its author; but as I was only a scribe echoing the harmonies of heaven in Divine Metaphysics, I cannot be super-modest of the Christian Science textbook."

If *Science and Health* were truly of divine origin, it would harmonize with the Bible—for God cannot lie or be confused. However, *Science and Health* denies essential teachings of the Bible. In summary form, it can be said that *Science and Health* denies a personal God, that God created the world, the Trinity, the deity of Christ, the Lord's true humanity, the substitutionary death of Christ at Calvary for sins, His resurrection, and His second advent. *Science and Health* denies an eternal punishment of the wicked and a day of judgment for the righteous.

What *Science and Health* affirms can also be summarized. There are four basic propositions, which may be stated in Mrs. Eddy's own words: "First, God is All in all. Second, God is good. Good is mind. Third, God's Spirit, being all, nothing is matter. Fourth, life, God, omnipotent, good, deny death, evil, sin, disease. Disease, sin, evil, death, deny good, omnipotent, God, life."

The great attraction for Christian Science is that it promised the mind could cure sickness, disease, and even death. Those who believed that mind is over matter, that sickness is an illusion, and that all pain in time and eternity is not real, did not want to be reminded that Mrs. Eddy was addicted to drugs for many years before her death, and that she relied upon dentists to help her with her teeth in her own old age.

Anyone listening to these teachings must be warned. The following story is just one example of what is really offered, in the end, as an alternative to the one true Gospel of God. Many years ago a Christian minister named Ivan Panin was sent for by a major in the Canadian army, who was dangerously ill in the hospital. The major had a friend who claimed to have been healed by Christian Science and was encouraging him to try it. The major asked Mr. Panin, "What do you advise?" and was shocked at the answer: "I would advise you to try Christian Science if you are prepared to pay the price."

"Price!" the major exclaimed, "what is money in comparison with health, or life itself?"

"I did not mean the price in money," replied Mr. Panin, "but you would have to give up the Lord Jesus as your Savior, for 'Science' denies sin, evil, Satan, and sickness as realities—and hence has no atoning blood nor redeeming grace nor assurance of salvation."

"Beware lest any man spoil you through philosophy and vain deceit, after the tradition of men, after the rudiments of the world, and not after Christ."
—COLOSSIANS 2:8

"And others save with fear, pulling them out of the fire; hating even the garment spotted by the flesh."
—JUDE 1:23

CHAPTER 38

A Return to Normalcy
A.D. 1858

An Antidote for Anti-Christian Teachings

Since the time when the flood gates of false doctrine were fully opened (c. 1830), the world has been inundated with fallacious theories of divine truth, so called. Neither time nor space permits a detailed examination of the multitude of heretical beliefs that have managed to inject themselves into the mainstream of religious life. It is sufficient to say that the Church has been, and is now being, challenged by many religious entities: Agnosticism, Annihilationism, Atheism, Baptismal Regeneration, British-Israelism, Buchmanism, Christadelphianism, Cooneyism, Evolution, Freemasonry, Humanism, Modernism, Spiritism, TheoSophie, Unitarianism, and the Unity School. In addition to these vain imaginations of men, Eastern mysticism has come with force to capture the souls of the unsuspecting. The Church is confronted with Astrology, Baha'ism, Buddhism, Confucianism, and Rosicrucianism, to say nothing of Islamic Fundamentalism.

Because this is true, a way must be found to protect the truth, as well as one's own heart. And God has shown the way: to stay close to Him (Isa 26:3). Knowledge of the Lord through knowledge of God's Word will protect the soul from an eternal separation from the Holy One (Psa 119:1–176).

As the Scriptures are constantly studied, something else must be done if the heart is to be kept from being led astray. The private life must be kept pure. It can be argued that every false teaching has its origin in moral failure. The basic theology of Joseph Smith, for example, was born of a lustful mind. Polygamy was not an afterthought to this man; it was one of the first thoughts when he realized that people would receive him as a prophet. The true essence of Mormonism, both past and present, cannot be correctly understood apart from the practice of polygamy.

Upon objective examination (John 7:24), the moral character of each of the men and women who have founded a cult or sect often reveals an inordinate amount of sexual licentiousness, pride, a pre-occupation with self, greed, and the need to control others about them. Set aside are the Christian virtues of sanctification involving purity of mind and heart, humility, Christ-consciousness, a spirit of giving, and the desire to serve others. The Word of God and a life of holiness, defined by the Scriptures and lived by the power of the Holy Spirit, serve as the best antidote for an anti-Christian message.

A Million Souls for the Savior

"The world has yet to see what God will do with a man fully consecrated to him."
—Henry Varley, British evangelist

Despite the fact that the cults arose to challenge the Church of the Living Lord, they did not prevail (Matt 16:18). The ministry of building-up the body of Christ continued through missions, personal witnessing, and the work of evangelism. One of the most used of all evangelists was D. L. Moody.

Dwight Lyman Moody was born February 5, 1837 in East Northfield, Massachusetts. His father died when he was four years old, leaving the family with many financial concerns. Mrs. Moody had seven children to care for; Dwight was number six. One month after the death of Dwight's father, Mrs. Moody gave birth to twins—making nine children to provide for. Times would be hard for the family, but Mrs. Moody was determined that they would all stay together. The older children could help with the younger ones; everyone could do something to help out. As a result of practical necessity, Moody went to work doing odd jobs at an early age, thereby missing out on the better part of a proper formal education.

At seventeen, Moody left home to find work with good wages. He went first to Clinton, Massachusetts, finding a job in a book store. Dissatisfied, he traveled to Boston, where his uncles owned a shoe-store. Perhaps they would give him a job. Moody had determined that someday he would be worth $100,000.

Willing to do whatever was asked without question, and agreeing to go to Church and not gamble or drink, Moody was given work in the shoe store. Upon discovering that he really was a good salesman, Moody turned even more towards being a successful businessman.

One day a humble Sunday school teacher walked into the store. He was from the church Moody was attending, and he had a question. Did Dwight know if he were saved? Was he sure of going to heaven when he died? Moody was not sure. Before Mr. Edward Kimball left the store that day, he had led Moody to a sure, saving knowledge of Christ (Prov 11:30).

Recently converted, Moody tried to join the Congregational Church (May, 1856). The Elders of the church were happy that Dwight wanted to be a member, but first he had to pass an oral examination on Christian doctrine. When unable to do that, Moody's membership was delayed until further knowledge could be gained. In the meantime, Moody decided he would move to Chicago. There he would engage in business and begin to make his fortune.

Moody did go to Chicago and he did engage in business. But something else happened. Moody began to win souls to the Savior. The revival of 1858 had come to the city and Moody wanted to be part of it. He rented extra pews at Plymouth Church and then he went into the streets of the city and invited the children to go with him to the services. Next, Moody opened a Sunday school in one of the poorest sections of the city in order to tell the little ones about Christ.

The Lord blessed, and soon Moody wanted nothing to do with any business except the business of preaching the Gospel and winning souls to Christ. Accordingly, in 1860, he left the shoe store to work full time with the YMCA. When the Civil War broke out, Moody ministered to the Union soldiers, again meeting with great success. Many hearts were converted or comforted in the hour of conflict. After the war Moody returned to Chicago, where he was able to transform a Sunday school into the independent Illinois Street Church. During this same time, from 1865 to 1869, Moody served as president of the Chicago YMCA.

His field of ministry was enlarged in 1871 when he began conducting revival meetings throughout the country. Until the time of his death in 1899, Moody would take the Gospel to every place the Lord led. He went to England and Scotland many times, always accompanied with his song leader Ira D. Sankey, who led the singing and introduced exciting new hymns to the crowds who came to hear Moody preach.

In his preaching Moody stressed three themes: Ruin, Redemption, and Regeneration.[1] He spoke of how sin had ruined man, how Christ had redeemed him, and how the Holy Spirit regenerates the soul—so that sins are forgiven, and life can be lived with joy and the knowledge of going to heaven. Moody spoke in simple language. His warmth and sincerity caused many people to consider the claims of Christ. And the Holy Spirit was pleased to open many hearts.

In addition to preaching the Gospel, Moody opened Christian boarding schools in Northfield, Massachusetts. In 1879 he founded a school for girls, and in 1881 established the Mount Hermon School for boys. In 1886 a Bible Institute was created to train effective Christian workers less formally than seminary training.

Bible conferences were held at Northfield beginning in 1880. At these meetings evangelism and holiness of life dominated the messages presented from some of the greatest Christian leaders from all parts of the world. These weeks of spiritual emphasis led to the Student Volunteer Movement in 1886. In the years to come a slogan would inspire many to do the work of an evangelist and go to faraway mission fields: "The evangelization of the world in this generation." It has been estimated that Dwight Lyman Moody, an obscure child from a poor fatherless family, grew up to reach 100 million people while leading a million souls to the Master. The world once saw what God will do with a man fully consecrated to Him.

Gospel Progress in the United Kingdom

The world is indebted to the Lord's mighty and continuing work in the British Isles during the 19th and 20th centuries. He has used great men in great movements for His purposes around the globe.

George Müeller (1805–1898). An unusual man of great faith, George Müeller was convinced that all of his material needs could be supplied through believing prayer alone. When he moved to Bristol, England, Müeller gave up his independent life to demonstrate that by faith and prayer alone God would supply for orphans (based upon Psa 68:5). His simple belief in a prayer-hearing God has encouraged and inspired the establishment of other ministries according to faith principles.

Horatius Bonar (1808–1889) was born at Old Broughton, Edinburgh, Scotland, whose brother was Andrew Bonar. Following his education at the University of Edinburgh, Horatius maintained an active and powerful ministry for more than half

---

[1] See *Ruin, Redemption, Regeneration*, an anonymous tract available from Chapel Library that captures these three themes.

a century, pastoring churches in that area until his death. Throughout his life, Bonar avoided all sensationalism, and was noted as calm, patient, sincere, solemn—and a steady writer. His tracts and books are finding their way back into print,[2] and he wrote 600 hymns, of which more than 100 are still in use.

Andrew Bonar (1810–1892). A Scottish minister, Bonar left the Church of Scotland in 1843 to help form the Free Church. Burdened for the salvation of the Jews, he labored to see them come to Christ. The author of many scholarly works, Bonar has been a source of blessing for his devotional writings. He is best remembered for the *Memoir and Remains of Robert Murray McCheyne* (1862), and for an edition of the *Letters of Samuel Rutherford*.[3]

Robert Murray McCheyne (1813–1843). Like Andrew Bonar, McCheyne continued to cultivate the Puritan heart through an exemplary life of self-discipline, fervent prayer, Bible study, and careful preparation for powerful preaching. It was said of this Scottish minister, "He cared for no question unless his Master cared for it; and his main anxiety was to know the mind of Christ."

Arthur W. Pink (1886–1952) was born in Nottingham, England in 1886, and born again of the Spirit of God in 1908 at the age of 22. He studied at Moody Bible Institute in Chicago, USA, for only six weeks before beginning his pastoral work in Colorado, then in California, Kentucky, and South Carolina, and then to Sydney Australia for a brief period, preaching and teaching. In 1934, at 48 years old, he returned to his native England. In 1940 he took permanent residence in Lewis, Scotland, remaining there 12 years until his death at 66. Most of his works, including *The Attributes of God*, first appeared as articles in his monthly *Studies in the Scriptures* published without interruption from 1922 through 1953. Pink was virtually unknown and certainly unappreciated in his day. Independent Bible study convinced him that much of modern evangelism was defective. When Puritan and reformed books were thrown out, he advanced the majority of their principles with untiring zeal. The progressive decline of his own nation (Britain) was to him the inevitable consequence of the prevalence of a gospel that could neither wound nor heal. Familiar with the whole range of revelation, Pink was rarely sidetracked from the great themes of Scripture: grace, justification, and sanctification.

---

[2] Contact Chapel Library for any of more than sixty tracts, sermon booklets, and paperbacks by Bonar.
[3] *Letters of Samuel Rutherford* – booklet with excerpts of thirty of the best letters is available from Chapel Library.

David Martyn Lloyd-Jones (1899–1981). Born in Newcastle Emlyn, Martin was reared as a Calvinistic Methodist and trained in medicine in London. After being converted to Christ, he studied for the ministry and accepted a pastorate at Port Talbot in Wales (1927–1938). During the difficult days of World War II, Dr. Jones served as an associate pastor with G. Campbell Morgan at London's Westminster Chapel. When Dr. Morgan retired in 1943, Dr. Jones continued to provide strong pastoral counseling while defending the faith. His many books include *Truth Unchanged, Unchanging* (1951), *From Fear to Faith* (1953), *Studies in the Sermon on the Mount* (two volumes, 1959–1960), and a number of commentaries including *Romans* and *Ephesians*. Dr. Martin Lloyd-Jones was a champion for the cause of Christ in the Church at the end of the twentieth century.

The General Next to God

"Go for souls and go for the worst!"—William Booth

There was still another movement that arose to challenge the formality of the Anglican Church. William Booth (1829–1912) was a former English Methodist minister who began the Salvation Army in Wales. Men and women who enlisted for service in the Salvation Army followed a soldier of the Cross of Christ, who was willing to go into the lowest dredges of society to win men and women, boys and girls to Jesus Christ. After conducting a successful revival ministry in Cardiff, Wales, Booth began a similar ministry in London (1878). Out of the work came an organization fashioned after the military—with distinguishing rank and job descriptions.

It was not an easy life. There were long days, jeering crowds, and low pay. The General told one graduating class, "I sentence you all to hard labor for the rest of your natural lives." His wife would tell others, "There comes a crisis, a moment when every human soul which enters the kingdom of God has to make its choice of that kingdom in preference to everything else that it holds and owns."

William Booth was an extraordinary man. During his life he traveled 5,000,000 miles and preached 60,000 sermons. As a vegetarian, he ate "neither fish, flesh, nor fowl." As a minister of the Gospel he was hungry for nothing but the salvation of souls (note John 4:32, 34). Booth wanted to save people not only from the penalty of sin, but its pollution as well. He wanted to terminate their hunger, poverty, drunkenness, unemployment and, most of all, their immorality. Booth led the fight against

London's open prostitution of teenage girls (ages 13–16). The 393,000 signatures he collected resulted in legislation that brought an end to "white slavery." He did more. He moved to minister to malnourished children—for "salvation from pinching poverty, from rags and misery, must be offered to all." His whole life was given to lifting up those who were cast down. When William Booth died, 150,000 people filed by the casket. Millions around the globe mourned his passing. More than 40,000 people attended his funeral.

Equally beloved was his faithful wife and companion, Catherine Booth (1865–1950). As a child Catherine Mumford Booth experienced long periods of illness, during which she read many books. Her mind was bright; she read theological and philosophical books far beyond her years. Before the age of 12 she had read the entire Bible. In later years, her wide knowledge and sharp wit would serve her well when applied with humor. During one street meeting, she responded to a man who argued that the Apostle Paul had said that it was a shame for women to speak in the Church. "Oh yes, so he did; but in the first place this is not a church, and in the second place, I am not a Corinthian; besides [she continued while turning to look with sympathy at the man's wife], Paul said in the same epistle that it was good for the unmarried to remain so."

During the most tumultuous days of an often thankless ministry, Catherine remained faithful to serving Christ, though she admitted it was not always easy. "What a deal there is of going to meetings and getting blessed, and then going away and living just the same, until sometimes we, who are constantly engaged in trying to bring people nearer the heart of God, go away so discouraged that our hearts are almost broken." Still, in the end Catherine would be able to say, "The waters are rising, but so am I. I am not going under, but over."

"The Prince of Preachers"

Charles Haddon Spurgeon (1834–1892), remains history's most widely read minister of the Gospel, often called "The Prince of Preachers." Converted as a teenager, Spurgeon began to preach shortly thereafter; by age twenty he had preached over 600 times. In 1854, the New Park Street Church in London, England, invited young Spurgeon to be its pastor for the congregation of 232 members. Thirty-eight years later, at the end of his pastorate, the congregation numbered 5,311, making it the largest independent congregation in the world. It has been estimated that Spurgeon preached to over 10,000,000 people during his lifetime. His sermons and books sold into the millions of copies. A pastor's college, an orphanage, and a publishing house were just some of the ministries associated with his endeavors. However, buildings and budgets, numbers and statistics do not tell the story—for Charles Spurgeon's was a life hidden in Christ. Someone once asked Mr. Spurgeon what was the success to his preaching. He replied, "I take every passage of Scripture and make a bee-line for the Cross."

According to his faithful wife Susan, Charles Spurgeon died an early death due to the Down-Grade Controversy (1887–1888). It was a dramatic episode involving the Baptist Union to which Spurgeon belonged. The controversy began when in March, 1887, Spurgeon published in his monthly magazine, *The Sword and the Trowel*, an article titled "The Down-Grade." Written anonymously by Spurgeon's friend, Robert Shindler, the declaration was made that some ministers were "denying the proper deity of the Son of God, renouncing faith in his atoning death ..." These ministers, said Shindler, were on a slippery slope, or down-grade. They were moving away from historical, essential evangelical doctrines.

The obvious question was asked by the leaders of the Baptist Union: "Who were these ministers that dare to deny the doctrines of the Church?" Spurgeon would not name names. His objective was focused and limited. Spurgeon simply wanted to warn against the rise of liberalism. He sincerely believed that three doctrines were being abandoned: the infallibility of the Bible, the substitutionary atonement of Christ, and the certainty of final judgment for those who died without saving knowledge of the Lord. When the Baptist Union met in October of 1887, the "Down Grade" was the main topic of conversation and concern. Rather than create a schism, Spurgeon resigned from the Baptist Union.

Unfortunately, this action was viewed as a public insult to the Union. Instead of dealing with the issue, Baptist leaders tried to recover their reputation as much as possible. On January 13, 1888, the Council of the Baptist Union passed a resolution known as the "vote of censure." Since Spurgeon would not give names and supporting evidence, the Council decreed that his charges should not have been made. Spurgeon felt betrayed, but remained resolute on the need to address the main issues. It did not matter that time vindicated Spurgeon's strong words of warning. The damage had been done; a very good man and a very important warning had been unfortunately diminished.

The Keswick Convention

The Keswick Convention began spontaneously in 1875 at a meeting in Keswick, a village in northern England. Since then the five day meeting has continued in much the same format each July. It has its foundations in the books of W. E. Boardman, *The Higher Christian Life* (1859), Robert Pearsall Smith, *Holiness through Faith* (1870), and his wife Hanna Whitehall Smith, *The Christian's Secret of a Happy Life* (1873). In addition, the religious climate in England had a marvelous awakening in the campaigns of D. L. Moody in every major city in 1873 and 1874.

Thus entered the Smiths, the real catalysts. Both were born and bred Quakers in Philadelphia, in 1827 and 1832 respectively, although he was a member of the Presbyterian Church most of his life. Eight years after their marriage both were converted, and were tried by an inability to have consistent victory over sin, being told by older Christians that a "sinning and repenting" cycle was the normative Christian experience due to the weakness of the flesh. Justification by faith was known and accepted, but "sanctification by faith" was a new revelation to them in 1867. This included committing not only one's eternal future to the Lord, but also one's daily life, "taking up one's cross daily," experiencing consistent victory over sin's power (see Rom 6 and 8).

Mr. Smith was a businessman, and both were without theological training, but natural gifts in teaching and writing won them wide audiences. They went to England in 1872 for a rest from too busy schedules. There they were invited to share at a series of breakfast meetings for pastors in London. In this way, 2,400 clergy heard their message. In 1874 and early 1875, several well attended conferences were organized at The Broadlands, Oxford, and Brighton. These clearly set forth the aim not to promote any new doctrine, but to experience real vitality within accepted conservative doctrine. The first Keswick Convention followed in July 1875, organized by the Evangelical diocese pastor at Keswick, Canon T. D. Harford-Battersby. It was entitled "Union Meetings for the Promotion of Practical Holiness," and was attended by all church affiliations. Great criticism began to pour in on the movement, and adherents had to be ready to be put out of some churches.

Over the years, Keswick has become the centerpiece for the movement of "Higher Life" teaching. Its original positions, speaking of a "second act of consecration," were modified over time to the more biblically-based position: that a complete surrender to Christ as Lord at conversion (the work of God in saving faith that includes repentance from sin and selfishness), proceeds to life-long daily commitment in denying self and serving Christ wholeheartedly, experiencing greater victory over sin's power (i.e., no longer slaves to sin). The sequence of teaching at every Keswick Convention is the same: one day for each of the exceeding sinfulness of sin (and encouragement to its abandonment), God's provision for sin (sin need not be a continual source of defeat), consecration of the Christian (in practical and scriptural holiness[4]), fullness of the Holy Spirit, and Christian service (including missionary responsibility). The Convention has received the support and participation of luminaries from a multitude of evangelical denominations such as Theodore Monod, Evan Hopkins, George Macgregor, Elder Cumming, Handley C. G. Moule, Andrew Murray, F. B. Meyer, Donald G. Barnhouse, W. Graham Scroggie, and G. Campbell Morgan. Both Hudson Taylor and Amy Carmichael came from the movement as missionaries.

---

[4] *practical and scriptural holiness* – "Holiness as understood by Keswick... is not a withdrawal from the world, nor a subjective pietism, nor striving after a vague mystical oneness with God, but spiritual wholeness and health that will issue in a practical walk in the Spirit and the daily doing of God's will."—Steven Barabas, Wheaton College, *So Great Salvation: The History and Message of the Keswick Convention* (Fleming H. Revell Co., 1952) p. 108.

CHAPTER 39

Challenges in the Twenty-First Century and Beyond

New Challenges

The beginning of the twentieth century brought many new challenges to the Church of Jesus Christ. Not all of them would be easy to meet.

The Challenge of Immigration

From 1865 to 1884 more than seven million immigrants came to the United States from Europe. This was good, for the "Land of the Free" wanted to welcome as many people as possible. However, as the immigrants arrived and settled throughout the country, they brought to America different religious concepts that would touch and transform established practices (the same phenomena is continuing in Europe as well).

There was, for example, the matter of worship on Sunday. Since colonial days, America practiced the "Puritan Sabbath" whereby the whole day was given to the Lord and religious activity. In contrast, there was the "Continental Sabbath" of the immigrants (advocated by Calvin)—Sunday morning may be given to church but the rest of the day was for rest and relaxation. Little by little the "Continental Sabbath" came to dominate the way Americans worshipped on Sunday.

There is an on-going pressure for populations to move from under-developed to developed countries for economic gain. Every immigrant brings his own culture and beliefs with him. And society, rather than teaching the new arrivals the great truths of Christianity, attempts to integrate, accommodate, and tolerate. In this we lose our push for evangelism, and the sense of the "absolute truths" of the Bible.

The Challenge of Evangelism in the Cities

With the rapid rise of city populations due to immigration and industrialization, it was inevitable that overcrowding take place in vast tenement districts. How could the Church personally and effectively minister to those who crowded into apartment buildings of the cities? Many of the new immigrants did not even speak the national language. In the United States in 1867, the Baptist Home Mission Society was established to lead the way in addressing this particular problem. Other denominations followed suit. New programs were devised to bring the Gospel to the tenements.

The Challenge of Affluence

The personal prosperity that many began to enjoy as a result of the Industrial Revolution brought its own concerns. It is possible for wealth to draw the heart away from the Lord (1 Tim 6:10), to cause people to become self-sufficient and think that they do not need God (Jas 5:1–6). It is also possible for much good to be done with money. Many wealthy Christians did want to do good and support the Church out of the blessings of God's grace to them. They helped to do innumerable good works at home and abroad, and to establish seminaries, universities, and colleges too. Some of these were designed to be Christian institutions, such as in the United States the McCormick Seminary, Cornell, Leland Stanford, Vassar, Smith, Wellesley, and Bryn Mawr universities. Unfortunately, the danger with affluence and the giving flowing from it, is that a business mentality crept into the ministry. Religious institutions were targeted for philanthropic work much like a Board of Directors would consider where to give money for a tax write-off. Successful businessmen were given places on the financial boards of churches, even if they did not met the scriptural qualifications set forth in 1 Timothy 3:1–14 and Titus 1:5–9.

The Challenge of Social Concerns

Because of the social crowding and the problems it brought to society, because of the growing affluence of the middle class, because of an increased wealth coming into the Church, it was inevitable that criticism be focused on that institution which proclaimed to be compassionate and caring for the poor and downtrodden. Horace Bushell, a Congregational minister, reminded the Church to pay closer attention to the training of young people in his work, *Christian Nurture*. While caring for others, the Church must care for its own as well.

Since man is both body and soul, conscientious Christians insisted that the Church do something to help society in practical ways. It was argued that local church assemblies and main denominations should consider ways to alleviate slum areas and reduce the cramped, disease infested conditions of the community. The outworking of these concepts led to the "Institutional Church."

A leading voice of the Institutional Church was the Episcopalian minister William A. Muhlenberg, great grandson of Henry Melchior Muhlenberg (1711–1787). The latter helped to establish the Lutheran Church in America during the colonial period. From 1846 to 1858 William Muhlenberg served as rector of the Church of the Holy Communion in New York City. Through his inspirational guidance several social works of lasting endurance were begun, such as the Sisterhood of the Holy Communion and St. Luke's Hospital.

Following his example, Thomas K. Beecher, pastor of the First Congregational Church of Elmira, New York, encouraged the community to come to his church for aerobics, lectures, and reading. Then there was Russell H. Conwell. In 1891 this pastor of the Baptist Temple in Philadelphia allowed the church facilities to be used for sewing classes, reading rooms, a recreational room, and a place for educational night classes to be held. Temple University grew out of this graciousness. The belief that the Institutional Church must do something in the community continued as the new century progressed. In 1908, the Federal Council of Churches of Christ in America adopted the *Social Creed of the Churches*.

While all this social activity was extremely commendable, it carried a danger. The programs offered were attractive to people, and in many churches have become an end unto themselves, rather than a means to an end. It was possible for the Church of the Lord to forget its main function of winning souls to Christ. It was possible for the Church to forget to preach the Gospel. It was possible for the Scriptures to be set aside in favor of sweet sermons that offended no one, because sin and the need of a Savior had been forgotten. The challenge that the Church faced was how to maintain its spiritual integrity while helping those in obvious need.

This has resulted in a historic drift away from the Scriptures and into liberal theology. We must all "serve one another," but only while carrying forward the teaching of true doctrines. When religious men disavow the necessity of the atonement, they are quite happy to be left with a "social gospel," in which all men will go to heaven. They focus on the love of God, and ignore the hatred of God toward sin and rebellion. This "social gospel" of love and good works, without the power of God unto salvation proclaimed in the Scriptures, has most unfortunately become the norm in many large denominations such as the Methodist Church and the United Presbyterian Church.

The Challenge of Secular Education

In 1925 a bill was passed in the state of Florida requiring daily Bible reading in all public schools and forbidding the teaching of the theory of evolution in public classrooms. Similar legislation was passed in the states of Texas and Tennessee. No one suspected that the stage was being set for one of the great trials of the century.

On Friday, June 10, 1925, at 9 A.M., in the quiet community of Dayton, Tennessee (pop. 2,000), court was convened to consider a challenge to the Butler Bill, which the State legislature had passed. The bill stipulated the penalty for any teacher found guilty of the misdemeanor. A fine would be imposed between $100 and $500. John Scopes had been charged with deliberately violating the new statute. The American Civil Liberties Union (ACLU) did not believe that Mr. Scopes should pay the penalty the bill imposed. The State of Tennessee disagreed. The "Scopes Monkey Trial," as it soon became known, would become the test case as to whether the statute would be upheld.

Coming to the defense of John Scopes at the request of the ACLU was Clarence Darrow, a liberal lawyer and "a stern foe of fundamentalists" according to one biography. When Darrow heard that William Jennings Bryan would argue the case for the State of Tennessee, he was delighted, saying, "I would like to meet Bryan in this case. I believe I could down him." He was partially right. On the final day of the trial the jury returned a verdict of guilty. John Scopes was to pay the court $100. However, in the "court of public opinion," Clarence Darrow had made a "monkey" out of William Jennings Bryan. He had led the public to believe that evolution was more "scientific" than biblical creationism.

Soon, the theory of evolution would replace the simplicity of the Scriptures in the classroom. The work of Charles Darwin first published in 1859, *The Origin of the Species*, had finally found a resting place in the fertile soil of a foolish society that rushed to embrace a godless philosophy, without fully considering all the evidence for scientific creationism. With all due respect for Mr. Bryan, he was a politician, not a theologian. Had he been better trained in the Bible, he would not have made some basic concessions that undermined his credibility, and gave away his case in the court of public opinion.

The Challenge of Modernism

Following the Scopes Monkey Trial, the relatively easy acceptance by the general public that evolutionary thinking should be allowed into the classroom is understandable. In part, liberal theologians had prepared the way. Thousands of people were being influenced Sunday after Sunday by liberal theology.

One of Modernism's most popular preachers was Harry Emerson Fosdick (1878–1979). During the 1920s he was an ardent champion of liberalism, which included the concept that the Church of Christ in the twentieth century was outdated. In a 1926 essay, "*What Christian Liberals Are Driving At,*" Fosdick argued that, "Not one of its historic statements of faith takes into account any of the masterful ideas that constitute the framework of modern thinking—the inductive method, the new astronomy, natural law, evolution. All these have come since Protestantism arrived." In other words, the Christian Church was "pre-scientific." Upon hearing things like this, and not knowing any better, many Christian were simply embarrassed and accepted the new ideas.

To stand firm against the attacks of the Modernists upon the Bible, there arose the *Fundamentalists.* They attempted to reduce the confusion by articulating the very most basic biblical doctrines that must be adhered to in order to remain "Christian." One such was Presbyterian theologian J. Gresham Machen, who was not embarrassed by the charges of Modernism. He was ready and able to challenge Modernism while defending the historic faith of the Church. Machen wisely pointed out that "The liberal attempt at reconciling Christianity with modern science has really relinquished everything distinctive of Christianity, so that what remains is in essentials only that same indefinite type of religious aspiration which was in the world before Christianity came upon the scene." Machen was right. There was no need for the Christian community to concede any truth it had proclaimed for two thousand years. The Church had nothing to apologize for. What it did need to do was think more clearly.

But the Fundamentalists had to do a better job of presenting their position. And this could be done because the problem was relatively simple: Fundamentalism was sending a mixed message to society. It was trying to hold two views at once (cp. Jas 1:8). One popular message argued that American culture was on the decline and under the judgment of God. Political solutions and human solutions to the problems of the world were only going to make matters worse. There needed to be a readiness to leave this life because the world was soon coming to an end. The Second Advent of the Lord was imminent. That was one message. The other message from the Fundamentalists was that America should be reformed. America was a chosen nation by God who had strayed from the right path. America needed to get back to God on her knees.

Many were confused. Either America was a Babylon under divine judgment, or America was a modern day Palestine, chosen by God to be the moral leader of the world. Either the Lord's coming was imminent and would happen at any moment, or it was impending and there was much work to do.

There was more confusion, for many Fundamentalists were no longer clear as to what constituted the basics of the Christian faith. In 1910 they had been clearer. In that year a series of small volumes was published with the title *The Fundamentals: A Testimony to the Truth.* Five basic doctrines were set forth:

- The Bible is free from error.
- Christ is Deity and was born of a virgin.
- Christ died a substitutionary death at Calvary to satisfy the wrath of God against sin.
- Christ arose from the dead on the third day.
- He will come again the second time for all who believe.

These were the fundamentals of the faith. But that was in 1910; by the 1920s there were new concerns. The "Roaring Twenties" made some conservative Christians think that perhaps "standards" should be included in the list of fundamentals of the faith. But if so, which standards? Who would be responsible for drawing-up the list of acceptable moral behavior by which one could be assured of salvation? Also, what about evolution? And war? And the holiness movement? The Fundamentalists had to do a better job of thinking through their own theology.

Realizing this, and weary with the Modernism that had crept in at Princeton Seminary, in 1929 Professor J. Gresham Machen united with other Christians to establish Westminster Theological Seminary in Philadelphia, Pennsylvania. The fight against Modernism would continue, but it would be conducted in the future by even more insightful individuals who had seriously considered the Scriptures.

The Challenge of International and Ecumenical Unity

Prior to World War I, World War II, and the Korean Conflict, the Modernists were sure that society was moving towards Utopia. To paraphrase popular liberal thought of the era, there was a religious belief that "every day and in every way societies were getting better and better." Maybe Communism would bring world harmony. Maybe the United Nations could solve people's problems, as diplomats sat down and talked about their differences. Maybe a World Council of Churches could show mankind the way to live in peace and harmony. One by one each of these secular and religious institutions arose to try. But time is showing once again that there is no substituting the effort or the institutions of men, for the regenerating work of the Holy Spirit in the hearts of men.

The Church Faces the Future

As the Church of Jesus Christ begins the twenty-first century, there are clever foes and formidable challenges that must be faced.

The Charismatic Movement

To issue a general warning about the Charismatic movement may appear to be unkind, but there is reason for concern among conservative Christians. For an insightful study of the foundation upon which this movement has been built, attention is directed to *Signs of the Apostles: Observations on Pentecostalism Old and New* by Walter J. Chantry, published by The Banner of Truth Trust, Carlisle, Pennsylvania, 17013. It is sufficient to say that feelings and experiences can take precedence over Scripture in some Charismatic churches (cp. John 15:15 with 2 Tim 3:16–17). Many Charismatic brethren are willing to follow after modern day "apostles," exalting men rather than Christ alone. There is a belief that the apostolic gift of being able to perform miracles to create signs and wonders is still valid (study 1 Cor 12:29–30). Also, it is taught that the manifestation of the filling of the Holy Spirit is demonstrated by speaking in tongues (cp. Luke 1:15; 1:41–42; 1:67–69). Since the extremes of Charismatic theology can redefine many historic Christian concepts and doctrines, careful discernment is required of anyone in this movement (Matt 7:22–23).

In addition, there is also an emphasis today on the "Health/Wealth" movement (or "Word/Faith" or Faith movement).[1] This is the teaching that our problems stem from a lack of faith, and to receive what we desire we need only "name it and claim it" by faith. But this totally ignores Christ's emphasis on *spiritual* blessing, and His promise of tribulation for His disciples, in order to keep our pride broken, us growing in faith, and us dependent upon Him alone. The Christian life consists not in getting what we want, but in serving a risen Master. Therein lies the only true joy.

Dispensationalism

The Congregational minister, Cyrus Ingerson Scofield (1843–1921), is widely credited with making popular dispensational teaching[2] by the publication of the *Scofield Reference Bible* in 1909. This theological system is based upon a seven-era method of "rightly dividing" the Scriptures. It was first proposed by John N. Darby in 1830 (see chapter 15). The system makes dramatic distinctions between seven dispensations, treating believing Israel and the believing Church as two distinct groups (rather than one body of believers). It also teaches two returns of Christ (cp. Heb 9:28) and two resurrections (cp. John 5:28). The key is this: the main Scriptures regarding the end-times can be interpreted two ways—in either the traditional reformed view, or the dispensational view, depending upon which Scriptures are emphasized as primary.

But the dispensational view has quickly led many people into four problems.

(1) Because of an impending "rapture," people tend to disregard their biblical responsibilities to impact society for Christ.

(2) And, because of the emphasis on this "age of grace," and the separation from the Old Testament Law as an invaluable guide to holy living, Dispensationalism encourages people to believe that they are "not under law, but grace," and therefore can continue to live life for themselves, seeking their own desires and interests, not seeking first the kingdom of God. This is called *anti-nomianism* (Greek *anti* – against, *nomia* – law).[3]

---

[1] For more on this, see *What Is Wrong with the Word Faith Movement* by Hank Hanegraff; available from Chapel Library.

[2] For more on this, see *Scofield or the Scriptures?* by Paul Sisco (1970) and *The Scofield Bible* by Albertus Pieters (1869–1955), both available from Chapel Library.

[3] Romans 6 demonstrates that "not under law" points to: not under law as a merit system to earn God's favor regarding salvation.

(3) In addition, most holding the dispensational view have embraced Arminian beliefs emphasizing man's free choice to "receive Christ," without also recognizing God's sovereign choice in electing them unto salvation (see chapter 12), becoming man-centered rather than God-centered.

(4) Finally, many who hold to Dispensationalism will emphasize "just make a decision for Christ"—receiving Christ as Savior becomes merely an intellectual assent to "believe," without a corresponding commitment to Christ as Lord. This is more accurately referred to as *Sandemanianism*, which began as a clear departure from the historical faith in the late 1700s (see chapter 15). It has re-surfaced in our day in the opposition to "Lordship Salvation."[4] Often within Dispensationalism, "becoming a disciple of Christ as Lord" is offered as an optional part of sanctification, instead of being a clear result of salvation initially. But the Bible associates "turning from sin" with "turning to God"—as a part of one in the same "turning." Historical orthodox Christianity views repentance from sin as an integral part of saving faith, all by the grace of God, submitting our will to Him as Savior and Lord.

Dispensationalism still remains popular, and thus can be a challenge for the Church when these problems enter in.

Legalism and Other Extremes

At the opposite end of the evangelical spectrum, there are extremes associated with a misunderstanding of "purity." In a mistaken self-inflated zeal for doctrinal purity, some have added many minor doctrines as a requirement for "unity," and proceeded to break off fellowship with other believers who disagree on only minor points, even branding them "heretics." There is today still much spiritual pride in head-knowledge of theology, without humility in application to the heart.

In addition, some have distorted the doctrine of God's free offer of saving grace, by insisting upon a season of "mourning and grieving over sin" before one is able to turn from sin to Christ. While the Holy Spirit may bring some through this, the application of the Gospel is in Christ's command to "Come unto me," without merit or condition (John 7:37).[5] This is the exhortation that must be proclaimed.

Also, in a mistaken zeal for practical purity, some have added long lists of rule-keeping, in order to demonstrate sanctification. But our obedience is always to be motivated by unfeigned love for God in gratitude of heart, as His servants. Rule-

---

[4] See *Letter to a Friend about Lordship Salvation* by John Piper, available from Chapel Library.
[5] See *Come unto Me* by Tom Wells, available from Chapel Library.

keeping only breeds a judgmental heart and superficiality in love-relationship with Christ.

Finally, in a mistaken interpretation of the sovereignty of God, some have adopted the belief that God will save His chosen (elected) ones, without consideration of the human *means*. This causes some to refuse to evangelize! But man *does* have responsibility to serve Christ with his whole heart; and God *will* sovereignly accomplish His purposes, independently of man's obedience. Both are perfectly true in the economy of God. His ways are high above our understanding.

Eastern Mysticism and the New Age

There are strange new religions that the Church of the living God must combat for the souls of men. The Unification Church, Hare Krishna, Zen Buddhism, and Transcendental Meditation were once religions of the Far East. Now, they are attracting the naive and the sophisticated in every nation in the Western world. Christians need to understand the opposition, and the competition, that the Church faces without being intimidated or overwhelmed. The clear Gospel message must not be surrendered. People still need the Son of Righteousness (Heb 1:1–4), not the "Moon" of Korea. Souls need Christ-consciousness, not the Hindu god of the Krishna-consciousness. The best way to witness is simply to tell others, "Come, see a man, which told me all things that ever I did: is not this the Christ?" (cp. John 4:29 with 3:16). As the claims of Christ and His redemptive work at Calvary are considered, He will be found more precious than silver and gold (1 Pet 1:18).

During the last two decades of the twentieth century, the New Age Movement has come out of the counter-culture into the mainstream of civilization to influence almost every facet of life—medical science, education, government, psychology, and religion. Combining Eastern mysticism with Western optimism, the New Age offers mankind an alternative to traditional beliefs and values. Its basic tenet is that man is intrinsically good, and that we must tolerate all behaviors as individual choices. It is the basis for the "one world order," and includes holistic health, trans-personal psychology, deified energy in physics, a politically unified world order, and a narcissistic (self-centered) spirituality. It claims that man can be happy without turning from his sin; in fact, its proponents claim that the very concept of sin is "outdated."

The Church faces the challenge of helping thoughtful people realize that behind the facade, there is only a bankrupt philosophy that will separate the soul from the

Creator. Contrary to the teaching of the New Age, people are not magnificent, and do not have great wisdom within themselves. People are sinful and selfish, and are in desperate need of a Savior.

Pragmatism and the Church Growth Movement

An interesting question has arisen for the Church at the end of the twentieth century. The question is this: "Can the local church grow, apart from the power of the Holy Spirit?" While the question is not really asked that blatantly, in essence that is exactly what is at issue. And the answer for many is a surprising, "*Yes!*" In hundreds of ways, thousands of ministers have now been told that the congregation can grow without having strong Gospel preaching, prayer, and soul-winning efforts. All that is needed is to be *pragmatic*, i.e., if a technique works in the world's eyes, then it is good and can be used to attract people. Of course, the techniques that work to attract people in the world, are the techniques of the world: the assembly must identify and target the community it is in, and then "find a need and fill it." With new concepts a flourishing industry has arisen to "build" the church. Today, the Church Growth Movement is well armed with popular music, charts, and "market" surveys; promotions, promises, programs, gimmicks, and gadgets; to woo and win the local community. All of this could also be said about many parts of the modern missions movement as well. Man's wisdom and "what works" has taken precedence over prayer and the Holy Spirit.[6]

The problem is this: often these techniques are simply "the world's ways" (and we are told to "love not the world," 1 John 2:15).[7] People respond to these methods because they are attracted to them in their flesh—it is "fun, food, and fellowship." Moreover, the pastor might tend not to preach sin and the need for salvation, because some might be offended by being called sinful, and might leave the local church. Therefore, the Gospel is changed into a "warm" message of love and kindness, without conviction of sin. In contrast, previous generations of Christians were convinced that "*the Lord* added to the church daily such as should be saved" (Acts 2:47, emphasis added).

---

[6] See *No Compromise* by C. H. Spurgeon (1834–1892), and *Ten Indictments against the Modern* Church by Paul Washer, both available from Chapel Library.

[7] See *Free Grace Broadcaster* "Love Not the World" and *Fleeing Out of Sodom* by Jonathan Edwards (1703–1758), both available from Chapel Library.

Psychological Seduction

One of the most powerful challenges to the Christian community today is that of psychology, which has fit right into the pragmatism discussed above. When the basic tenets of psychology are assembled, they make a direct assault upon the fundamental doctrines of the Bible. Psychology teaches, in part, that man is inherently good; society, not self, is ultimately to blame for the problems of life; sin is simply low self-esteem; self becomes a god; beliefs, not behavior, should change—even if the behavior involves casual sex or an aberrant lifestyle; values are relative; and there are no absolutes (note Rom 1:18–32; 3:10; 6:23; 2 Tim 3:1–7). We are taught to "love ourselves" before we can love others!

But when Jesus said "love others as you *love yourself*," He was simply using the natural care we take for our bodies and interests, as the measure to love others, not giving a new command to "love ourselves."[8] We are told many times in Scripture instead that "the first will be last" and to "deny yourself" (Matt 19:30; 20:16; Mark 9:35; 10:31; Luke 13:30; Matt 16:24; Mark 8:34; Luke 9:23). Self-denial in Christ's power, not self-love, is the key to following Christ. The basic problem with psychology is twofold: (1) it identifies a different problem—others, not personal sin, and, (2) it offers a different solution—self-esteem, not Christ. The Church must find a way to disentangle Christianity from the psychological religion, a false religion that has confused many by intertwining itself with the true Gospel message of Christ's redeeming self-sacrificing love.

The Battle for the Bible

Throughout the twentieth and into the twenty-first century, there has been a relentless attack upon the authority of the Bible itself. If the Bible can be shown to have errors, or to be less than the authoritative Word of God, then man is justified in conforming his life to the commands of the Scripture *only partially!* We see that man will do anything to avoid submitting his life 100% to God's authority. So today we have those that say the Bible can be *interpreted* in many ways, so that obedience to biblical instruction in righteousness becomes just a matter of personal interpretation! However, the Word of God is not to be handled so carelessly. There are proper Bible study methods to follow. These include: (1) staying in context

---

[8] See *The Biblical View of Self-esteem* by Jay Adams, available from Chapel Library.

(historical and narrative), (2) using the original language word meanings, and (3) following the original language grammar.[9]

We also have those who say the Bible is *infallible* (incapable of error in the areas in which it claims authority), but not *inerrant* (completely without error). By this they mean the Bible is without error in faith and practice, but can have error in science and history. This allows them to disregard the Genesis account of creation, Noah's flood, and miracles such as Jonah and the whale. In fact, it opens the door to re-interpret any aspect of biblical truth. The fact of the matter is, that whenever the Bible and science have seemed to collide, and further scientific investigation has revealed new facts, the Bible has been proven to be correct.[10]

To be very clear in this day of abundant distortions, we must say four words: that we hold to the *verbal, plenary inspiration* of the *inerrant* Scriptures. "Verbal" means the written words (in the original languages), not the intended or spiritual meaning (which is a matter of correct interpretation). "Plenary" means every word, not just most. "Inspiration" means God-breathed: the words in the original language were written by men who were guided by the Holy Spirit to write the very words that God intended (yet reflecting their own personalities!).

In the words of C. H. Spurgeon:

> However this sacred Book may be treated nowadays, it was not treated . . . questioningly by the Lord . . . He continually quoted the Law and the prophets...with intense reverence . . . How much more should we! [Moreover,] the utmost degree of deference and homage is paid to the Old Testament by the writers of the New. We never find an apostle raising a question about the degree of inspiration in this book or that.[11]

The Sovereignty of God

An emphasis on "man's free will" has caused many believers today to accept a mistaken view of who God is, even without realizing it. Historically, Christians have held that God is both omnipotent (no limit to His power) and sovereign (no limit to His authority), as in Revelation 19:9—"The Lord God Omnipotent Reigneth." This will be our song in heaven; why should it not also be now? But all the influences mentioned in this chapter have caused the common Christian culture of today to

---

[9] See the study course available from Mount Zion Bible Institute: *Methods of Bible Study*.
[10] See *Is the Bible Reliable?* by John Piper, available from Chapel Library.
[11] Sermon from *Metropolitan Tabernacle Pulpit*, vol. 34, no. 2013.

become occupied with personal desires, preferences, and plans. We desire to be "in control" (a virtue in the world system), and we get frustrated with bad circumstances, even angry! Many now see God as desiring good, but constantly thwarted by sin, to the point that He is only watching, and it is up to us to strive to make things better, using our own strengths (Deism all over again). People say, "He helps us to do good as we see it." But this view destroys faith, and causes us to look to ourselves.

The Bible, on the other hand, consistently presents God as "in control," completely and with no exceptions. He accomplishes His will on earth, not ours. We are called to submit our will to Him in all things, and serve Him as bond-slaves (2 Cor 4:10–12; Rom 12:11; 14:18). We live for His will, not our own (Matt 6:10; Heb 12:1; 1 Pet 4:2). He uses *everything*, even the acts of sinful men, for our good (Rom 8:28–29). What a blessing this truth is to the saints—it means we can have peace and joy (John 14:27; Rom 15:13) as we "trust His heart even when we cannot trace His hand." Prayer and peace can replace planning, pressure, and power-plays![12]

The Next Chapter

Despite these very real challenges, the Church will yet march on from victory to victory. The "old old story of Jesus and His love" shall always be told, because the Holy Spirit moves in men to avoid the past being forgotten.

One day multitudes will stand to honor and salute individuals who have worked to preserve the past, while maintaining the purity of doctrinal truth. One day the King of Glory will return to earth. He will find faith because individuals of courage and conviction have been busy about their Father's business.

By remembering the faithfulness of God in the past, the Church can face the future with great confidence—despite the many challenges to its creeds and conduct. True disciples of Christ must rise up and follow Him afresh. Individuals of purity and passion are needed just as much as ever, to lead souls out of spiritual darkness into the glorious light of the kingdom of God.

More than one Bible commentator has noted that the book of *Acts* ends rather abruptly. It seems as if the manuscript were left unfinished. Perhaps there is a reason for this; perhaps the last chapter of the "book of the Acts of the Holy Spirit" has yet to be written. The story of the Church is not yet finished. If the Lord tarries, the Church today will be the next chapter that future generations will read about.

---

[12] See *Does God Rule Everything?* by Arthur Dent (1706) and *Self-denial* (*Free Grace Broadcaster*), both available from Chapel Library.

Therefore, let us leave a legacy of lasting glory. Let us with the first century saints both ...

> "continue steadfastly in the apostles' doctrine and fellowship."
> —ACTS 2:41

And,

> "go ... into all the world, and preach the gospel to every creature."
> —MARK 16:15

Amen!

Soli Deo Gloria
To God Alone Be the Glory

www.ingramcontent.com/pod-product-compliance
Lightning Source LLC
Chambersburg PA
CBHW081913170426
43200CB00014B/2720